TURNING
ARCHIVAL

A book in the series
Radical Perspectives:
A Radical History Review book series

Series editors:

Daniel J. Walkowitz, New York University

Barbara Weinstein, New York University

Duke University Press *Durham and London* 2022

TURNING ARCHIVAL

The Life of the Historical in Queer Studies

EDITED BY DANIEL MARSHALL AND
ZEB TORTORICI

Designed by Courtney Leigh Baker
Typeset in Garamond Premier Pro and Din
by Westchester Publishing Services

Library of Congress Cataloging-in-Publication Data
Names: Marshall, Daniel, [date] editor. | Tortorici, Zeb, [date] editor.
Title: Turning archival : the life of the historical in queer studies /
[edited by] Daniel Marshall and Zeb Tortorici.
Other titles: Radical perspectives.
Description: Durham : Duke University Press, 2022. | Series: Radical
perspectives | Includes bibliographical references and index. Identifiers:
LCCN 2021059689 (print) | LCCN 2021059690 (ebook) ISBN
9781478015345 (hardcover)
ISBN 9781478017974 (paperback)
ISBN 9781478022589 (ebook)
Subjects: LCSH: Gay and lesbian studies—Archival resources. | Gays—
History—Sources. | Gays—Research. | Queer theory. | BISAC: SOCIAL
SCIENCE / LGBTQ Studies / Gay Studies | HISTORY / World
Classification: LCC HQ75.15 .T837 2022 (print) | LCC HQ75.15 (ebook) |
DDC 306.76/6—dc23/eng/20220404
LC record available at https://lccn.loc.gov/2021059689
LC ebook record available at https://lccn.loc.gov/2021059690

Cover art: Danielle Brathwaite-Shirley, *H1 (haunting Ebun Sodipo)* and
H2 (haunting Tobi Adebajo), 2021. Video hologram diptych. Installation
dimensions variable. Edition of 4, with 2 AP. Courtesy of the artist.

Contents

Acknowledgments

Turning Archival has been a long time in the making, and we are grateful to those who—over the years—made this project possible. The idea for the book came about after we, with Kevin P. Murphy, coedited two special issues of *Radical History Review* (no. 120 from 2014 and no. 122 from 2015) on the topic of "Queering Archives," and we wish to thank Kevin for his unflagging support for that project and for contributing thoughts and ideas to this book. We also would like to thank Tom Harbison and the editorial board of RHR for their help and support along the way toward publishing those two issues. We thank Duke University Press for permission to republish revised versions of the articles of María Elena Martínez, Martin F. Manalansan IV, and Joan Nestle here. Special thanks go to Sarah Gualtieri, who offered the support, consultation, and close readings that enabled us to publish an expanded version of Martínez's article in *Turning Archival*. We are grateful, too, to Joan Nestle, who provided inspiration, ideas, and encouragement for this project. Special thanks are reserved for both Gisela Fosado and Alejandra Mejía, our editors at Duke University Press, who have stuck with us throughout this project, offering critical support, feedback, guidance, and patience along the way. As always, it has been a pleasure—personally and intellectually—to work with them toward the realization of this book. Our contributors too have been patient as we have brought this book into the world, and we thank them for all their work and for the vibrancy of their ideas which have been a powerful motor for this project. Anonymous readers of this manuscript, and the Duke University Press Editorial Advisory Board, provided generous and generative feedback and we gratefully acknowledge their input, which has made this a better book. We are thankful as well to several scholars, archivists, and activists who, in one way or another, left their mark on this project: Sara Ahmed, Tamara Chaplin, Jonathan Ned Katz, Oraison Larmon, Deborah Levine, Tavia Nyong'o, Susan Stryker, Marvin J. Taylor, and Jeffrey Weeks, among others. In Melbourne, the Australian Queer Archives and Deakin University's School of Communication and Creative Arts and its Gender and Sexuality Studies Research Network provided a nourishing intellectual environment supporting this work; and Daniel also thanks Valda Marshall, Roger Marshall, Gary Jaynes, Mary Lou Rasmussen, Anna

Hickey-Moody, Michal Morris, Don Hill, Dino Hodge, Geoffrey Robinson, Eliza Smith, Peter Aggleton, Rob Cover, Benjamin Hegarty, Timothy Jones, and Duane Duncan. In New York City, the Department of Spanish and Portuguese Languages and Literatures at New York University has been a supportive intellectual environment to carry out this work. Zeb wishes to acknowledge the help of the archivists at the Archivo General de Centro América, and especially Anna Carla Ericastilla for her unflagging support. Last, we are extremely grateful to the NYU Center of the Humanities, and especially to Ulrich Baer and Molly Rogers, for supporting this project with a book subvention grant, and to Jen Burton for assisting with the indexing of the book.

The book's cover artwork is based on art by Danielle Brathwaite-Shirley: *H1 (haunting Ebun Sodipo)* and *H2 (haunting Tobi Adebajo)*, 2021, video hologram diptych. These pieces are featured in the artist's exhibition *Get Home Safe* at David Kordansky Gallery. Situated throughout *Get Home Safe* are video portraits composed using motion capture data, which records the movement of objects and people. Here, Brathwaite-Shirley records data from Black trans people and converts the data into text, which, in turn, gives the human form in these works a new, readable body. The portraits speak to visitors of the exhibition and depict Black trans people from a range of source materials, both found by and given to the artist. Also included are images of people Brathwaite-Shirley meets; each participant receives compensation for their time and the personal stories they share. The portraits are both homages and testaments to the power of speaking about the fullest range of life experiences. Likewise, they document the process of assuming agency for the ways in which one is remembered and identified by the community at large.

Introduction

(Re)Turning to the Queer Archives

DANIEL MARSHALL AND ZEB TORTORICI

This anthology centers on the queer archival turn at the intersection of feminist and queer studies, literary and cultural studies, and history. The book is born from the relationship between ideas of archives and the cultural, political, and embodied work of *turning*.[1] We focus on how ideas about the archive have been shaped by rhetorics and practices of specific types of turns, and on the work of turning itself as part of epistemological, historiographical, and archival production. In this light, the book interrogates the cultural politics of *turning to* the archives—the roles and functions that archives and archival knowledges are pressed into to serve a multitude of shifting demands. It also analyzes multiple turns among and away from archives. Our contributors trace overlapping and at times contradictory sequences of turns, where diverse physical objects deposited into (or excluded from) the archives get turned into forms of knowledge, which are then deployed and put to work by a wide range of investigative turns to "the archive" as a site for the imagining and writing of history about sex, gender, and sexuality. Archives are places where material gets *turned into* something else: evidence or loss, history or an inspiration to do history differently. We are interested, then, in the transformative histories echoing inside the term "to turn," and in how "the archival" gets turned into a distinct form of archival endeavor when the records being archived focus explicitly on sex, gender, and sexuality. Indeed, insofar as the queer archival turn might be inseparable from people's experiences of being *turned on*, intellectually or erotically, by what one discovers in the past, it is also inseparable from developments which have seen this emphasis change understandings of what an archive is (or what it *can be*).

The so-called archival turn in the humanities typically refers to the frenetic pace of interdisciplinary interest in notions of "the archive" following the 1995 publication of Jacques Derrida's *Archive Fever: A Freudian Impression*.[2] Yet as Ann Laura Stoler writes, "the archival turn has a wider arc and a longer durée. *Archive Fever* compellingly captured that impulse by giving it theoretical stature, but Jacques Derrida's intervention came only after the 'archival turn' was already being made."[3] The "archival turn" might best be seen, then, as a part of the broader reimagination of the archive in the humanities and the social sciences in the final decades of the twentieth century.[4] As Ruth Rosengarten notes, "The trope of 'the turn' has coloured the history of the humanities for over half a century: we've had quantitative, linguistic, cultural and spatial turns in the academy. The figure of a corporeal change of position and orientation is used, then, to make intelligible a structure of reflexivity, and importantly, with it, a shift in aesthetic and cognitive direction, if not paradigm."[5] The figuration of this "turn" to the archives has, of course, been shaped by disciplinary perspectives by those whose fields have not traditionally involved archives in the first place. Part of the controversial nature of this so-called turn is the always immanent risk of erasing the work in core disciplinary fields like library and information studies (or archivistics) and history, where archival theory and praxis have been most fully developed. Contentiously, as other disciplines turned on to the archive, what they often brought with them was at least an implicit critique that archives had up until then circulated within their natural disciplinary homes as largely uninterrogated "depositories of documents."[6] The "archival turn" has often been framed in general terms not only as an engagement with archival knowledges and methods from fresh disciplinary perspectives, but also as an aggressive project of theorization that problematically often imagined archives as "virgin territories" ripe for fresh theoretical cultivation. It is precisely the performative elements of this work that interest us here—unpacking how the archival turn has generated particularly queer ways of knowing archives and the bodies and desires they house. Some of the many operations through which people and things "turn archival" become evident in the ways that the chapters of *Turning Archival* trace the life of the historical in the field of queer studies.

What *queer* means, of course, is not straightforward. Since the arrival of the term into a range of disciplines in the 1990s, queer has been contested, especially within LGBTQ history.[7] Part of the controversy of queer as it emerged in some early formations was its centering of a narrow set of privileged perspectives and presumptions under the sign of a purportedly radical deconstruction. As many historians and scholars persuasively argued, early deconstructionist work in queer theory routinely decontextualized the study of sex, gender, and sexuality, ahistoricizing scholarship and privileging a mode of critique that problemati-cally often reproduced uneven power relations that gender and sexuality stud-ies had historically sought to trouble (the privileging of white perspectives or the marginalization of critical engagements with class in some early queer studies are examples of this). In much of the earlier scholarship in gay and lesbian stud-ies and queer studies—and indeed, much scholarship today—*queer* has often been taken as an unstated default, a presumption of a white, able-bodied, cis-normative, middle-class subject of Eurocentric modernity, whose "queerness" nonetheless falls outside certain norms. In these deployments of queer, its rep-utation for subversion came to rest, problematically, on an effacement of a raft of dominant power relations that much queer scholarship has since sought to bring into focus. The conceptual union between turning and queer is a gen-erative one, then, because it indexes movement within queer studies to turn the focus of critique to neglected perspectives and marginalized knowledges. Part of this turn within queer studies over the last quarter-century has been a refreshed engagement with materialism and materialist critique, and a reap-praisal of the significance of lived experience. This (re)turn to the materiality of the body and how it intersects with sex, sexuality, and gender has brought renewed attention to the practices and politics of embodiment that have been so crucial in the cultural politics and histories of gender and sexuality studies.

The problematic functioning of queer as reinstating a set of unstated default presumptions turned into, especially in the 1990s and early 2000s, an impetus to reshape the boundaries, subjects, and methods of queer studies from within. Work in a range of disciplinary fields—and especially born out of feminist stud-ies and queer of color critique in its early years—*turned to* the archives precisely as a way of documenting the presence of difference to challenge queer's false normativities and to help foster the development of the material conditions to support the staging of critiques that broadened the scope of queer. Work in the exponentially growing field of trans studies, for example, illustrates this ap-proach through efforts to develop approaches in community LGBTQ archiving and in the simultaneous development of both public and scholarly archival knowledges (Susan Stryker's work is a powerful example of how queer stud-ies has been reshaped by moves within trans studies to turn to the archives).[8] Part of what is so radical about the intersection of trans studies and queer of color critique in relation to the archive is that it has excavated what the ar-chive means and how archival knowledge gets produced. Our reading of the performativity of the queer archival turn draws on how scholars like C. Riley Snorton have theorized archival knowledges as active sites of meaning-making, where trans and blackness achieve significance to each other in part through their apprehensions in the archives. For Snorton, "'black on both sides' refers to the temporal, spatial, and semantic concerns that are multiplicatively redoubled—between, beside, within, and across themselves—in transitive and transversal relation."[9] For the contributors to *Turning Archival*, then, the queer archival turn is a meaning-making maneuver that provides new ways of theorizing the idiom of the archive and new forms of embodiment in relation to it.

Similarly, the field of critical disability or crip studies has also reshaped the archive through notions of embodiment, questions of access, and notions of crip time. This notion of crip time challenges understandings of the archival through critical reflections on embodied experiences of how differently abled bodies move through archival space and time in particular ways: "*Crip time is time travel.* Disability and illness have the power to extract us from linear, progressive time with its normative life stages and cast us into a wormhole of backward and forward acceleration, jerky stops and starts, tedious intervals and abrupt endings."[10] Through the insights of crip studies and its elaboration of diverse practices of embodiment, notions of the archival have been reshaped by reappropriated engagements with historical notions of archival (dis)order, exposing the poverty of an unreconstructed archive studies which relies on the fictive presumptions of an unchallenged ableism. Records creation and archival description, as Gracen Brilmyer has shown, have long played a role in documenting and surveilling "disabled" and other non-normative bodies and minds.[11] Yet through crip interventions in the archive, the once-regulatory archive gets turned into something larger, something more capacious, to accommodate the diverse embodied histories it contains. These very same archives become places to find and connect with the "knowledge learned through one's own disabled insights as well as those of crip kin and ancestors."[12] And as Ryan Lee Cartwright shows, crip time in the archives breaks and reassembles order in the archives in line with the embodied experience of turning to the archive: "The disabled researcher's shaking, seizing, stimming and drooling have been deemed 'impediments' to the important work of the archive and its orderliness."[13] Through varied modes of living and experiencing crip time—outside of the archives, and within—it is not only that the archive expands to house unruly disorder but that all of this diverse embodiment reshapes the archive itself, exposing the limitations of ableist archival imaginaries. Centering and prizing such diverse archival "impediments," we are engaging with queer, then, in the same way that we are engaging with the archival: as ideas in motion, they function as terms of a critical destabilization which has been manifest in queer studies through the growing diversity of embodied experience that now characterizes the field. And while the referents of the queer archival turn may necessarily be "unfixed," what centers the queer archival turn is this figure of the body and how critiques, rejections, friendly amendments, and cautions regarding queer at some level revolve around questions of embodiment—the racially minoritized, gendered, classed, cripped, transed bodies—that push back on queer's unstated body-norms.[14] Turning to the queer archive, then involves turning away from it—we want to turn away from queer's unstated body-norms to bring into focus other bodies, other archived desires, other histories, and our work here is informed by critiques that help us expand how we understand links between archives and embodiment. *Turning Archival* turns to the life of the historical in queer studies in the spirit of how these disciplines have turned the archive back on itself to invent new archival studies for the future, and revised understandings of the archival through reflections on the generative labor and preservation of embodiment itself.

*

To think about the "archival turn" in queer terms is to understand how the idea of the archives turns on this notion of turning—it is to put the very notion of the *turn* itself front and center. The idea of *turning* resists easy immobilization; instead it encompasses multidirectionality, and movements and frictions that traverse space and time. The wide semantic range just lurking under the definitional veneer of the "turn" illustrates its twisting analytical potential. As a verb of motion, "to turn" might signify—as it did in the late Old English *turnian* and the Middle English *tournen, tornen,* and *turnen,* which absorbed their meanings from earlier Old English terms that separated out their meanings (and directions) of motion—either "the motion of turning back to the direction of the place from which the subject came" or "to go (on in the same direction)."[15] The very idea of the turn, in its late Old English etymological roots, thus already represents the proliferation of directionalities, the fecund capacity of multidirectionality, that we associate with the term. *Turn* is partly derived from the Latin *tornare,* which signified "to turn in a lathe" and is related to the Latin word for a "turner's wheel," that is, a machine for shaping wood or metal by means of rotation.[16] In modern English, the word *turn* turns up a complex assemblage of connotations, ranging from the (literal and figurative) "turning point," a place or time at which a decisive change takes place; a turn (of a river) as a "place of bending"; to "take a turn" as in a sudden alteration in the state or ability of the body or mind; and to "turn up," as deployed early in this sentence, to convey an arrival or appearance. Key instantiations of *to turn* denote change and transformation through some form of rotation, as the Proto-Indo-European root of the word—*tere-,* meaning to rub, drill, pierce, and twist—suggests.[17] *Turning Archival* capaciously plays with these many meanings, investigating how turning *to* the archives can be understood in terms of friction, pleasure, and desire, always caught up in unsteady—and relentlessly generative—processes of transformation.

The work of turning is similarly yoked to regimes of power that produce transformations, in different scales and with different implications. This is one reason there is something inherently queer about turning: its obsessive orientation toward transformation means that the work of turning often involves taking simplified options—usually binary options—and knitting or kneading them together, turning so many figurative threads into a shawl or a few ingredients into a dough. Like queerness, practices of turning constitute the lability of whatever constituent elements are at hand. Turning often involves taking disparate elements and producing something different from their almost alchemical combination; turning is often described in magical terms (as the magician turns, say, a handkerchief in a hat into a rabbit, so too are discoveries in the archives often described as turning into something of a different order than what the archival thing is in and of itself). Turning invokes ideas about transformation in other registers, too. For example, the phrase "to turn oneself in" (or to be "turned in") references an individual's subjection to particular types of authorities, a process that typically sets in motion an archivable documentary trail that transforms the juridical subject (e.g., from free citizen to prisoner), providing a clear illustration of links between ideas of turning and bureaucratic regimes of power. From juridical judgment to esoteric magic, and from knitted blankets to baked breads, the cultural history of turning is replete with so many different routines for alterations in signification that the changes produced by turning in—donating, giving up, selling, losing, or bequeathing—an object to the archive, and then turning to it for one use or another, might appear to be just one other illustration of the work of transformation in the long cultural history of turns and turning. Yet there is something specific about turning *queerly*. The deep attachments inspired by the specifically *queer* archival turn—evidenced by its successful career both inside the academy and outside of it—invite more direct exploration of the constitution and resonance of its particular significance. For us, the notion of *turning archival* frames an investment in exploring how, through a kind of mutual reliance, certain things turn into something that can be named both "queer" and "archival." In other words, the notion of *turning archival* calls up or designates practices of reflection through which we might come to more closely track the diverse ways notions of queerness and the archive are iteratively produced through our turns to them. A key project of the queer archival turn becomes the work of turning to reflect on itself and the myriad ways in which the cultural politics of archives, archival practices, preserved material things, classificatory structures, their epistemological limits, and diverse rationales driving users to turn to the archives all get stitched together in discrete, often fleeting, and always mobile moments of signification and meaning-making. In *turning archival*, the queer archival turn turns toward a wall of mirrors or, perhaps, a mirage.

The proliferation of what an archive might be is a defining characteristic of the popularization of archives over the past half-century. As Kate Eichhorn notes, "Since the archival turn in the early 1990s, researchers have reconfigured everything from collections of graffiti under highway overpasses to the human genome as types of archives. The plasticity of the concept has opened up new avenues through which to question the authority of the archive while simultaneously legitimizing non-institutional collections as important sites of research and inquiry."[18] It has thus become commonplace, as Geert-Jan Van Bussel and Marlene Manoff respectively discuss, to hear of configurations including the "social archive," the "raw archive," the "postcolonial archive," the "popular archive," the "ethnographic archive," the "geographical archive," and the "liberal archive."[19] To this list we might add the "intimate archive," the "affective archive," the "porn archive," the "ethnopornographic archive," the "medical archive," the "torture archive," the "poetic archive," the "performative archive," the "rebel archive," and so on.[20] Indeed, the term's ubiquity threatens to empty it of a precise significance. Unsurprisingly then, the "queer archive" more often than not serves as a black box, an ambiguous signifier into which the deployer of the term pours their hopes, fantasies, and anxieties. Valentines are written to the queer archive, and it is set out as a familiar site for cultural lamentation. Almost half a century after the establishment of community LGBTQ archives, the notion of the queer archive is seen by some as an idea that has lost useful specificity. But like the zombies in *The Return of the Living Dead*, queer archives refuse to die as the knowledges they signify get reanimated, over and over. We return to the archives queerly, then, to explore how the fragments of the past—all that ephemeral dust, desire, and documentary incompletion—get turned, again and again, into material to feast on in the present.

The possibilities—of the *X* archive—are, no doubt, interminable. And rather than grieve this excess and try to grasp toward some kind of arbitration regarding what an archive is or is not, we share a view with Eric Ketelaar, who in his "Archival Turns and Returns: Studies of the Archive" emphatically proclaims: "Let anything be 'as archive' and let everyone be an archivist. The important question is not 'what is an archive' but how does this particular individual or group perceive and understand an archive?"[21] Ketelaar discusses the archival turn as characterized by acknowledging archives as subjects of study: How is it that we might come to know archives as "things"? How archives have come to be known as queer things is a key question for the authors whose chapters we include here. Ketelaar considers a range of archival turns—linguistic, social, performative, representational, and so on—and his discussion of the archival turn as having produced archives as "things" with "agency" brings up the conditions under which archival agency itself is produced and made legible. Explicitly tied to broader regimes of power governing the context within which any archival endeavor emerges, "archival agency" is necessarily shaped by the cultural politics pertinent to an archive's collection and situation, suggesting how queer archival agency is freighted with specific historical contests in relation to authority, gender, and sexuality more generally. Similarly, Ketelaar's observation that the archival turn has been characterized by a turn to the body—such as in his discussion of reenactments and embodiment—invites further reflection on the particular significance of this development from a queer perspective.[22] Queer bodies have, of course, been subjected to unique and complex histories of erasure, regulation, modification, and amplification in the archives. Indeed, an enduring imperative of queer archival work has been to challenge and reconfigure the terms under which bodies and their desires have archival existences. The importance of the body and practices of archival embodiment that Ketelaar observes as being central to the archival turn have added significance when that turn goes queer.

Turning Archival emerges out of a series of long-running conversations with people working in and outside of queer archive studies, which is reflected partly in our prior coediting of two special issues of *Radical History Review* on "Queering Archives" (see articles by archivists including Rebecka Taves Sheffield, Peter Edelberg, and others). Archival science and library studies scholars have been at the forefront of exploring the implications of the increased preservation and conservation of LGBTQ materials, and some of the most important interdisciplinary queer studies work on archives is directly indebted to library and information studies. See, for instance, recent scholarship by those whose earlier work appeared in our *Radical History Review* issues, including Robb Hernández's *Archiving an Epidemic: Art, AIDS, and the Queer Chicanx Avant-Garde*; Cait McKinney's *Information Activism: A Queer History of Lesbian Media Technologies*; and Rebecka Taves Sheffield's *Documenting Rebellions: A Study of Four Lesbian and Gay Archives in Queer Times*, among others.[23] *Turning Archival* has strategically assembled a group of humanities scholars at the intersection of queer studies and disciplinary boundaries, working on a range of temporal and geopolitical contexts. In their own ways the chapters trace the career of the queer archival turn in humanities scholarship (especially queer studies and gender/sexuality studies) and serve as a companion piece to the expanding field of queer archives scholarship in library and information studies.[24] In *Turning Archival* we are foregrounding these turns between, among, and toward the multiple disciplines constituting queer archive studies not only as performative turns through which the subjects of our analysis are produced, but as hopeful turns toward further transdisciplinary collaboration.

*

Histories of LGBTQ archiving are enmeshed in overlapping histories of activism, research, and theoretical work that has sought to examine experiences of difference, especially in terms of class, race, and citizenship status as they intersect with gender and sexuality. Queer archive studies—and archive studies in general—is indebted to much longer histories of scholarship examining racism, slavery, colonialism, class injustice, and migration. As McKemmish and Gilliland observe, the archive-oriented critical theory that has emerged over the past half-century has developed techniques "for theorizing about both the role of the Archive in social conditions and forces such as colonialism, oppression, marginalization and abuse of human rights, and the part that it might play in postcolonial, post-trauma and post-conflict societies."[25] It is in this critical tradition of paying attention to questions of history and power, and institutions and their subjects, that *turning archival* is framed as a critical posture that invites us to more carefully attend to the ways in which archives are not only situated within the context of the cultural politics of gender and sexuality, but also how knowledges generated through turning to the archive play active roles in these political struggles.

Born first from liberation-era struggles to turn away from histories of omission, queer archiving gained its footing by making a stand on the grounds of evidence—that gender and sexual difference had left historical traces and the renegade preservation of the dissident historical knowledge such traces informed could be the basis for new ways to recognize the past and set the terms for a desirable future. Despite these early affirmations of the political power of documented proof of historical sexual and gender difference, the question of evidence has, of course, always been controversial in histories and cultural politics of gender and sexual difference. This is largely because the idea of evidence has so often been used so powerfully against women and queers, especially Indigenous people and people of color, working-class communities, and those with disabilities. These troubling histories mean that appealing in any straightforward way to the merits of evidence risks incorporation within those historical and often juridical structures of power that have policed and regulated queer life in both the past and the present. Queer critique thus must stay alert to the diverse and often nefarious ways in which evidence has been mobilized against queers, and this speaks to the political importance of examining the performative work of *turning* sexual and gender difference into archival evidence that this book explores. Such analyses can ultimately help expose, in the words of Marisa J. Fuentes, both "the machinations of archival power" and the ways that the archive always "conceals, distorts, and silences as much as it reveals."[26]

Put simply, queer archive studies is a struggle against reading evidence straight, not least because the very idioms and institutions for the production of archival knowledge continue to be so deeply enmeshed in colonial matrices of value, authority, access, and power. As Ann Cvetkovich oberves, so many "foundational texts for the archival turn predate queer theory" and many of these texts—from Gayatri Spivak's "Can the Subaltern Speak?" to Michel-Rolph Trouillot's *Silencing the Past: Power and the Production of History*—are grounded in the epistemological and political concerns of postcolonial critique (and the lingering aftereffects of empire).[27] More than a diffuse desire to turn extant understandings of archives into something else by replacing them with a more or less benign, banal kind of poststructuralist proliferation, decolonizing queer critiques of the archive and archival practice seek to alter the idiom through which the subjects of the archive are constructed as part of broader anticolonial political struggles. As Anjali Arondekar observes in this volume, concerns with reading queer pasts "are especially pressing for the lives of sexual minorities as the legal and economic right to be here and now is often authorized by the evidence of histories past." The legacies of the complicity of colonial archives in turning diverse subjects around the world into racialized, sexualized, and gendered others endure in marked and umarked ways today. As LGBTQ archiving achieves increased state sponsorship in different national contexts, more and more questions are being asked about the implications of turning state histories into LGBTQ histories and vice versa. The tracing of the diverse functions and effects of these "turns"—as both rhetorical expressions and epistemological practices—helps to illustrate some of the ways that the queer archival turn has given shape to contemporary racialized understandings of sex, gender, sexuality, and archives while also generating a site for turning the queer archival turn to reflect on its own histories and complicities and examine the colonial contours of its own desires and discoveries.

By turning to reflect on the queer archival turn itself, this collection reflects on the terms and practices through which sex, gender, and sexuality are understood as having *turned archival*. This critical reflection can guide us away, we hope, from an earnest and straightforward celebration of the "queer archive" and toward a more expansive consideration of the productivity of the queer archival turn itself. As the queer archival turn considers its mirrors—and its mirages—what comes into focus is how the queer archival turn produces its varied forms of knowledge, and, enticingly, we also catch glimpses of assemblies of queerness and the archival that diverge from the disciplinary motions, temporalities, and spatialities that have been enforced through normative practices of turns and turning. In these ways, the works presented here seek to diversify relationships between archives, gender, and sexuality while also critically reflecting on how time and again, the cultural politics of gender and sexuality have turned to archives to harness their knowledge-producing power within often tightly confined knowledge pursuits. The explorations in this book, then, might be thought of as experiments or explorations in mapping out what we might call a *postarchival* tendency in queer and feminist studies—explorations in the life of the historical in feminist and queer studies in the wake of the archival turn— and one that contributes to other scholarly efforts to reflect on the productive work of the historical, methodological, political, and personal injunction to turn to the queer archive.[28] The chapters here take turns at working through the turn to the archival in queer and feminist studies as means to explore diverse ways of engaging historical knowledge and experience in contemporary cultural politics of gender and sexuality. And the turns engaged and performed by each chapter give body to, and flesh out, different visions of what *turning archival* looks like.

Seeking to press against the disciplined expectation to turn to the archive in normative ways, the feminist and queer scholarship in this book digs deeper into links between ideas of feeling and motion, which often mobilize relations between the archival and gender and sexuality. The turn to the archive in queer studies has often been examined as so many practices of emotion and affect, and what interests us here is the importance of ideas about motion and movement to affective engagements with the archive—a relationship that a critical reflection on archival turns helps bring into focus. Anecdotally, it is common to remark on how one is "moved" by a turn to the archive—moved by experiences of witnessing historical lives and events that invoke a diverse array of feelings from horror to admiration and pleasure to fear. The messiness of emotional movements denoted by the queer archival turn means that any analysis of the productivity of turning to the archive cannot be bound to any conclusive, straightforward feeling—every moment of archival pride is shadowed by archival shame. This proliferation of archival feelings is symptomatic of the performativity of turning archival. By exploring multiple ways in which the turn to the archive is generative, producing multiple coexisting forms of knowledge that rub up against each other, we can recall Sedgwick's theorization of the per-formativity of "thinking beside" (as opposed to "thinking beyond") in *Touching Feeling: Affect, Pedagogy, Performativity*.[29] Here, Sedgwick extends her theoriza-tion of performativity in *Epistemology of the Closet*, which she presented as a theoretical alternative to critical accounts that believed in the conclusive turn represented by the idea of a "great paradigm shift" (as illustrated, for example, by apparently contrasting critical discussions about "homosexuality today").[30] In other words, our focus here is not the destination, or final significance, of any given turn, but rather a reflection on the pluralizing epistemologies and embodiments that are generated by frictive archival turns when understood as performative motions of change and transformation.

As the historical deployment of a language of "movement" reminds us, from the women's movement to the Black Lives Matter movement and beyond, his-tories of sexual and gender difference have often made explicit how emotion is constituted, in part, by motion itself. And if we examine the motions contained within the emotion of the archival turn, we can reflect on how the union be-tween the archival and gender and sexual difference has been sharply shaped by ideas about turning as a regulated form of motion. By exploring how the motion of turning disciplines the way that the archival is thought about and practiced from the perspective of gender and sexuality studies and politics, we might better be able to understand the enduring power of thinking about en-gagements with the archive through a rhetoric of turns, and thus sponsor less regulated forms of engagement between archives, gender and sexuality, and subsequent knowledge production. *Turning Archival* seeks to denaturalize the relationship between feminist and queer studies and the archives by turning to explore some of the implications of this turning work itself. How do objects get materially and discursively altered once they are turned into a given archive? How have different meanings and authorities been produced for feminist/LGBTQ research, politics, and researchers by the turn to the archive? Relatedly, how has the archival turn helped us move away from problematic notions of the historical as authentic and authorizing in particularly self-legitimizing ways?

*

Turning Archival focuses on the significance of the very *act of turning*, rather than the idea of the queer archival turn as some kind of discrete historical pe-riod or event. Sara Ahmed asks us to reflect on what "we could call 'the politics of turning' (and turning around), and how in facing this way or that the surfaces of bodies and worlds take their shape."[31] Certainly, how some historical subjects do (or do not) become "archival" is itself a reflection of how bodies and desires take shape in relation to archival technologies of conservation, reproduction, and dissemination. Turning thus partly constitutes, and partly unfixes, each and every archival subject, as the following chapters demonstrate. Every turn to the archive is a witnessing of the archive turning into something else, and that something else can often be nothing at all, with the degradation of archival materials reminding us of how the turn to immateriality is the immanent ghost of the material archive. While the archive, in the words of Francis X. Blouin Jr. and William G. Rosenberg, is "a place of imagined and unexpected possibilities," it is also a place where the inevitable destruction of material records is slowed down (through processes of conservation).[32]

This emphasis on archival loss in the queer archival turn means that the historical project imagined within its terms has often fixated on the limits of historical knowledge, generating influential insights into historical erasure as well as the problematic reproduction of methodological and political assumptions about historical invisibility. More generatively, the emphasis on the ephemerality of queerness has meant that queer archive studies has drawn attention to the elusiveness of many queer historical knowledges, identifying how such knowledge has often been historically expressed through knowledge systems that have not been decipherable to all (e.g., work in queer Indigenous studies and decolonizing approaches emphasize these observations more forcefully; also, other work by people like Samuel Steward illustrate the historical development of approaches to the preservation of queer knowledge which often included specific barriers to access).[33] Thus the queer turn in archival studies, building on Muñoz and others, has emphasized the ephemerality of gendered and sexual life, demonstrating how contemporary understandings of histories of sexual and gender difference as histories comprised of fragments have been shaped by the patterning motion of the archive as a place one turns to for piecing together something that is presumed from the outset to be broken and retrievable, at least in part, but only piece by piece. What it also emphasizes is the way in which archives in general are queer because ephemerality has been queered (that is, structured by knowledges of queerness) through the emphasis on queerness as signifying an epistemological gap or pregnant absence. Queer as a critical approach has helped to give sense to the ephemerality of archives, and as all archives are systems spanning different expressions of lack, all archives become sites of queer potential. In short, the queer archival turn has helped to bring archives studies within a register of desire.

Since the advent of the archival turn in queer studies, the intense relationship between queer studies and archive studies has turned on this notion of turning. Taking Ahmed's method of confronting an idea's persistence by following it around, the queer archival turn invites similar reflection on the work that the idea of turning is performing, not least because the recession of that moment into the recent past means that addressing it requires a different type of turn in attention.[34] Turning to the queer archival turn as an object of curiosity, a historical moment, a critical and methodological tendency within a nested set of intersecting fields of intellectual inquiry, yields a variety of generative propositions. Why, for instance, does the idea of turning bridge understandings of the queer and the archival? Certainly, the emphasis on historical scholarship in North American gay and lesbian studies of the 1970s and 1980s is one explanation for this powerful association, reflecting as it does how studies of homosexuality turned to historical methods and knowledges to consolidate and grow themselves. Indeed, the profound influence of disagreements between essentialist and social constructionist positions throughout the 1980s underlines how studies of sexuality have been shaped by an apparently inexhaustible project of returning, again and again, to some earlier historical point or figure so that it might be interrogated for the sexual and gendered evidence it could manifest.

This repetitive return to the historical as constitutive of foundational gay and lesbian studies is, of course, only one of the ways that can help us think about the success of "turning" as a way of framing the relationship between "queer" and "archive." While returning to this or that moment of history points to the ways in which the importance of history to queer studies has been largely understood in terms of history's *exteriority*, that is, queer studies' relationship to history as a set of external happenings, what the idea of "returns" also speaks to is the way in which the relationship between "queer" and "archives" has been characterized by understandings of the archive as a space where historical knowledges return something in an *interior* or internalized way—such as an affirmation of identity—to the queer subject in the archive. This diversity of turns reminds us of the variety of meanings suggested by the term discussed earlier in this introduction. Turning is a powerful idea because the action of pivoting that underpins it suggests change across a variety of scales and registers: a change in how we understand the past, a change in how we understand the self, changes within and without. It is little wonder then that the queer and the archival have been yoked together by a concept so centrally concentrated on reinvention and the plurality of meaning given the fashioning of both queer cultural politics and archival endeavors as projects focusing on the production of new knowledge and experience.

This abiding queerness of archives is observable in the ways in which archival materials are deployed to illustrate queer historical presence. Powerfully, queer archive studies asks questions of how gender and sexual difference manifest in the historical archive. We are asked to look at the precise ways in which both queerness and the archival are put to work to illustrate each other. How, in the mechanics of archival apprehension and analysis, are illustrations of gender and sexual difference composed? A study of this question of the illustrative turn—the illustration of queer presence in the archives—reveals how understandings of queerness and the archive are stitched together. As Cvetkovich writes, "Ephemeral objects have that power—gesturing to affective meanings that are attached to objects but not fully present in them, while also making immaterial ephemeralities material."[35] In this way archival objects are deeply generative, helping to materialize "immaterial ephemeralities"—it is through the queer archive that certain expressions of queer life find an expression or realization that would otherwise remain elusive. In other words, it is only by turning archival that certain forms of queer life become knowable and possible. The critical impulse encourages us to tug on those tight stitches marked by the hyphenation of the "queer-archival": by picking at those stitches we learn more about the production of queerness itself which is so often stitched up by turning to the archive.

By turning to the ways in which the archival turn is queered through its expression across feminist and queer archives, we can explore how queerness gets constituted through processes of "turning archival" while simultaneously queering what such turns mean. As feminist and queer historians have demonstrated, queer and feminist history has historically been structured by the absent presence of sexual and gendered difference. What turns up in the archive, then, is also a queer question because it raises questions beyond the mere appearance of something in the archive, asking us to think about histories of acquisition, power, loss, and production behind such appearance. If the queer archive is often understood through its emphasis on the contingency, instability, and ephemeral nature of archival material, it is also understood as a place in which meanings and histories are often made concrete, stable, and real. The rationale for many feminist and gay and lesbian archives emerging from the 1970s was to create a historical repository that would bear witness to the reality of people's lives: *we are here* (to take the title of a 2018 exhibition drawing on the collection of the Australian Queer [then Lesbian and Gay] Archives).[36] That the queer archive is often characterized by such deeply held affective and political attachments dramatizes the queer archival turn in unique ways—the queer archival turn is often about queer people turning to the archive, seeking out in the archive others who are themselves. *It is thus a turning outward as a way of turning in*. The queer archival turn has often been a turn to the past as future-building practice. That many people have a lot at stake in the queer archival project freights the work of turning with a great deal of political and personal significance and is a key reason why the archival turn has had such a prominent career in the rise of contemporary queer studies over the past four decades.

That the queer archival turn might be said to have multiple different starting points, or what we might call hinge moments, is only fitting in the context of queer studies where the ideas of teleological development and universal paradigm shifts have been problematized by scholars pointing to the performative interplay of multiple simultaneous epistemological formations: *turns beside turns*, to recall our discussion of Sedgwick earlier. *Besides*, then, straight histories of the queer archival turn that might posit the turn as happening at some static historical point in time, this collection meditates on the evasive allure of turns, and how different accounts of them function generatively. It encourages us to critically reflect on the work of turning, and what might make it attractive in the first place. Like turning over a new page, the idea of the archival turn has often carried with it the allure of the new, suggesting that a turn toward the archives signals a turn away from an older, deficient approach. The pleasures produced by this rhetorical formulation are illustrative of some of the seductive power of turning archival. A postarchival approach to these questions brings these archiving pleasures within our critical view for analysis and exploration.

This turn to archiving pleasures was, after all, in many ways a key starting point for this book, growing as it did out of earlier work Daniel Marshall conducted with Joan Nestle, the author of the coda for this collection, and explored as it was in previously mentioned special issues of *Radical History Review* on "Queering Archives" that we coedited with Kevin P. Murphy. In this earlier work we sought to think through some of the reasons relationships between queers and archives can often be so sticky and the emotions of turning so messy. This guided us to reflect more deeply on how desire and pleasure get produced through turning archival, and this in turn turned us to think more about turning itself, recalling our etymological gloss from earlier: *to go this way or that, to come and to go, to be turned and worked on as if in a carpenter's hand, to rotate with friction, to be as a "place of bending," to rub, drill, pierce, and twist.* With Sedgwick in mind, her theorization of performativity as diverse models of knowledge rubbing as they coexist "beside" each other offers a useful way to entertain all this "heat" produced by the interactions of so many diverse knowledge formations. Maybe turning archival turns people on through so much shared performative burn, like flesh heated up when a fabric twists against it just quickly enough. Wanting to place frictive engagements with the queer archival turn side by side, this collection has assembled a promiscuous movement between disciplines, theorists, and periods, collecting together diverse pieces to rub against each other, to turn against each other, and to produce that friction burn of queer significance and queer desire, helping us to rethink how gender, sexuality, and the archive are shaped, felt, and lived by the constant urge to turn.

*

The fecundity of the "turn" as a productive set of motions within queer studies is illustrated in *Turning Archival* by the diverse ways in which the historical has been put to work in queer studies across a range of contexts in North America, Latin America, South Asia, Africa, and Europe. Invoking the mercurial character of turning archival, this collection opens with a meditation on the theme of lost-and-found in two paired chapters, respectively by María Elena Martínez ("Archives, Bodies, and Imagination") and Zeb Tortorici ("Decolonial Archival Imaginaries"), which illustrate one archival turn in particular: the loss and subsequent turning up of Juana Aguilar in the Archivo General de Centro América. Martínez's chapter—written in 2013, shortly before her death—is coupled with a recent chapter by Tortorici that offers a particular type of return to Guatemala's colonial archives. Martínez offers a reflection on how disciplinary and classificatory regimes within historical and archival scholarship routinely suppress queer archival knowledge, focusing on one archival document in particular: the 1803 medical report published by the male surgeon who probed the body parts of Aguilar, a suspected "hermaphrodite" (in the language of early nineteenth-century criminal courts and medical reports) who was tried by the Royal Court in colonial Guatemala. Responding to the (then) archival absence of the original criminal trial transcripts, Martínez uses performance studies to move beyond traditional historical methodologies and reimagine lost archival knowledges. Yet as Tortorici asks, what happens when the long-lost records unexpectedly turn up in the archives?

Sometime in 2012, Sylvia Sellers-García, historian of colonial Guatemala, came across a card catalog descriptor of Aguilar's trial transcripts in the Guatemalan national archives—a fact that was unbeknownst to Martínez, Tortorici, and other historians who had previously looked for them, to no avail. Tortorici's chapter reflects on this peculiar, though not uncommon, archival twist, focusing his analysis on what happens when much desired missing archival documents—and the historical subject within—are suddenly uncovered, found again, and then filtered through the public sphere. Tortorici shows, despite having finally "found" Aguilar in the archives, the narratives we spin about them can still be just as imaginary as those written and performed prior to when the transcripts surfaced. If these documents do bring us any closer to Aguilar, they do so partly (and paradoxically) through negation—that is, through Juana's own embodied evasions of the medical and colonial bureaucratic incursions into their body and life. Yet the new details we learn about their life allow, at the same time, for a more nuanced microhistorical image of a fascinating historical figure, about whom we may one day yet know more.

Scholars of colonialism, slavery, and sexuality have long been attentive to archival economies of loss, paucity, and devaluation, turning the "archival trace" into the preferred value form through which sexuality's pasts accrue meaning. In "Telling Tales," Anjali Arondekar calls for scholars working on the history of sexuality to be attentive to how "archival consumption and dissemination" unfold in relation to minoritized historiographies, including how they privilege rhetorics of loss and recovery. Arondekar expands on the problematic significance of loss, rarity, or absence for queer archive studies by illustrating some of the implications when the lost object in the queer archive gets found, and when the lure of absence which has enticed queer archive studies for so long is overwhelmed by plenitude. Arondekar asks what makes something an archival event/situation as opposed to a mere gestural instance or example, and why does the history of sexuality take on particular narrative forms? The task here is to treat the archival trace as other than something that might allow for historical recuperation or stabilization. In Arondekar's chapter we glimpse such a turn to the hermeneutical, through the archival trace of the "evil ladies of Girgaum," in early twentieth-century South Bombay, where local Indian taxpayers complain to the colonial Commissioner of Police about the growing presence of "common prostitutes" in nearby buildings and rented rooms. Both sides argue about the in/visibilty of the problem, leading Arondekar to show how the archival trace becomes "laden with the challenges and possibilities of historical visibility," and always imbued with fantasies of value/capital that come to be implicit in the very form of the archival trace itself. This archival turn toward capital, value, and worth is one that we find both within archival documents themselves and in their materiality (leading us to think, for example, about which archives purchase which collections, and through what means). The "evil ladies" of Girgaum are, as Arondekar shows, representationally and archivally tied to "their corruption of the family form as value," and herein lies part of their queer nature, always caught between the real and apparent—caught within archival representations, among the traces, in other words.

Carrying these reflections on the affordances and constraints of institutionalized archiving in a different direction, Ann Cvetkovich—whose book *An Archive of Feelings* was influential in setting in motion the archival turn in queer studies—turns again to the archives, this time to the June L. Mazer Lesbian Archives, now housed at the special collections library at the University of California, Los Angeles.[37] In "Ordinary Lesbians and Special Collections," Cvetkovich explores what happens when grassroots lesbian feminist archives are brought into major university research libraries, turning both things into something different along the way. Recounting her intimate, archivally mediated contact with the once private epistolary exchanges between June Mazer and her lover Bunny MacCulloch, Cvetkovich describes breathing in "a queer form of archival dust," gesturing toward Carolyn Steedman's *Dust: The Archive and Cultural History*, in which the author meditates in part on historians and archivists breathing in "the dust of the dead."[38] When the lesbian archive enters the institution, or the dusty archival glitter gets breathed in by the archive visitor, what do they turn into? Throughout this chapter, Cvetkovich reflects on how turning to or being turned into the archive has transformative effects. For example, when archival materials literally refuse to "fit into a box," Cvetkovich gestures toward the ways in which this experience of *not fitting in*—a common queer turn if there ever was one—alters the significance of both institutional archival space as well as the status of the archived thing. (And remember, the original etymological roots of "turn" gesture toward rotation, trying to get objects to fit with each other.) Similar to a proposal to donate water from a gay sauna that was closing down to the Australian Queer Archives (AQuA), materials evidencing queer historical lives can be misfits, as in Cvetkovich's illustration, or leaky, to use the AQuA example, risking not only escape from proper archival collection but threatening its very order and preservation. And it is the productivity of this immanent threat to normative archival order posed by queer historical life that is foregrounded in Cvetkovich's chapter. Cvetkovich conjures up an image of "animated" archival materials jostling against their archival ordering, recalling the state-altering sense of the term turn discussed at the start of this chapter: queer archives so often invite us to think of them as archives "taking a turn"; convulsing, as if having a fit, the objects agitate. What could make more sense for archives built, as they so often are, on the preservation of histories of malady and pathology, and rage and protest? Indeed, yet undead, queer archives are animate, alive, bearing "traces of the flesh and blood pulse of both the people in the archives and the cataloguers."

Following Cvetkovich's chapter, Javier Fernández-Galeano ("Performing Queer Archives") extends this meditation on visiting queer archives through a reflection on his own experiences as a researcher in police archives—specifically, the Instituto de Clasificación, now housed in Argentina's Penitentiary Museum Antonio Ballvé—researching so-called deviant sexual activities. There, given that no photographs of written transcriptions were permitted, the author had to record himself reading archival documents out loud in order to make a copy of them. Reflecting on his experiences of reading out prisoners' responses to psychological tests, in front of the archival authorities, Fernández-Galeano theorizes the performance of archival sources as a generative archival method arguing that "the performance of dissonant voices" enables us to "better appreciate ambivalence in the face of surveillance." As becomes clear, ambivalence—the resistance to easy scrutiny—forms a key part of queer (archival) survival:

The best thing . . . I never say;

What hurts me . . . I don't show;

In secret . . . nothing.

Lo mejor . . . nunca lo digo

Lo que me duele . . . No lo demuestro

En secreto . . . nada.

Taking turns as both researcher and as the archival subject under scrutiny, Fernández-Galeano identifies how queer archival work is often propelled by ambiguous, pulsing turns flicking from guilt to desire and back again: between "the guilt that I feel for using sources that are the direct result of state violence" and "my desire to access the stories that they contain" lies a complicated archiving pleasure linked to what Emmett Harsin Drager describes as the "fugitivity" of the queer past.

In "Looking After Mrs. G," Harsin Drager extends this cultivation of a counterpathologizing, anti-authoritarian turn to the archive by focusing on the medical gaze at university-based clinics of the 1960s and 1970s through a study of the Robert J. Stoller Papers (also housed at the UCLA special collections library). This chapter advances *Turning Archival*'s reflections on the complex way in which the queer archival turn has been shaped by simultaneous attempts to turn outward to the archive as part of a technology of the self, a way to turn more into one's self: "We look in order to be found." Troubling this kind of straightforward turn to the archive, Harsin Drager second-guesses the merits of seeking out the transsexual traces in archival clinical cases as a political methodology for inverting historical logics of transsexual pathologizing because what this approach actually requires is a renewal of the historical injury of subjecting gender diverse subjects to archival scrutiny. The chapter turns the critical gaze on Stoller, the archived clinician himself, embracing this kind of queer archival inversion. The power of the clinician is thus wrapped up with both therapeutic and archival authority. Gesturing toward "a queer ethics of looking *after* rather than looking *for*," Harsin Drager turns toward an ethics of turning away, of accepting that queer life may sometimes require not archival preservation of its traces, but archival loss.

Building on such discussion of archives as urgent sites of reckoning with unfreedom in the present, Elliot James, in "Naming Afrika's Archive 'Queer Pan-Africanism,'" relates their earliest experiences of archival research—and of uncovering deep-seated histories of anti-black racial violence in their college town—at the Northfield Historical Society in the Midwest of the United States. Building on and contributing to other queer Africa-based scholars' conceptualizations of Afrika—with a "k"—as a politicized cultural space that cuts across rigid geopolitical (often ex-colonial) borders, James fashions the queer archival turn as a movement for cultivating the decolonization of sex, gender, and sexuality. The decolonizing archive then becomes more a set of shared social relations and experiences than a "depository of documents,"[39] to recall an earlier formulation, and one founded on the political and pedagogical power of recognizing Afrikan transnational solidarities across continents and oceans, partly mediated by the specter of slavery. Through a retrospective narration of a series of live events, James begins to map out what an archive of queer Pan-Africanism might look like, and how such an archive might be assembled within a cultural politics of resistance that links the contemporary moment to the historical efforts of activist "ancestors." Through this activist deployment of the notion of ancestry, James reflects on how the queer archival turn might be regarded as a movement, then, not only because of what and whom it moves, but because of those relations that move through it, back and forth across time, calling up future ghosts of queer, decolonized hope.

As time-spaces in which histories get handed on and as places where the ethics of how such histories get handled can come sharply into focus, archives are often places that get understood through a language of hands. That each archive requires the work of many hands reminds us that turning archival entails a cultural politics of handling and handing around, in more or less sophisticated ways. Daniel Marshall, in "Secondhand Cultures, Ephemeral Erotics, and Queer Reproduction," picks up this rhetoric of hands—firsthand, secondhand—to think through some of the implications of the circulation of objects among a diversity of handlers. Following Ahmed's methodological encouragement to follow "turning" around, we come across so many different hands; it seems "handy" to think about the archival turn in terms of hands not only because turning seems often to rely on hands but because turning to the language of hands tends to help us handle the subject of the archive. Eichhorn illustrates this in her invocation of a popular conception of the archive as a space "in which to locate myself in histories I never experienced firsthand." Theorizing archives through an epistemological framework of firsthand, secondhand, and the installation or restitution of significance in ephemeral objects through processes of object circulation, Marshall reflects on secondhand record collecting to think about how historical queerness becomes understood through people's relationships to objects. Taking the movement of secondhand David Bowie records from user to user, the traveling Bowie archive and the circulation of public feelings in the wake of Bowie's death as illustrative moments, Marshall develops discussions about what queer chains of inheritance might look like through theorizations of the secondhand and, relatedly, how these things might help us deepen understandings of relationships between archival materials and the enacted cultural life of queer legacies. Examining how objects get turned into different things through the various ways they are handled over time, Marshall offers a reading of queer archival engagements in terms of queer reproduction, where turning archival and all its sordid relations between first and second hands function as movements to proliferate queerness.

Providing an elaboration of secondhand cultures and diverse modes of cultural and economic (re)production and circulation, Iván A. Ramos turns to the archival implications of punk, in its political and artistic manifestations, in late twentieth-century Mexico City, by linking piracy, imaginatively illicit reproduction, and questions of access to remixed forms of cultural production. In "Pirates and Punks," bootlegging (for many of the artists discussed) is an inherently archival practice—one that resonates with DIY forms of feminist cultural production discussed by both Eichhorn and Cvetkovich here as well—because it "attempts to leave its own traces scattered as unfaithful remnants of what once was." For Ramos this longing for the imagined purity of an archival "once was" (made necessarily irretrievable by conflicting experiences and expressions of historical and contemporary desire and representation) shapes the archival turn as a recognition of "not having been there." That queer engagements with the archive foreground the failure to ever really arrive in a firsthand sense to "once was" moments renders queerness as something which is always partly out of reach, and Ramos links this to a propulsion toward queer futures based on the elusiveness of queerness, as we see in the work of José Esteban Muñoz in *Cruising Utopia*. Of course, such valorizations of queerness as incomplete and ephemeral find their natural expression through archival materials and practices because incompletion and elusion flood archives and queerness alike. Finding signs of queer life in the imperfect record, Ramos's exploration of the bootleg archive returns to concerns raised earlier in the collection about what happens when LGBTQ materials get turned into institutional collections, a theme that is shared throughout many of the chapters in *Turning Archival*.

In "Unfixed," Kate Clark and David Serlin critically situate these discussions about object circulation and queer significance within the urgent context of queer crip archive studies. "Unfixing" archival objects from their lodgment within histories built around desires for normative models of bodies and desires, Clark and Serlin work through the roles that these "queer" objects have had in co-producing forms of disabled subjectivity, while excavating promise from the painful histories of what they describe as a "disappeared aesthetics." Recalling the counterpathologizing maneuvers that characterize the queer archival turn for Fernández-Galeano and Harsin Drager, Clark and Serlin turn back to objects lodged in therapeutic histories in order to extract them through the force of their own theoretical reframing. One example of this is the work they perform recontextualizing historical wartime bandages that had been "used and destroyed" before they could be preserved as artifacts in a "disappeared" queer crip archive. Recalling Marshall's reflections on secondhand object circulation, Clark and Serlin invoke the image of "the material circulation of the bandage on the battlefield as it moves between the hands of soldiers trained for warfare but not for welfare" to bring it within the purview of the queer crip archival, arguing that it indexes not "sexual practices" but "new forms of same-sex intimacy and socialization" forged "on the battlefield in the intimate skills of triage." The work of "unfixing" advocated by the authors—the work of decontextualizing archival objects from normative archival lodgment and recontextualizing them within an analytical framework that intersects queer and crip investments in the historical—involves a kind of archival labor which the authors allegorize through reference to the figure of the nursing soldier in triage. Archival unfixing emerges, then, in a queer turn and allegorized in the care work of triage, as a way to try to fix archival injury, to tend archival wounds and work for historical healing.

Opening this introduction, we reflected on the etymology of the turn, and read in its promise of rubbing and grinding, drilling and twisting, a kind of Sedgwickean performativity, where Clark and Serlin's renegade appropriations of objects into a queer crip archive generate new, suggestive archival knowledges that rub up beside those fostered by the normative historical knowledges within which such objects have previously been "disappeared." With the "intimacy and industriousness" of the soldier's triage work both as an object of their analysis (insofar as such care work is residualized in the archival bandage) and as an analogy for their method, Clark and Serlin's queer archival turn inverts the norm-work of historical therapeutics, displacing it with the critical care work of a contemporary politics of archival un/fixing. The queer archival turn is thus rendered in urgent terms, with the friction produced by proliferating knowledges manifesting in every sense a struggle, a struggle for non-normative life made material at the site of the archive itself, and a struggle that sponsors the question: How might we all best nurse the archives we inherit? How might we tend to a world so that it might be fit to care for the queer histories it inherits?

As is clear in Clark and Serlin's discussion of the queer archive as an archive of "the thrown away" and "the cast off," and in Arondekar and Marshall, the queerness of archives links tightly to the ways in which these archival practices challenge normative understandings of archival value. In "An Archival Life," Martin F. Manalansan provides a different kind of reflection on what Clark and Serlin describe as the "queerness of detritus" in his reflection on archives as lived phenomena, explored through extended ethnographic research with members of queer undocumented immigrants' households in New York City. Through thick description, Manalansan offers analytical reflections of his fieldwork conducted between 2003 and 2012 as "a queer take on 'dwelling in the archives' as the quotidian becomes the fuel for animating capacious engagements with queer undocumented immigrants as 'impossible subjects' of history." For Manalansan, queer experience can be indexed in part through what he terms "archival life," where people's lives are saturated with everyday things that mark their contemporary situation and their historical traces as racialized subjects living under racist governance structures. Detached from institutions and enacted in the personal space of the home, these queer archives turn normative understandings of archives inside out as they refuse routine distinctions between public and private, institutional and personal, and exterior and interior. Focusing on the "stuff" that makes up the "archival life" of queer migrants, Manalansan traces a shifting set of practices of collecting and caring, placement and displacement, acquisition and loss. These documented accounts perform their own archiving work, collecting and preserving entangled and messy intimacies between space, time, objects, and people as a record of archival life amid a crisis in citizenship—crises that have only been exacerbated by the recent growth of alt-right and fascist ideologies around the globe (and the ongoing elections of right-wing populist leaders that do their best to curtail the rights of immigrants and turn nativist sentiments against them, often regardless of immigrants' own legal status). Through turning to this mode of dwelling in history, Manalansan offers a meditation on archival ecologies of affective events, atmospheres, and object uses that are "awash in the fluid and ambivalent forces of modernity," nationalism, normativity, morality, legality, and pleasure.

As set out at the start of this introduction, one set of critical interests that gave rise to this book was the desire to reflect on the career of the archival turn within queer studies. In "Reassessing 'The Archive' in Queer Theory," Kate Eichhorn turns us back to those questions through an examination of the rise of the archive as a critical trope within largely North American queer theory and cultural theory. Situating her own work within this historical deployment while also calling attention to its implications, Eichhorn investigates some of the ways that queer studies can revise its engagement with the archive by paying more attention to the specificities of archival labor. Under these terms, Eichhorn revisits queer people's involvement in the "recirculation" of archival materials that promise proximity to histories that can't be "experienced first-hand," asking how queers thus build an understanding of the archive through such uses. Queers may be "at home in archives," as per Eichhorn's contention, but on what foundations are these homes built and occupied? Or, put another way, under what labor terms have queers been turned into historical evidence and archives turned into queer resources? Queer studies can revitalize its engagement with archives and archival knowledge, Eichhorn argues, by focusing on the work of turning—all those hands—and mapping out renewed recognitions of the ways in which "archives are deeply embedded in power structures" and thus "engaged in the production of subjects, the conditions of language, and the possibility of alternative histories and countergenealogies."

As several chapters demonstrate, the political usefulness of a deconstructed understanding of the queer archive has rested in large measure on a common queer experience of queer subjects, users, and knowledges being excluded from archival collections, and queer archives have often been shaped as responses to these exclusions. However, as greater attention has been given to the queerness that has been preserved within archives, the archival turn has been experienced in more diffuse and often ambivalent ways, as expectations of triumphalist historical discovery have given way to exposure to more diversity and ambiguity. Indeed, the archival turn in queer studies can be understood as a process of turning toward and away from a clear sense of what queerness in the archive is, and what archives themselves are. Like a chimera, established ideas about queerness are often undone by the turn to the archives (just as it is in reverse). Looking there, the imagined vision of historical queerness often vaporizes—emerging as a much less stable proposition than beforehand. In "Crocker Land," Carolyn Dinshaw and Marget Long take up the notion of turning archival by exploring it as a logic of motion driving queer studies, which they explore through a discussion of the archival pursuit of a mirage, which functions much like an archive: "It refracts, duplicates, shifts, distorts, expands our vision." The mirage itself—not unlike the desires that come to be simultaneously represented within and obscured by archives and their systems of classification—"shimmers but cannot be corralled, contained, saved, or stored," which prompts a rethinking of archival practice "as an ongoing, perpetual revelation." This invocation recalls the transformative magic inhering in the turn to the archives that we foregrounded at the start of this introduction, where the indeterminacy and lability of queer material in the archives is a specified way to understand the more generalized performativity of sex, gender, and sexuality. The authors conjure up "our old friend the mirage" as they reflect on the vagaries of archival sleuthing, and it is the tenderness of the expression that is moving, for so often, for so many of us, we have turned to the archives in search of some kind of connection. That this connection might, as it turns out, be fostered less by what is found when we turn to the archive and more by involvement in a shared practice of turning, of searching, of hoping and then troubling what is found, endures as what might still make archival turns queer.

Starting with the problem of sameness and the desire for something we recognize, the queerness of archives presents us with difference, ultimately requiring us to recalibrate the terms of our initial turn or quest in the first place. Turning to the archive, we are turned into something else ourselves and invited into the world of the past not because of what we have in common with it but because of a shared sense of how different we are from it. That our engagements with archives, as with mirages, might routinely be characterized by elusion and evasion is, as Dinshaw and Long demonstrate, a key part of their value and what compels us to turn to them, again and again. Perhaps, they suggest, gender and sexual difference may need to remain at least in some respects unreachable (lost in the archive) if desire is to be preserved. Does securing gender and sexual difference in the archive vanish or dilute the desire that animates it? If desire is understood as a longing, then can desire be preserved—archived—when that act of preservation necessarily "fixes" the object in place (to recall Clark and Serlin), effectively diminishing desire through the consummation of archival "discovery"? In short, does the queer archive freeze the desires it saves in the act of making them archivable and available? Do the material limits of the archived thing reduce queerness to the limits of evidence? If queerness is to be preserved as that which, to use Dinshaw and Long's words, "beckons, but . . . can't ever be reached," then a key challenge for queer archive studies is to consider how we might turn to archives without arresting their desire, without making it necessary to "drain the liveness."

To bring historical materials within a queer frame of perception, Dinshaw and Long talk about looking "askew": discussing one particular image they describe literally inverting it—and inversion is such a fitting queer turn because in its punning way it turns us to look back on the histories we inherit. This reminds us that humor, after all, endures as a necessary archival (e)motion and one that often carries us through histories marked so often by pain and penalty, triaging archival injury. Even though each archive is a record of its own losses, humor might be a fix when queer archive studies has so often been caught up in its hauntings—a different (e)motion to move us when we get stuck. In finding the humor in the hurt, in looking askew at the archive, in hunting the ever-receding mirage, we might turn to the queer archive not to repair its losses but, as Dinshaw and Long argue, to "value the *unsaveable*." Such work involves a turning away from an "expansionist" or incorporative approach that has too often sought to assimilate the archival into preexisting knowledges, categories, and desires and to reject the fantasies of empire and conquest that such incorporations too easily risk sliding into. Instead, at journey's end, surrounded by so many maps to mirages, we might chart a course for the enduring promise of defamiliarization and difference which the archival encounter fosters, finding at last, like Dinshaw and Long, that "'we were strange to ourselves and strange to others.'"

In the coda to this collection, "Who Were We to Do Such a Thing?," Joan Nestle draws a different kind of map of archival hope and defamiliarization, recalling her work with the Lesbian Herstory Archives and how her lived history now reframes that work: "Queer archives of the future perhaps will give evidence that it is harder to live with a history than without one." Rubbing beside those foundational hopes for historical reparation through archival accumulation are "new questions, new uncertainties," which redraw a hope in a set archival destination with a desire for the queer archival to always unsettle itself, to keep turning, to keep the friction burning: "The queer archives must be a border crossing in all directions."

The archival turn is thus so many turnings understood anew: a turning back to take up those things that resource new futures, and a turning away from certain turns taken. Nestle emphasizes how the queer archival project has pivoted on these friction points of liberation and dissent, of exclusion and incorporation, and she turns these histories into archival histories themselves, as she herself "is now the archived." As the contemporary moment folds into the past, under what terms might we ourselves concede to turn archival, to become distilled into some kind of trace fragment or broken out as a kind of signal for some kind of queer future? Under what terms should the contemporary queer moment yield to its own archival processing? Turning back to any given archive, we are reminded, of course, that seldom does the archived subject have the opportunity to determine the terms of their own preservation. And it is amid these ambiguities, turning between the archived and the archivist, the lost and the found, that we see again and again how historical traces of the queer past get turned into new knowledges and experiences which, in turn, sponsor hope that the past and the future will turn into different things, time and time again.

Notes

1 This anthology is also born out of our extended conversations with Kevin P. Murphy, with whom we coedited two earlier issues of *Radical History Review* on the topic of "Queering Archives" and to whom we are grateful for suggesting the title *Turning Archival* for this anthology. We sincerely thank Gisela Fosado and Alejandra Mejía at Duke University Press for her vision and support, and the anonymous readers who improved the book as a whole.

2 Derrida, *Archive Fever*.

3 Stoler, *Along the Archival Grain*, 44.

4 McDonald, *The Historic Turn in the Human Sciences*, 1.

5 Rosengarten, *Between Memory and Document*, 11.

6 Arondekar et al., "Queering Archives: A Roundtable Discussion," 214.

7 For more on this discussion, see Weeks, "Queer(y)ing the 'Modern Homosexual.'"

8 See, for instance, the documentary *Screaming Queens: The Riot at Compton's Cafeteria*, directed by Susan Stryker and Victor Silverman, and Stryker's *Transgender History*. Fieldmaking publications by Stryker and others—such as *The Transgender Studies Reader*, *The Transgender Studies Reader 2*, and the founding of the journal *TSQ: Transgender Studies Quarterly* in 2014—have also centered engagements with the archives as key to the development of trans studies. See Stryker and Whittle, *The Transgender Studies Reader*; Stryker and Aizura, *The Transgender Studies Reader 2*; and *TSQ: Transgender Studies Quarterly*.

9 Snorton, *Black on Both Sides*, 11.

10 Samuels, "Six Ways of Looking at Crip Time."

11 Brilmyer, "Archival Assemblages."

12 Cartwright, "Out of Sorts," 64.

13 Cartwright, "Out of Sorts," 67.

14 For more on the (queer) archival body, see Lee, "Be/longing in the Archival Body."

15 Ogura, *Verbs of Motion in Medieval English*, 22.

16 Skeat, *The Concise Dictionary of English Etymology*, 528.

17 Partridge, *Origins*, 717.

18 Eichhorn, "Archival Genres," 3.

19 Van Bussel, "Theoretical Framework," 24, and Manoff, "Theories of the Archive," 11.

20 See, for instance, Dean, Ruszczycky, and Squires, *Porn Archives*; Sigal, Tortorici, and Whitehead, *Ethnopornography*; Palladini and Pustianaz, *Lexicon for an Affective Archive*; and Dever, Vickery, and Newman, *The Intimate Archive*. On the "rebel archive," see Hernández, *City of Inmates*.

21 Ketelaar, "Archival Turns and Returns," 239.

22 Ketelaar, "Archival Turns and Returns," 241.

23 Hernández, *Archiving an Epidemic*; McKinney, *Information Activism*; and Sheffield, *Documenting Rebellions*.

24 See, for instance, Cifor, "Stains and Remains."

25 McKemmish and Gilliland, "Archival and Recordkeeping Research," 92.

26 Fuentes, *Dispossessed Lives*, 1 and 48.

27 Arondekar et al., "Queering Archives: A Roundtable Discussion," 219.

28 For a different discussion of the "postarchival," please see Cooper, "Imagining Something Else Entirely."

29 Sedgwick, *Touching Feeling*.

30 Sedgwick, *Epistemology of the Closet*.

31 Ahmed, *Queer Phenomenology*, 201.

32 Blouin and Rosenberg, *Processing the Past*, 3.

33 See, for instance, Driskill, Finley, Gilley, and Morgensen, *Queer Indigenous Studies*. On Samuel Steward, see Spring, *Secret Historian*.

34 Ahmed, *Willful Subjects*.

35 Cvetkovich, "Ephemera," 183. For more on queer ephemera, see Muñoz, "Ephemera as Evidence."

36 "We Are Here: Contemporary Artists Explore Their Queer Heritage," State Library of Victoria, accessed March 3, 2022, https://www.slv.vic.gov.au/whats-on/we-are-here -contemporary-artists-explore-their-queer-cultural-heritage.

37 Cvetkovich, *An Archive of Feelings*. See here for the June L. Mazer Archives: http:// digital2.library.ucla.edu/mazer/, accessed March 3, 2022.

38 Steedman, *Dust*, 38.

39 Arondekar et al., "Queering Archives: A Roundtable Discussion," 214.

Works Cited

Ahmed, Sara. *Queer Phenomenology: Orientations, Objects, Others*. Durham, NC: Duke University Press, 2006.

Ahmed, Sara. *Willful Subjects*. Durham, NC: Duke University Press, 2014.

Arondekar, Anjali, Ann Cvetkovich, Christina B. Hanhardt, Regina Kunzel, Tavia Nyong'o, Juana María Rodríguez, Susan Stryker, Daniel Marshall, Kevin P. Murphy, and Zeb Tortorici. "Queering Archives: A Roundtable Discussion." *Radical History Review* 122 (May 2015): 211–31.

Blouin, Francis X., Jr., and William G. Rosenberg. *Processing the Past: Contesting Authority in History and the Archives*. Oxford: Oxford University Press, 2011.

Brilmyer, Gracen. "Archival Assemblages: Applying Disability Studies' Political/Relational Model to Archival Description." *Archival Science* 18 (June 2018): 95–118.

Cartwright, Ryan Lee. "Out of Sorts: A Queer Crip in the Archive." *Feminist Review* 125 (July 2020): 62–69.

Cifor, Marika. "Stains and Remains: Liveliness, Materiality, and the Archival Lives of Queer Bodies." *Australian Feminist Studies* 32, nos. 91–92 (2017): 5–21.

Cooper, Danielle. "Imagining Something Else Entirely: Metaphorical Archives in Feminist Theory." *Women's Studies* 45, no. 5 (2016): 444–56.

Cvetkovich, Ann. *An Archive of Feelings: Trauma, Sexuality, and Lesbian Public Cultures.* Durham, NC: Duke University Press, 2003.

Cvetkovich, Ann. "Ephemera." In *Lexicon for an Affective Archive*, edited by Giulia Palladini and Marco Pustianaz, 179–83. Bristol, UK: Intellect, 2017.

Dean, Tim, Steven Ruszczycky, and David Squires, eds. *Porn Archives*. Durham, NC: Duke University Press, 2014.

Derrida, Jacques. *Archive Fever: A Freudian Impression*. Chicago: University of Chicago Press, 1995.

Dever, Maryanne, Ann Vickery, and Sally Newman. *The Intimate Archive: Journeys through Private Papers*. Canberra: National Library of Australia, 2009.

Driskill, Qwo-Li, Chris Finley, Brian Joseph Gilley, and Scott Lauria Morgensen, eds. *Queer Indigenous Studies: Critical Interventions in Theory, Politics, and Literature*. Tucson: University of Arizona Press, 2011.

Eichhorn, Kate. "Archival Genres: Gathering Texts and Readings Spaces." *Invisible Culture: An Electronic Journal for Visual Culture* 12 (2008). http://www.rochester.edu/in_visible _culture/Issue_12/eichhorn/eichhorn.pdf.

Fuentes, Marisa J. *Dispossessed Lives: Enslaved Women, Violence, and the Archive*. Philadelphia: University of Pennsylvania Press, 2016.

Hernández, Kelly Lytle. *City of Inmates: Conquest, Rebellion, and the Rise of Human Caging in Los Angeles, 1771–1965*. Chapel Hill: University of North Carolina Press, 2017.

Hernández, Robb. *Archiving an Epidemic: Art, AIDS, and the Queer Chicanx Avant-Garde*. New York: NYU Press, 2019.

Ketelaar, Eric. "Archival Turns and Returns: Studies of the Archive." In *Research in the Archival Multiverse*, edited by Anne J. Gilliland, Sue McKemmish, and Andrew J. Lau, 228–68. Clayton, Victoria: Monash University Publishing, 2017.

Lee, Jamie A. "Be/longing in the Archival Body: Eros and the 'Endearing' Value of Material Lives." *Archival Science* 16, no. 1 (2016): 33–51.

Manoff, Marlene. "Theories of the Archive from across the Disciplines." *portal: Libraries and the Academy* 4, no. 1 (2004): 9–25.

McDonald, Terrence, ed. *The Historic Turn in the Human Sciences*. Ann Arbor: University of Michigan Press, 1996.

McKemmish, Sue, and Anne J. Gilliland. "Archival and Recordkeeping Research: Past, Present and Future." In *Research Methods: Information Management, Systems, and Contexts*, edited by Kirsty Williamson and Graeme Johanson, 79–112. Cambridge, MA: Elsevier, 2018.

McKinney, Cait. *Information Activism: A Queer History of Lesbian Media Technologies*. Durham, NC: Duke University Press, 2020.

Muñoz, José Esteban. "Ephemera as Evidence: Introductory Notes to Queer Acts." *Women & Performance: A Journal of Feminist Theory* 8, no. 2 (1996): 5–16.

Ogura, Michiko. *Verbs of Motion in Medieval English*. Cambridge: D. S. Brewer, 2002.

Palladini, Giulia, and Marco Pustianaz, eds. *Lexicon for an Affective Archive*. Fishponds, UK: Intellect, 2017.

Partridge, Eric. *Origins: A Short Etymological Dictionary of Modern English*. Milton Park, UK: Routledge, 2002.

Rosengarten, Ruth. *Between Memory and Document: The Archival Turn in Contemporary Art*. Lisbon: Museu Coleção Bernardo, 2012.

Samuels, Ellen. "Six Ways of Looking at Crip Time." *Disability Studies Quarterly* 37, no. 3 (2017). https://dsq-sds.org/article/view/5824/4684.

Sedgwick, Eve Kosofsky. *Epistemology of the Closet*. Berkeley: University of California Press, 1990.

Sedgwick, Eve Kosofsky. *Touching Feeling: Affect, Pedagogy, Performativity*. Durham, NC: Duke University Press, 2003.

Sheffield, Rebecka Taves. *Documenting Rebellions: A Study of Four Lesbian and Gay Archives in Queer Times*. Sacramento, CA: Litwin Books, 2020.

Skeat, Walter W. *The Concise Dictionary of English Etymology*. Hertfordshire, UK: Wordsworth Editions, 1993.

Sigal, Pete, Zeb Tortorici, and Neil L. Whitehead, eds. *Ethnopornography: Sexuality, Colonialism, and Archival Knowledge*. Durham, NC: Duke University Press, 2020.

Snorton, C. Riley. *Black on Both Sides: A Racial History of Trans Identity*. Minneapolis: University of Minnesota Press, 2017.

Spring, Justin. *Secret Historian: The Life and Times of Samuel Steward, Professor, Tattoo Artist, and Sexual Renegade*. New York: Farrar, Straus and Giroux, 2011.

Steedman, Carolyn. *Dust: The Archive and Cultural History*. New Brunswick, NJ: Rutgers University Press, 2001.

Stoler, Ann Laura. *Along the Archival Grain: Epistemic Anxieties and Colonial Common Sense*. Princeton, NJ: Princeton University Press, 2009.

Stryker, Susan. *Transgender History*. Berkeley, CA: Seal Press, 2008.

Stryker, Susan, and Aren Z. Aizura, eds. *The Transgender Studies Reader 2*. London: Routledge, 2013.

Stryker, Susan, and Victor Silverman, dirs. *Screaming Queens: The Riot at Compton's Cafeteria*. San Francisco, CA: KQED/Independent Television Productions, 2005.

Stryker, Susan, and Stephen Whittle, eds. *The Transgender Studies Reader*. New York: Routledge, 2006.

Van Bussel, Geert-Jan. "The Theoretical Framework for the 'Archive-As-Is': An Organization Oriented View on Archives. Part I. Setting the Stage: Enterprise Information Management and Archival Theories." In *Archives in Liquid Times*, edited by Frans Smit, Arnould Glaudemans, and Rienk Jonker, 17–41. Amsterdam: Stichting Archiefpublicaties, 2017.

Weeks, Jeffrey. "Queer(y)ing the 'Modern Homosexual.'" *Journal of British Studies* 51, no. 3 (2012): 523–39.

1. ARCHIVES, BODIES, AND IMAGINATION

The Case of Juana Aguilar and Queer Approaches to History, Sexuality, and Politics

MARÍA ELENA MARTÍNEZ

In July 1803, the *Gazeta de Guatemala* published a report written by the surgeon Narciso Esparragosa y Gallardo of the sexual body parts of Juana Aguilar, a suspected hermaphrodite who was being tried by the Real Audiencia (Royal Court) for committing *pecados nefandos*, or "abominable sins," with women.[1] Esparragosa, an enlightened creole (descendant of Spaniards), had been commissioned by the Protomedicato (the colonial medical tribunal) to study Aguilar's anatomy and offer his opinion on her sexual status. After several sessions of observing her body and probing her vagina, ovaries, and especially her clitoris, Esparragosa concluded that she was not a hermaphrodite, as was rumored and had been affirmed by midwives and physicians who had inspected her before he had. Although Juana "la Larga" ("the Long")—as she had been nicknamed by townspeople presumably because of her genitalia—did have an enlarged clitoris, the *protomédico* (protomedic or royal physician) asserted that she did not have a "union of the two sexes" and therefore was not both a man and a woman.

However, because Aguilar had not developed the full sexual and reproductive organs of either a man (her clitoris could not become erect or emit semen) or a woman (her vagina lacked an opening), she also could not be considered either male or female. Instead, Esparragosa concluded, she was sexually "neutral," like some bees. Convinced that his conclusions were rational and enlightened, informed by the most advanced knowledge on sex and nature that "wise men" such as the French naturalist Comte Georges-Louis Leclerc de Buffon had produced in the previous century, the doctor ended his report by noting that because the law (and in particular the crime of *pecado nefando* or the "nefarious sin" of sodomy) required that the parties involved be of one or another sex, the court should exonerate Aguilar.[2] Esparragosa presented his opinions to the Audiencia in February 1803, along with a note offering to also submit illustrations of Aguilar's sexual organs that he had commissioned a local artist to draw. Because the papers from the criminal trial are missing and other documents on the accused have not yet surfaced, it is impossible to know what impact his report had on the court's ruling, let alone what her fate afterward was. Murkier still are the details of Aguilar's life before her legal persecution, which apparently took place in El Salvador in the early 1790s and eventually forced her to flee to Guatemala in search of more freedom.

Despite (and because of) the dearth of documents on Aguilar, the case raises a number of intriguing historical questions about her life, discourses of sex and sexual difference in late colonial Spanish America, and the influence of the new or "enlightened" science on theories of the sexed body in different parts of the Atlantic world. This chapter alludes to some of these topics, but does not discuss them or Esparragosa's report in detail, as they have been analyzed elsewhere.[3] Rather, its main objective is to use the case to explore a series of problems related to the colonial archive and queer history, including the power dynamics involved in the production and preservation of documents, the structural limitations that they place on studying sexuality in the past, and the possibilities and challenges that approaching them from different angles, disciplines, and performative acts can present for both history and politics. Interweaving discussions of theoretical scholarship on the archive, the violent processes by which most cases of sodomy and other non-normative sexual practices became part of the historical record, and parts of conversations with the Mexican theater director and actress Jesusa Rodríguez about how she is using the Aguilar case on- and offstage to critique homophobia and other forms of discrimination in Latin America, the chapter focuses on the role of the imagination in historical reconstruction and the place of embodied or performative practices in radical queer art, history, and politics. It also reflects on some of the ethical questions that using history to make political claims raises for historians, performers, and others who mediate between the past and present publics.

The (Aguilar) Case for the Repertoire

I first turned to the Juana Aguilar case in 2011, as part of my research on race, sex, and gender and the Enlightenment in the eighteenth-century Spanish Atlantic world. Since that time, the investigation has taken some unexpected turns not only in terms of the historical and theoretical questions the case led me to formulate, but because of the discussions I had about it with Rodríguez, one of Mexico's most accomplished cabaret and political performance artists.

For fifteen years she and her longtime partner, the singer and actress Liliana Felipe, operated the legendary Teatro Bar El Hábito, an alternative performance space in Mexico City, and during that time took some of their shows to the United States, Europe, Canada, and other parts of Latin America. Rodríguez's performances, which encompass and often blend different theatrical genres (elite and popular, Greek tragedy and cabaret, indigenous and other Latin American aesthetic traditions, and so forth), have earned her numerous awards and fellowships. The insertion of piercing social critiques in many of her shows also established her reputation as one of the most politically uncompromising and influential voices in Mexico's cultural scene.[4]

Since closing El Hábito in 2005, Rodríguez has continued to utilize performance, satire, and her body on and off the stage to denounce the Mexican political system's corruption and lack of democracy, the Catholic Church's views toward women and sexuality, and more generally social inequality, discrimination, and injustice. As part of her involvement with Resistencia Creativa, a movement that she founded after the contested 2006 presidential elections and that uses art as a weapon of peaceful resistance, she regularly stages "mass cabarets" with searing political critiques in Mexico City's Zócalo (central plaza) and other public spaces. Whether on a theater stage or civil rally, Rodríguez has thus turned to theatrical performance—part of what performance studies scholar Diana Taylor calls "the repertoire" of practices performed by human bodies that can be linked to knowledge and memory but that Western culture distinguishes from "the archive" because of their ephemeral nature—to make political claims and try to enact social change.[5] Even her weddings (which include a symbolic ceremony in 1991 when Mexico City passed a domestic partnership law and a more formal one in 2010 when the capital city legalized same-sex marriages) to Felipe have been performative public events or *espectáculos* meant to proclaim the rights of gays and lesbians in Mexican society and incite debate about the history of what the poet Adrienne Rich called "compulsory heterosexuality" and its profound implications for people who have not fit or rejected sexual norms.[6]

When during a casual conversation in Mexico City I first brought up the Aguilar case with her, Rodríguez seemed to be immediately captivated, as if she was already picturing it on the stage. It was the theatricality of the name *Juana la Larga*, she later explained in a workshop: "There is the word's sonority and the strong imaginary that it unleashes, because it is at once concrete and derogatory and yet can take your mind in so many possible directions."[7] In the months that followed, we continued to talk about the case and its potential as a performance piece. Rodríguez studied Esparragosa's report, and subsequently she and Felipe used parts of it in a presentation they gave in a panel on "diversity" at the Fourth Iberoamerican Congress on Public Cultures in Argentina in September 2011.

Titled "Diversity and Equality," the presentation, which opened with Felipe reading a lengthy passage from the report graphically referring to Aguilar's clitoris and vagina, was intended to provoke a discussion of contemporary politics, sexuality, and violence (gendered and otherwise) in Latin America. In particular, it aimed to critique the "obsolete" gender norms, biological definitions of sex, and homophobia that persist in the area, notwithstanding the relatively recent legalization of gay marriage in Argentina, Uruguay, Mexico City, and Brazil. With the Uruguayan writer Eduardo Galeano's 1971 historical-literary text *Open Veins of Latin America: Five Centuries of the Pillage of a Continent* as a reference point, the presentation also made parallels between the repeated subjection of Aguilar's body to invasive physical probes and the history of European and US imperialism in Latin America, between her forcibly opened legs and the violently "opened veins" of the region:

> Apart from the resonances that the case of Juana la Larga can have with [current] issues of diversity and human rights, I am asking everyone to participate in an exercise of "geographic transgenderization" [*transgenerización geográfica*]. On the body of Juana la Larga we could [imagine] the map of Latin America: a different cosmovision, a different body, misapprehended by Western canons, morbidly probed, masturbated, and humiliated by surgeons intent on placing into preconceived models live objects that don't fit their classifications. That is how the occident has treated [Latin] American cultures, as deformed entities, exotic fancies, and inexistent hermaphrodites. They have opened our legs to see what operation should be executed or even more accurately to open mines with unbridled abandon. For centuries, conservative forces aligned with the perverse Catholic Church have dedicated themselves to probing the genitals of human beings, always with the objective of enabling social control and economic exploitation . . . To Western minds and in particular to neoliberalism, Latin American cultures are not made of men and women, but of strange entities lacking the "pleasure" of knowing real culture, entities that should be pitied and classified for the sake of progress.[8]

Playing with the idea of transgendered human and geopolitical bodies, the exercise in "geographic transgenderization" emphasized the European creation of categories for American territories and peoples as acts of control and domination, thereby calling attention to classification as a type of violence. According to Rodríguez, the audience (which included government functionaries, artists, intellectuals, academics, and political activists from twenty-two countries) had a strong reaction to the presentation during both the reading of Esparragosa's text and in the discussion that followed. Attributing listener interest to the peculiarity of the text and the different angle that the Aguilar case—as an example of how sexual difference has been treated in the distant past—provided for the topic of sexual diversity in the present, Rodríguez believed that the presentation had the desired result of offering new lenses for thinking about contemporary sexual discourses and their links to other forms of power. If nothing else, she observed, it managed to jolt the audience out of the typical conference stupor that sets in after hours of hearing speeches and lectures.[9]

After the event in Argentina, Rodríguez and Felipe continued to entertain the idea of turning the Aguilar case into a theatrical performance and took advantage of a trip to Guatemala in January 2012 to visit the country's national archive, where they consulted Esparragosa's original report and discovered that the story of "Juana la Larga" was part of local folklore. An archivist told them that the house in which she had lived was well known and that her nickname implied that she was a thief and cheat because that is what the word *long* can connote in Guatemala (as in to have long arms and be wily or deceitful, *tramposa*). At a bookstore the couple also purchased a copy of Carlos Martínez Durán's 1941 *Las ciencias médicas en Guatemala. Origen y evolución*, which devotes several chapters to the *protomédico*'s contribution to medical science in that country.[10] By then, Rodríguez was finding the colonial doctor an equally, if not more, compelling figure than Aguilar, and the idea of a performance began to revolve around him. At a symposium on "Race and Sex in the Eighteenth-Century Spanish Atlantic World," held at the University of Southern California (USC) on April 12, 2013, she gave a preview of that show, turning herself into Esparragosa before an interactive audience that weighed in on how he should look during a workshop discussion on archives, history, and theatrical performance.

At that discussion, Rodríguez explained that the case interested her not only because of its unusualness (in particular the size of Aguilar's clitoris, she quipped) and dramatic components (among them the doctor's conclusions), but also because of her concern with confronting discrimination and colonization, past and present. Esparragosa's reading of Aguilar's body through European lenses and a Western medicine that labeled her as strange and monstrous to exert its authority over her, she pointed out, as well as his misogyny, homophobia, and paternalism, offer the opportunity to think critically about the continued prevalence of those problems in Latin America and how to dismantle them, including through art/performance. When asked what was fair game in terms of using the past in performance for political purposes, her answer, not surprisingly (given her notorious irreverence), was that pretty much anything goes.

Actors and artists in general are not shackled by rules of historical writing and argumentation, Rodríguez noted, but she did concede that the representation of a particular past has to seem feasible. Taking license with some details—for example, the racial status of Aguilar, which is not specified in existing sources—is acceptable, Rodríguez stated, as is using the case to raise present political and social concerns. Her process of turning the Aguilar case into a theatrical piece thus raises a set of issues pertaining to history and performance, among them the possibilities and limitations of traditional archives for the study of the "queer past," the role that the imagination (and uniting the archive with the repertoire) can play in reconstructing that past, and the uses of history for present politics, queer and otherwise.

Queer Sex and the Colonial Archive

In the past three decades, the traditional archive—generally defined as a place where documents deemed to have historical value are stored and organized, usually by government or other institutions, and made available for consultation[11]—has been subject to much theorization and critique by scholars in different disciplines, among them philosophy, literature, and anthropology, and in "postdisciplines" such as performance studies. These scholars have emphasized, for example, the strong relationship between institutional archives and state projects (sovereign or liberal); the power dynamics and silencing effects involved in the collection, organization, and use of written sources; and the ways in which privileging writing as a site of information and knowledge comes at the expense of other forms—oral, visual, and "embodied" or "performatic"—of constructing historical memory and meaning.[12] Driven in part by the postmodern suspicion of the evidentiary status of historical documents, scholarship on the archive has highlighted its role in shaping the politics of both the past and present, thereby undermining its status as an innocent bystander in history and turning it into an object of inquiry rather than just a source of information.

Historians, for the most part, are not oblivious to the politics and limitations of archives and their implications for historical study. A questioning of sources is in fact part of the "craft." It is true that the discipline privileges written sources and that some of its practitioners approach the archive with the confidence of a nineteenth-century positivist that they will find clear facts, certainty, and unmediated access to the past there. But there is no one way of writing history, and different approaches (social, intellectual, economic, political, and cultural to name a few) can involve various methods (including textual and discursive analyses as well as more empirical ones such as statistics) and sources (among them oral and visual), as well as healthy doses of doubt. The bogeyman that the historian becomes in conversations outside the field in which the discipline is dismissed as antiquated, politically and intellectually conservative, naively empiricist, and so forth, more often than not turns out to be a strawman.

Perhaps because of the particularly challenging nature of their subject matter, historians with the most suspicious approaches to the archive tend to be those that focus on history "from below" or histories of (nonelite) women, slaves, peasants, colonized populations, and others who until relatively recently did not normally get to produce written sources with their views on events and themselves. Historical scholarship on colonial Latin America, for example, has long recognized—in part through the influence of social history and more recently subaltern and colonial/postcolonial studies—that documents must be examined carefully, taking into account who produced them and why, that any information they contain about ordinary people is mediated (say by royal officials, inquisitors, local political leaders, priests, or notaries), that they can be read from different angles, and that different ones can reveal contrasting views on the same event.[13]

The insight that the politics and structural limitations of archives can hinder as much as allow the study of the past has thus not been lost on historians themselves and some have warned about considering archived documents the only source of knowledge about history. To mitigate those problems, they turn to analytical strategies such as reading "against the grain" (for problematizing imperial and other dominant perspectives lodged in sources), emphasizing the interpretative nature of historical analysis, and scrutinizing not just the content of documents but their form (such as narrative techniques in legal sources) and the context in which they were produced.[14] The need for these strategies becomes all the more evident when venturing into topics as charged and filtered as that of same-sex desires and relationships in colonial situations because of the way that sexuality, together with race, class, and gender, were central organizing vectors in colonial social orders and in the very constitution of their archives. In most cases, archived documents were not only produced by or for colonial authorities or institutions, but are testaments to the administrative technologies devised to produce and reproduce racial and gender categories.

Most colonial Latin American archives, for example, are replete with birth and marriage records, tribute lists, censuses, medical examinations and reports on sexual status, legal procedures to determine race/caste, genealogies, and other sources that reflect the colonial archive's function less as place than as process and epistemic practice; its embeddedness in, and collusion with, systems of rule.[15] In these archives, in which the presence of the state and church (their laws, institutions, projects, officials, and categories) looms exceedingly large, when people with same-sex desires or more generally who are rendered as "queer" (because their sexual organs, behavior, or longings don't seem to conform to dominant definitions of the normal) appear, it tends to be because they were subjected to investigation, discipline, and punishment.[16] The church and state considered same-sex desires to be unnatural and acting on them a sinful crime (labeled *sodomía* or *pecado nefando*) that when tried often required ordering a medical examination of the accused to ascertain if the deviance was located in her or his body. "Making it" into the historical archive therefore was normally not a sign of positive developments for the person associated with those desires or acts. Given the juridical, theological, and medical processes and discourses that influenced how "queers" normally entered into the archive and the way they are inscribed in the sources themselves, what (if anything) can be known or recovered about them as real people?

Aguilar, for example, became material for historical study mainly because of Esparragosa's report, in which fragments of her life, and especially of her body, appear through different filters, among them colonial, misogynist, and homophobic. She is present in the archive because of efforts by the doctor and others to inspect, classify, and regulate her, and the archival source does not provide "access" to Aguilar's person, sexual practices or desires, or thoughts. It mainly reveals a series of assumptions about gender and sex that shaped the way the *protomédico* perceived and examined her and ruled on her body's potential to commit "sodomy" with other women. These assumptions, the central one being that a man or woman is defined fundamentally by the capacity to reproduce, stemmed from colonial Latin America's patriarchal culture of honor, Christian views of sex and marriage, and the preoccupation among eighteenth-century naturalists, anatomists, and physiologists with reinforcing the binary of male and female and basing it on sexual organs.[17] Esparragosa's views were also colored by what Katherine Park and Robert Nye refer to as a "phallocentric science" which, since the high Middle Ages, set "procreative, heterosexual sex at the heart of the natural universe and associated sodomy with heresy, as a rejection of the physical and metaphysical order created by God."[18]

The sources on Aguilar illustrate both the possibilities and limitations of the colonial archive for queer history. The documents provide rich historical material about, among other things, the importance of sexuality and its control in late colonial Guatemala; the circulation of new scientific texts and theories about the sexed body in parts of Spanish America; and the role of certain eighteenth-century sexual and medical discourses in determining the boundaries between the normal and the anomalous, the natural and the unnatural (or artificial), and the human and the monstrous. The sources also hint at how an early modern Spanish American "technology of the body" developed mainly by the clergy to study, determine, and punish sinful conduct (especially in women linked to witchcraft, mysticism, and sexual deviance) was connected to, and altered by, the Enlightenment period's secular obsession with observation and classification and incessant probing of non-normative bodies.[19]

Throughout the Atlantic world, not just hermaphrodites but also albinos, "spotted blacks" (people of African ancestry that developed white marks or the skin pigment condition now called vitiligo), and other "types" that seemed to defy established sexual or racial schema and binaries supporting them were the subject of relentless scrutiny and debate on the part of natural historians, anatomists, and other eighteenth-century thinkers.[20] Underlying the acute preoccupation with these bodies was not just a fascination with what was perceived and labeled as odd (part of a longer history of the construction of the "abnormal"[21]) but a desire to identify the roots of, and thus criteria for, sexual and racial difference through the rational study of nature. Race and sex being sociohistorical constructions, identifying such criteria proved to be a vexing problem (then and now). Although generally anatomists and physiologists made sex and race binaries more rigid during the latter half of the eighteenth century,[22] the period gave way to the profusion of categories and theories: some located racial difference in the blood, skin, skull, or maternal imagination, and others located sex in genitalia, humoral processes during fetal formation, or other anatomical or physiological characteristics.

As tortuous, confused, and futile as the eighteenth-century impulse to permanently fix criteria for sexual and racial difference was, however, it not only had real consequences for the people slotted into non-normative categories but was linked to and helped mold emerging modern medical-legal discourses on sexuality and race. When Esparragosa concluded that Aguilar was sexually neutral, for example, he hoped that category would exonerate her (he pitied her "condition" and the twisted sexual desires it might have led her to have), but even more so that it would be recognized by the law and thus be subject to proper regulation. By contending that the accused should be liberated because the law recognized only two sexes and implying that only with the official creation of the category of sexual neutrality could the court legitimately punish her for her alleged behavior, the doctor's arguments point to the potential that classification has to produce subjects subject to regulation—the power dynamics, exclusions, and violence that categorization, even when ostensibly well intentioned, can enable.

Beyond helping to unravel important aspects of the complex relationship of medicine, law, and science in the history of sexual classification, the written sources for the Juana Aguilar case provide a powerful example of how queers are produced by and through multiple operations of power, including the archive. More to the point, they demonstrate how queerness does not exist independent of the processes—here including legal and medical investigations, reports that claim authoritative opinions about the sexed body, and the archival storage and use of those documents—that construct it. Moreover, placing Esparragosa's report within the light of the longer history of colonial Latin American society's production of heteronormativity in different aspects of public and private life (law, religion, medicine, intimacy) and in the traditions of narrativity in archival and other documents (such as medical reports on sexual "deviance") can further illuminate how heterosexual relations were produced and made to seem natural and the most normal option for sexual, marriage, familial, and communal arrangements. In short, through attentiveness to operations of historical and discursive power, the archive can be used to expose the socially and politically constructed nature of heterosexuality—an approach with radical potential because it helps not only to historicize it but to denaturalize it.

But if critical reading approaches can destabilize the logics of positivism, colonialism, and heteronormativity in written sources by denaturalizing heterosexuality and other socially constructed categories, the question of the limits of historical archives and methods for understanding the past still remains. In the Aguilar case, for example, the documents make evident the futility of trying to find the real—the real person, the real story, the real history. Her life is and will remain a mystery and through their categories, silences, and gazes, the sources shape, if not determine, the terms of historical discourse. Can applying analytical strategies and categories from other disciplines or approaches enrich understandings of the Aguilar case and history more generally?

What would happen, for example, if there were more trans- or postdisciplinary convergences, to borrow Taylor's terms,[23] and historians paid greater attention, say to embodiment (acts, practices, and rituals performed by human bodies) as scholars of performance studies do; or consciously allowed themselves to engage in practices of the imagination, as say a theater performer trying to give a historical figure flesh on stage might? How would those eclectic—and in some respects methodologically and epistemologically disobedient—approaches to the archive affect the historian's relationship not only to history but in particular to bodies in the past? Stated differently, what effects would relying on different types of archives, altering the way we normally read sources, and expanding definitions of knowledge have on how we understand and write history and especially on the past lives we decide to study?

Archives, Bodies, and the Imagination, or Fine Line between History and Fiction

The archaeologist has in his hands the power to give life to that which has died and to come face to face with what it once was. That is how he comes to confront the face of death to give it life.—EDUARDO MATOS MOCTEZUMA, *Vida y muerte en el Templo Mayor*

Different disciplines and professions have their ways of making history "come alive" or "channeling the voices" of the dead. Historians' conceit of reconstructing past lives and worlds through documents is matched, for example, by that of the archaeologist piecing together (sometimes literally with stones) ancient societies through analyses of material remains such as buildings, pottery, and bones in order to "give life to that which has died," or by that of an actor staging a historical drama/performance and drawing on historical sources as well as their own bodies to embody dead people on stage. Referring to her first incursion into a historical archive and search for details about Aguilar, for example, Rodríguez stated that she wanted to find out whether she was indigenous, had breasts, "and all those other things you ask yourself because you are going to embody [*personalizar*] this person, to put her in your body, so you have to imagine what she was like . . . and every detail matters."

Historians, archaeologists, and performers may all attempt to "access" and represent historical figures, but their methods, expectations, and standards of evidence are different. The first two don't usually think of using their bodies as sources for their scholarship, and actors and other artists are granted creative license, especially when there is no pretense, in their work, of historical accuracy. Even when dealing with historical topics, the performance, novel, or film can be cast as an artistic interpretation, and as such there is flexibility (and often little accountability) in terms of correctly depicting the details of a historical person, event, or context. The imagination can be explicitly summoned, recognized, and valued as a source and resource and in performance the body can function as a kind of archive, such as when acting, singing, or dancing serves to access and transmit knowledge.

These aspects of performance were described by the Mexican theater director Ludwik Margules (1933–2006). In a documentary about his work, he explained that when his actors were preparing for their characters, he demanded that they reach their own innermost interior spaces, the limits of their physical and mental selves, until they were able to "detonate their imaginations" to create images and meaning that spoke to aspects of the human condition.[24] In this creative process, images, meaning, and truth are to be achieved through the knowledge and memory that the body has stored. Evoking Derrida's psychoanalytic approach to the archive in which he compares it to the Freudian unconscious, the body and the psyche act as repositories of information connecting the past to the present. The analogy has its limits, among other reasons because archives and human memory do not function in the same way,[25] but is nonetheless useful for thinking about how the relationship of two "archives"— the one that stores documents and other historical fragments and the one that stores human memory—is at the heart of all connections to the past.

At the aforementioned USC workshop, Rodríguez discussed the conscious and unconscious components that had drawn her to the figure of Dr. Esparragosa, including her recollection of her father's practices as a thoracic surgeon. She remembered how for decades the latter performed five to seven operations on tuberculosis patients almost daily and came to treat the cutting up of bodies in detached and routine ways, which in retrospect helped her understand the colonial doctor's views of Aguilar and how the handling of her body, including the rubbing of her clitoris to see if it would become erect, in all likelihood seemed natural to men with his training. The *protomédico* could not see what an utterly "delirious scenario, at once comical, tragic, and terrible, it all was: the enlightened, impeccable, unpolluted Dr. Narciso Esparragosa trying to study this woman's body with clinical distance while having to masturbate her repeatedly!"

Rodríguez elaborated that because she was very close to her father, as a child he would take her to his surgeries, which were

> sheer butchery because back then they would slice open the back entirely, rip all its layers, tear some ribs, and go into the lungs . . . And I was thrilled to see the heart, lungs, all of it was beautiful because the human body is very beautiful inside too . . . So perhaps this proximity to surgeons that I had as a child influenced my interest in Esparragosa and how I understood him . . . And as I learned more about him . . . he was no longer a kind of inquisitor over Juana but a very human physician, full of prejudices and with a colonial mindset but with a measure of sensibility . . . and genuinely committed, as a doctor, to the case.

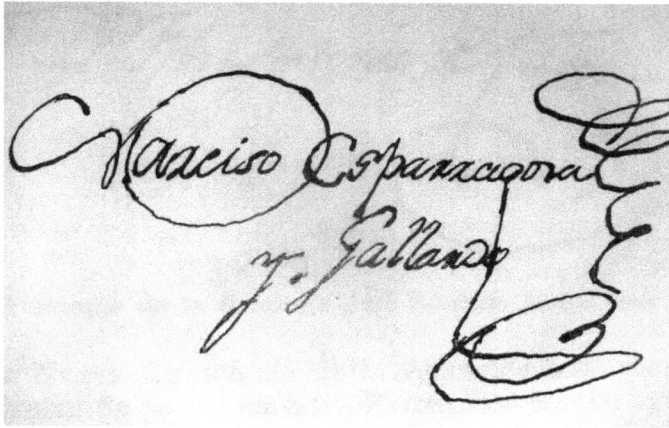

FIGURE 1.1. Esparragosa's signature, *Las Ciencias médicas*, 226.

In the sources Rodríguez also found details that had sparked her imagination about Esparragosa's character, including his name (*"Narciso*, how appropriate!"), his signature ("every letter and detail meticulously drawn and that 'O' encircling his first name, how anal retentive!") and his Bourbon-era doctor's jacket ("how Francophile!") (Figures 1.1 and 1.2).

Personal experiences, details of the case in archival sources, and the imagination allowed her to humanize Esparragosa while not letting him off the hook for his paternalism, heterocentrism, and phallocentric views toward women's bodies and sexuality. Rodríguez's use of the Aguilar case in performance would rely on humor and gesture to ridicule some of the *protomédico*'s views, in particular about women's inability to experience pleasure while engaging in nonheterosexual or nonreproductive sex. By turning him into the object of the gaze she would subvert his authoritative voice in the medical report, his claim to enlightened reason and objectivity, and his presence in the archive as the normal, ideal, and unmarked body. Insofar as it succeeds in making audiences reflect on the ways in which heteronormativity has been constructed and functioned historically and into the present, or at least on the violence it has often implied for people who do not conform to established definitions of the normal, such a union of the archive and the repertoire, of historical sources and performative acts, would be in the service of "politics," a queer imaginative use of history for provoking thought on current social concerns and change.

Some historians cringe at the thought of unleashing the imagination on the past, especially for present political purposes. The main fear is that having a

FIGURE 1.2. Esparra-gosa's coat, *Las Ciencias médicas*, 427.

"political" agenda can contaminate history, and lead to the mapping of pre-sent categories and concerns onto past societies in which different ones op-erated, to a highly selective and self-serving use for sources that conveniently ignores those that have information that does not fit the intended argument, or to an "anything goes" approach where historical claims are made without any grounding and outright invention replaces informed interpretation. The concerns with anachronism and evidence are at least partly legitimate. After all, what would history be if it did not *at least try* to understand the past on its own terms? What would it accomplish if it did not attempt to carefully chart concepts, practices, and social relations over time and their changing cul-tural and political meanings? How could that charting be achieved without the consultation of written documents and other material remains? But if history cannot dispense with the archive, the great unease that some historians express with the imaginative and political components of their craft often ignores the fabricated dimensions and dialectical relationship between past and present that are part of any historical study.

Although it is not acknowledged much (and is sometimes exceedingly diffi-cult to detect), the use of the imagination is not absent from historical writing, particularly but not exclusively when it is in narrative or story-based form. The limited information that documents provide on a given event or life, the dif-ficulty of doing justice to lived time (to represent its passage with only the written word), the need to decide what and whom to foreground and describe in detail—these and other factors involve selection, interpretation, and the imagination. These factors, however, tend to be underplayed in the profession because recognizing their role not only risks wresting objectivity from the craft, but also calls attention to its fictional components and to the part that the historian's own life experiences plays in shaping her or his understandings of the past. The discipline involves a kind of performance of objectivity, among other ways, through standard writing practices such as the use of the third-person voice, which creates an omniscient and invisible narrator and distance from the subject matter, and through the almost ritualistic and surgical approach to documents that many archives require, such as the wearing of gloves and masks when untying bundles of papers and "treating" or "examining" manuscripts (Figures 1.3 and 1.4). In form, if not effect, these practices resemble those of the enlightened *protomédico*, his apparent distance to the object of study, his authoritative voice but unmarked presence, his blindness to the ways his biases and normative ways of understanding the world shaped his analysis of Aguilar, his fictions.

History's fictional components derive not from falsehoods necessarily but from its fragmented and representational nature. Because there are no real events or people in archival documents, only their textual representations, narrativizing by necessity involves filling in gaps in the story, taking informed guesses on aspects of the given event based on clues in the sources, and deciding on how to organize the description.[26] Furthermore, determining what things, people, places, and developments to highlight, and what plot/argumentative structure, temporality, and importance to grant the given case or event also involves, consciously or not, reading that historical topic not just through tools gained in academic training but through one's other life experiences and more generally through the memories, conceptual categories, and world understandings archived, living, and fluctuating in the historian's own body and psyche.

FIGURE 1.3. Bound colonial documents in Mexico's Archivo General de la Nación. Photograph taken by author.

Despite some differences in methods and evidentiary requirements, then, the ways that a historian and an artist approach the past are not necessarily that different, and to some extent we are all looking for truth, not for the "real" or absolute truth, but for "truths," studying historical processes and people to understand aspects of the past, the present world, and the human condition. Historians, however, don't normally think about their craft as a process that entails the imagination and use of the body and experiential knowledge as (re)sources. It was not always that way. Various ancient societies had professions that recognized certain bodies as "living archives." The folk singer and poet-chronicler of classical antiquity who belted out songs, poems, or stories with epic content, for example, or the Mesoamerican specialist in codices who read them in public performances that could involve singing and dancing, transmitted historical knowledge that linked the community's past, present, and future.[27] Historical memory resided in their bodies and minds and was shared through speeches and embodied acts, and that knowledge was supposed to orient the community on its purpose and destiny. In this approach to the past, history is not divided into discrete periods and the body is the great articulator of different temporalities.

In eighteenth-century Europe, when history as a modern Western discipline was born and the first archives surfaced as manifestations of centralized power and enlightened despotism, older forms of preserving historical memory—and memory itself—lost ground to the written document, its apparent permanency equated with reliability.[28] "As a historian," responded Eric Hobsbawm when asked (shortly before he died) by Mexican journalist Sylvia Lemus why he did not talk much about his own life, "I know not to trust memory."[29] But the privileging of writing by historians cannot entirely conceal the interpretative and imaginative dimensions of historical writing, the role that the experiential knowledge lodged in our bodies and minds plays in shaping how we understand and write about the past, and the ways that the study of history in turn influences how we view the present.

Indeed, there is a corpus of scholarly literature that recognizes those aspects of the craft.[30] Engaging in more inter- or postdisciplinary discussions, however, can serve not only to make them more apparent and productive but also to expand definitions of archives to include embodied and other sources of historical memory, and more generally to make bodies more central in historical analysis. Paying greater attention to how broad historical processes such as colonialism, slavery, racism, scientific revolutions, and so forth may have affected people in the flesh in turn would serve to heighten awareness of the different forms of violence those processes implied for colonial, raced, queer, and other non-normative bodies, of how we connect to their lives, and of the ethical responsibilities of how we represent them.

The Limits, Violence, and Politics of Historical Representation

Whether we rely on traditional or alternative archives to consider different readings of past lives and worlds, what are our obligations, if any, to both the past and the present? For if the two are indeed inseparable, then all historical representations carry the responsibility of thinking not just about how they are colored by present categories, memories, and political concerns but about how they can avoid enacting or reenacting forms of historical violence. Whether for historians, artists, or others who represent people who lived in the past, what is acceptable in terms of what is projected onto those bodies, in terms of what is assumed and claimed about them, and in terms of what they are made to symbolize, particularly if they are used to draw political lessons or points for present politics, queer and otherwise? More to the point, what are our ethical obligations as scholars, performers, and/or activists, to raced or sexed bodies like those of Juana Aguilar and the way we deploy images of them that are inextricably tied to the violent logics of domination?

In Aguilar's case, for all the mysteries surrounding her life, the documents make clear, first, that her body—its alleged sexual anomalies, excesses, and relations with other women—was central to her criminalization and, second, that because of her body's presumed queerness, she was subjected to different forms of historical violence. The violence of being shamed by members of different towns for her supposed sexual organs and practices was followed by the violence of being disciplined by the courts, physically probed by different medical authorities for a period of about ten years, and publicly exposed by the trial and Dr. Esparragosa's publication of his assessment in the Guatemalan gazette. The enlightened doctor might even have disseminated the illustrations of her genitals that he reportedly commissioned and had in his possession.

The archive did some damage too. Not only was Aguilar inscribed in the written record mainly as the object of the surgeon's gaze, but when the twentieth-century historian Carlos Martínez Durán used the colonial surgeon's report to refer to her life, he reproduced some of its main heterosexist and paternalistic assumptions about her body and behavior.[31] A Guatemalan doctor and scholar, Martínez Durán considered Esparragosa the founder of modern medical science and surgery in his country and thus devotes much of *Las Ciencias médicas en Guatemala. Origen y evolución* to lauding his work. He was less interested in Juana Aguilar as a historical subject in her own right than in what the colonial doctor had published on her, which he conceived as a brilliant contribution to forensic science.

Whereas in Martínez Durán's historical text Esparragosa is made to stand as a kind of founding father of modern medicine and surgery in Guatemala, in his brief section on Aguilar she figures as the pathetic hermaphrodite with queer desires who was saved from the shackles of the law by the *protomédico* but whose "tragic" life and ending (by virtue of her deviance) was basically preordained. One body stands for the nation and modernity, the other for the abnormal, abject, and doomed. Martínez Durán's postindependence historical recuperation of Aguilar, which is marked by pity and slippages between Esparragosa's heteronormative discourses on her sexual organs, sex, and sexual desires and his own, underscores again the importance of distancing historical claims and narratives from archival ones that can sometimes arrive at conclusions without a critical examination of sources and power.

Avoiding the collusion with power, however, can be trickier than it seems precisely because of the difficulty of disentangling social, archival, and historical inscriptions—of dismantling the archive's transformation of social markings into historical ones. Given the ways in which the non-normative tends to figure in archival sources, how can treatments of bodies as "texts," as metaphorical expressions of the effects of power (patriarchy, conquest, colonialism, racism, etc.), avoid reducing them to disembodied fragments, to mere parts like Esparragosa does when he produces a report that inserts Aguilar into the archive—and thus to history—essentially as sexual organs? The crux of the problem is that of exposing historical violence and power without reproducing their forms.

In studying or using cases such as Aguilar's, which requires reproducing at least part of what is in the colonial archive (after all, as historians also like to think, the devil is in the detail), the challenge for scholars and nonscholars alike is how to lessen the possibility that whatever is generated does not simply provide salacious or "juicy" information about raced and/or sexed bodies or reduce them to just that. Even a well-intentioned provocation such as the public sharing of parts of Dr. Esparragosa's report by Rodríguez and Felipe at the Fourth Iberoamerican Congress on Public Cultures in Argentina has to contend with tensions stemming from the fine line that can exist between subverting and reproducing images birthed through sexual and/or racial power and violence and therefore connected to some kind of pain. And yet fragments of lives are all that archives offer, if that. The connections of record-keeping practices, power, and history, or traps set up by the "long arm" of the archive, can be tenacious, deceitful, and wily indeed.

As has been suggested throughout this chapter, one strategy to avoid colluding with power is to subject the source to a relentless scrutiny, treat the archive as an ethnographic subject itself, and use critical reading practices to deconstruct heterosexuality and other dominant discourses. Another is to turn the historical gaze around through creative approaches, as Rodríguez decided to do with Esparragosa in her performance. That is not to say that anything goes—not even for artists, for to the extent that they are implicated in politics they too have a responsibility to the past and present and to think about the ethical or other problems that might be involved in their representational strategies. Deciding to use the term *lesbian* to refer to Aguilar in order to make her more accessible to a nonacademic audience or simply to make her a part of "gay and lesbian history," for example, does not just risk committing an act of historical anachronism. It can also imply succumbing to a classificatory impulse not unlike that which is present in Esparragosa's investigation and report on Aguilar, thus reproducing the very practice a radical queer approach to the archive aims to critique and dismantle.

Apart from summoning the imagination to explore different forms of subverting the terms and categories of power embedded in archival documents, then, such an approach involves thinking about the links between classification and power both in the past and present, how the two might be connected, and what the possible implications of treating concepts such as "man," "woman," "lesbian," "homosexual," and so forth as transhistorical and transcultural might be for our understandings of sexuality, subjectivities, and social arrangements. The act of mapping a category onto subjects who may not have recognized the practices, lifestyles, notions of body and self and so forth that it references, for example, aligns itself with a genealogy of power—one that imposes, distorts, or forecloses certain desires, identifications, and experiences. It can also entail missing an opportunity to discover in the past human possibilities and imaginings that were suppressed or left unfulfilled but that can provide guidance in the present for creating better worlds in the future.

For historians, creative archival approaches and thinking strategies do not imply inventing details but focusing—indeed, insisting—on the possibility of different readings, being more cognizant of the role of our subjectivity in our work, and paying greater attention to bodies in history and how we connect to them. More than empathy for people who lived in the past, more than attempts to understand them within and in relation to their historical context, a queer approach to archives requires an exercise of the mind that endeavors hard to treat classification schemes not just as abstractions but systems of power that have multiple effects on lives and bodies.[32] It also entails recognizing that we can only begin to imagine the memories and histories that those bodies can contain, unleash, and perform.

Trans-, inter-, and postdisciplinary conversations about the archive and the repertoire can advance our thinking on these and other problems of historical investigation and representation. The workshop at USC, for example, showed that performers and academics who engage with history but don't normally think about problems related to archival uses and abuses can benefit from discussions with historians, and that the latter can learn a great deal from actors, performance studies experts, colleagues in different disciplines, and people who are trained to think about bodies and embodiment and how to focus on the bodily life, as opposed to the "head life," of humans. The workshop cleared a space to talk about our continued need to classify, in academic writing and otherwise, and the dangers that operation can carry with it, as well as about methods, the place of experience and political concerns in connections to the past, and alternative ways of approaching the violence of Enlightenment rationality. In the process, it revealed the potential that conversations about the archive and the repertoire have not just to inform our understandings of the past and ignite our collective imaginations but to take our work and gazes in unexpected directions.

In hearing Rodríguez discuss her decision to feature Esparragosa in her performance, for example, it became evident that her approach to the case could well serve to get at certain problems related to the archive onstage. Although she explained the decision mainly in terms of her childhood memories of her father and the better understanding of the *protomédico* than of Aguilar that they afforded, it was impossible not to see that it was also partly dictated by the nature of the sources for the case, especially the report, which say much more about the doctor than about Aguilar. Rodríguez's transformation of the case into a performance (which she had ready in late 2014) featuring Dr. Esparragosa giving a "master class on anatomy" in which the authoritative physician provides a long lecture on a human subject that never appears onstage can powerfully dramatize this problem of archival presence/absence and lead to discussions about it with audiences in the question sessions that the artist normally has after her shows.

The workshop also placed the lens on historians in unexpected ways. For me at least, when Rodríguez vividly referred to being struck by Esparragosa's detached tone while describing his probing of Aguilar's body; by his lack of awareness of how his subjectivity and understandings of the world shaped the way he approached, understood, and classified her; and by the performative aspects of his "scientific objectivity," she inadvertently made some telling parallels between the figure of the enlightened doctor and that of the professional historian come to the surface. Given that the historical period that produced him also started to give life to modern medicine and history as a profession, perhaps the parallels should not be surprising but worth further exploration, as is the role of sentiment in historical research and writing. The general expectation that the historian has to have a rational, objective approach to historical sources and apply methods that rely on reason more than emotion to study past lives and subjects might have more than a little relationship to the importance of the rationality/passion dichotomy in the early modern world, one that in colonial contexts was mapped on to both gender and race (with reason coded as masculine and passion/emotion as feminine).

If the workshop discussion productively shifted the focus of the queer critical gaze from the doctor to the historian, it also ironically led to a valorization of the traditional historical archive, for when Rodríguez described her visits

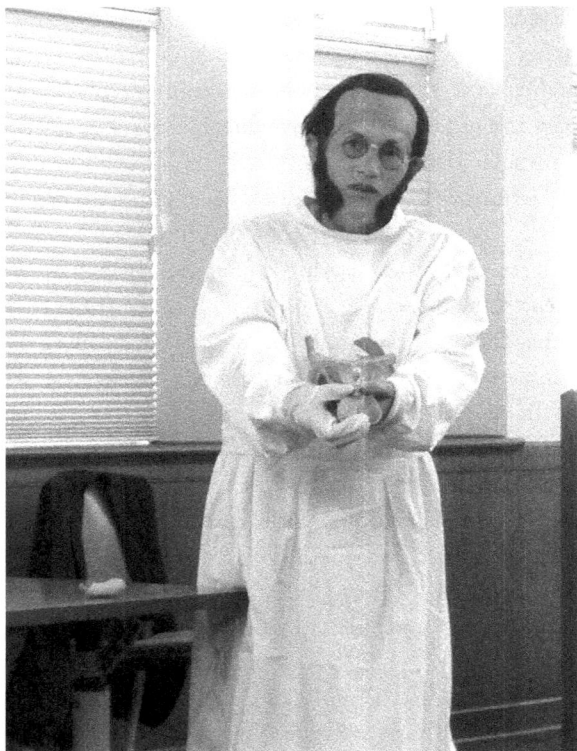

FIGURE 1.4. Rodríguez as Dr. Esparragosa lecturing on sexual organs at the USC workshop. Photograph taken by Laura G. Gutiérrez.

to Guatemala she essentially confessed to contracting the historian's "fever" or feeling at once euphoric by the "treasures" to be discovered and overwhelmed by the vastness of information.[33] Although she has embodied historical characters before (Mexican president Francisco Madero, Charles Darwin, and Leonardo da Vinci among them), this was her first experience at a physical archive and she found it nothing short of fascinating and enlightening, describing it as "the process of realizing all that can be discovered from a single detail [you find in a document] and the different threads that exist in a story and how if you start to pull one you find that you can keep pulling and find an infinite bundle of threads until you get to the bottom of things." And then there was the materiality of the objects, "because one thing is to read a typed or printed copy of a report . . . and another to get the original manuscript, open its pages, and read it in its own handwriting and ink on an old parchment, all these elements and textures and smells affect you too."

In describing the potential mental, emotional, and sensorial components of being with some of the material fragments of the past—or archival work as embodied practice—Rodríguez demonstrated how, for all of its associations with power, one archive can serve to denote the imagination of the other and the possibilities that their convergence can have for history and its performance. As a whole, the workshop served to highlight different forms of recording, remembering, and representing history and how disobeying disciplinary boundaries and sharing different methodological techniques can be enlightening, in a postenlightenment way, for all involved in the discussion. Rodríguez's theatrical approach to Juana Aguilar and Esparragosa played a key part in the conversation because it showed that though it might take creative license with some historical details, use humor and irreverence as critical weapons, and last only for the hour or two that it is performed on stage, it was not necessarily less insightful and consequential than that which a historian might produce on paper. After all, if embodiment can be linked to memory and knowledge and if the body can act as an archive that articulates the past, present, and future, then the act of representing Esparragosa on stage, critically making him the object of the gaze, and parodying the discourses that shaped his colonial and phallocentric mentality, is part of the process of radically making and remaking history and politics, no matter how ephemeral.

A Final Note to and about Audiences

From when it first took place to the present, the Juana Aguilar case has had multiple audiences, among them the Audiencia officials for whom Esparragosa wrote the report and the imagined enlightened community (scientific and otherwise) that he wished to impress when he published his findings in *La Gazeta de Guatemala*. It is not clear how the Audiencia judges responded because the legal dossier for the case is missing, just as it is also difficult to assess how the readers of the gazette responded because no one wrote to the editor or author to register a reaction (and if they did, the letters were not published in subsequent issues). Not that there was no reaction at all. The publication of the report scandalized at least one not-so-enlightened reader of the gazette, Manuel Antonio Borjas, to the point that he denounced it to the Mexican Inquisition. Borjas, whose identity is mysterious but most likely was a resident of Guatemala, objected to the publication of the report because he considered its content scandalous and obscene, its matter so detrimental to the souls of those who read it that it should not be allowed to circulate. In his letter to the Holy Office, he included a copy of the report, which is how it made its way into an inquisitorial dossier that is now part of Mexico's Archivo General de la Nación.[34] (Various other archives that have copies or originals of the *Gazeta de Guatemala* also have copies of the report.)

Though reactions to the report by the broader *Gazeta*'s readership and colonial legal authorities are hard to determine, it is clear that Esparragosa wanted to impress those audiences in order not only to bolster his status as a knowledgeable and enlightened doctor but to leave his mark in history. A regular contributor to the *Gazeta de Guatemala*'s medicine and surgery section, lauded in the gazette for his pedagogy and celebrated locally for his contributions to certain medical procedures (such as the introduction of elastic forceps to deal with difficult births), the report promised to ensure him a place in posterity. For the *protomédico*, the apparent unusualness of the case (and of Aguilar's body) coupled with what he saw as his unique findings (at least from a local perspective, for he borrowed the category of sexual neutrality from European commentators on hermaphroditism) were to spark great public interest and put not only Aguilar but him in the archive.

Another audience for the case has consisted of academics that have learned about it from what historians who have studied it have written or said about it. Having presented on it myself, it seems that the interest the case generates among this public is also partly due to a general sense that the Aguilar case is unique, an archival rarity that allows for some fascinating if disturbing glimpses at sexual discourses of the past as well as some amusing moments (such as when the nickname "La Larga" is mentioned). Finally, there are the audiences for Rodríguez's uses of the case, whether in cultural events like that in Argentina or on the stage when it fully materializes as a theatrical performance. If Rodríguez's assessment of the reaction to the reading of parts of Esparragosa's report in Argentina is correct, then these audiences too will be captivated in some measure by the "unusualness of the case."

Assuming that the different readings of audience interest in Juana Aguilar are correct, what the vastly different publics for the case seem to share, then, is the perception that it is exceptional or unique. This perception is correct in the sense that, like all cases or events in history, it has its particularities (here these might include the ten years of investigations, the escape to Guatemala, and the doctor's publication of the report in a gazette). But as many early modernists who work on sexuality and the history of medicine, natural science, anatomy, or criminality know, in many respects it is not unusual. Although the quantity should not be exaggerated, there are plenty of cases of people tried for non-normative sexual practices and hermaphroditism in various parts of the Atlantic world and, as discussed earlier, during the eighteenth century and beyond the heightened preoccupation with classification among certain scientific circles and a broader enlightened community led to the observation, study, and probing of countless bodies that fell outside the norm.[35]

At least for Spain and Spanish America, these cases and topics had not, until recently, received much attention, in part because they are "hidden" in the archives, not classified in such a way as to make it easy to find them or at all, but mainly because only in the past few decades have they gained significant legitimacy as subjects of inquiry. That more scholars are turning to those cases can mainly be attributed to the growing presence and theoretical interventions of gender studies, queer studies, and transgender studies in academia and related current discussions in the humanities about, among other things, sexuality, the performativity of gender, and archives, power, and knowledge.[36] As more cases of criminalized non-normative bodies and sexual practices are brought to light, examined with critical queer lenses, and made available to different audiences through different venues, not only will the idea that a case like that of Aguilar is unique be dispelled, but more occluded histories, knowledges, and experiences will be unveiled and new narrative and interpretative frameworks for understanding past and present produced. That, at least, is the case for uniting the archive and the repertoire, history and performance, queer theory and politics.

Notes

Editors' Note: A version of this chapter, with the same title, was published in *Radical History Review* 120 (Fall 2014): 159–82. The chapter you read here, with minimal edits (and shortened footnotes) by Zeb Tortorici, is the slightly longer version that María Elena wanted to publish back then but had to truncate for the journal. We are grateful to Sarah Gualtieri, the executor of María Elena Martínez's estate, who granted permission to publish an expanded version of that article in *Turning Archival*.

Author's Note: Research for this essay was made possible by a 2012–2013 Fulbright Scholars Fellowship. Parts of the essay were presented at the symposium "Race and Sex in the Eighteenth-Century Spanish Atlantic World," held at the University of Southern California on April 12–13, 2013, and at the conference "Embodied Politics: Race, Sexuality, and Performance" of the Tepoztlán Institute for the Transnational History of the Americas, held in Tepoztlán, Mexico, on July 26, 2013. I am grateful to the participants at both events for their comments as well as to the anonymous reviewers of the *Radical History Review* for their suggestions.

1   The gazette's publication of the report can be located in a number of places, including Mexico's Archivo General de la Nación, Mexico City (hereafter AGN), Indiferente Virreinal, Caja (Box) 5216, Folder 12.

2 In the early modern Atlantic world, the concept of sodomy was mainly linked to anal penetration, but it referred to nonreproductive or non-normative sexual acts more generally, and thus was applied to different kinds of sexual activities between women. For more on the category of "female sodomy," see Martínez, "Sex, Race, and Nature."

3 In addition to Martínez, "Sex, Race, and Nature," see the pathbreaking article by Few, "'That Monster of Nature.'"

4 For more on the work of Rodríguez and Felipe refer to the website of the Hemispheric Institute of Performance and Politics, which has a digital archive of photos, videos, and written documents pertaining to their performances, see Hemispheric Institute, Mission Statement, https://hemisphericinstitute.org/en/mission (last accessed January 23, 2022); and Gutiérrez, *Performing Mexicanidad*.

5 Taylor, *The Archive and the Repertoire*, 3–8. For performativity and video, Muñoz, *Disidentifications*. For performance, theater, and gay politics in the United States, refer to the works of David Román, particularly his *Acts of Intervention*.

6 Rich, "Compulsory Heterosexuality and Lesbian Existence."

7 Unless otherwise indicated, all quotes of Jesusa Rodríguez are from a workshop discussion on archives, history, and performance held at the University of Southern California on April 12, 2013, and the translations are mine.

8 The text for the presentation was written by Rodríguez and read by Felipe. It ended with "a short epilogue on Mexico" in which Rodríguez and Felipe denounced the government of Felipe Calderón for its tactics for dealing with drug traffickers, for its ties with big financial interests and multinationals, and for its human rights violations, as well as for the efforts by its institutions to control cultural production and co-opt artists and intellectuals. For Argentine newspaper coverage of the presentation, see Dillon, "Entrevista."

9 Personal conversations with Rodríguez about the cultural event in Buenos Aires, fall 2011 and 2013.

10 Martínez Durán, *Las ciencias médicas en Guatemala*, 423–73.

11 Besides public ones run by state institutions there are many other kinds of archives, including church, family, and personal ones, and some scholars define an archive as anywhere the past has left some of its traces, whether in written form or not. For an introduction to some of the literature and debates on the subject, see Hamilton and Harris, *Refiguring the Archive*, and the special issue on the archive in *History of the Human Sciences* 12, no. 107 (1999).

12 Scholarship on the topic is too vast to cite all of it here, but on the archive and its relationship to the law and authority, see Derrida, *Archive Fever*, especially the opening note; and Foucault, *The Archaeology of Knowledge*, 129–31. On power dynamics in the preservation, collection, and interpretation of sources, see Trouillot, *Silencing the Past*. And on written and other archival sources versus embodied culture, see Taylor, *The Archive and the Repertoire*.

13 Recent examples include Vos, *La Guerra de las dos vírgenes*, and Burns, *Into the Archive*.

14 See, for example, Davis, *Fiction in the Archives*; Steedman, *Dust*; and Burton, *Dwelling in the Archive*.

15 On colonial Latin American archives and race/caste classifications, see Martínez, *Genealogical Fictions*, 142–70; on archives, notarial culture, and power in colonial Peru, see

Burns, *Into the Archives*; and on the colonial archive more generally, see Stoler, *Along the Archival Grain*.

16 This use of the term "queer" underscores its social constructed-ness and interdependence with discursive operations and regimes of normality.

17 Martínez, "Sex, Race, and Nature." On eighteenth-century science reinforcing the two-sex binary, see Laqueur, *Making Sex*, and Schiebinger, *The Mind Has No Sex?*

18 Park and Nye, "Destiny Is Anatomy," 56.

19 The term "technology of the body" is from Franco, *Plotting Women*, 74.

20 Particularly as of the 1750s, albinos, hermaphrodites, and "spotted blacks" were displayed as human curiosities in European cities such as London and Paris as well as studied (sometimes just through painted images) by naturalists and physicians. The extensive literature on the eighteenth-century obsession with studying, probing, and classifying raced and sexed bodies includes Schiebinger, *Nature's Body*; Curran, "Rethinking Race History"; Haidt, *Embodying the Enlightenment*; Hudson, "From 'Nation' to 'Race'"; and Lafuente and Moscoso, *Monstruos y seres imaginarios en la Biblioteca Nacional*.

21 Foucault, *Abnormal*, especially 55–80.

22 See Schiebinger, "The Anatomy of Difference."

23 Taylor, "Performance and/as History," 71.

24 See the documentary *En Batalla: El teatro de Ludwik Margules*, directed by Verónica Quezada.

25 Steedman, "The Space of Memory," 66.

26 In addition to Davis, *Fiction in the Archives*, see Ginzburg, *Threads and Traces*.

27 Florescano, *Memory, Myth, and Time in Mexico*, 30–64.

28 See Le Goff, *History and Memory*, 51–100, and Osborne, "The Ordinariness of the Archive," 55.

29 Hobsbawm made his comments in an interview on Lemus's television program *Tratos y Retratos*, which aired on Mexico's Canal 22 on October 10, 2012.

30 In the English tradition, literature on the dialectical relationship between the past and present, or role of the historian's subjectivity in "reconstructing" the past, goes back to Collingwood, *The Idea of History*. For more recent treatments, see Lowenthal, *The Past Is a Foreign Country*; Le Goff, *History and Memory*, 120–21; and Van Young, "The Cuautla Lazarus."

31 Martínez Durán, *Las Ciencias médicas en Guatemala*, 463–65.

32 Following Foucault, Stryker eloquently stresses this point in "(De)Subjugated Knowledges," 3.

33 Rodríguez likened the archival experience to finding a precious pre-Columbian object in an archaeological site, which served as a reminder of the profoundly strong connection between archaeology and indigenous history in Mexico since the late eighteenth century, and the relationship of both with its national history after independence.

34 AGN, Indiferente Virreinal, Caja (Box) 5216, Folder 12. In the AGN's catalogues, the report can be found in the "Inquisition" and "Indiferente Virreinal" sections. Similar to "Indiferente General" in Seville's Archivo General de Indias, the latter is a free-for-all category containing documents from the colonial period that archivists have not reviewed or find too difficult to classify because of their content or another reason,

or that simply have made their way there through serendipitous or other mysterious processes.

35 As Velasco points out, there are numerous representations of "female homoeroticism" in early modern Spanish historical and literary texts as well as secular and inquisitorial court cases involving women tried for having sexual relations with other women (in relation sometimes to other "deviant" domains, such as prostitution and witchcraft). *Lesbians in Early Modern Spain*, 1 and 7–8. Also refer to Daston and Park, "The Hermaphrodite and the Orders of Nature."

36 It is not possible to do justice to all the contributions in these studies, but for an insightful recent discussion of debates about historicism in queer studies, see Traub, "The New Unhistoricism in Queer Studies." And for an introduction to transgender studies, see Stryker and Whittle, *The Transgender Studies Reader*; and Stryker and Aizura, *The Transgender Studies Reader 2*.

Works Cited

Burns, Kathryn. *Into the Archive: Writing and Power in Colonial Peru*. Durham, NC: Duke University Press, 2010.

Burton, Antoinette. *Dwelling in the Archive: Women Writing House, Home, and History in Late Colonial India*. New York: Oxford University Press, 2003.

Collingwood, R. G. *The Idea of History*. Oxford: Clarendon Press, 1946.

Curran, Andrew. "Rethinking Race History: The Role of the Albino in the French Enlightenment Life Sciences." *History and Theory* 48 (October 2009): 151–79.

Daston, Lorraine, and Katharine Park. "The Hermaphrodite and the Orders of Nature: Sexual Ambiguity in Early Modern France." *GLQ: A Journal of Lesbian and Gay Studies* 1, no. 4 (1995): 419–38.

Davis, Natalie Zemon. *Fiction in the Archives: Pardon Tales and Their Tellers in Sixteenth-Century France*. Stanford, CA: Stanford University Press, 1987.

Derrida, Jacques. *Archive Fever: A Freudian Impression*. Trans. Eric Prenowitz. Chicago: University of Chicago Press, 1998.

De Vos, Jan. *La Guerra de las dos vírgenes. La rebelión de Los Zendales (Chiapas, 1712): documentada, recordada, recreada*. Mérida: Centro Peninsular en Humanidades y Ciencias Sociales, 2011.

Dillon, Marta. "Entrevista: El coctel Felipe." *Página 12* (Buenos Aires), September 23, 2011.

Durán, Carlos Martínez. *Las ciencias médicas en Guatemala. Origen y evolución*. Guatemala: Tipografía Sánchez & De Guise, 1941.

Few, Martha. "'That Monster of Nature': Gender, Sexuality, and the Medicalization of a 'Hermaphrodite' in Late Colonial Guatemala." *Ethnohistory* 54, no. 1 (2007): 159–76.

Florescano, Enrique. *Memory, Myth, and Time in Mexico: From the Aztecs to Independence*. Trans. Albert G. Bork. Austin: University of Texas Press, 1994.

Foucault, Michel. *Abnormal: Lectures at the Collège De France 1974–1975*. Ed. Valerio Marchetti and Antonella Salomoni. Trans. Graham Burchell. London: Verso, 2004.

Foucault, Michel. *The Archaeology of Knowledge*. New York: Vintage Books, 2010.

Franco, Jean. *Plotting Women: Gender and Representation in Mexico*. New York: Columbia University Press, 1989.

Ginzburg, Carlo. *Threads and Traces: True False Fictive*. Trans. Anne Tedeschi and John Tedeschi. Berkeley: University of California Press, 2012.

Gutiérrez, Laura G. *Performing Mexicanidad: Vendidas y Cabareteras on the Transnational Stage*. Austin: University of Texas Press, 2010.

Haidt, Rebecca. *Embodying the Enlightenment: Knowing the Body in Eighteenth-Century Spanish Literature and Culture*. New York: St. Martin's Press, 1998.

Hamilton, Carolyn, and Verne Harris, eds. *Refiguring the Archive*. Cape Town: Kluwer Academic Publishers, 2002.

History of the Human Sciences 12, no. 107 (1999).

Hudson, Nicholas. "From 'Nation' to 'Race': The Origin of Racial Classification in Eighteenth-Century Thought." *Eighteenth-Century Studies* 29, no. 3 (1996): 247–64.

Lafuente, Antonio, and Javier Moscoso. *Monstruos y seres imaginarios en la Biblioteca Nacional*. Madrid: Biblioteca Nacional, 2000.

Laqueur, Thomas Walter. *Making Sex: Body and Gender from the Greeks to Freud*. Cambridge, MA: Harvard University Press, 1990.

Le Goff, Jacques. *History and Memory*. Trans. Steven Rendall and Elizabeth Claman. New York: Columbia University Press, 1992.

Lowenthal, David. *The Past Is a Foreign Country*. Cambridge: Cambridge University Press, 1985.

Martínez, María Elena. "Sex, Race, and Nature: Juana Aguilar's Body and Creole Enlightened Thought in Late Colonial New Spain." Paper presented at the symposium "Race and Sex in the Eighteenth-Century Spanish Atlantic World" at the University of Southern California, April 12–13, 2013.

Muñoz, José Esteban. *Disidentifications: Queers of Color and the Performance of Politics*. Minneapolis: University of Minnesota Press, 1999.

Osborne, Thomas. "The Ordinariness of the Archive." *History of the Human Sciences* 12, no. 2 (1999): 51–64.

Quezada, Verónica, dir. *En Batalla: El teatro de Ludwik Margules*. Mexico City, Centro de Investigación Teatral Rodolfo Usigli and Instituto Nacional de Bellas Artes, 2013.

Rich, Adrienne. "Compulsory Heterosexuality and Lesbian Existence." *Signs: Journal of Women in Culture and Society* 5 (Summer 1980): 631–60.

Román, David. *Acts of Intervention: Performance, Gay Culture, and AIDS*. Bloomington: Indiana University Press, 1998.

Schiebinger, Londa L. *The Mind Has No Sex?: Women in the Origins of Modern Science*. Cambridge, MA: Harvard University Press, 1989.

Schiebinger, Londa L. "The Anatomy of Difference: Race and Sex in 18th-Century Science." *Eighteenth-Century Studies* 23, no. 4 (1990): 387–405.

Schiebinger, Londa L. *Nature's Body: Gender in the Making of Modern Science*. New Brunswick, NJ: Rutgers University Press, 2006.

Steedman, Carolyn. "The Space of Memory: In an Archive." *History of the Human Sciences* 11, no. 4 (1998): 65–83.

Steedman, Carolyn. *Dust: The Archive and Cultural History*. New Brunswick, NJ: Rutgers University Press, 2002.

Stoler, Ann Laura. *Along the Archival Grain: Epistemic Anxieties and Colonial Common Sense*. Princeton, NJ: Princeton University Press, 2009.

Stryker, Susan. "(De)Subjugated Knowledges: An Introduction to Transgender Studies." In *The Transgender Studies Reader*, edited by Susan Stryker and Stephen Whittle, 1–17. New York: Routledge, 2006.

Stryker, Susan, and Aren Z. Aizura, eds. *The Transgender Studies Reader 2*. London: Routledge, 2013.

Stryker, Susan, and Stephen Whittle, eds. *The Transgender Studies Reader*. New York: Routledge, 2006.

Taylor, Diana. *The Archive and the Repertoire: Performing Cultural Memory in the Americas*. Durham, NC: Duke University Press, 2003.

Taylor, Diana. "Performance and/as History." *Drama Review* 50, no. 1 (2006): 67–86.

Traub, Valerie. "The New Unhistoricism in Queer Studies." *PMLA* 128, no. 1 (2013): 21–39.

Trouillot, Michel-Rolph. *Silencing the Past: Power and the Production of History*. Boston: Beacon Press, 1995.

Van Young, Eric. "The Cuautla Lazarus: Double Subjectivities in Reading Texts on Popular Collective Action." *Colonial Latin American Review* 2, nos. 1–2 (1993): 3–26.

Velasco, Sherry. *Lesbians in Early Modern Spain*. Nashville, TN: Vanderbilt University Press, 2011.

2. DECOLONIAL ARCHIVAL IMAGINARIES

On Losing, Performing, and Finding Juana Aguilar

ZEB TORTORICI

What happens when the long-lost records, sometimes even fetishized in (or *because of*) their absence, unexpectedly turn up in the archives? This chapter, building on María Elena Martínez's previous chapter, is partly about how the performative, symbiotic acts of archivization and historical narration—from the late eighteenth century to the present—can function as forms of fabrication, fantasizing, and imagining that, nonetheless, paint a better picture of an elusive historical figure. I am partly interested in how truth claims and historiographical fabrications come to be produced by and through absences and gaps in colonial archives, particularly in relation to trans history—a term that I use in its most open-ended and capacious sense, and which points to the "possibility of being confronted with the deep alterity of the past," especially in relation to "early gendered, gender-nonconforming, and transgender experience" into the eighteenth century.[1] I too am interested in how the unexpected *turning up* of Aguilar in the archives—and Aguilar's own repeated *turning away* from colonial criminal authorities, and hence the bureaucratic impulses behind colonial archives—radically shifts the archival terrain of that which we can say or know about them. I trace how Juana Aguilar—suspected, in the language of the criminal courts, of being a hermaphrodite in late colonial Guatemala, at the close of the eighteenth century—has been written about, performed, and archived over time. Martínez's 2014 *Radical History Review* article, published here in *Turning Archival* in expanded form, offers what we might call queer microhistory at its very best. In this chapter, I hope to follow in those footsteps. It appears that Guatemalan historians first wrote about Aguilar in 1941, though since 2007 they have been written about at a frenzied pace. In recent years, Aguilar has also been publicly performed repeatedly—first by Mexican performance artist Jesusa

Rodríguez between 2011 and 2014 in Canada, Argentina, and the United States, and perhaps most recently by several academics at the 2017 meeting of the Tepoztlán Institute of the Transnational History of the Americas in Tepoztlán, Mexico, which was in honor of María Elena Martínez, one of the collective's founding members.

Because the transcripts of the late eighteenth- and early nineteenth-century criminal trials against Aguilar were long thought by several historians—myself and María Elena Martínez included—to have been missing until they were rediscovered in recent years, many of the writings on Aguilar (and performances of them) have theoretically been framed by and through questions of archival absence, which enacted particularly queer readings and methods to reimagine the possibilities of Aguilar in the very first place. This chapter first offers a genealogy of these writings and performances, revisiting some of the texts analyzed by Martínez, but in a different light. It then looks at the archiving—and descriptive metadata—of Aguilar by analyzing both the archival description of the trial and, for the first time since 1941, the original transcripts of these criminal trial records, presumed to have been lost by so many historians (myself included) to the ravages of time. I argue, on the one hand, that despite historians having uncovered, once again, the 1802 criminal records (which actually span from 1792 to 1803) containing Aguilar's original testimony, we come only partly closer to understanding Aguilar's own intersecting identities in the past. Several attempts to narrativize, perform, and archive Aguilar contribute to a growing assemblage of myths and distortions—falsehoods and (de)colonial fantasies—that have been heaped upon them, as a historical subject with political potential, over time. Yet at the same time we gather some crucial information about Aguilar, which give us clues into the worlds that they constructed around them at different points in time. We are left with overlapping archival slivers of an elusive historical subject who, for decades, survived and prospered as a merchant—key information that was previously unknown about them—and who actively escaped colonial authorities on several occasions. Throughout, I am interested in how Juana Aguilar simultaneously turns toward and away from us in the archives—a productive archival instability that mimics Aguilar's own multiple intersecting identities, mediated by race, class, gender, profession, and a range of other factors.

As we will see, however, "fabrication" and "falsehood" in such narrative and performative contexts are not necessarily the opposite of "truth" or "authenticity," but rather a partial reimagining and fantasizing of them. We see this much, for instance, in Narciso Esparragosa's conclusion that Aguilar was neither man nor woman. Aguilar, in this sense, was someone that in some ways resisted

Enlightenment taxonomies, and in doing so exhibited a range of complex markers of intersecting and shifting and sometimes contradictory identities that Aguilar embodied (and had to in order to thrive). Throughout, I am attuned to the shifting political and archival stakes of such gestures, the decolonial impetus behind them, and the archival classifications through which Aguilar has been documented and described in both the Mexican and Guatemalan national archives.

The eighteenth-century criminal prosecutions of Aguilar, the twentieth-century archiving of their "crimes," and the historiographical writings and performances surrounding them are all partly built up around whether or not Aguilar, as historical subject, fits the categories of "man," "woman," "hermaphrodite," "trans," "queer," or something else, today as in the past. As several scholars have shown, the surgeon and medical doctor Narciso Esparragosa y Gallardo, whom the Guatemalan criminal courts called upon to examine Aguilar's body in the early 1800s, concluded that they were "neither man nor woman."[2] And while Martínez in the previous chapter refers to Aguilar as "she," throughout my chapter, I use "they," which in some paradoxical way might even resonate with Esparragosa's own nonbinary assessments and negations of Aguilar's lived gender. From the outset, Aguilar resists easy categorization, yet whereas for late colonial Guatemalan medics and criminal courts, Aguilar presented somewhat of a biological conundrum, today with the advances in modern medical science, we might perhaps best understand Aguilar today as someone who was intersex. The original transcripts of the criminal trials seem to intimate that Aguilar's own identities and embodiments of gender shifted over time and depending on context. In the recently surfaced 1792 court records, the initial criminal complaint registered by the court is against "a woman named Juana" for the "ugly sin of cohabiting with the same *feminine* gender."[3] Yet Aguilar themself, recording their plea at one point in the first person, acknowledged that they—an *yndia mestiza*, or a mixed-race indigenous woman—were imprisoned for having been "taken for [being] a man and dressing in women's garb [*en trage mugeril*], and similarly for having had carnal copulation with one or two indigenous women."[4]

Throughout the testimonies Aguilar gave, for instance, "she" *appears* to use feminine pronouns and adjectives in Spanish self-referentially (as do scribes and doctors referring to Aguilar in the third person). It is, however, difficult for the readers of the archival document to know the extent to which these gendered pronouns at times might have been imposed upon Aguilar by the notary or scribe who recorded their own words, especially given that Aguilar most frequently gave their testimony in the first person, yet they came to be recorded by the notary in the third (e.g., "She said her name was Juana Antonia de Aguilar, about thirty years old, single [*soltera*], day laborer"). As Kathryn Burns tells us, throughout colonial Latin America "notaries produced a shaped, collaborative truth—one that might shave, bevel, and polish witnesses' words a bit here, a bit there, as they were 'translated' into writing."[5] With each new attempt to find or fix Aguilar in the archives—to write about or to perform them—we also correspondingly lose something of them, partly fictionalizing them and their desires. Such distortions, as we will see, are inevitably produced by the very processes of writing, performing, and archiving Juana Aguilar, and at the very same time that we do, little by little, get to know more and more about Aguilar and their life. Scholars, activists, and archivists (perhaps not unlike notaries and medics who described Aguilar) all construct collective imaginings around—and desires through—Aguilar. At the same time, however, we can trace crucial contours of the life and experiences of Aguilar, especially with the tools familiar to microhistory, and in doing so come to understand Aguilar and their world and palimpsestic subjectivity a little bit better.

Much of the writings on, and performances of, Aguilar initially came about as a response to a presumed archival absence that now no longer pertains: in 2012, historian Sylvia Sellers-García's research into the life of Dr. Narciso Esparragosa—who first examined Aguilar's body—unexpectedly turned up a card catalog descriptor of Aguilar's trial transcripts in the Guatemalan national archive, the Archivo General de Centro América (hereafter AGCA). Based on this archival "find," as I will relate, the further that one delves into these recently surfaced archival documents about Aguilar, the more one realizes that Aguilar, in their everyday life, simply wanted to be left alone by colonial authorities, medical doctors, invasive procedures, and prying public eyes. These archival records shed important light on Aguilar's life, giving up clues about how they lived and survived, restoring some of the dignity and agency that Esparragosa and others have taken away from Aguilar. The transcripts of the criminal trials allow us to fill in the blanks of Aguilar's life and experiences a little bit more than was previously possible, yet much remains unknown. Historical speculation—even when done in ways that are sympathetic to the historical subject in question—can inadvertently contribute to the cross-temporal accretion of myths, stereotypes, and misinformation about the historical subject in question, showing us how acts of historical narration can often trade in voyeurism, fantasy, fiction, and fabrication. Around multiple issues, Aguilar (of their own volition) resists our very desires to know more about them. Recognizing this illegibility, I argue, should be at the heart of any attempt to decolonize our own archival imaginaries about Aguilar. At the very same time, the recently surfaced archival records outline the life of a trader, shopkeeper, and merchant who more often than not appears to have blended in, and been at home with, the environs and inhabitants of late colonial Guatemala. As the records themselves show, Aguilar clearly resisted (at several moments in time) colonial intrusions on their life and body, and at the very same time—as a merchant and shopkeeper on the margins and frontiers of the Viceroyalty of New Spain—was one of the quotidian enablers and movers of colonialism itself. Aguilar thus participated in the colonial processes—facilitating the exchange of goods—at the same time that they, for many years, evaded colonial authorities. Aguilar's own identities thus intersect at multiple points and in shifting and unstable ways with racial identification, gender identity, sexual desire, and with other colonial projects and colonized subjects.

The very notion of "decolonial archival imaginaries," through which I read the archiving and historical narration of Aguilar, merges ideas of how both decolonial praxis and archival theory can, in a gesture toward Benedict Anderson among others, be productively redeployed through the concept of the imaginary.[6] Emma Pérez, for one, conceptualizes the *decolonial imaginary* as "that time lag between the colonial and postcolonial, that interstitial space where differential politics and social dilemmas are negotiated. The decolonial imaginary is intangible to many because it acts much like a dark shadow in the dark. It survives as a faint outline gliding against a wall or an object. The shadow is the figure between the subject and the object on which it is cast, moving and breathing through an in-between space."[7] As we trace the shadows and contours of Aguilar through archival descriptors, historiography, and performance art, we will see how they inhabit exactly the type of post/colonial time lag—a mere shadow upon a shadow of, and within, the archive—that Pérez gestures toward.

Aguilar simultaneously inhabits what Anne J. Gilliland and Michelle Caswell term *impossible archival imaginaries*, which can refer to the "individual and collective imaginings about the absent or unattainable archive."[8] Aguilar, I argue, will continue to embody "a kind of never-actualized record" despite the fact that the long presumed-to-be-lost archival records about them have now turned up in the archives—a fact that will, no doubt, prompt many new histories to be written about them.[9] The archival representations of Aguilar that María Elena Martínez and I examine in our respective chapters—alongside the archival imaginaries that we too spin—are forever poised between past and present; colonial violence and decolonial promise; archival subject and archived object.

Writing Juana

As Martínez lays out in her chapter, in 1802 in Guatemala City, Aguilar was accused of having committed the crime of "concubinage" (living together outside of wedlock) with a woman. The Royal Tribunal of the Protomedicato—the board of physicians in colonial Latin America that regulated medical practitioners and inspected apothecaries—in Guatemala called upon two medical doctors, Narciso Esparragosa and José María Guerra, on September 15, 1802, to "assess" Aguilar's body to determine their "true" gender. Both men, *and several midwives*, repeatedly examined Aguilar's body—probing their vagina, ovaries, and what Esparragosa deemed a "prominent" clitoris—in order to determine Aguilar's sex and whether or not they were indeed a hermaphrodite, all to resolve the allegations that Aguilar was even physiologically capable of committing sodomy. Such court-sanctioned invasive medical examinations amount to forms of violence enacted on the body of a gender-nonconforming individual. For as Marisa Fuentes notes, violence is the historical material that animates historiography and historical narration "in its subtle and excessive modes—on the body of the archive, the body in the archive and the material body."[10] Such an observation is especially applicable to Aguilar, whose body is textually and visually fragmented—*turned archival*—partly by and through Esparragosa's widely circulating medical reports published in the *Gazeta de Guatemala*.

It was Esparragosa's assessment that entered the public sphere because he published his medical reports in two separate articles in the late colonial newspaper, the *Gazeta de Guatemala*. Given that the original transcripts of Aguilar's trial records only surfaced recently, the bulk of what scholars previously knew about Aguilar came from these two articles. Published respectively on July 4, 1803, and on July 11, 1803, the articles were both titled "HERMAFRODITAS" (Figure 2.1) and became, according to Martha Few, "a means to circulate information about Aguilar's exotic, exceptional body, both to the legal court and to the broader public."[11] As Martínez here points out, Aguilar first turned into material for historical study because of Esparragosa's report, "in which fragments of her life, and especially of her body, appear through different filters, among them colonial, misogynist, and homophobic." Esparragosa presented his opinions to the court in February 1803, along with detailed illustrations of Aguilar's genitalia (of which no trace exists). Esparragosa noted that Aguilar had an enlarged clitoris, lacked a defined vaginal canal, and whose "menstruations of watery blood" originated from the same orifice as urine. He documented "two oval-shaped glandular bodies, each about the size of a cacao bean" inside of Aguilar's labia, which he posited were either inchoate testicles or malformed ova-

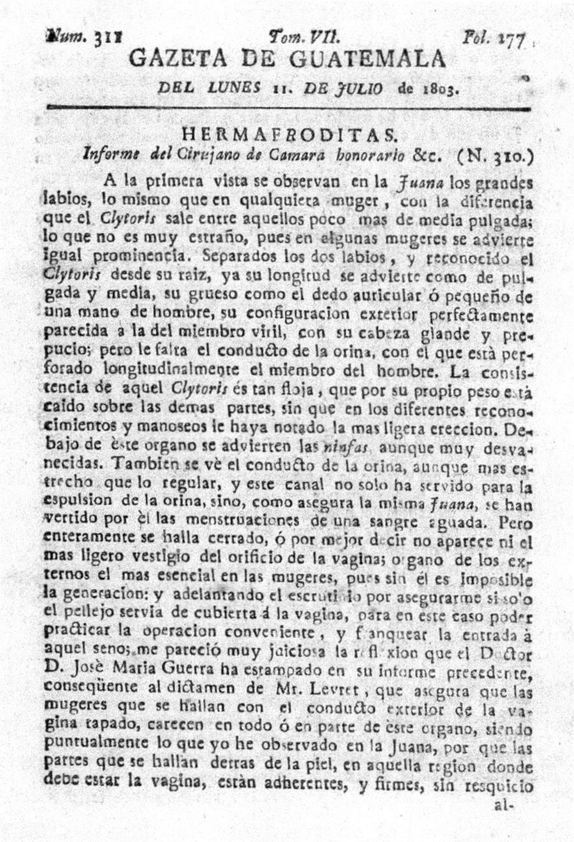

FIGURE 2.1. Article published by Dr. Narciso Esparragosa in the *Gazeta de Guatemala* on July 11, 1803, on the topic of "HERMAPHRODITES."

The figure shows a newspaper article with the following visible text:

Num. 311   ***Tom. VII.***   *Fol. 277*

GAZETA DE GUATEMALA

DEL LUNES 11. DE JULIO de 1803.

HERMAFRODITAS.

Informe del Cirujano de Camara honorario &c. (N. 310.)

A la primera vista se observan en la *Juana* los grandes labios, lo mismo que en qualquiera muger, con la diferencia que el *Clytoris* sale entre aquellos poco mas de media pulgada; lo que no es muy estraño, pues en algunas mugeres se advierte igual prominencia. Separados los dos labios, y reconocido el *Clytoris* desde su raiz, ya su longitud se advierte como de pulgada y media, su grueso como el dedo auricular ó pequeño de una mano de hombre, su configuracion exterior perfectamente parecida a la del miembro viril, con su cabeza glande y prepucio; pero le falta el conducto de la orina, con el que está perforado longitudinalmente el miembro del hombre. La consistencia de aquel *Clytoris* es tan floja, que por su propio peso está caído sobre las demas partes, sin que en los diferentes reconocimientos y manoseos le haya notado la mas ligera ereccion. Debajo de este organo se advierten las *ninfas,* aunque muy desvanecidas. Tambien se ve el conducto de la orina, aunque mas estrecho que lo regular, y este canal no solo ha servido para la espulsion de la orina, sino, como asegura la misma *Juana,* se han vertido por él las menstruaciones de una sangre aguada. Pero enteramente se halla cerrado, ó por mejor decir no aparece ni el mas ligero vestigio del orificio de la vagina; organo de los externos el mas esencial en las mugeres, pues sin él es imposible la generacion: y adelantando el escrutinio por asegurarme si solo el pellejo servia de cubierta á la vagina, para en este caso poder practicar la operacion conveniente, y f anquear la entrada á aquel seno; me pareció muy juiciosa la reflexion que el Doctor D. José Maria Guerra ha estampado en su informe precedente, consequente al dictamen de Mr. Levret, que asegura que las mugeres que se hallan con el conducto exterior de la vagina tapado, carecen en todo ó en parte de este organo, siendo puntualmente lo que yo he observado en la Juana, por que las partes que se hallan detras de la piel, en aquella region donde debe estar la vagina, están adherentes, y firmes, sin resquicio al-

ries.[12] Esparragosa paints his image of Aguilar in terms of both "lack" (*defecto*) and "excess" (*excesso*), concluding—or fantasizing—that "she is a truly unhappy [*verdaderamente infeliz*] person, for nature having denied her the reproductive organs that every individual appreciates."[13] All this demonstrated, to Esparragosa's satisfaction, that Aguilar could *not* have consummated sodomy: "being neither man nor woman, Juana is incapable of incurring a crime that necessarily demands the existence of one of the two sexes."[14]

Here, it is worth reflecting briefly on how these two late colonial newspaper articles circulated, both as archival documents and as newspaper print, throughout New Spain. How did these two articles on Aguilar, originally published in Guatemala City, end up in the national archives of both Guatemala and Mexico, and why? Whereas Guatemala's Archivo General de Centro

América maintains a complete set of the print run of the *Gazeta de Guatemala*, Mexico's Archivo General de la Nación (hereafter AGN) holds only a handful of complete issues, all from 1808, which in the archive's finding aid are classified simply as "*Gazeta de Guatemala*, numbers 24, 25, 26, and 27." The two 1803 *Gazeta* articles on Aguilar are, in contrast, archived separately, and they have been excised from the newspapers in which they were originally printed. They are couched, instead—as Martínez showed in the previous chapter—inside a very different archival classification: a one-page, handwritten formal complaint by a certain Manuel Antonio Borjas against the newspaper, filed with the Mexican Inquisition on August 3, 1803, only a month following their publication. In his complaint, Borjas critiqued the *Gazeta* for "containing a report related to a certain Juana Larga, who is taken by some of the common people as a Hermaphrodite . . . for they [the articles] appear to me obscene and provocative, material far from that which should be [printed] in the *Gazeta* in the hands of all, and they cannot be read without grave ruin to one's soul."[15] Aguilar's body—depicted as *obscene and provocative*—is here archived by means of a moral judgment, which registers yet another archival imaginary about them and their desires.

The Mexican Inquisition, it appears, did not follow up on the complaint, yet it came to be archived among the files of the Inquisition along with Esparragosa's articles. Nonetheless, the entry's framing of Esparragosa's writings on Juana Aguilar as both "obscene and provocative" show how some readers viewed the text—and, we can assume, Aguilar's own body—as having an ethnopornographic function when put into mass circulation. Here obscenity is defined not solely by the intent to sexually arouse or to provoke lust, but rather by the potential to shock, to disgust, and to end up "in the hands of all" thereby provoking "grave ruin." The language of the complaint specifies that the problem was not solely the graphic nature of Esparragosa's medical reports, but rather the circulation of such knowledge among the masses. The recently uncovered court records of Juana Aguilar, Esparragosa's writing on Aguilar's body, and even the placement of Esparragosa's *Gazeta* articles within the files of the Mexican Inquisition (as part of an obscenity complaint), show how Aguilar's archived could attain overlapping juridical, scientific, popular, and pornographic meanings when circulated among diverse audiences.

As important as historical records these 1803 articles published by Esparragosa in *La Gazeta de Guatemala* are, they have been sufficiently treated at length by several scholars.[16] What interests me here is both how Aguilar first entered public consciousness in the early nineteenth century and how they entered historiographical consciousness in the mid-twentieth through a multiplicity of falsifying and conflicting narratives about them. As Martínez briefly discussed in her chapter, the earliest historiographical traces of Aguilar are found in *Las ciencias médicas en Guatemala. Origen y evolución*, published in 1941 by Carlos Martínez Durán, a Guatemalan researcher and medical doctor who first transcribed Esparragosa's testimony from the original criminal trial transcripts. Martínez Durán's imagining of Aguilar initiates a chain of fictionalizing distortions and misinscriptions of Aguilar. Martínez Durán titled the thirty-second chapter of his book "Narciso Esparragosa y Gallardo, founder of Legal Medicine in Guatemala," and it quickly becomes clear with whom Martínez Durán's own sympathies lie.[17] Martínez Durán glorifies the late colonial doctor, noting that "The report of our illustrious surgeon on the case of Juana la Larga is a masterpiece." The first falsification is that he refers to Aguilar with the malicious nickname that they came to be known by: "Juana la Larga" or "Juana the Long," a name that was supposedly used in reference to their elongated clitoris. This is a nickname that Esparragosa used repeatedly in his 1803 *Gazeta de Guatemala* articles, and one that Martínez Durán not only takes at face value, but seems to revel in—seamlessly switching between using both Aguilar's real name and the pejorative nickname with no rhyme or reason.

Martínez Durán then goes on, in his brief introduction to Esparragosa's report, to weave his fictionalizing narrative (based on, but greatly deviating from, the trial transcripts). He sets the scene for his readers:

> Juana la Larga lived in several towns throughout the province of El Salvador, and in all of them she was accused of *pecados nefandos* ["nefarious sins" of sodomy]. Just as long [*Larga*] as her nickname was her scandalous life. The year of 1792 had been so full of tranquility for the peaceful citizens of [the town of] Cojutepeque. On one sad and rainy morning in September, a woman named Juana Aguilar arrived in town, and she set up her *achimería* business [i.e., a shop selling trinkets]. Soon many clients came, the most assiduous of whom was Feliciana María Mejía. This woman had a very honest friendship with Aguilar, and on one ill-fated [*desgraciado*] day, she was violated and trapped in one of the interior rooms by the audacious shopkeeper. It is not known exactly what took place in that room, but shortly thereafter news of the scandal spread and a thousand tongues spoke of Juana Aguilar who, though she dressed as a woman, she flirted with [*requería*] those of her same sex, with whom she practiced coitus as a man.[18]

Here, Martínez Durán introduces a wide range of narrative fictive elements into Aguilar's story, so as to impress upon his readers the immorality of illicit acts and desires. His unequivocal assertion that "Both [doctors] affirmed that Juana la Larga had a man's penis, but one that lacked the duct to expel semen" is contradicted by Esparragosa himself, who notes that Aguila's clitoris *resembled* a penis but was not one. The transcripts of the criminal trial, to be certain, make no mention of "sad and rainy" weather on the day of Aguilar's arrival into the town of Cojutepeqeue (nor do they even discuss this arrival). The "tranquility" and "peaceful" nature of its (presumably cisgender, heterosexual) citizens too is a figment of Martínez Durán's imagination.

So too, then, is the violence with which Aguilar imposed themself upon the first witness, Feliciana María Mejía, a young married indigenous woman who, in Martínez Durán's account, was "violated and trapped." Martínez Durán writes, for instance, that Feliciana Mejía "assured that she had been violated [*violentada*] by Juana, [and] enjoyed the act as if it had been performed by a man. The indignation of the town spread like fire. Men were no longer feared [by women] now that Donjuanesque violence inhabited the body of a woman."[19] In the recently surfaced trial transcripts, however, Mejía did not describe the encounter in any such terms—she simply described having not wanted "to be with her [Aguilar]" because Mejía herself was married, and "she had heard it said that she [Aguilar] loved other women."[20] According to Mejía's own testimony, Aguilar did "achieve her aim on one occasion, taking her by the hand which she'd grabbed, and although she [Mejía] resisted, excusing herself . . . she [Aguilar] offered to bother her no more, only on that one occasion, in which she succeeded in appeasing her appetite."[21]

The misogynistic violation imagined—or fantasized—here by Martínez Durán is problematic on several levels. Furthermore, he contradicts himself: he admittedly states that the archival documents are vague about what went on between Aguilar and Mejía, yet he subsequently infers that Aguilar—enjoying the sexual act as if "she" were a man—could only have "violated" Mejía. These are some of the many narrative distortions whereby Martínez Durán obliquely archives his *own* affective reactions to (and disgust toward) "hermaphrodites" and intersex individuals in the mid-twentieth century, alongside his readings of sodomy and its attendant illicit desires in Guatemala's colonial past. Of Aguilar, Martínez Durán concludes: "Grave misfortune would be her life, tragic and desperate until death"—a fanciful claim that partly recycles Esparragosa's discourse on how "truly unhappy" Aguilar must have been, given that Nature denied "her" either of the two sexes supposedly natural to all species. Such claims persist, despite the fact that we know relatively little about Aguilar's robust life after they were ultimately exonerated and set free in 1803. This is, in essence, gossip-mongering masquerading as historiography.

I have here used Martínez Durán's 1941 writings on doctor Narciso Esparragosa and Juana Aguilar as an example of how the earliest historical narratives of Aguilar are imbued with falsifying desires, imagination, and distortion to serve particular points of view (and are seen in stark contrast to the authority and truth claims of colonial medical science). This is perhaps unsurprising, especially given Martínez Durán's own elite status as a surgeon and medical doctor in mid-twentieth-century Guatemala and his own envisioned role as a purveyor of knowledge about the history of medicine in colonial Guatemala. It is clear that Martínez Durán sees himself in a great chain of medical expertise and scientific authenticity, stretching back to Enlightenment-era Esparragosa as its "founder" in late colonial Guatemala. For a long time—at least until Sellers-García located the case in the AGCA several years ago—Esparragosa's 1803 newspaper articles and Martínez Durán's 1941 history were the only records we had of Aguilar, leading scholars and activists to radically reimagine the contours of their life, though with very different goals in mind.

Performing Juana

Based on Esparragosa's newspaper articles, historian Martha Few published an article titled "'That Monster of Nature': Gender, Sexuality, and the Medicalization of a 'Hermaphrodite' in Late Colonial Guatemala" in *Ethnohistory*, which first thrust Juana Aguilar into the twenty-first-century public sphere and collective imaginary, provoking a sort of scholarly fascination with Juana Aguilar (and with the missing archival records about them). Few's incisive article—written from the perspective of a historian of science—traced how Esparragosa classified Juana Aguilar, partly through racializing discourses of monstrosity, debunking what he saw as ignorant ideas about hermaphrodites that circulated among midwives, surgeons, and the masses. Yet in her writing of that article, Few ran up against the problem of archival absence: she rightly posited that "it appears from this background information provided by Martínez Durán that he had access to the original court records and other documents, and that he may have even selectively quoted from them."[22] Yet despite several attempts to finds those trial records, Few was unsuccessful—as was I, years later, when I too waded through the thousands of index cards found in the AGCA *fichero* (index card catalog) to write my own monograph, *Sins against Nature: Sex and Archives in Colonial New Spain*.[23]

The late historian María Elena Martínez was also frustrated in her search for Aguilar's criminal trial records, though, as we saw in the previous chapter, she took a different methodological approach from Few and others to explore the role of the imagination in the theorizing and writing of queer history. What Martínez could say about Aguilar, back in 2014 when she wrote the chapter, was thus directly conditioned by this same archival absence: "Because the papers from the criminal trial are missing and other documents on the accused have not yet surfaced, it is impossible to know what impact his report had on the court's ruling, let alone what her fate afterward was."[24] Martínez has, as the previous chapter showed, infused Aguilar with new possibilities through conversations with performance artist Jesusa Rodríguez. Rodríguez subsequently performed parts of the Juana Aguilar piece—embodying doctor Esparragosa rather than Aguilar themself—at several conferences around the world: at the Fourth Iberoamerican Congress on Public Cultures in Argentina in September 2011; at the symposium "Race and Sex in the Eighteenth-Century Spanish Atlantic World," held at the University of Southern California (USC) in April 2013; and at the Hemispheric Institute of Performance and Politics annual Encuentro in Montreal, Canada, in June 2014 (where she performed alongside Liliana Felipe), among other venues.[25]

These performances too have come to be the focus of several scholars, often in a justifiably critical vein, adding yet another complex narrative layer to the story of Juana Aguilar.[26] The Montreal Encuentro performance, for instance, became highly charged when some conference attendees saw Rodríguez's use of a mannequin (Figure 2.2) to represent the "trans" body of Aguilar as highly problematic. Others became justifiably infuriated when—in an awkward twist not seen in her previous performances—Rodríguez interjected her personification of Esparragosa with a racialized performance of a Japanese Dr. Katsuhiko Hayashi. She did so in unabashed yellowface, which she rendered visually legible by squinting her eyes, feigning buckteeth, and speaking, according to several conferencegoers, in an overtly stereotypical accent. According to Lok C. D. Siu, some conference attendees and participants who had witnessed Rodríguez's performance there, titled *Juana La Larga*, "described a scene in which different people expressed disappointment, anger, and hurt around a cluster of issues, with the two most salient being the treatment of the transgender subject and the 'yellowface' performance of a Japanese doctor."[27] What Rodríguez possibly meant to be a form of "comic relief" used to "induce humor" directly clashed with the ways this aspect of the performance was deeply offensive to several international members of the audience. Although Diana Taylor notes that the very idea of yellowface may have simply been entirely unknown to Rodríguez, who "said that the facial expression was [the same] one she used to represent the late Mexican president Luis Díaz Ordáz, who was noted for his pronounced overbite," the reality is not so simple.[28]

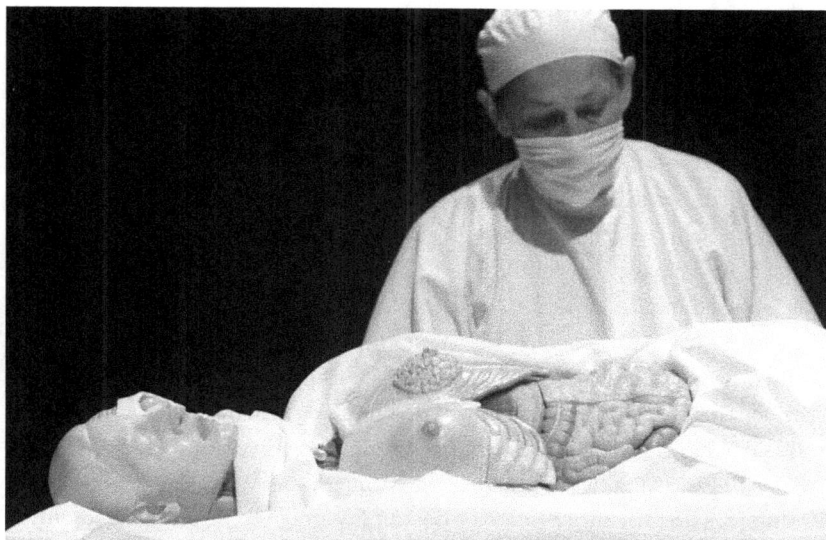

FIGURE 2.2. Jesusa Rodríguez playing Doctor Esparragosa and the medical mannequin representing Juana Aguilar, at the Hemispheric Institute's Encuentro in Montreal, 2014. Photograph courtesy of Marlène Ramírez-Cancio.

To address some of the many explosive issues that arose in the performance, organizers of the Hemispheric Institute in Montreal decided to hold a town hall meeting—a Long Table format that staged a "performance of a dinner party" informally titled "Representing Bodies and Experiences"—in which twelve rotating individuals at the table, including Jesusa Rodríguez, engaged (through translators) in conversation for some ninety minutes.[29] As Siu notes in her reading of the performance, at the subsequent town hall meeting "the majority of the discussion focused on the treatment of the transgender subject as a disembodied, voiceless object."[30] Performance artist Dan Fishback, one of the participants, noted that regarding the mannequin used to stand in for Aguilar, "the corpse of a gender non-conforming body (a woman who appears to have a penis), who was not given a voice/subjectivity, plus various jokes making fun of her anatomy, in the context of a world where trans women are regularly murdered and then mocked in public, added up to a show that felt dismissive of the very people it wished to champion."[31] Diana Taylor writes, "Through the performance, however, the artists make clear that Juana Aguilar has once again become an object of display—a pretext to tell another story about gender violence."[32]

We see how the performing of Aguilar (and of Esparragosa), as well as the audience's reactions to the performative reinterpretation of Esparragosa's writings, unintentionally participate in a certain degree of mythmaking, distortion, and misinformation, which creep into each and every representation of Aguilar and their life. Although it was the Royal Tribunal of the Protomedicato of Guatemala—an entirely secular court with no ties to inquisitorial or ecclesiastical tribunals—that tried Aguilar, several scholars have erroneously and repeatedly claimed that "the Spanish Inquisition" (which had no jurisdiction over New Spain!) was responsible for the policing and eradication of "queer" subjects in the past. Jesusa Rodríguez, for one, inaccurately notes that Aguilar was "accused of criminal excess and persecuted by the Inquisition" in colonial Guatemala (they were not).[33] Taylor too mistakenly writes that Aguilar "was accused by the Inquisition of committing 'abominable sins' with women" and that, for this very crime, inquisitors "tried to execute Juana la Larga."[34] Aguilar was said to have fled from "the merciless scrutinizing powers of the Inquisition."[35] Alice Ming Wai Jim, who attended the Montreal performance, observed that Rodríguez's performance depicted a doctor, Esparragosa, who "appeared during the staging of the surgical procedure ordered by the Inquisition to remove Aguilar's female sexual organs."[36] This suggestion—wherever it may have originated—that the "Inquisition" would have executed someone like Aguilar in late colonial Guatemala, or mandated any type of surgical procedure to remove their (or anyone else's) clitoris for being a "hermaphrodite" speaks more to inaccurate, ahistorical stereotypes of the Inquisition than anything else.

Such misguided assertions unintentionally set up the "Black Legend" of the Spanish Inquisition as part historical straw man (and, in this case, it was not even the Spanish Inquisition that had jurisdiction over colonial Guatemala, but rather the Holy Office of the Mexican Inquisition, established in 1571 in Mexico City). To clarify, neither the Mexican nor the Spanish Inquisition had anything to do with Aguilar's secular Guatemalan criminal trials. Such assertions, however, by scholars nonetheless indicate the extent to which popular histories and misperceptions of a supposedly monolithic institution known as "the Inquisition" have come to be wrapped up with scholars' desires to challenge the criminalization of illicit bodies, acts, and desires in both the past and the present. As Taylor writes, "queerness and trans have always been with us, although the same inquisitorial forces that tried to execute Juana la Larga have attacked and literally demonized it (as *cosas del diablo*) for over five hundred years."[37] It thus becomes impossible to separate out these popular perceptions of the Inquisition (and other forms of colonial justice, more broadly, as carried out on "sodomites," "hermaphrodites," and other "queer" subjects in the past), from the present-day writings and performances of Juana Aguilar. As Irene Silverblatt notes, "No act painted the Spanish Inquisition with greater infamy than torture. Yet like its peer institutions throughout Europe, the Inquisition believed torture was a means to the truth—albeit, in the Spanish case, a means that was used reluctantly. Contrary to the stereotype, torture was more supervised and less likely to be practiced in Spain than in other nations we associate with Western civilization."[38] To be clear, as the original trial transcripts show, at no point was Juana Aguilar either tortured (or threatened with torture) by criminal justices in colonial Guatemala, yet assertions to the contrary set up yet another level of narrative mythmaking around the historical subject of Aguilar themself.

Such mythmaking too has circulated, perhaps even more unexpectedly, in the realm of literature. In 2011, for instance, renowned Uruguayan novelist and writer Eduardo Galeano—author of the highly influential 1971 *Open Veins of Latin America*—published a collection called *Los hijos de los días* (translated as *Children of the Days: A Calendar of Human History*), which reunited 366 stories, each inspired by the calendar dates of individual years over time. He dedicates one of those days/stories to Aguilar. Citing no references to the scholarship on Aguilar, Galeano gave "4 February" the title of "The Threat." The story, in its entirety, reads:

> Her name was Juana Aguilar, but she was called Juana the Long, for the scandalous size of her clitoris.
>
> The Holy Inquisition received several denunciations of that "criminal excess," and in the year 1803 the Royal Audience of Guatemala sent a surgeon, Narciso Esparragosa, to examine the accused.
>
> This expert in anatomy warned that such a clitoris could be dangerous, as was well known in Egypt and other kingdoms of the Orient, and he found Juana guilty of "flouting the natural order."[39]

The cultural imaginary behind the repeated myth of Aguilar's chimerical prosecution by the Holy Inquisition is somewhat baffling but telling: for it subtly shows the ways that the vast assemblage of the disparate institutions known popularly today as "the Inquisition" (in Spain and its overseas colonies) are still associated with a backwardness and with the eradication of "queer" subjects in the past. That is to say, each and every "fact" recorded in the archives—or purported to be so—is highly susceptible to manipulation and misunderstanding. To be clear, I cite these examples not to critique the scholars who have unintentionally misunderstood this historical distinction, but rather to show how with each new telling of Aguilar's story, new distortions, myths, fears, stereotypes, and untruths unavoidably creep into the historical and archival narratives (and certainly my own writing at times is no exception here).

Now, what happens when performances of Aguilar go wrong, as I would say some did at the 2017 annual meeting of the Tepoztlán Institute for Transnational History in Tepoztlán, Mexico? That year, the conference theme was "Colonialisms: Legacies and Futures. A Conference in Honor of María Elena Martínez," who passed away in 2014 from a rare cancer, just shortly after the publication of her "Bodies, Archives, and Imagination" in *Radical History Review*. According to the conference organizers, the conference in her name offered participants "the opportunity to consider continuities and discontinuities from the colonial period until today, and possible decolonial/postcolonial futures, fantasies, and utopias."[40] As such, all of the theory groups—that is, multiple groups of scholars who read and debated shared sets of readings— deeply engaged with Martínez's *Radical History Review* article as assigned reading. Given the Tepoztlán Institute's unique structure and format, on the Saturday night in the middle of the week-long conference, each of the houses (made up of approximately fifteen to twenty graduate students, professors, and independent scholars) is invited to "perform" some aspect of the theoretical readings for that semester. Each year the performances tend to be satirical, irreverent, and good-spirited, but some nonetheless proved problematic in terms of misrepresenting and performing Aguilar.

It may come as no surprise that several of the groups, in their attempts to incorporate the scholarship of María Elena Martínez into their performances, turned to the trope of Aguilar—though instead of being represented by a mannequin, they were now represented, at times, by cis-gender men wearing makeup, dressed in drag, and, on one occasion, sporting blown-up balloons in a pair of shorts (seemingly signifying Aguilar's enlarged clitoris), and even giving birth, with water breaking at the end of one performance. Although there was no maliciousness on the part of those who acted out Juana Aguilar in the context of satire, certain aspects of these performance made me, and several others at the conference, uncomfortable. I could not help but wonder what María Elena Martínez's own reaction might have been, should she have been with us (especially given the extent to which she critiqued the types of voyeurism that framed the writings about Aguilar in the past). My frustration then with some friends and colleagues at this moment stemmed from the fact that Aguilar became, yet again, the butt of our jokes and the titillating target of our laughter. My point, however, is not that these performances were inherently problematic, but rather that each and every performance and iteration of Juana Aguilar constructs and produces new possibilities for reimagining, fictionalizing, and even satirizing the archived colonial past and its relation to the politics of the present. Some performances did this well, and others, in my opinion, far less so. And of course, lurking behind each and every decolonial historiograph-ical or performative gesture is the inherent and very real danger of recolonizing some other aspect of the past.

Archiving Aguilar

Gilliland and Caswell's notion of *impossible archival imaginaries* seems partic-ularly applicable to the ways that Juana Aguilar is suspended in a constant state of *turning archival*—being uncovered, exposed, lost, and found again in the ar-chives: "for as long as they [the much desired records] remain either inaccessi-ble or their contents or very existence remains purely speculative, the records as imagined or anticipated can inspire all sorts of narratives, suppositions, aspira-tions, longings, fears and distrust."[41] What, however, happens when the long fetishized missing archival documents are suddenly uncovered, making their way unexpectedly into the public sphere? In this final section, I briefly examine these recently surfaced archival records and trial transcripts of Juana Aguilar, alongside the specific language of archival description deployed in the cata-logs and finding aids of the AGCA.[42] How does this recent archival discovery invite us to rethink all that had previously been thought and written about Aguilar? Do they rectify some fantasies and falsehoods, serve to amplify them, or do both? Despite Juana Aguilar having finally turned up in the archives, I argue that any narratives we spin about them are inevitably just as imaginary as those written and performed prior to the transcripts having resurfaced. If these documents do bring us any closer to Aguilar, I argue that they do so par-adoxically through negation—that is, through Juana's own embodied evasions of and resistance to the medical and colonial bureaucratic incursions into their body, life, experiences, and desires. Aguilar, as we will see, repeatedly frustrated the attempts of colonial authorities to locate them and imprison them, and in doing so ruptured the impulses of the archive.

When Sellers-García fortuitously came across the card reference to Agui-lar's criminal trial several years ago, it was not because she was looking for Juana Aguilar, but rather was "scanning through the thousands of cards and pulling out what looked interesting. Juana's case seemed worth photographing because of how it was described . . . Then I became interested in the case because it fea-tured Narciso Esparragosa, who was also a central figure in the principal case I had begun working on."[43] Sellers-García generously alerted Martha Few, who kindly shared this information with me, and so goes one chain of the archival rediscovery of Juana Aguilar. Here, I reflect on how and why I—just like Mar-tha Few, María Elena Martínez, and others before us—may have all failed to find Juana Aguilar in the AGCA's card catalogs and physical finding aid (Figure 2.3). The AGCA has a card catalog finding aid system known as the Fichero Pardo, made up of 562,603 individual *fichas* (index cards). The documentation from the colonial period, identified with the classification *Signatura A*, makes up a significant portion of this. The research process itself, as one might imagine, is daunting.

The Fichero Pardo itself is the result of the "Herculean labour that went into its organization by the late José Joaquín Pardo, the man responsible for classifying much of the documentation extant for the colonial period."[44] Pardo himself, who had no formal archival training but showed incomparable dedication, did most of this organization and classifying between 1935 and 1964, when he was director of the then Archivo General del Gobierno de Guatemala, which had been established in 1846 as a repository of documents with little to no previous system of organization.[45] Prior to 1848, the archives were known as the Archivo de la Capitanía General y Escribanía de Cámara,

FIGURE 2.3 Several of the Fichero Pardo card catalog cabinets and drawers at the AGCA, organized chronologically, patronymically, and geographically. Photograph taken by the author in 2019.

which during the colonial period (1519–1821) safeguarded all of the documentation pertaining to the *audiencia* of Guatemala. This was, in essence, all of the documentation produced during the colonial period by the Capitanía General del Reyno de Guatemala (the General Captaincy of the Kingdom of Guatemala), which then fell under the jurisdiction of the Viceroyalty of New Spain. Finally, in 1968 the archives were placed under the control of the Ministry of Education and renamed the Archivo General de Centro América, which is the name it bears to this day.[46]

It was within this particular archival context that I, like so many others, had failed to see any reference to Juana Aguilar or to their presumed crime of "concubinage," though I spent several days individually reading each of the thousands of card catalog entries that pertained to colonial criminal records. On the one hand, in retrospect, I am certain that my eyes simply glazed over the word *concubinato* (concubinage) since that was not a topic that had previously interested me as I searched for the terms *sodomía* (sodomy), *bestialidad* (bestiality), and *pecado nefando* (nefarious sin) for my own book on the "sins against nature" in New Spain. But this brings me to the more profound reason that I think I failed to see this reference to Aguilar in the card catalog. In my own encounters with thousands of individual index cards, there was something specific in the Pardo Fichero's archival description of Aguilar that rendered them (and the reasons they entered the archive) even more illegible (Figure 2.4).

As one peruses the index card description in the figure, it reads: "*era emafotdita y usaba traje de mujer*," which translates (in an ungendered way given the lack of gendered pronouns) to "s/he was a hermaphrodite and used women's clothing." However, upon encountering this key term, I didn't recognize the Spanish word *emafotdita* (with its multiple misspellings and a crossed-out letter "t") as the modern-day Spanish word *hermafrodita* ("hermaphrodite"). Once again, there are multiple layers of abstraction and distortion that go into each and every attempt to describe Aguilar, their body, and their desires. Is it possible that this was a minor typographical error on the part of Pardo, or whomever took on the task of describing this particular case in the card catalogs? Or might this misspelling and crossed-out letter signal a certain conceptual unfamiliarity with, or confusion around, the term "hermaphrodite"—a confusion that resonates from the past to the present? The misreading (or simple typo/mistranscription) of the word *[h]ermafrodita* from the cover page of the 1801 trial records (Figure 2.5), to the *emafotdita* on the card catalog description, is illustrative of the ways that Aguilar herself is partly distorted with each and every act of representation. As we have seen throughout, the work of fabrication and distortion is enacted both symbolically and descriptively, pushing Aguilar

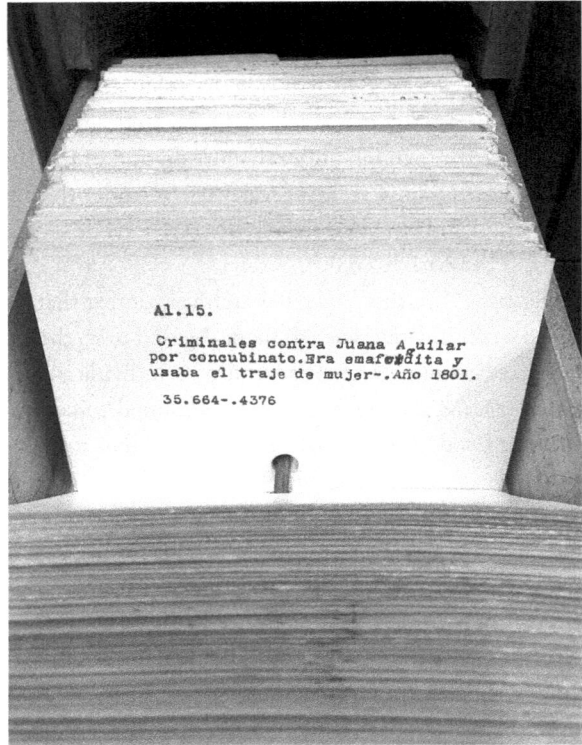

A1.15.

Criminales contra Juana Aguilar
por concubinato. Era emafedita y
usaba el traje de mujer-. Año 1801.

35.664-.4376

to simultaneously—and repeatedly—enter into and disappear from the colonial archives.

This brings us, finally, to the contents of the recently surfaced trial records, and to that which we learn from them. Although the 1801 criminal trial itself is relatively lengthy—the file is composed of forty-four folios, which is eighty-seven pages of actual text between the recto and verso sides—my goal here is not to delve fully into the case. Rather, I want to speak briefly about what new information the case offers its readers (in addition to those details of Mejía's accusation shared earlier) that expands our knowledge of Aguilar's lived experiences. Aguilar, so far as we know, first entered the colonial archives through the denunciation made by the indigenous governor of the town of Cojutepeque, Marcos Perdomo, in 1792, for sexual relations with two women, Mejía and Petrona Pérez. This initial denunciation, when Aguilar was still living in El Salvador, set in motion a chain of documenting, archiving, and fictionalizing Aguilar and their life. Aguilar was first placed in custody in 1792,

FIGURE 2.5. Title page of Juana Aguilar's criminal trial, 1801. AGCA, Sig. A1, Leg. 4376, Exp. 35,664, "Criminales contra Juana Aguilar, alias Larga, por concubinatos no obstante de ser ermafrodita y de bestir traje de muger," 1801. Courtesy of the Archivo General de Centro América, Guatemala City, Guatemala.

with all of their personal goods—including a mattress, clothing, culinary items, tobacco and cigars, tobacco containers, glass bottles, yarn, a mirror, soap, and sheets—embargoed by the criminal court. Aguilar was placed *en depósito*, that is, in the custody of the local *cabildo* or town council as they awaited trial.

What comes up next brings us to the crux of how Aguilar navigated their everyday yet extraordinary world. It turns out that 1792 was not the first denunciation against Aguilar, though it is the first recorded denunciation that has thus far been uncovered. In the report about their suspect's past, colonial authorities mention that Aguilar was also briefly imprisoned in 1790 (though no supporting documentation is included), supposedly for having been accused of amorous relations with two women, and also for having been accused of being a man who dressed in women's clothing. Citing a lack of evidence, the court determined that Aguilar be set free that same year. Aguilar then related how subsequently, in the Salvadoran town of Sensuntepeque, a local deputy named

Manuel Jiménez also subjected them to physical examinations by *peritos*, or medical experts, "for appearing to him more man than woman according to the height of my body, for which defect I am not guilty."[47] Aguilar too asserted that the medical examiners "found nothing other than some minor defect [*leve defecto*] of nature." Aguilar denied any wrongdoing with either María Mejía or Pérez, saying that Pérez was a roommate, but nothing more. Here, at heart we find competing truth claims to the nature of physiology of Aguilar's body: they stated there was merely a "minor defect" of their genitalia while Esparragosa rendered Aguilar a false man, false woman, and false hermaphrodite. The court asked if Aguilar knew why they had been imprisoned, and Aguilar replied they had been mistaken for a man, for wandering around in women's clothing, and for engaging in sexual relations with two indigenous women, according to the charges against them.[48] Aguilar, however, denied all of these charges, referring to the crime of which they had been accused as "an ugly and enormous crime" that they would never commit.

That which most emphatically resists the falsifying historiographical narratives of Aguilar, however, is their own repeated negations of colonial authorities (and consequently, their unyielding resistance to being examined and documented, inscribed onto paper and into the archives, and even narrated or coerced into the histories we write). Time and time again, for instance, Aguilar actively evaded colonial authorities and in doing so resisted at least several of their many encroachments on their body and life. On December 27, 1792, one of the local sheriffs of the town of Cojutepeque lodged a complaint with the criminal court: "That Juana Aguilar, imprisoned for this [criminal] case, had escaped from the prison in which she was being held, for which reason it should be demanded from the local *alcaldes* [officials with judicial functions] and other subaltern justices of this region."[49] He also reported that although he mandated that Aguilar be put in chains in the jail cell, when they asked to be briefly let out "because she wanted to defecate or do the necessities [i.e., urinate], they removed her chains, and from the common area [of the prison] she fled running."[50] As Sara Ahmed writes, "One becomes a subject through 'turning around' when hailed by the police . . . Turning might not only constitute subjects in the sense that the 'turning' allows subjects to misrecognize themselves in the policeman's address, but it might also take subjects in different directions. Depending on which way one turns, different worlds might even come into view."[51] Aguilar's repeated turning away from their captors radically altered the many ways that Aguilar does turn archival, as well as the ways that they constructed their everyday life, made different worlds come into view, and turned into a historical subject in the very first place. By my use of *turning archival* here, I refer not only to the many ways that Aguilar ultimately came to be documented and recorded (entering newspapers, histories, literature, conferences, performances, and roundtable discussions), but also to the many interminably possible ways that they could have otherwise been archived (and punished) had they *not* successfully evaded their captors for so many years, creating new worlds of possibility in the process.

Aguilar, it seems, evaded colonial authorities *for nearly a decade*(!), until they were recognized in 1801, then living in the town of Santa Ana, Guatemala. There Aguilar was outed by someone from Cojutepeque who denounced them in April 1801 for being an *hombre disfrasado*—"a man in disguise"—who had had "carnal relations" with several women some years earlier. In an almost picaresque twist, on August 14, 1801, Aguilar *once again*(!) successfully fled their captors, though this time from a private home instead of a local prison. This time Aguilar succeeded in evading authorities for nearly a year until, on July 13, 1802, they were captured once more in Guatemala City and immediately sent to the prisons of the Real Sala del Crimen—the highest ranking criminal judicial institution in Guatemala—with all of their goods embargoed. By 1802, it is clear that Aguilar had climbed the social ladder considerably: their embargoed goods now included hundreds of items including 70 gold-plated crosses, rings, 120 rosaries, 68 pieces of white metal, and many other items. Aguilar's upward social mobility through successful business dealings as a merchant over the course of a decade is certainly a far cry from the sad image painted by Martínez Durán in his assertion that "Grave misfortune would be her life, tragic and desperate until death."

It was ultimately at this point—Aguilar now likely in their forties—that doctors Esparragosa and Guerra were called upon by the Royal Tribunal to assess Aguilar's body. Those reports penned by Esparragosa are the very ones that he eventually published in the *Gazeta de Guatemala*, and that became the basis for almost all previous scholarship on Aguilar (with the exception of Martínez Durán who, in the late 1930s and early 1940s, had access to Aguilar's original trial transcripts). Though there is still so much more to be said about the invaluable transcripts of the criminal trial, this is the topic of my ongoing research. I turn here to one final unexpected archival turn: Aguilar's ultimate fate (and to the reasons that they will always continue to resist our fictionalizing impulses). While several scholars and performance artists have rightly criticized doctor Esparragosa for his elite, racist, and misogynist tendencies, perhaps paradoxically it was his own testimony—along with that of the other male medic, Guerra—that played a crucial role in exonerating Aguilar from the crimes of which they were accused. This is absolutely key, especially given that Aguilar's fate was not previously known by historians, nor was the role that Esparragosa's (or Guerra's) reports had in determining it.

In 1803 both doctors submitted their assessments of Juana Aguilar, asserting that they were not a "true" hermaphrodite, but rather someone to whom nature had denied either the male or female sex, and that therefore they could *not* legally be found guilty of the crime of sodomy. Shortly thereafter, on February 19, 1803, the *fiscal*, or prosecutor of the tribunal, concluded "that Juana Aguilar, alias Larga, is worthier of compassion than deserving of punishment, although it has been believed that she is [both] woman and man, at the same time, and this notion has been widely spoken; in reality, she is neither one nor the other, as shown by Doctors Don J[ose]ph Maria Guerra and Don Narsiso [*sic*] Esparragosa in their respective reports: an individual of the rational species, to whom nature, as one of its rarities, has denied the two sexes [*xesos*]; it is undeniable that she be unhappy for the [remaining] days of her life given that she can count herself among neither men nor women."[52] Here, we gain some insight into why Martínez Durán, in his *Las ciencias médicas en Guatemala*, echoes the court's assessment that the rest of Aguilar's life must have been plagued by unhappiness and desperation. And while it seems safe to assume that—especially given Aguilar's resilience, ingenuity, and resistance over so many years—nothing could have been further from the truth, I too must admit that my own desires that Aguilar, after being exonerated, lived out a gloriously fulfilling life until death, are also part of the collective fantasizing about Aguilar as a surviving queer, trans subject in the past. To imagine Aguilar as such perhaps speaks more to the nature of my own desires than to the historical realities and prejudices of the past. We will, fortunately or unfortunately, never know. Perhaps the ultimate irony of the colonial archive here is that Esparragosa—so intent on probing Aguilar's body, circulating graphic, racist, and misogynist reports—is what ultimately exonerated them.

To conclude, I want to return briefly to Jesusa Rodríguez's decision to represent Aguilar with a medical mannequin, for which she was amply criticized at the 2014 Hemispheric Institute Encuentro in Montreal for having somehow silenced (and objectified) a trans subject, an intersex person, and a gender nonconforming person in the past and the present. For me, far from disrespecting Juana Aguilar, this conscientious gesture points to the epistemological and interpretive gaps that separate us from them, satirically and mordantly showing how despite our (best?) attempts to learn more about Aguilar, to hear about their desires and affects, Aguilar will partly evade us and the interpretive regimes we might otherwise place upon them. This too is one of Juana Aguilar's potentially decolonizing gestures and negations of us (and of our own political goals in the present). Aguilar's own negations—of colonial authorities, of classificatory regimes, of the fictionalizing impulses of archive, historiography, literature, and performance alike, of efforts to probe and document their body, and ultimately of the stories we might want to tell about them—coalesce with the extant archival documentation and archival descriptions about them, which is ultimately what structures our knowledge about Aguilar, their life, desires, and experiences.

These negations must be taken absolutely seriously (and analytically). That Juana Aguilar has turned up in the archives—and turned archival in ways previously unimaginable—and that scholars have now rediscovered the long-missing criminal trial transcripts do not offer any pretense of unmediated access to Aguilar as historical subject (and to be fair, the archival records were always in Guatemala City's Archivo General de Centro América, sitting right under researchers' noses all along). Rather, they highlight even more gaps in what we could ever possibly know about them. At the very same time, these documents do offer us new, crucial information about Aguilar, ultimately pointing to how they simply wanted to be left alone, allowed to live their life as they pleased. It is my utmost hope (and likely that of the readers of María Elena Martínez's and my chapters) that this is indeed what happened.

Aguilar lived their life in ways that resonate with, but also deviate from, so many of the narratives about them—archival, historiographical, performative, literary, and political. Far from coming off as someone who was "unhappy" (as Esparragosa, colonial authorities, and later historians like Martínez Durán presumed) because of their intersexed body and ambiguous genitalia, Aguilar was a bold and defiant individual who actively resisted the grip of colonial authorities and medical incursions as long and as persistently as they could. If even some of the allegations about Aguilar were true, we gain a brief archival glimpse of an individual who, over the course of several decades, had a number of short- and long-term female lovers, and who succeeded in becoming a successful merchant and shopkeeper, a practice to which they very likely returned after being exonerated. After being set free by the criminal courts in 1803, Juana Aguilar seems to drop out of the archives so far as we know.

The impossible and de/colonial archival imaginaries that have risen up around Aguilar did so, in part, *because* of the very allure of the missing documents about them. An alluring archival absence inspired queer historical methods, performance, and literary license. And the finding of the original trial transcripts negates none of that, but rather adds to it. The previously known archival fragments about Aguilar—and even the recently surfaced trial transcripts—invite new ways of reimagining Aguilar, and what their story might teach us in the present, at times filling in the gaps with hopes and desires for what we (or others) wanted (or feared) Aguilar to be. These pieces do not fit comfortably into a whole—that is to say, the accumulation and joining together of all these disparate fragments of (misrepresentations of) Juana Aguilar will never be able to fully represent Aguilar's life and lived desires. These overlapping archival imaginaries about Juana Aguilar simultaneously coalesce and fracture, offering an always refracted, kaleidoscopic view of one archived subject whose own desires we may never separate from our own.

To return to Emma Pérez's evocative metaphor in *The Decolonial Imaginary*, Juana Aguilar moves almost seamlessly between past, present, and future—simultaneously inhabiting both coloniality and decolonial promise—"like a dark shadow in the dark" whose outlines we can still barely begin to trace. Being repeatedly lost and found in the archives—constantly turning and unturning archival, being written about, performed, and archived across time—has temporally fractured Juana Aguilar as a historical subject, rendering them a colonized subject (who actively resisted colonial authorities and also participated in colonial processes) who holds so much decolonial allure for us in the present. Gilliland and Caswell have shown that "*impossible archival imaginaries* and the affect associated with the *imagined records* produced within those imaginaries, offer important affective counterbalances and sometimes resistance to dominant legal, bureaucratic, historical and forensic notions of evidence that so often fall short in explaining the capacity of records and archives to motivate, inspire, anger and traumatize."[53] The contents of the long-lost records about Juana Aguilar may no longer need to be imagined or fantasized, but our own decolonial archival imaginaries about them may have only just begun, both facilitated and frustrated by what the archives do and do not give up, as Aguilar turns archival again and again.

Notes

1 LaFleur, Raskolnikov, and Klosowska, "Introduction," 3.
2 Few, "Monster of Nature," 172.
3 Archivo General de Centro América, Guatemala [AGCA], sig. A1, leg. 4376, exp. 35,664, f. 1. In the original, the word *femenino* is underlined.
4 AGCA, sig. A1, leg. 4376, exp. 35,664, f. 11.
5 Burns, *Into the Archive*, 34.
6 Anderson, *Imagined Communities*.
7 Pérez, *The Decolonial Imaginary*, 6.
8 Gilliland and Caswell, "Records and Their Imaginaries," 55.
9 Gilliland and Caswell, "Records and Their Imaginaries," 56.

10 Fuentes, *Dispossessed Lives*, 7. For more on how medical examinations in colonial Latin America might have been experienced as invasive forms of violence by the victims of sexual violence, see Tortorici, "Sexual Violence."

11 Few, "Monster of Nature," 161.

12 Archivo General de la Nación, Mexico [AGN], Indiferente Virreinal 5216, exp. 12, f. 2.

13 AGCA, sig. A1, leg. 4376, exp. 35,664, f. 37v.

14 AGN, Indiferente Virreinal 5216, exp. 12, f. 8.

15 AGN, Inquisición, caja 5216, exp. 12: "contiene en ellos un informe relativo a una d[ic]ha Juana Larga, a q[uie]ⁿ se tenia p[o]ʳ algunos del vulgo pʳ Hermafrotida . . . p[o]ʳ parecerme obzeno, y provocativo, materia mui agena de andar en Gazeta en manos de todos, y q[u]ᵉ no puede lerse en grave ruina de las almas."

16 Few, "Monster of Nature"; Martínez, "Archives, Bodies, and Imagination"; and Giraldo, "Sexualidades intermedias."

17 Martínez Durán, *Las ciencias médicas*, 267–77.

18 Martínez Durán, *Las ciencias médicas*, 268.

19 Martínez Durán, *Las ciencias médicas*, 268.

20 AGCA, sig. A1, leg. 4376, exp. 35,664, f. 3v

21 AGCA, sig. A1, leg. 4376, exp. 35,664, f. 3r–3v.

22 Few, "Monster of Nature," 173.

23 Tortorici, *Sins against Nature*.

24 Martínez, "Bodies, Archives, and Imagination," 160.

25 Jesusa Rodríguez and Liliane Felipe's June 23, 2014, performance at Concordia University in Montreal, Canada, can be viewed in its entirety here: http://archive .hemisphericinstitute.org/hemi/es/enc14-performances-esp/item/2330-enc14 -performances-rodriguez-felipe-juana.

26 Siu, "Hemispheric Raciality"; Taylor, "We Have Always Been Queer"; and Jim, "Fashioning Race."

27 Siu, "Hemispheric Raciality," 163.

28 Taylor, "We Have Always Been Queer," 213.

29 The entire Long Table discussion, held on June 24, 2014, can be viewed at Hemispheric Institute, "Representing Bodies and Experiences," https://cdnapisec.kaltura.com/html5 /html5lib/v2.8/mwEmbedFrame.php/p/1674401/uiconf_id/23435151/entry_id/1 _ioy712rn?wid=_1674401&iframeembed=true&playerId=kaltura_player&entry_id=1 _ioy712rn&wid=1_esxj53lj&flashvars%5bmediaProtocol%5d=rtmp&flashvars%5bstrea merType%5d=rtmp&flashvars%5bstreamerUrl%5d=rtmp://www.kaltura.com:1935&fla shvars%5brtmpFlavors%5d=1&amp.

30 Siu, "Hemispheric Raciality," 169.

31 Cited in Assaf, "Intervention 2."

32 Diana Taylor, *¡Presente!*, 162.

33 Rodríguez, "Juana la Larga," 359.

34 Taylor, "We Have Always Been Queer," 205 and 210.

35 Taylor, *¡Presente!*, 160.

36 Jim, "Fashioning Race," 89.

37 Taylor, *¡Presente!*, 160.

38 Silverblatt, *Modern Inquisitions*, 70.

39 Galeano, *Children of the Days*, 40.

40 Tepoztlan Institute, Colonialisms Conference Call for Participants, 2017, https://www
    .tepoztlaninstitute.org/2017-conference.html.

41 Gilliland and Caswell, "Records and their Imaginaries," 54–55.

42 This is the topic of my current book project, and for this reason I merely analyze some
    aspects of the trial transcripts here, rather than offer a full exegesis.

43 Personal communication with author on April 28, 2017. For the murder and dismem-
    berment case involving doctor Esparragosa, see Sellers-García, *The Woman on the
    Windowsill*.

44 Lovell, *Conquest and Survival*, 271.

45 Franks and Bernier, *The International Directory of National Archives*, 148.

46 Fry, *Historical Dictionary of Guatemala*, 49.

47 AGCA, sig. A1, leg. 4376, exp. 35,664, f. 11.

48 AGCA, sig. A1, leg. 4376, exp. 35,664, f. 11.

49 AGCA, sig. A1, leg. 4376, exp. 35,664, f. 21.

50 AGCA, sig. A1, leg. 4376, exp. 35,664, f. 22.

51 Ahmed, *Queer Phenomenology*, 15.

52 AGCA, sig. A1, leg. 4376, exp. 35,664, f. 41.

53 Gilliland and Caswell, "Records and Their Imaginaries," 55–56.

Works Cited

Ahmed, Sara. *Queer Phenomenology: Orientations, Objects, Others*. Durham, NC: Duke
    University Press, 2006.

Anderson, Benedict. *Imagined Communities: Reflections on the Origins and Spread of Na-
    tionalism*. London: Verso, 1983.

Assaf, Andrea. "Intervention 2: The Ethics of Humor, and Staying in the Conversation."
    Alternate Roots. August 24, 2014. http://alternateroots.org/alternate-roots-encuentro
    -with-the-hemispheric-institute-values-practices-interventions/.

Burns, Kathryn. *Into the Archive: Writing and Power in Colonial Peru*. Durham, NC: Duke
    University Press, 2010.

Few, Martha. "'That Monster of Nature': Gender, Sexuality, and the Medicalization of a
    'Hermaphrodite' in Late Colonial Guatemala." *Ethnohistory* 54, no. 1 (2017): 159–76.

Franks, Patricia C., and Anthony Bernier, eds. *The International Directory of National
    Archives*. Lanham, MD: Rowman & Littlefield, 2018.

Fry, Michael F. *Historical Dictionary of Guatemala*. Lanham, MD: Rowman & Littlefield,
    2018.

Fuentes, Marisa J. *Dispossessed Lives: Enslaved Women, Violence, and the Archive*. Philadel-
    phia: University of Pennsylvania Press, 2016.

Galeano, Eduardo. *Children of the Days: A Calendar of Human History*. New York: Nation
    Books, 2013.

Gilliland, Anne J., and Michelle Caswell. "Records and Their Imaginaries: Imagining the
    Impossible, Making Possible the Imagined." *Archival Science* 16, no. 1 (2016): 53–75.

Giraldo, Daniel. "Sexualidades intermedias en la prensa colonial hispanoamericana: Tres estudios de caso." *Tinkuy: Boletín de investigación y debate* 14 (2010): 119–38.

Jim, Alice Ming Wai. "Fashioning Race, Gender, and Desire: Cheryl Sim's *Fitting Room* and Mary Sui Yee Wong's *Yellow Apparel.*" In *Desire Change: Contemporary Feminist Art in Canada*, edited by Heather Davis, 76–95. Montreal: McGill-Queen's University Press, 2017.

LaFleur, Greta, Masha Raskolnikov, and Anna Klosowska, "Introduction: The Benefits of Being Trans Historical." In *Trans Historical: Gender Plurality before the Modern*, edited by Greta LaFleur, Masha Raskolnikov, and Anna Klosowska, 1–23. Ithaca, NY: Cornell University Press, 2021.

Lovell, George. *Conquest and Survival in Colonial Guatemala: A Historical Geography of the Cuchumatán Highlands, 1500–1821.* Montreal: McGill-Queen's University Press, 2004.

Martínez, María Elena. "Archives, Bodies, and Imagination: The Case of Juana Aguilar and Queer Approaches to History, Sexuality, and Politics." *Radical History Review* 120 (Fall 2014): 159–82.

Martínez Durán, Carlos. *Las ciencias médicas en Guatemala. Origen y evolución.* Guatemala City: Editorial Universitaria, 1941.

Pérez, Emma. *The Decolonial Imaginary: Writing Chicanas into History.* Bloomington: Indiana University Press, 1999.

Rodríguez, Jesusa. "Juana la Larga." *Debate Feminista* 50 (October 2014): 351–66.

Sellers-García, Sylvia. *The Woman on the Windowsill: A Tale of Mystery in Several Parts.* New Haven, CT: Yale University Press, 2020.

Silverblatt, Irene. *Modern Inquisitions: Peru and the Colonial Origins of the Civilized World.* Durham, NC: Duke University Press, 2004.

Siu, Lok. "Hemispheric Raciality: Yellowface and the Challenge of Transnational Critique." *Asian Diasporic Visual Cultures and the Americas* 2, nos. 1–2 (2016): 163–79.

Taylor, Diana. "We Have Always Been Queer." *GLQ* 22, no. 2 (2016): 205–14.

Taylor, Diana. *¡Presente!: The Politics of Presence.* Durham, NC: Duke University Press, 2020.

Tortorici, Zeb. "Sexual Violence, Predatory Masculinity, and Medical Testimony in New Spain." *Osiris* 30, no. 1 (2015): 272–94.

Tortorici, Zeb. *Sins against Nature: Sex and Archives in Colonial New Spain.* Durham, NC: Duke University Press, 2018.

3. TELLING TALES
Sexuality, Archives, South Asia

ANJALI ARONDEKAR

For the past few years, much ink (toxic and otherwise) has been expended on how to read historical archives. From a diatribe against the hermeneutics of suspicion or reading against the grain (where all readings are necessarily symptomatic readings of something that is missing or erased) becoming the new hegemony, to a rallying call for surface readings and readings along the archival grain (where the surface of the texts bears witness to the violence of the moment), there is a shared sense that how and why we make meanings out of the past must constantly be debated.[1] That the most trenchant challenges to our consumptions of times past have overwhelmingly come from scholars working on histories of slavery, sexuality, and colonialism who are attentive to archival economies of loss, paucity, and devaluation, is hardly surprising. Scholars such as Jennifer Morgan, Indrani Chatterjee, and Beth Povinelli, to name a select few, have foregrounded the fervent born-again historical materialism (if you will) that has plagued, indeed haunted, histories of slavery and colonialism, contrasting it with more robust informal and imaginative economies of survival that are often ignored or elided in such readings. They have variously problematized the triumphant demand for conventional economic histories (even if they are directed to liberatory ends) that preserve rather than trouble the vexed calculus of gender, labor, and capital.[2]

Even as I write this, archival economies of devaluation abound, as state-sponsored campaigns to purify India of cultural pollution (*sanskritik pradushan*) have become the mainstay of a Hindutva-fueled polity. Within such state formulations, the pollution of the Indian populace derives from its historical amnesia, from its refusal and erasure of proper historical vernaculars, cast in the loss of Sanskrit as mother tongue, or in the aspiration of a *swachh bharat*, emptied of the corrupting forces of alternative sexualities. Now more than ever, the past founds the moral authority of the Indian nation-state where all forms of difference are coercively shunted aside to make way for a new India shining. When it comes to historical evidence any shoddy travesty of research appears to pass muster, as is evident in the recent appointment of Professor Y. Sudershan Rao as chairperson of the Indian Council for Historical Research (ICHR).[3] For Rao and his ilk, Indian historians need to abandon their Marxist and Western historiographical ways to make way for a Hindutva-infused empiricism that would eschew archival ambivalences and establish historical dates for the "factual" events of the Ramayana and Mahabharatha.[4] Such concerns, with the manipulation, erasure, and refusal of diverse pasts, are especially pressing for the lives of sexual minorities as the legal and economic right to be here and now is often authorized by the evidence of histories past. One has to only recall the past legal challenges around the repeal of the so-called anti-sodomy statute, Section 377, that remained embroiled in debates around the presence/absence of alternative sexualities in India's past.[5] As historians of sexuality, we are thus called upon to insist on a protean and diverse past that rejects an instrumentalist and triumphalist Hindutva worldview.[6]

To put it mildly, the reading of sexuality's past(s), has now clearly become a complicated affair, a balancing act between an embrace of sexuality's munificent incommensurability (divergent temporalities are fodder for theories of queer difference) and a capture of its genealogical sameness (the past surrenders lineages of our queer presents). The cornerstone of such writing is of course the idea of the archive—more specifically, the archival trace—as the preferred value form through which we accrue meaning. Even as it is almost commonplace, particularly for those of us who work within colonial archives, to argue that historical archives must be read more as registers of selection than empiricism, there is less debate around forms of archival consumption and dissemination, particularly as they unfold in minoritized historiographies.[7] I want to begin then with one such narrative form that continues to inaugurate most historiographical and ethnographic projects: the problem-event, the detail, the legal case, the anecdote—in other words, an archival trace that is often a tantalizing obstacle to clarity, which then comes alive through our reconstructive hermeneutics.[8] Most often than not, the turn to such an inaugural problem-event becomes an exemplifying narrative, pointing to something bigger, a critical encounter that opens up potentialities that we as scholars want to and most often figure out.

For scholars working at the interstices of multiple minoritized historiographies, such as myself, the problem-event often becomes a crucial way of resolving the crisis of marginality where the scarcity of historical evidence is refused by the hermeneutical performance of plenitude—where you recover the archival trace for the promise of historical precedence and futurity. In my previous work, I wrote about the pressing impasse that haunts our recuperation of the historical archive, about the hermeneutical demands placed on histories of sexuality, and about the double binds and possibilities that emerge from within such recuperative practices. In this chapter, I want to think more about the analytical forms through which recuperative historiographies gather their salutary force, especially as they service minoritized communities that lack adequate rights and representation. The challenge here is to marshal a queer historiography, as I have previously argued, that "paradoxically adds value to a sedimented historical form (minoritized archives must be resurrected, found, produced for future gains) precisely by staging interest in its modes of reproduction."[9]

In what follows, I want to talk more about what exemplifying readings of problem-events mean for the way in which we encounter archives, particularly as is the case here, archives of sexuality. Simply put, what makes something an archival event/situation, and not a merely gestural instance, illustration, or example, and, following Lauren Berlant, how to "query the adequacy of an object to bear the weight of an explanation worthy of attending to and taking a lesson from"?[10] By this I mean to say, why does the writing of a history of sexuality, as will be the case here, take a particular narrative form, and what creates obstacles to its lithesome storytelling? What are the hermeneutic demands placed on its telling? The provocation of my title, "Telling Tales" is an invitation to move with the archival trace without presuming it as a mode of historical stabilization or recuperation. My efforts here are directed at resisting the impulse (by now well sedimented in sexuality studies) to overread archival evidence (particularly in the historical past) as obdurately and enticingly sparse. Indeed the seductions of such paucity accrue a certain value where you cede to historical difference precisely to lay aside the epistemic work such difference does. In other words, how might we relay something of the messy misalignments that the archival trace offers, without revisiting routinized habits of analysis, even as we attend to the generation of value/capital that is implicit in the form itself? After all, as Jacques Derrida reminds us, "every example must necessarily fail to do its job."[11]

More Imagined than Real

Let me begin then with one archival problem-event. A public meeting of the residents and ratepayers of Girgaum (in South Bombay) is hastily convened on July 16, 1911, with the express purpose of protesting "against the growing evil of women of bad repute coming to reside in increasing numbers in Girgaum." Four unanimous resolutions are passed (under the leadership of Sir Bhalchandra Krishna) and in turn forwarded to the Secretary of Government, Bombay. The resolutions argue (1) that it is "highly objectionable that women of ill-fame should at all be allowed to occupy houses even on main roads and thoroughfares, and generally in quarters inhabited by respectable families and they emphatically deprecate the recent increase of this evil in Girgaum," (2) that "effective steps should be taken to induce house-owners to refuse to let their houses or premises be used for immoral purposes," (3) that the "Commissioner of Police should use all the powers given to him by law to reduce this evil" and "fresh legislation" should be passed to further "empower him," and (4) last but not least, that a committee consisting of the gentlemen from the association, should be appointed to take any steps necessary to "carry out the object of the meeting."[12]

Responding with some testiness, the Secretary to the Government, C. A. Kincaid, writes a long and disciplining letter (dated November 13, 1911) to the ratepayers of Girgaum. In the letter, Kincaid applauds the "spirit" of the resolutions against the "evil of prostitution," but cautions against the inflammatory rhetoric used by the ratepayers, and argues that "he has reason to believe that the growth of the evil is more apparent than real." He further adds that in the "absence of definite statistics" there is no indication that the evil of prostitution has in fact increased in Girgaum—the more obvious explanation for the threat being that "ill-houses of fame" had been shut down in North Girgaum and forced the "women to scatter and invade the southern part of the ward." In case the ratepayers still think it is incumbent on the Commissioner of Police to take action, the Secretary further adds that the Commissioner cannot use the "power invested in him by the law" to take action against a large proportion of these immoral women who are more "kept mistresses/devadasis" than "common prostitutes." And further, even if the women are redistributed and moved to other parts of the city, it would interfere with the goals of the City Improvement Trust that does not have a particular investment in providing "harlot's quarters." To do so would be to endorse such vice, and perhaps, the letter snidely questions, is that what the ratepayers want?

The letter ends with a final flourish, saying that "prostitution in Girgaum is a subject which usually comes in for publicity during the monsoon season when there is not much going on in Bombay and the Government are away in Poona." Castigating the ratepayers for their own involvement in the "apparent" evil of this vice, Kincaid adds that the houses in which the women reside are owned and supported by the very ratepayers advocating these resolutions. And moreover, in his own "experiences" of Bombay, "the very gentleman who presided over the meeting recommended to Government the other day for an honour an individual who counts among his nearest female relations three ladies who according to my Criminal Investigation Department must be classes among those who, in Census parlance, are following dishonourable professions." In a last note, he also reminds the ratepayers that the Government must act "with great caution," especially as the Commissioner of Police is still recovering from "being hauled into court by a woman upon whom he has served a notice" and being told that he had acted *ultra vires* and that the woman is not a "common prostitute." And in an effort to erase any doubts on this question, Kincaid writes that he himself has visited similar houses accused of being "disorderly brothels" in response to like complaints, only to find that one of the members who visits the house is "a member of a Parsi Purity Brigade or Vigilance Committee."

At the heart of the debate between the two sides is a rather peculiar crisis of representation embedded in an even more fascinating palimpsest of arguments. The hermeneutical demand on either side is to make visible or eradicate an object of sexuality that is for all considered "apparent"—a paradoxical term that traffics equally in the realm of the obvious and of the elusive (we know the evil ladies exist but the force of their threat may or may not be real). For someone like myself who is writing a book on these "evil ladies of Girgaum," this exchange inevitably becomes an archival trace laden with the challenges and possibilities of historical visibility. Surely, I must insist, fueled by a corrective historiographical impulse, that what is lost in the back and forth of this exchange are the material histories and contexts of the very object of knowledge that is being debated. The slipperiness of the arguments made on both sides (are they or are they not prostitutes, are they "kept mistresses" or *Devadasis*?) could become the perfect foil for the "real" history of sexuality that needs telling: that to reduce these women to the confines of this debate is to limit our analytical horizons; to forget that these so-called evil ladies became in the decade or so after this event founders of one of the most successful collectivities in Bombay, the Gomantak Maratha Samaj, earning them the moniker of a model minority.

Let me say more about what I mean. I am currently writing a historiography of a *Devadasi* diaspora, the Gomantak Maratha Samaj. *Devadasi* is a compound noun, coupling *deva* or god with *dasi* or female slave; a pan-Indian term (falsely) interchangeable with courtesan, dancing girl, prostitute, and sex worker. Often referred to as *kalavants* (literally carriers of *kala*/art), these women moved between Portuguese and British colonial India for over two hundred years, in search of artistic training and professional enhancement. The Gomantak Maratha Samaj (henceforth the Samaj) is an OBC (Other

Backward Castes) community and was established as a formal organization in 1927 and 1929 in the western states of Goa and Maharashtra, respectively. It officially became a charitable institution in 1936. The Samaj continues its activities to this day and has from its inception maintained a community of ten thousand to fifty thousand registered members. Of singular importance is that the history of the Samaj never disappeared or was erased, as is the case in more well-known historical accounts of *Devadasis*, particularly in South India. Instead, the Samaj, from its inception, has maintained a continuous, copious, and accessible archive of its own emergence, embracing rather than disavowing its past and present attachments to sexuality. The Samaj's archives (housed in Panaji and Bombay) constitute an efflorescence of information in Marathi, Konkani, and Portuguese, ranging from minutes of meetings, journals, newsletters, private correspondence, flyers, and programs all filled with details of the daily exigencies and crises that concerned the community. Often referred to as Bharatatil ek Aggressor Samaj (an aggressive community in India), this *Devadasi* diaspora is routinely lauded (by the left *and* the right in India) for its self-reform and progress. From the immortal Mangeshkar sisters (Lata and Asha), to the first chief minister of independent Goa, Dayanand Bandodkar, there are few sectors of Indian society where the presence of Samaj members cannot be felt.[13]

The Properties of Evil

Several historical accounts from the period allude to the "evil ladies" of Girgaum as being the progenitors of this successful and celebrated Samaj. Padma Anagol, for example, situates such community efforts to read the evil ladies as morally contagious within a larger respectability movement, orchestrated by largely middle-class (and mostly upper-caste) women. Within such narratives of reform and progress, the evil ladies become purveyors of a curiously fecund set of cultural threats. Here the evil of the ladies shifts from the corruptions of sex to the debasement of *kala*/art, a shift that needs to be rerouted (and stabilized) through a more heteronormative marriage economy. On the one hand, the evil ladies trouble cherished distinctions between *kalavants*/*naikins*/artists and prostitutes; after all, if they are primarily repositories of arts (*kala*), then their growing presence cannot be regulated within anti-prostitution regulation, and the resolution of the Girgaum ratepayers holds no ground. On the other hand, the rise of such evil ladies and their clientele demonstrates the need for a more robust cultivation of arts/*kala* within middle-class women themselves. In this vein, middle-class men become clients of evil ladies in search of artistic enrichment, not sex, a turn that rouses middle-class women to claiming the domain of the arts/*kala* for themselves. For Anagol, groups such as the Maharashtra Mahila Mandal (founded in 1902) embody the tensions of such concerns as they plot efforts to both train in the arts and organize against the presence of the evil ladies. Vernacular newspapers of the day, such as *Bodh Sudhakar* and *Subodh Patrika*, Anagol writes, equally register the scale of these efforts, carrying accounts of middle-class women trying to oust the evil ladies from their residences, even as others such as *Indu Prakash* and *Dnyan Prakash* run editorials extolling the bravery of the *naikins* in resisting eviction.[14]

Ethnographic and travel accounts of colonial Bombay similarly record the troublesome and vexing history of the evil ladies. Govind Narayan's *Mumbaiche Varnan* (1863) documents the author's migration to Bombay from Madgaon through a series of lush accounts of the city's shifting urban landscape. In a chapter describing the rise of arts and theater in Bombay (circa 1861), Narayan writes with great disgust about the rise of "dancing girls" who appear to have garnered clientele across the city, with their "numbers increasing daily." Of great concern to Narayan is the successful dancing girl's acquisition of properties and her vulgar display of wealth. As he writes, "she spent nearly four thousand rupees" on an initiation ceremony for her daughter to become a *Devadasi*, reminding him of the "stories of the matriarchates mentioned in the Puranas."[15] K. Raghunathji expresses a similar articulation of shock and awe in his documentation of the rise of Bombay dancing girls. Writing for the *Indian Antiquary* (1884), Raghunathji provides detailed descriptions of these dancing girls (who are both Hindu and Musalman) and their practices, noting that a large percentage of the Hindu girls appear to have migrated "from Goa and the places around it."[16] He notes that the "Hindu dancing girls are of four sects, viz: Naikins, Bhavins, Murlis and Kasbins. Of these the first two belong to Goa and villages round it, being natives of that district." Unlike Narayan, Raghunathji paints a more flattering picture of these women, extolling their beauty and their generally "intelligent pleasing appearance."[17] While they arrive in Bombay speaking "Goanese" (which we are mysteriously told differs from the "language of Bombay"), they quickly acclimatize and soon read, write, and even compose songs in Marathi. As in Narayan's account, Raghunathji too emphasizes the "large sums of money" that the women appear to have access to, describing in excruciating detail the gold ornaments the women routinely wear.[18] Even as such anthropological accounts are to be consumed with some trepidation (after all, we are rarely provided with any sources for the information that is provided!), references to the women's growing presence and appetite for wealth can also be found in other genres of archival records. Even more recent scholarly studies on the migration into and rehabilitation of "prostitutes in Bombay" (with a "reference to family background") applaud the positive efforts of the evil ladies of the Samaj, and contrast them sharply with other organizations like the Association of Tawaifs and Deredars that continue to use "singing girls" as "shield" to propagate more "unscrupulous" and unlawful activity. But the study notes (with some irony) that "the majority of their respondents" are migrants from Goa, whose mother tongue is Konkani, and therefore to be taken with a grain of salt.[19]

Of equal interest are also several legal appeals filed on behalf of these evil ladies petitioning the state for support in their claims for maintenance from the families of dead patrons or *yajemans*, residing in or around Girgaum. As in the accounts discussed earlier, the focus continues to be on the acquisition of ill-gotten wealth by the evil ladies and the threat it poses to the sanctioned circulation of capital within family formations. One series of appeals, in particular, stand out in their detailed listing of monies acquired and requisitioned from the family of an upstanding member of society (very much kin of the Girgaum ratepayers association I began with) after his untimely death in 1919. In *Bai Monghibai vs Bai Nagubai*, Bai Monghibai (widow of the deceased Vasanji Madhavji Thakar, who died on November 21, 1919) appeals a previous judgment of Mr. Justice Kanga that awarded monthly maintenance of Rs. 400 to Bai Nagubai Manglorkar as "the permanent concubine of the deceased."[20] According to the details of the previous judgment, the deceased "possessed of moveable and immoveable property of a very large value," had abandoned his family domicile in Vadgadi and had come to reside with Bai Nagubai, a Goan *naikin*, "in her house in Girgaum and that he continued to reside there until the day prior to his death." Bai Nagubai claimed monthly maintenance and "alleged that a sum of Rs. 25,000 was specially promised by the deceased" for the benefit of her and her daughter after his death. In the series of legal skirmishes that followed the original judgment of Justice Kanga, much effort is made to determine if Bai Nagubai was the "exclusive mistress" of the deceased, and if she maintained sexual chastity even after his death. Bai Monghibai, the deceased's widow, argues that the deceased merely visited Bai Nagubai in her Girgaum residence, and was permanently domiciled elsewhere. Acting Judge Lallubhai Shah, who reviewed the widow's appeal, concurs with her claim even as he is "willing to admit that Bai Nagubai used to live in a house near Kennedy Bridge at Girgaon where the deceased Vasanji used to visit her regularly . . . prior to his death and used to pay her some monthly allowance." The crux of the appeal relies on the status of Bai Nagubai's residence in Girgaon/Girgaum: Is it or is it not the primary residence of the deceased? For Shah, the true nature of the deceased's relationship with Bai Nagubai cannot be ascertained without "knowing the nature of his visits" to the Girgaum residence. True companionship, for Shah, can only be determined through open and continuous cohabitation with Bai Nagubai, something that the facts of the case do not appear to corroborate. Shah's judgment is appealed further by Bai Nagubai; she provides evidence that the deceased had rented the Girgaum residence "in her name . . . and that he was nursed there during his last illness and only removed shortly before his death."[21]

As the story of these evil ladies unfolds in multiple historical accounts of the period, it becomes apparent that the "real" archival substance of their evil unfolds in variegated scenes of capital. From their ostentatious displays of wealth, to their corruption of the family form as value, the evil ladies appear to play exemplary roles in what Mariam Dossal has called Bombay's "theatre of conflict."[22] At the time of the ratepayers' complaint against the evil ladies of Girgaum, the city of Bombay appears mired in various struggles around land expansion and reclamation, gentrification, and the increasing demands of native franchise. Preeti Chopra, for instance, argues that the expansion debates pivot around the "joint public realm" where native elites collaborate with the colonial state (with varying degrees of success) to create public institutions of finance.[23] One key stage of such financial ventures circles precisely around the acquisition and control of lucrative land such as the properties the evil ladies of Girgaum inhabit.[24] Prashant Kidambi reminds us that this is also the period when the Bombay Improvement Trust (BIT) emerges as the central force in shaping the city's physical landscape. BIT was an ambitious colonial enterprise that was largely a response to the sanitation risks of overcrowding that had come to the forefront in the devastating aftermath of the Bombay plague. One of its key projects was the construction of thoroughfares such as the Princess Street Scheme II and the Sandhurst Road Scheme III, which opened up a wide corridor in the otherwise crowded locality of Girgaum. Such efforts were however continuously mired in multiple property disputes around land acquisitions as native landlords and homeowners rushed to capitalize on the increasing value of their assets.[25]

Elided also in our focus on the evil ladies of Girgaum is their emergence in the context of a precarious and controversial period of property tax legislation in Bombay Presidency. The crux of the controversy revolved around the famous Girgaum Memorial Memorandum of 1870 that called for the abolition of occupier's and house taxes, and what more reformist newspapers at the time such as *Native Opinion* derisively called the "landlord's movement." The memorandum principally involved the tax levied on house property by the colonial state and asked for a reduction of the taxes from 7 percent to 4 percent.

The Bombay Municipal Act of 1872 further complicated matters by allowing the upper echelon of ratepayers (primarily landlords and businessmen) to be elected members of the Municipal Corporation. Leading up to 1911, the year in which the Girgaum residents and ratepayers association filed the public resolutions against the evil ladies of Girgaum, the tax rate legislation on property continued to be heavily disputed, with property values escalating (as mentioned previously) thanks to the redistribution of lands due to the institution of the City Improvement Trust. In such a context, the evil ladies' occupation of homes in the main thoroughfares of Girgaum needs to be more carefully examined.[26] According to the census of 1901, the number of prostitutes in Girgaum had significantly diminished in numbers (dropping from over 1,200 or so in the late 1890s to about 235 in 1901; figures cum grano, of course, given the unreliability of census reports at the time).[27] So the Secretary to the State is right in arguing that a statistical case cannot be made for the rise of evil ladies in Girgaum. Alternately, what the private archives of the Gomantak Maratha Samaj (which contain many property deeds and genealogies of inheritance and distribution) reveal is that the evil ladies of Girgaum occupied and then gradually took possession of the multiple residences they were inhabiting, thanks to their complex negotiation with their *yajemans*/patrons, of a payment system that bypassed cash payments for property deeds.

The association of the Girgaum residents and ratepayers lists as its members prominent Saraswat shetias, Mohammedan merchants, and a few converted Christians and Eurasians, a motley crew of caste and races that is reflected in the current geography of Girgaum.[28] In the back and forth between the members of the Girgaum association and the Secretary to the Government, no such skirmish over tax rates and property values is made visible.[29] Instead, the repeated and apparent invocation of "vice" and prostitution seamlessly covers over the economics and exigencies of the Samaj women's day-to-day survival. It is thus with some pleasure that I add here that the economic success of the Samaj is also largely built on their acquisition in the early 1900s of prime property all over Bombay Presidency, particularly in the areas of Girgaum, Gamdevi, and Chowpatty.[30]

Even as I write this, I continue to discover new archival evidence that can further unpack the telling tales of this problem-event. Generous colleagues working on histories of policing and surveillance in colonial Bombay reference (with great confidence, I would add) the presence of numerous classified files on these evil ladies of Girgaum that still lie outside of the realm of public consumption. As of now, such files remain sequestered within the bureaucratic walls of police archives, their content, like the material of this problem-event, offering the promise of multiple readings.[31] Such invocations of classified (and therefore potentially explosive evidence) further concatenate the value accrued around the problem-event. After all, any new historical reading, especially of sexuality's pasts, surely benefits from the continued promise of archival evidence. To hold such evidence in narrative abeyance makes possible further heroic reconstructions of the event, bypassing any narrative-stopping closure of an always-impending authentic history.

In light of such concerns, the scandal now shifts from an evaluation or disputation of the "evil" of the ladies of Girgaum to the apparent entanglements behind their invocation. Let me be clear: reading sexuality here as a cover story is not merely to make the familiar but necessary argument for sexuality's material contexts. It is more an attempt to think of these contexts themselves as being equally locked in the dialectic of the apparent and the real. Within such imaginaries, the matter of the evil ladies of Girgaum works not as an exemplary case that resolves historical ambivalence or loss through its successful recognition and emergence, but rather as a narrative that inserts epistemic discontinuity in how and why we write histories of sexuality.[32] Even as the story of the evil ladies morphing into the successful emergence of the Gomantak Maratha Samaj is a crucial and inspiring one, it is more than just another exercise in recuperative and redemptive historiography. Rather, it pushes us to consider the archival trace less as a marginalized, erased archival trace of sexuality and more as evidence of the hegemonic intercalation of property, caste, and sexuality. The exemplar of the evil ladies thus does not affirm or erase their liminality as archival objects; rather it simply presses against our desire for an archival hermeneutics that will recover to restore value to a lost form/collectivity. In this case, the collectivity, as I have noted, is never lost or erased, or missing an archive. As is clear by now, not only do these evil ladies exist in multiple archival forms, but they also maintain and sustain an archive of their own making. Instead, the evil ladies of Girgaum function (then and now) as a fetishistic screen whereby we return over and over again to the vice of sexuality as the familiar place of historical redress and reform. What would it mean to refuse such habits of occlusion, to uncouple sex from the safety of its "evil" form, and to summon its ordinary plenitude within public discussions of culture, capital, and historiography? What would it mean to read the evil ladies not as a seductive exemplar, nor as an exceptional case study that needs decoding (which is of course the preferred form)? After all, there remains the enduring allure of a virtuoso reading (within which I too am mired) that will somehow unravel the secrets of sexuality. Instead, as we have seen, the exemplar of the evil ladies speaks more to a history of sexuality that is unfinished and messy, upending sedimented mandates of restoration and representation. Bypassing the heroics of recuperative historiography, the exemplar here is less a record of lost lives and more a potential epistemology for how we know, relate, and intensify our relationship to the past. Let us try to imagine that history together.

Notes

1 See Best and Marcus, "Surface Reading"; Ricoeur, *Freud and Philosophy*; and Stewart, "The Hermeneutics of Suspicion."

2 See Chatterjee, "When 'Sexualities' Floated Free of Histories in South Asia"; Povinelli, *Economies of Abandonment*; and Morgan, "Accounting for the 'Most Excruciating Torment.'" Within South Asian studies, in particular, the early work of the Subaltern Studies Collective attended to the elitist compositional and distributive logics of archives in colonial and postcolonial India. Yet for the most part, the focus of the collective has still largely been recuperative and reparative, and only more recently supplemented by the work of feminist historians such as Indrani Chatterjee and the emphasis on more discrepant and gendered histories of labor, governmentality, and affect.

3 For a prescient reading of this appointment, see Thapar, "The Appointment of a Historian Whose Work Is Unfamiliar." The ruling Bharitiya Janata Party's litany of mistakes, backflips, controversies, and denials of India's diverse past is by now well known and too extensive to be rehearsed here in its entirety.

4 "Historians Raise Questions," *Firstpost*.

5 For an extended exegesis on the use of historical archives in the efforts to repeal Section 377, see Arondekar, "Time's Corpus" and Kapur, "Unruly Desires, Gay Governance, and the Makeover of Sexuality in Postcolonial India." For further reading, see Nagar and Dasgupta, "Public Koti and Private Love."

6 When I first conceived of this chapter it was 2017, and we lived in a pandemic-free world. Since then, much has changed for all of us, but the authoritarian manipulation of our pasts continues unabated in Narendra Modi's India. Now, Modi's propaganda machine routinely merges historical fiction with scientific facts, arguing for the primacy of a Hindu science amidst the unfolding health drama in the world. See "'Cow Urine Is Pure Elixir': To Fight Coronavirus, Hindu Mahasabha Hosts 'Gaumutra Party,'" *Outlook India*, March 15, 2020, https://www.outlookindia.com/website/story/india -news-cow-urine-is-pure-elixir-to-fight-coronavirus-hindu-mahasabha-holds-gaumutra -party/348809.

7 Stoler, *Along the Archival Grain*, 32–33.

8 Berlant, "On the Case." See also Damousi, Lang, and Sutton, *Case Studies and the Dissemination of Knowledge*.

9 Arondekar, "In the Absence of Reliable Ghosts."

10 Berlant, "On the Case," 666.

11 Derrida, *Of Grammatology*, 47.

12 All records of the event were found in an unmarked file at the Mumbai offices of the Gomantak Maratha Samaj. The file was buried in a box containing paperwork on the acquisition of the Samaj building in Girgaum. The available records contain typewrit-

ten letters from the Residents and Ratepayers of Girgaum (July 16, 1911) and a response from the Judicial Department (dated November 13, 1911). What is curious about the contents of the file is that the letters contain corrections that have been penciled in, with no indication of whether the letters were revised and resent. The official record can be located in the papers of the Judicial Department, Maharashtra State Archives, and is titled "Protest by the rate payers and residents of Girgaum, Bombay against the evil of women of bad repute, 1911," J. D. Volume 208/1911, 235. The bulk of the archives is now housed at the Gomantak Maratha Samaj Society building in Mumbai, India. In 2004, the Samaj offices were moved from Gomantak Maratha Samaj Sadan, 345 V.P. Road, Bombay 400004 to Sitladevi Co-op. Housing Society Ltd., 7-16/B Wing, D. N. Nagar, New Link Road, Andheri (W), Mumbai 400053. A partial archive can be found at the Gomantak Maratha Samaj, Dayanand Smriti, Swami Vivekanand Marg, Panaji 403001, Goa.

13 For more historical detail on the emergence of the Samaj and on the presence of *Deva-dasis* in Western India, see Arondekar, "Subject to Sex." Other texts that gloss briefly on the history of the Samaj include Bhobe, *Kalavant Gomantak*; Khedekar, *Gomantak Lok Kala*; and Satoshkar, *Gomantak Prakriti Ani Sanskriti*. The brief history of the Samaj I provide here is one that I narrate repeatedly and verbatim in all work that touches on the Samaj's exemplarity. Part of the challenge of writing about a collectivity that is known and not known all at once is that historical details become routinized only through their constant repetition.

14 Anagol, *The Emergence of Feminism in India*, 123–37.

15 Ranganathan, *Govind Narayan's Mumbai*, 261–62. The original Marathi text utilizes more lavish and efflorescent language.

16 Ranganathan, *Govind Narayan's Mumbai*, 166.

17 Ranganathan, *Govind Narayan's Mumbai*, 167.

18 Raghunathji, "Bombay Dancing Girls."

19 Punekar and Rao, *A Study of Prostitutes in Bombay*, 169, 160. For a broader understanding of late colonial debates on prostitution in Bombay, see Tambe, "Brothels as Families."

20 *Bai Monghibai vs Bai Nagubai*, August 11, 1922.

21 *Bai Monghibai vs Bai Nagubai* (1922) 24 Bombay Legal Reporter (BOMLR) 1009 and *Bai Nagubai vs Bai Monghibai* (1926) 28 BOMLR 1143. Other cases that deal with questions of maintenance and similar "evil ladies" include *Bai Appibai vs Khimji Cooverji* (1936) 38 BOMLR 77 and *Yashvantrav vs Kashibai* (1888) Indian Law Reports 12 Bom 26. Kunal Parker, writing on similar questions, proposes that colonial courts in India augmented *Devadasi* reform through innovative and often unprecedented translations of the law. Legal norms that previously applied to different castes represented within Brahmanical taxonomies were extended to include an innovative set of patriarchal norms with respect to the sexual behavior of Hindu women. For example, the *Devadasi* was cast less as a "temple dancing girl," and more as a "Hindu girl" engaging in sexual activities outside of marriage. Such a shift from the "tradition" of *Devadasis* to the aberration of their sexual practices allowed the courts to legislate against the *Devadasis* as prostitutes without engaging their more complex functions as repositories of art,

culture, and religion. According to Parker, these concerns substantially impacted the interpretation of the 1861 Indian Penal code with reference to the *Devadasis*. By focusing on the prostitution of minors dedicated to temples, Parker suggests that *Devadasi* reform groups rerouted provisions intended to protect minors, to nullify adoption by *Devadasis*, and to outlaw any and all dedications of girls to deities. Such a turn to the protection of minors became a crucial part of the judicial reform movement aimed at eliminating *Devadasis*. See Parker, "'A Corporation of Superior Prostitutes.'"

22 Dossal, *Theatre of Conflict, City of Hope*. See specifically chapter 7, "Urban Planning or Crisis Management? 1860–1930."

23 Chopra, *A Joint Enterprise*.

24 In a similar vein, Padma Anagol notes that "residents of various towns and cities often sent complaints to police authorities to remove kalavantins from what they considered respectable neighborhoods and to house them outside the city or town limits." Anagol cites the example of a complaint carried by Ahmadnagar residents against prostitutes. See *Nagar Samachar*, February 23, 1878, and *Dandio*, March 22, 1879, Native Newspaper Reports (NNR), 1878–79; NNR was a weekly report of Indian-language newspapers compiled by the British colonial state for distribution amongst its civil servants.

25 Kidambi, "Housing the Poor in a Colonial City." See also Kidambi, *The Making of an Indian Metropolis*, 70–76.

26 Rao, "Community, Urban Citizenship, and Housing in Bombay, ca 1919–1980." See also Rao, *House But No Garden*. I am grateful to Nikhil Rao for providing early feedback on property disputes in Bombay. For a broader historical view of the twists and turns of the ratepayer/landlord's movement, see also Dossal, "A Master Plan for the City" and Dossal, *Imperial Designs and Indian Realities*; Batley, "The Need for City Planning"; Haynes, *Small Town Capitalism in Western India*; and Wacha, *Rise and Growth of the Bombay Municipal Government*.

27 Ashwini Tambe, *Codes of Misconduct*, 60 and 168.

28 Pace, *Elites in South Asia*, 89.

29 S. M. Edwardes provides the following detailed description of the topography of Girgaum in *The Gazetteer of Bombay City and Island, Vol. 1., 1873–1927*, Bombay, Printed at the Times press, 1909–10:

> The Girgaum section is bounded on the North by Girgaum Back road, on the south by Thakurdwar road, on the east by Girgaum Back road and Bhuleshwar road, and on the west by Back Bay and Charni road. Like Chaupati and Phanasswadi its interior portion has arisen upon the side of ancient parts, such as Borbhat and Mugbat, with the old Girgaum village as its original nucleus. Its most noteworthy buildings are the Muhamadan sanitarium at the corner of Queen's road, the old Police Court on Girgaum back road, the Allbless Bagh on Charni Road and the Portuguese Church opposite the Trans terminus. The latter building which actually lies just outside the sectional limits was founded in 1773 and rebuilt in its present form in 1836. The neighbourhood of Charni road has of late years been taken up to some extent of the building of middle-class Parsi flats; but the bulk of the section still retains its old character as a Brahman settlement. (41–42)

30 A recently curated exhibition by Tejaswini Niranjana and Surabhi Sharma, "Making Music, Making Space," documents musical histories of Girgaum, giving their audiences a small glimpse of the rich and networked worlds of these *naikins* and *kalavantins*. In the exhibition, the audience is also provided with an annotated map of Girgaum that marks all the residences and buildings occupied by collectivities such as the "evil ladies." See India Foundation for the Arts, 2015, http://www.indiaifa.org/events/making -music-making-space-june-15-17-2015-studio-x-mumbai.html.

31 I am grateful to Shekhar Krishnan, a wonderful chronicler of the varied histories of Bombay, and his deep familiarity with police and municipal archives. Krishnan, for some time, has been attempting to help me gain access to these notorious classified files that he tells me have been seen but not catalogued. For a taste of Krishnan's wide-ranging knowledge of colonial Bombay, see his website at http://shekhar.cc/, accessed February 28, 2022.

32 Durba Mitra has brilliantly reminded us that the exemplarity of prostitutes/evil ladies and their kin is constitutive to the very making of colonial epistemologies and the structure of the archive itself. For more detailed analysis, see her second chapter on "Repetition: Law and the Sociology of Deviant Female Sexuality," in Mitra, *Indian Sex Life*.

Works Cited

Anagol, Padma. *The Emergence of Feminism in India, 1850–1920*. Burlington, VT: Ashgate, 2005.

Arondekar, Anjali. "Time's Corpus: On Temporality, Sexuality and the Indian Penal Code." In *Comparatively Queer: Crossing Times, Crossing Cultures*, edited by Jarrod Hayes and William Spurlin, 143–56. New York: Palgrave, 2010.

Arondekar, Anjali. "Subject to Sex: A Small History of the Gomantak Maratha Samaj." In *South Asian Feminisms*, edited by Ania Loomba and Ritty A. Lukose, 244–66. Durham, NC: Duke University Press, 2012.

Arondekar, Anjali. "In the Absence of Reliable Ghosts: Sexuality, Historiography, South Asia." *Differences: A Journal of Feminist Cultural Studies* 25, no. 3 (2015): 98–121.

Batley, Claude. "The Need for City Planning." *Journal of the Indian Institute of Architecture* 1, no. 1 (April 1934): 11–20.

Berlant, Lauren. "On the Case." *Critical Inquiry* 34, no. 2 (2007): 663–71.

Best, Stephen, and Sharon Marcus. "Surface Reading: An Introduction." *Representations* 108, no. 1 (Fall 2009): 1–21.

Bhobe, Gopalkrishna. *Kalavant Gomantak*. Goa: Kala Academy 1972.

Chatterjee, Indrani. "When 'Sexualities' Floated Free of Histories in South Asia." *Journal of Asian Studies* 71, no. 4 (2012): 945–62.

Chopra, Preeti. *A Joint Enterprise: Indian Elites and the Making of British Bombay*. Minneapolis: University of Minnesota Press, 2011.

Damousi, Joy, Birgit Lang, and Kattie Sutton. *Case Studies and the Dissemination of Knowledge*. New York: Routledge, 2015.

Derrida, Jacques. *Of Grammatology*. Corrected Edition. Translated by Gayatri Chakravorty Spivak. Baltimore: Johns Hopkins University Press, 1997.

Dossal, Miriam. *Imperial Designs and Indian Realities: The Planning of Bombay City, 1845–1875*. Bombay: Oxford University Press, 1991.

Dossal, Miriam. "A Master Plan for the City: Looking at the Past." *Economic and Political Weekly* 40, no. 36 (September 3–9, 2005): 3897–3900.

Dossal, Mariam. *Theatre of Conflict, City of Hope: Bombay/Mumbai, 1660 to Present Times*. New Delhi: Oxford University Press, 2010.

Edwardes, S. M. *The Gazetteer of Bombay City and Island, Vol. 1, 1873–1927*. Bombay: Times Press, 1909–10.

Haynes, Douglas. *Small Town Capitalism in Western India: Artisans, Merchants and the Making of the Informal Economy, 1870–1960*. Cambridge: Cambridge University Press, 2012.

"Historians Raise Questions About ICHR's New Boss Prof Y Sudershan Rao." *Firstpost*, July 14, 2014. https://www.firstpost.com/living/historians-raise-questions-about-ichrs -new-boss-prof-y-sudershan-rao-1617971.html.

Kapur, Ratna. "Unruly Desires, Gay Governance, and the Makeover of Sexuality in Postcolonial India." In *Global Justice and Desire: Queering Economy*, edited by Nikita Dhawan, Antke Engel, Christoph H. E. Holzhey, and Volker Woltersdorff, 115–31. New York: Routledge, 2015.

Khedekar, Vinayak. *Gomantak Lok Kala*. Goa: Government Press, 1980.

Kidambi, Prashant. "Housing the Poor in a Colonial City: The Bombay Improvement Trust, 1898–1918." *Studies in History* 17, no. 1 (2001): 58–79.

Kidambi, Prashant. *The Making of an Indian Metropolis: Colonial Governance and Public Culture in Bombay*. Burlington, VT: Ashgate, 2007.

Mitra, Durba. *Indian Sex Life: Sexuality and the Colonial Origins of Modern Social Thought*. Princeton, NJ: Princeton University Press, 2019.

Morgan, Jennifer. "Accounting for the 'Most Excruciating Torment'": Gender, Slavery, and Trans-Atlantic Passages." *History of the Present* 6, no. 2 (Fall 2016): 184–207.

Nagar, Ila, and Debanuj Dasgupta. "Public Koti and Private Love: Section 377, Religion, Perversity and Lived Desire." *Contemporary South Asia* 23, no. 4 (2015): 426–41.

Parker, K. M. "'A Corporation of Superior Prostitutes': Anglo-Indian Legal Conceptions of Temple Dancing Girls, 1800–1914." *Modern Asian Studies* 32 no. 3 (1998): 559–663.

Povinelli, Elizabeth. *Economies of Abandonment: Social Belonging and Endurance in Late Liberalism*. Durham, NC: Duke University Press, 2011.

Punekar, S. D., and Kamala Rao, *A Study of Prostitutes in Bombay (With Reference to Family Background)*. Bombay: Lalwani Publishing House, 1962, 1967.

Raghunathji, K. "Bombay Dancing Girls." *Indian Antiquary* 13 (June 1884): 165–78.

Ranganathan, Murali, trans. and ed. *Govind Narayan's Mumbai: An Urban Biography from 1863*. Delhi: Anthem Press, India, 2012.

Rao, Nikhil. "Community, Urban Citizenship, and Housing in Bombay, ca 1919–1980." *South Asia* 36, no. 3 (2013): 415–33.

Rao, Nikhil. *House But No Garden: Apartment Living in Bombay's Suburbs 1898–1964*. Minneapolis: University of Minnesota Press, 2013.

Ricoeur, Paul. *Freud and Philosophy: An Essay on Interpretation*. New Haven, CT: Yale University Press, 1970.

Satoshkar, Balakrishna Dattaraya. *Gomantak Prakriti Ani Sanskriti Vol. 1*. 2nd ed. Pune: Subhda Saraswat, 1988.

Stewart, David. "The Hermeneutics of Suspicion." *Journal of Literature and Theology* 3 no. 3 (1989): 296–307.

Stoler, Ann Laura. *Along the Archival Grain: Epistemic Anxieties and Colonial Common Sense.* Princeton, NJ: Princeton University Press, 2009.

Tambe, Ashwini. "Brothels as Families: Reflections on the History of Bombay's *Kothas.*" *International Journal of Feminist Politics* 8, no. 2 (June 2006): 219–42.

Tambe, Ashwini. *Codes of Misconduct: Regulating Prostitution in Late Colonial Bombay.* Minneapolis: University of Minnesota Press, 2009.

Thapar, Romila. "The Appointment of a Historian Whose Work Is Unfamiliar to Most Historians Shows Scant Regard for the Impressive Scholarship That Now Characterises the Study of Indian History and This Disregard May Stultify Future Academic Research." *India Today,* July 11, 2014. http://indiatoday.intoday.in/story/romila-thapar -smriti-irani-old-history-baiters-of-bjp/1/370799.html.

Wacha, D. E. *Rise and Growth of the Bombay Municipal Government.* Madras: G. A. Natesan, 1913.

4. ORDINARY LESBIANS AND SPECIAL COLLECTIONS
The June L. Mazer Lesbian Archives at UCLA

ANN CVETKOVICH

What happens when a grassroots lesbian feminist archive finds its way to the special collections of a major university research library? Does it lose its counter-archival aura, or can it carry its powers of critical intervention into new spaces? This chapter takes up these questions through the case of the June L. Mazer Lesbian Archives, many of whose collections are now housed and cataloged at UCLA (University of California, Los Angeles) as part of a partnership that began in 2009 with the digitization of some of the Mazer collections in order to make them more accessible. The Mazer Archives emerged from the West Coast Lesbian Collections founded in Oakland, California, in 1981 with the mission of collecting "anything a lesbian ever touched," a sensibility that also inspired Brooklyn's steadfastly independent Lesbian Herstory Archives (LHA). Faced with economic and logistical challenges, the collections were rescued in 1987 by members of the Connexxus/Centro de Mujeres in Los Angeles, including June Mazer's lover Bunny MacCulloch, who initially brought them to their Altadena home. In 1989, the archives were given space in a building donated by the city of West Hollywood and since then have been maintained primarily by dedicated volunteers; UCLA's resources are now giving them further stability.

Although the archival turn is often understood to mean the turn toward theoretical critique within archival studies and research, for me the archival turn has also meant the turn from theory to an archival practice. In *An Archive of Feelings*, I developed the concept of "an archive of feelings" as a challenge to conventional institutions with their boxes and paper documents and finding aids and tightly restricted security measures, and I used the term "archive" quite loosely to mean any kind of document or ephemera collected for purposes of emotional memory, and to indicate the potential impossibility of archiving "feelings."

The LHA was my "gateway" archive, and I use the drug metaphor intentionally because I discovered the seductive and even addictive lure of archival work for those who seek lost histories and people, and especially for those who love paper cultures and their organizational systems. As I was researching *An Archive of Feelings* in the late 1990s, partnerships between grassroots archives and university research collections were getting underway, and I developed a keen interest in how archival and institutional practice could be transformed by a new wave of queer collecting by universities and public libraries.[1] My archival turn has thus taken the form of what I think of as fieldwork (including ethnography) in community-based archives and special collections dedicated to LGBTQ lives and histories, but it has also been guided by a critical relation to archives, which has often taken the form of an affective turn to the sensory and tactile dimensions of archival research.

June Mazer's Ephemera

With my questions about collaboration in mind, particularly the question of whether and how institutionalization benefits the independent archive, I set out to research the Mazer through its presence at UCLA—to see what it's like to encounter a lesbian feminist archive in a research collection. On a previous research trip, I had visited the Mazer's home base in West Hollywood and appreciated the informal and welcoming atmosphere. There, I was free to wander the open stacks and to browse the posters, buttons, T-shirts, and other ephemera on display amid the books and boxes on the shelves, while my guide, Angela Brinskele, was only too happy to answer questions about the collections. I was amused to see June Mazer's Birkenstocks on display (albeit protected by a plastic bag), and I was especially drawn to a room divider screen that Ester Bentley had decorated with photos of her friends, an exemplary case of an archive of feelings. Like many LGBTQ collections, the Mazer functions as a museum and community center as well as a site of research, and the space itself becomes integral to the research unlike the more impersonal reading rooms in libraries where special collections boxes are only available one folder at a time. This time, I wanted to see what it would feel like to access lesbian lives in a more conventional archive with its bureaucratic rules and regulations. Such visits require sometimes tedious advance preparation, including tracking through online finding aids and catalogues in order to figure out what boxes to request so that they can be retrieved from storage in time for your visit.

The lesbian feminist archive is distinguished by its focus on "ordinary" women—the Mazer, for example, actively solicited material from any woman who wished to donate to the archives and its publicity material often references this ideal. Interested in what this principle means in practice, I decided to focus on the ordinary lesbians who found their way to the archive, beginning with the woman, June Mazer, whose name it bears. The Mazer does, of course, have numerous collections that are of obvious or conventional public and historical interest, including the records of political organizations, such as Daughters of Bilitis (donated to the WCLC by Phyllis Lyon and Del Martin), National Gay and Lesbian Task Force (in LA), Los Angeles Women's Community Chorus, Old Lesbians Organizing for Change (OLOC), National Lesbian Conference, Lesbian Nurses of Los Angeles, Lesbian Schoolworkers, Lesbian Catholics Together, and the Woman's Building. The holdings also include alternative publications, such as Broomstick Magazine Records, the Carol Waymire Collection, and the very substantial Barbara Grier Periodical Collection, which provide visible evidence of a public lesbian print culture, and which were often carefully accumulated by amateur collectors who understood their value. In addition to these more public records, central to the Mazer's holdings are also many collections of personal papers, often donated directly by individual women writers and activists, who, even if they are not well known, could, through archival research, become historically important in their own right or in connection with the organizations or cultural movements to which they contributed. The Mazer collections provide a valuable picture of how the lesbian feminist organizing and print cultures that were catalyzed in the 1970s continued into the 1980s and 1990s, when much of the collection's foundation was produced and gathered, and they hold great potential for more complex histories of lesbian feminist cultures in a time before the internet and the groundswell of 1990s activisms. For purposes of this inquiry, though, I was looking for what has found its way into the archive that remains somewhat tangential or resistant to conventional kinds of historical research, and for how the lesbian feminist archive, with its commitment to ordinary lives that are not of conventional historical value, interrupts archival business as usual.

I thus began my research with June Mazer herself, whose name was given to the collections as a posthumous memorial in 1987. After June's death, her lover Bunny MacCulloch, drawn, like many activist lesbians, to the preservation of historical records, devoted her time to building and cataloging the collections before her own premature death, also from cancer, in 1989, and she donated two boxes of June Mazer materials. When looking at queer archives, I gravitate toward ephemera, not just the occasional paper documents for which archivists use the term, but the material artifacts that press up against the conventional boundaries of the archive and hint at ephemerality as that which escapes it. I was thus particularly intrigued by the following list in the finding aid: "Box 2, Folder 1: Ephemera. 1970–78. Physical Description: small knife, jewelry, ribbon, two bound books." The scope and content note elaborates further, offering details that are unusual, especially given the modest nature of the objects: "Contains June L. Mazer's address book, a small knife, a silver butterfly necklace, an award ribbon for June and Bunny's dog and a small book on the 'Springs of Friendship.'"

I requested the box with the ephemera but was mistakenly given Box 1 rather than Box 2, and thus began with the more conventional overview of June's work as an activist and a professional. The paper documents bring to life her work as an occupational therapist, and I was intrigued to discover that she was interested in somatic approaches to healing, including a workshop called "Exploring How A Think Feels" [sic]. Scattered amid the folders that contain copies of her article publications and workshop notes is personal correspondence, including love notes between her and Bunny. I pulled out a batch of paper Valentines—the kind that children give each other in grade school. I carefully removed the colored paper clip that holds them together and saw that they were all from Bunny, who wrote funny messages inspired by the animal images on each one—"Leos love Crabs," says the lion. After spreading them out across the manila folder in order to take a photograph, I put them back as carefully as I could but little sparkles of glitter had been deposited on the bright orange paper provided by the library for taking notes. A queer form of archival dust, the glitter leaves a material trail of testimony to my intimate contact with June and Bunny's exchange.

As I made my way through the two boxes, there were many other discoveries that provided evidence of queer affects and intimacies. One folder contains a lengthy transcript of an astrology reading for June, who was a triple Cancer with "oceans of feeling." In addition to her involvement with drama therapy, June's creative activities included sketches of her domestic life with Bunny—their garden and hot tub, Bunny milking their pet goat, and their beloved cats and dogs. Things took a more somber turn in the final folders, which document June's illness—medical records and caretaking logs, condolence letters from friends, receipts from her funeral, and more signs of dust—the plastic plaque that identified her ashes. Although it is sad to read of a life and love cut short, it is also in the lesbian feminist spirit of the Mazer to make this ordinary life special; by testifying not only to June's accomplishments but to her daily activities, the boxes also make a case for the value of every lesbian life.

When I finally got to the ephemera folder, I took the silver butterfly necklace out of its tiny plastic bag, unsheathed the pearl-handled knife, opened up the

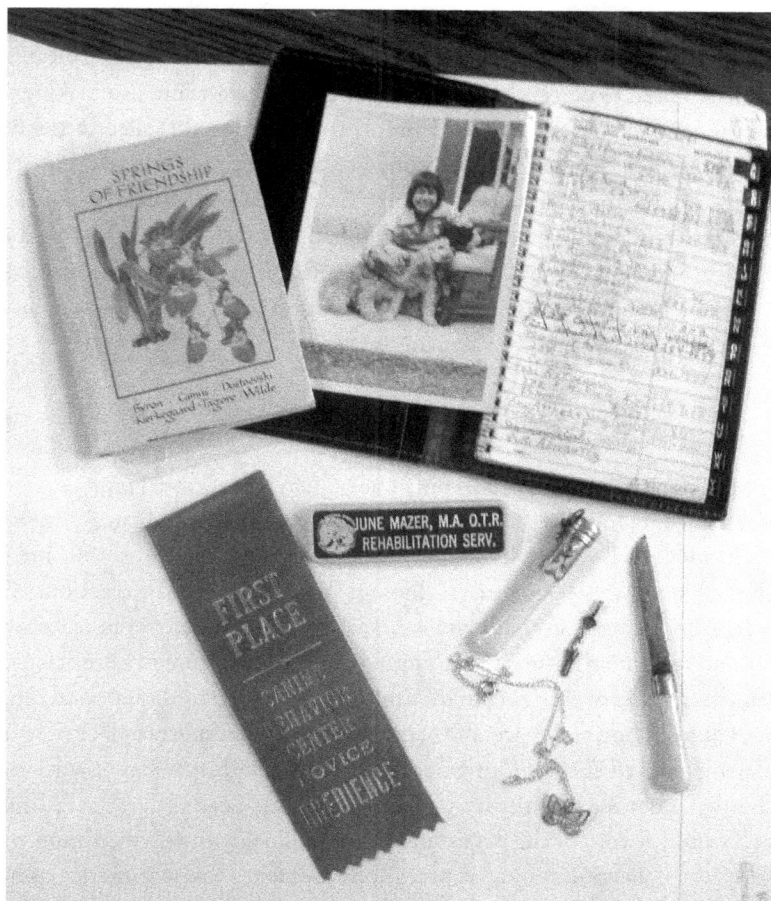

FIGURE 4.1. Ephemera, June L. Mazer Papers (Collection 2136). Library Special Collections, Charles E. Young Research Library, UCLA. Photograph by Ann Cvetkovich, published with permission of June L. Mazer Lesbian Archives.

address book that includes a photo of June, and placed them alongside the other objects to take a picture of the resulting collage (Figure 4.1). The mute objects and their odd juxtapositions spoke to me, providing a sense of a life that lies beyond the folders. Personal and affective value is what matters in this mini-collection—the award ribbon for the beloved dog is as important as the name tag that represents June's professional status and the address book that reveals her wide circle of friends and contacts. Even though I couldn't really know what they mean, the necklace and the knife—gifts perhaps—no doubt represented other significant relationships and memories. To touch these objects is to imagine receiving a personal message from June about what she thought was important. Ephemeral objects have that power—gesturing to affective meanings that are attached to objects but not fully present in them while also making immaterial ephemeralities material. Here in UCLA's Special Collections where I could only handle one folder and one box at a time, and where the materials thus remain sometimes quite literally remote, I was gratified to be able to touch the strange and random objects that had found their way into this space and thus to feel that June Mazer's simultaneously humble and remarkable life still matters. As concrete as a pearl-handled knife, the lesbian feminist archive's commitment to ordinary lives remains intact in the research library.

The Mazer Archives before UCLA

The Mazer's presence at UCLA is only one of many transitional moments in its history since its founding in Oakland as the West Coast Lesbian Archives in 1985, its move to Los Angeles in 1987, and the debates about a possible merger with the University of Southern California (USC) and ONE International Gay and Lesbian Archives in the late 1990s. That the Mazer Archives have survived at all, and particularly as an autonomous organization, is somewhat miraculous given the number of times when they might have folded or disappeared due to lack of funds, labor, and space, and sometimes internal disputes or lack of strong leadership, as well as the shifting status of lesbian feminist values of autonomy and independence. The history of the Mazer, which can only be told briefly here, is often a story of the persistence of individual women who found ways to keep the collections going at precarious moments and a reminder of how much grassroots organizations can be contingent on the everyday acts of ordinary people, not just collective action.

I have been especially interested in the Mazer's partnership with UCLA because when I was researching *An Archive of Feelings* and such collaborations were just beginning, the ONE archives and the June L. Mazer Lesbian Archives were negotiating with USC to provide space for their collections, although it was not then clear whether the university would be able to provide any additional resources for processing collections and making them more accessible. What was a question mark two decades ago has subsequently developed into a fully fledged collaboration for the ONE archives, which began a process of moving their collections to the USC campus, where they are now housed in a former fraternity house that has become a thriving research center with full-time staff, not just volunteers and that also includes an exhibition space.

In 2012, ONE officially joined USC's libraries, while also maintaining the autonomy and visibility afforded by having their own space.[2]

The Mazer, however, chose a different path at that critical juncture in the 1990s, ultimately deciding to maintain its independent status. The Mazer's reluctance to join ONE in its move to USC stemmed from the politics of separatism and autonomy that are part of its lesbian feminist sensibility. Its current partnership with UCLA, which began over a decade later, is thus all the more remarkable. The Mazer's innovative partnership with UCLA began with a grant to digitize some of the collections, a relatively modest and circumscribed project that only very slowly led to major portions of the Mazer collections moving to UCLA's special collections with the support of funding from the National Endowment for the Humanities. Especially important for addressing fears about loss of autonomy was a model of postcustodial holding where the university would sustain the free-standing archive. In 2009, Kathleen McHugh, director of UCLA's Center for the Study of Women, was looking to establish community partnerships and approached the Mazer on the recommendation of one of her graduate students who had been doing volunteer work there. In collaboration with library staff, she was successful in applying for a UCLA Community Partnership Grant to digitize five collections from the Mazer so as to make them accessible through UCLA's Special Collections. They chose collections that represent the Mazer's activist connections—Connexxus/Centro de Mujeres (which was actively involved in its move to LA), Southern California Women for Understanding (whose members also included many of those active with the Mazer), and Women Against Violence Against Women (WAVAW), as well as some key lesbian scholars—Margaret Cruikshank and Lillian Faderman—whose collections would be of scholarly interest. The digitization process not only made the collections more publicly visible on the UCLA campus, available through its own website portal, but provided valuable research experience for the graduate students who scanned and cataloged them. It also enabled a postcustodial arrangement where the original documents would stay with the Mazer while also being accessible through UCLA's digital portal, thus addressing the potential fear from grassroots archives, particularly those shaped by lesbian separatist values, about losing independent control over their collections.[3]

The utopian dream of the grassroots archive as an accessible site of knowledge and community for ordinary people rather than professional researchers often has to confront numerous material challenges. The collaboration with UCLA was ultimately very encouraging for the Mazer, which like many independent archives struggles to find the resources to maintain its collections—not just space for ongoing acquisitions but, equally important, labor to process and make them available to researchers and community members. Happy with UCLA's support, the Mazer agreed to the ambitious project of transferring some of its collections to a permanent home in the university's libraries, and McHugh and others applied successfully for an NEH grant that made this work possible. By 2014, over eighty collections, the bulk of the Mazer's holdings, had been physically moved to Special Collections, and UCLA has also begun acquiring new collections, such as Margaret Cammermeyer's papers, in collaboration with the Mazer. In many cases, the boxes arrived having never been processed in the ways that are routine for research collections, although not necessary in the same way at the Mazer because they were available for browsing on the open shelves. Their acquisition by UCLA included cataloging and the creation of professional finding aids that are available online and make it easier for researchers to determine whether the collections might be of use to their projects.

Looking back on the early history of the Mazer from the vantage point of its presence at UCLA is important for reckoning with its reputation as a community-based archive that differs from most university and research collections because it collects the lives of "ordinary lesbians" and values documents and artifacts that might otherwise be neglected. Indeed, the early history of the Mazer as the West Coast Lesbian Archives suggests both the direct influence of the model of the LHA, as well as the difficulty of sustaining that vision over time because of the need for space and labor beyond what a small group or domestic space can accommodate. While some knowledge of that early history seems important for researchers at UCLA to appreciate, so as not to lose the Mazer's ties to grassroots collecting, it is not easy to construct.

The archives emerged from the West Coast Lesbian Collections (WCLC) founded in Oakland in 1981 by Lynn Fonfa, Cherrie Cox, and Clare Potter, who were inspired by the sensibility guiding the mission of Brooklyn's steadfastly independent Lesbian Herstory Archives. Like LHA, the WCLC, which included organizational records from the region, opened its doors in a home, that of Cherrie Cox. Faced with economic and logistical challenges once she was no longer able to keep them there, the collections were brought to Los Angeles in 1985 partly through the intervention of Bunny MacCulloch who, along with her lover June Mazer, was an activist with a strong interest in archives. Bunny arranged for Connexxus/Centro de Mujeres, a women-run organization providing services for lesbians with which she was involved, to take them over. The collections were housed briefly in their Altadena home after June's death from cancer in 1987 and through the period of Bunny's illness and death in 1989, during which time the house was open to tours by visitors in a version of public domesticity so common for gay and lesbian archives. Connexxus was also relatively short-lived, closing its doors after six years in 1991, but some of those involved in the archives project, including Irene Wolt, Degania Golove, Yolanda Retter, and Lillian Faderman, worked to make sure that the archives had space in a building donated by the city of West Hollywood, and they were moved there in 1989. They have remained there since then, having undergone a major transition in the mid-1990s as the board debated the possible move to USC, after which Ann Giagni became board president. The hiring of Angela Brinskele as a staff person in 2007 has also contributed to the stability of the Mazer, and the relative permanence of the space has made its survival possible even with a skeletal paid and volunteer staff and periods of relative inactivity.

This very brief thumbnail sketch is a partial and potentially inadequate history not only because of its brevity but because it is hard to tell the story in a way that doesn't skew it toward a celebration of either resisting institutions or embracing them, and hence beg the very question I am hoping to address here. There is a persistent tendency within histories of LGBTQ archives to tell stories of heroic survival against the odds that smooth over internal conflicts and the absence of people who are no longer actively involved, in a version of what Kate Orazem has called the "romance of the archive."[4] There are many twists and turns to the story of what's in the Mazer collections and how it got there, as well as many different small but critical moments in the history of its leadership and its different homes. In relaying this condensed account, I am indebted to Rebecka Sheffield's more extensive research on the history of the Mazer prior to its collaboration with UCLA as part of a book on gay and lesbian archives that seeks to address some of the same questions about institutionalization that also motivate my work.[5] Through interviews and other archival sleuthing, Sheffield pieced together the early history of the Mazer, including its Oakland origins, its transfer to Los Angeles, and the internal debates about whether or not to partner with USC, information that was often unknown even by its current board members and directors and not available even from the relatively extensive documentation that the UCLA partnership produced. Sheffield not only fills in blanks that are present in the Mazer's own records and publicity but also suggests how an archival collection's own history can be erased as it shifts hands and locations especially if, as in the case of the Mazer, there are gaps in continuity of leadership between its original founders and its current organization.[6] At the risk of obscuring the Mazer's earlier (and sometimes messy) history by focusing on the collaboration with UCLA, I hope in my own way to consider what the ongoing legacy of the lesbian feminist archive might be even when it doesn't exist in an autonomous space. While Sheffield's wide and deep history of the Mazer is one valuable way to assess the encounter between community-based and institutional archives, my research has taken me to the collections themselves, where I have sought to focus on its personal rather than organizational records in order to explore the value of the lesbian feminist archive as a document of "ordinary lives."

Self-Archiving: Michelle Johnston and Tyger-Womon

Alongside the papers of community activists (and amateur archivists) such as Bunny and June, the Mazer collections include a number of donations from ordinary lesbians, that is, women who don't seem to have the claims to distinction, such as publications or activist and organizational work, that are common in conventional archives, especially because such activities often leave a documentary paper trail that is considered to have historical value. Instead, the Mazer collections are often the result of what I would call acts of self-archiving; they consist of materials that women chose to donate to the archives in order to represent themselves in the historical record, in some cases in response to calls from the Mazer for contributions from any and all lesbians.

Responding to this outreach in 1993, for example, Michelle Johnston proposes to donate records of her participation in internet bulletin boards and listservs such as Prodigy, early forms of social networking that allowed people who didn't know each other to form collective connections. In correspondence with the Mazer included in her files, she explains that "it seems there is a lack of information about average (ie, not famous) lesbians." She mentions that she can't submit records from one of her groups because the exchanges are confidential, but she is able to secure individual permissions from some of her Prodigy correspondents. Johnston is thus engaging in very deliberate acts of self-archiving as a result of thinking about how her ordinary life might have historical value.

Independent of their content, the results of Johnston's work are a fascinating case for media archaeology. She transferred the electronic medium to a paper form that could become an archival document by printing out the chats in hard copy, with one exchange per page, onto the perforated paper used in the dot matrix printers common for home use in the 1980s and into the 1990s before inkjet and laser printers became the standard. To those acquainted with the technology of that fleeting moment, the digital typeface appears simultaneously familiar and archaic. A cover page that gives a brief description of the interlocutor for each exchange also includes the tag line "these are ordinary dykes not famous celebrities." Although they are like letters, the exchanges, which are funny, flirtatious, and irreverent, have the frequency and informality now familiar in electronic social networks but still in the process of being forged as a new kind of intimacy.

But what do these ordinary dykes talk about? Celebrities! A major staple of the exchanges are moments of lesbian visibility in mainstream media. A huge k. d. lang fan, Johnston engages in lengthy discussions of the erotic scenes in the film *Salmonberries*, which although critically panned was still of interest to fans because of lang's presence. Johnston's care in collecting these conversations provides a historical record of a moment when lesbian celebrity, prior, for example, to the watershed moment of the *Ellen* show's coming out episode in 1997, was a subcultural phenomenon waiting to burst into the mainstream. Moreover, the paper documents provide a valuable print record of early uses of the internet to build fan cultures that establish a collective sense of lesbian identity; what might otherwise be an ephemeral digital technology, as well as an ephemeral cultural phenomenon, is rendered more stable, and hence more historically legible, by its conversion to paper. Although Johnston's contribution ultimately blurs the distinction between the ordinary and the celebrity, it also makes its case for the value of the ordinary.

Another self-archiver is the mysterious Tyger-Womon, about whom little is known other than her self-identification as Native American, which makes her papers stand out as one of the few from women of color in the Mazer collections. The materials date mostly from the early 1990s, when Tyger-Womon had what appears to have been a brief but highly productive relationship with the Vietnamese American artist Hanh Thi Pham, with whom she made a number of artist books that form the bulk of the collection.[7] Described in the finding aid as "chapbooks," the volumes turn out to be rather humble self-produced artifacts whose material forms are at least as interesting as their content. Some of the earlier volumes consist of handwritten poems and short essays, which are turned into collections by being placed in three-ring binders. One self-made book, titled "Of Heart and Herstory," consists of ten pages of carefully handwritten text crafted by ripping out the other pages from a red spiral-ring notebook. These collections consist of multigenre writings—poems, prose statements, letters, and songs—that might seem random but for their being combined together. A letter titled "Dear Friend" deplores the loss of parkland and speaks of ceremony: "Tonight is the holiday set aside for ancestors to travel across time, space, dimension. It is a most sacred holiday. Most people do not realize it; but you knew."[8] Tyger-Womon establishes a form of intimate public address by framing her comments as a letter to a friend (who because they are not named could be anyone, including the reader), and the act of collecting her writings also frames them for public circulation.

Tyger-Womon appears to have acquired access to a word processor at some point because later volumes are typed and printed, although sometimes in fonts that resemble handwriting and hence convey a sense of personal handcraft. As with Johnston's files, the materials bear the mark of a particular, and now largely obsolete, moment in print reproductive technologies—the copy shop with its choice of bindings and paper colors and the early word processor with its variety of fonts, including script.[9] Tyger-Womon took advantage of the copy shop's aesthetic charms to create very limited editions (sometimes as few as three copies) of the slim volumes, using the fastback binding common for theses and course packs and combining a white cover with bright pink pages for one volume and a green cover with green pages for another. The experience of reading these chapbooks within the archive resides as much in handling them as material objects as it does in absorbing their content, although the writing also suggests that Tyger-Womon is writing for posterity: "'I'm ready to be revolutionary' is a statement I have made for over twenty-five years, and lived it. Now I'm tired. I did my time as an anarchist. I'm going to try to relax, once in awhile, and let the young people take over. I just don't have the energy (or the heart) anymore."[10] Had Tyger-Womon not turned her words into books, they might well have seemed like journal entries or drafts; the act of creating books resembles the forms of material preservation that are also part of the archival process, and new forms of self-publishing made possible by computers and copy machines also lend themselves to self-archiving.

Before desktop computers and laser printers made high-quality reproduction of photographs possible at home, the copy shop was also the source for crude reproduction of photographs. Like the zines of the same period, some of Tyger-Womon's chapbooks include xeroxed photographs of her and Pham. In one book titled "A Day in the Life" and composed almost entirely of photos, the two experiment with costumes and gender roles, posing for each other to create their own intimate archive. Indeed, their desire to document stems from a sense of the historical and social value of their lives and work; Pham identifies with Asian American forms of masculine and multigendered identities, and in some of the prose, they write about being in a cross-cultural relationship and about the cultural specificity of their complex and shifting relation to gender.[11] In one of the photos, Pham, wearing dark sunglasses and a sleeveless denim vest with her tattooed arm exposed, is posed at the entrance to the Mazer, suggesting that the couple conceived of their work of self-archiving with this repository as a destination. Putting these self-published limited editions in the archive is another way of circulating them, and as a prospective destination, the archive serves as an incitement to cultural production—providing a broader public for one's work in the same way that small presses, bookstores, and artist collectives have also done. Drawing on the encouragement of self-expression in prose, poetry, and photography that is part of lesbian feminist cultural politics, Tyger-Womon understands her writing and photographs to be a form of creative production worth "publishing," and part of her distribution strategy includes archiving.

Boxes Inside Boxes: Ester Bentley's Personal Collections

As it became clearer to me that I was interested in the special collections of ordinary lesbians and their self-archiving practices, I decided that I wanted to focus on at least one large personal collection. I had already been intrigued by Ester Bentley because of the creative and affective process of self-archiving so materially evident in her screen, which, as I mentioned earlier, did not make the move to UCLA but instead sits in the Mazer's Hollywood home base, on display among the shelves because, having become an "oversize" material artifact, it can't be fit into a box or a folder. Adorned with the title "Celebrating the Women in My Life," the screen documents Bentley's friendships through photographs that she has lovingly cut and collaged onto backgrounds of colored paper, with each of the rectangular grids framing the different clusters as though it were an archival box (Figure 4.2). The inspirational messages also suggest its power as an archival collection: "Each picture will be to the last a fleeting moment rescued from the past." Just as Bentley herself might have lived with these images on display in order to have a material reminder of her social networks, the screen now sits at the Mazer as testimony to the importance of friendship as a foundation for lesbian culture and to Bentley's conviction that "I am a composite of all those who have touched my life." As Stacy Wood has discovered, the screen also provides important archival clues about the connections among some of the women in the collections, many of whom are present in the Mazer because of their friendships.[12] (Indeed, looking to the Mazer collections for a comprehensive or inclusive survey of Southern California lesbian cultures may be inappropriate because they are the result of a bounded social network composed of specific friendships.)

Ester Bentley's transformation of photographic images into a material artifact is a reminder that print and photographic documents are also objects. It suggests why ephemera in the form of objects play an important role in the Mazer collections but also present something of a challenge for transfer to

FIGURE 4.2. "Celebrating the Women in My Life, 1915–200?," collage on screen created by Ester Bentley shown by Angela Brinskele at the June L. Mazer Lesbian Archives. Still from video used by permission of the June L. Mazer Lesbian Archives.

collections like UCLA, where everything must fit into a box rather than being open to view as they are at the Mazer, which with its buttons and posters and flags and other objects readily on display alongside boxes is a cross between museum and archive. Already charmed by Bentley's screen, I was intrigued to see her full collection at UCLA, especially because it was large—at seventeen boxes one of the biggest personal collections in the Mazer—and quite a vast number for a relatively ordinary lesbian, whom the finding aid describes as a longtime social worker who was very active in Catholic ministries and gay and lesbian organizations after retirement. The finding aid lists boxes that include photographs, correspondence, and professional papers, as well as ephemera; although Bentley's screen didn't make it to UCLA, a number of her personal effects did, and these constitute little treasure boxes (of actual treasure boxes) for the researcher. Starting my research with one such box, for example, I unpacked the following objects that had been carefully arranged in the container so that everything would fit despite the lack of uniform sizes: a sampling of books on religion, women, and songs; a Gay Pride flag and an American flag; an address book; a box of greeting cards that contained the notes and other mementoes from Ester's sister Mildred's death in 1996 (Mildred lived with her for many years); a plastic apron with a rainbow bow; a name tag from an event; a small blue wooden box with a rainbow sticker on the lid and small trinkets inside; an empty green metal box with the words Ester Bentley and Private scratched on the top; a No Smoking sign; and a wooden carving of the words "Ester (heart) Gayle." The biggest item is a wooden writing desk with storage for mail that appears to be a gift from Ester to Gayle; there is a card (with a Virginia Woolf quotation) taped on the top that flips over to reveal the message, "Whenever You Want or Need Me You Will Find Me in the Box—See Note Enclosed Love Ester," and the lid opens to reveal a wooden carving of the name "Ester" below a colorful sticker that reads "I Love You."

What might be the historical value of these artifacts? A great deal, I would suggest: the friendship networks and love of a long-term couple, the traces of LGBTQ identity and politics in rainbows and Gay Pride mementoes, and the entanglements of affective relations and social histories are animated through their presence in these objects, which surrounded their owners and were embedded in their daily lives. It is important to preserve these objects along with the papers and photographs, even though their materiality can be cumbersome and their meanings may be less immediately available than those of more discursive print documents. In their unwieldiness, too, they suggest some of the ways in which the community-based and personal archive doesn't necessarily "fit" into the conventional archive, keeping alive the tension between the animated states of objects in daily life and their enclosure in boxes.

The ephemera box is also a box of boxes, offering testimony to the forms of storage that lend themselves to the self-archiving practices of ordinary lesbians—whose culture is marked by a penchant for saving things. These include forms of storage and recycling that repurpose containers for archival purposes: a greeting card box holds important correspondence, or a bank checkbook holder becomes a container for address labels. Equally notable are the forms of decoration and crafting—the rainbow flag on the box of trinkets, the personal messages that decorate the mailbox—that signal intentional forms of storage and that use boxes as texts and signs of communication, especially signs of love. Just as professional archivists are skilled craftmakers of boxes (indeed, one of the pleasures of unpacking ephemera are some of the ingenious modes of storage), so too is the self-archiving lesbian someone who understands the power of the box or container as a way of saving and keeping. That Ester's own boxes are stored together without being reboxed is a way of indicating the labor that has already gone into preservation prior to UCLA's archival processing. The careful storage by the cataloger, Stacy Wood, who keeps the rainbow box as-is with its little collection of artifacts—a shoelace, a mini-maraca, green staples, stamps with toys—that are not valuable in themselves but are evidence of a lifetime of saving, is a way of preserving this everyday practice of archiving.

Archival Biography: Constructing Ester Bentley's Life

As Melanie Micir has suggested, for those whose lives are not known in other ways, an archival collection can be a form of biography.[13] Although it took some time to get through all of the boxes, I was ultimately able to assemble a picture of Ester's life not only from more public records and print documents, which include papers from her professional life as a social worker and her involvement in organizations such as the California Organization for Older Lesbians (COOL), but also from more personal materials, such as correspondence with friends and colleagues and photographs.

Born in 1915 in Louisville, Ester Bentley was able to go to college at a time when many women did not, although she stayed local (at University of Louisville and Catherine Spalding College) and her postgraduate study was in a field—social work—that was more readily available to women and closely connected to the Catholic Church, which enabled not only professional trajectories for women but women-only spaces that fostered lesbianism. In her connections with the military, Ester also seems to fit the model of John D'Emilio's argument that World War II service allowed people to move and hence to create openly gay communities.[14] Ester's work as a USO director during World War II took her away from Kentucky, and in 1949 she graduated with an MA in social work from the Catholic University of America in Washington, DC. Her professional training as a social worker allowed her to remain economically independent and move to Southern California sometime in the early 1950s, where she worked as a district director for the San Bernardino County Council of Community Services and later as a case worker for the California State Department of Social Welfare. Her affiliation with UCLA's School of Social Welfare as a field consultant and student supervisor from 1966 to 1974 just prior to her retirement is prominently featured in her biographical notes and in the papers.

As someone who was openly out by the 1940s and who then participated in lesbian and feminist organizing in the 1960s and 1970s that brought her into contact with the Mazer archives, Bentley is an interesting case of an ordinary lesbian whose ability to live an openly lesbian life nonetheless represents a noteworthy history. Her presence in the archives is also a function of her generational status as an "older lesbian," one of the categories that is especially pronounced in the Mazer's holdings, which seem to be driven by the efforts of Mazer volunteers to document those who came before them as they start to age—or to gather materials from their own aging friendship circle, since many of those active in the Mazer were older. Inspired by the spirit of the LHA, which places value on preserving earlier generations, their outreach to the community to donate their materials to the Mazer is a form of collective self-archiving, and Ester was part of the social network that surrounded the Mazer in its initial years in LA. Although quite a bit older than those who came of age in the 1960s and 1970s, Ester was also active in lesbian feminist circles, especially since she was retired and had the time (and the temperament) to be involved in community organizing as an extension of her identity as a social worker (a profession prominently featured in the Mazer's collections).

It's thus important to consider what kind of ordinary lesbian makes it into the archives—those who were active in organizations, those who were openly lesbian, those who were older. While Ester may be ordinary, there's a specificity to the ordinary lesbians represented in the Mazer's personal collections, most of whom had direct ties through organizational and activist connections that brought them to the archives. This dynamic also helps explain why the Mazer's collections are predominantly white, since they mirror what is often a de facto segregation of lesbian social networks. The personal collections in the Mazer, which were mostly acquired during the period when it first moved to LA, may ultimately come to represent a bounded and relatively brief history of the category "lesbian." Emerging in the 1970s and 1980s, and backdated to earlier periods, lesbian identities began shifting in the 1990s with the rise of butch-femme, (gender)queer, and trans identities, and many younger people no longer identify with the term *lesbian* as a way to name their identities. As time goes by, despite its ambition to represent all lesbians, the Mazer may instead be more valuable as a record of a particular period in the history of gender and sexual identities, and the very specific affective and social networks, including friendship groups, out of which the category lesbian emerged. Included in that history would be the links between the lesbian and the desire to preserve ordinary lesbians through archival practices.

Ordinary Lesbians and Their Personal Papers

While one way to read Ester Bentley's collection for its historic value would be to construct a biography that positions her as both ordinary and exceptional, my affective attachment to her screen and her boxes of ephemera, even without knowing much at all about the facts of her life, suggests an alternative "archive of feelings" method of archival research. The screen that records Ester's lesbian affective networks and social relations—with friends as well as lovers—is an entry point onto the more personal materials, especially the vernacular photos and the notes and correspondence, that are central to the collection. The historical value of Ester's archival materials lies in the vivid documentation of her personal life and extended social circle through both the correspondence and the photographs. While her status as a professional woman enables her identity as a lesbian, she is most visible as a lesbian in her intimate life, and the artifacts that document it—greeting cards, correspondence, photos—are thus of greater historic value for this kind of collection than they might be for writers, artists, and other public figures whose professional work is often the focus of archival documents. Five of the seventeen boxes feature photographs, some in albums or sleeves but many simply loose and culled from a range of times. These snapshots document a rich social life that encompasses not only the intimacies of couples and lovers but the groups of friends whose gatherings in private homes rather than more public spaces are also part of the broader cultural formation of lesbian life in mid-twentieth-century US cultures. Also very prominent in the collections (as with June Mazer) are personal papers, including not just formal correspondence but notecards, lists, sketches, creative writing efforts, and other paper records. The tendency to value written documents, sometimes for sentimental reasons, offers further evidence of the strong relations between the lesbian and the archive, including the emphasis on literacy that drives lesbian feminist institutions of print publication, such as periodicals, publishing companies, and bookstores.[15]

One of my most surprising discoveries in the files was Ester's longtime relationship with Martha Foster, a poet whose papers are also one of the Mazer's collections. Foster's collection features prominently in the research guide published by UCLA because it includes a number of very glamorous photographs of her posing for the camera—an unusual glimpse of mid-century femme identities. But the guide and the finding aids don't mention the connection between Bentley and Foster—and I didn't understand that they had been lovers until I came across a small folder of love notes and correspondence that dates from their initial involvement in 1963 and 1964. Their early connection seems to have been around the romance of a shared interest in poetry—and they trade poems back and forth, with Martha the more experienced poet clearly an inspiration for Ester. On a postcard, a poem from her begins: "Walking talking rolling sea / Picture gallery you and me / Petting Susie; fingers meet / No choice now for fast retreat."[16] The records are sketchy—and were it not for the transcript of an oral history interview in which Ester explicitly describes their relationship, I might not have pieced it together from the available documents.[17] It appears to have been a somewhat stormy but persistent relationship. They never lived together, and at some point they ceased being lovers, but they remained close friends until Martha's death in 1987, as evidenced by the records of Ester's role as executor of her estate. Reading the two collections together makes for an intriguing story of an intimacy that is ordinary but also complicated and that testifies to the forms of commitment that lesbians have provided for one another that lie outside conventional understandings of both love and friendship. Foster's collection is less comprehensive than Ester's and reveals that she was an alcoholic who became something of an eccentric recluse in her old age, but Ester clearly remained a steadfast support to the friend and former lover who did not have other family. Indeed, I suspect that Foster's papers must be in the Mazer because Ester saved and donated them as another gesture of love and care—appreciating their archival (and lesbian) value in a way that a family member might not have. Ester's role as the keeper of Foster's papers is another form of coupledom or long-term relationship that falls somewhere between romance and friendship.

In searching for further evidence of Ester's and Martha's history, one of my most evocative finds was a black and white snapshot of Martha posed in front of her cabin at Lake Arrowhead (Figure 4.3). Like the portraits in her collection, she looks like a glamorous movie star but the setting is her home, albeit a place in the San Bernardino mountains where Hollywood often vacationed. She's wearing pants but elegantly so—the wide legs enable her to kneel comfortably, and she's paired them with a wool sweater that clings to her breasts, which are accentuated by the light and shadows of the photo. She's accessorized by her dog in one hand and a cigarette in the other. So often it's the pet that is the lesbian reveal—the little terrier is up on its hind legs with its head cocked toward her and nestled on her shoulder as her companion animal. The cigarette adds to the Hollywood glamor; her arm is held straight to show it to advantage and her hand is gracefully turned up like a dancer's. Although it might just be a cover for her unkempt hair, her head is wrapped in a scarf that makes her look even more exotic.

The archive invites affective connections to the paper traces of love and passion. The photograph of Martha is the punctum for my experience of the collection, affirming the value of the archive of feelings that exceeds the historical record of an ordinary lesbian life and its use for biographical information or documentation of facts. Even without knowing who Ester and Martha were, the photograph as both image and material artifact speaks to me as a message from the past. What is the lesbian life that is recorded here? It's not just about the individual people and the biographical facts of their lives but about the setting and the material aesthetics of the photographic image. It's a snapshot but also a mise-en-scène or a curatorial arrangement that creates a moment in

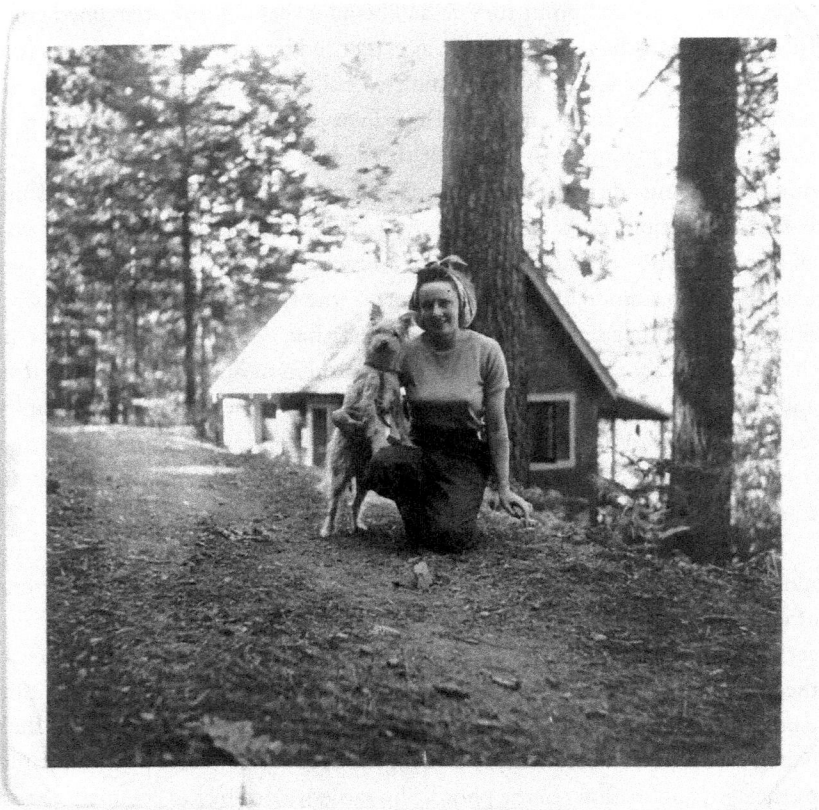

FIGURE 4.3. Photograph of Martha Foster (likely taken by Ester Bentley) at Lake Arrowhead cottage, Ester F. Bentley Papers (Collection 1981). Library Special Collections, Charles E. Young Research Library, UCLA. Photograph of photograph by Ann Cvetkovich, published with permission of June L. Mazer Lesbian Archives.

time that becomes historical. As a work of art, an expression of fantasy, and a gendered performance, it provides the reach across time illuminated by theorists of queer affect and temporality.[18]

Resource Guides and Finding Aids

My ability to describe the Mazer collections as a whole has been enabled by UCLA's publication of a resource guide titled *Making Invisible Histories Visible*, another valuable result of the collaboration that might not otherwise have been possible.[19] Published in conjunction with the completion of the project, the guide helps transform the archive from what could be inert material to knowledge to be used. In its own way, it is an archive—not only a document of what is in the collections but a document of the process by which they were transferred from the Mazer to UCLA. It includes a history of the Mazer Archives and the UCLA project through brief articles from a variety of perspectives: UCLA scholars, such as Kathleen McHugh, then director of the Center for the Study of Women; Mazer volunteers, including Ann Giagni, longtime president of the board, and Angela Brinskele, the primary paid staff member; UCLA's librarians and archivists, such as Sharon Farb and Lizette Guerra; and, especially significant, students who worked on the project. This kind of backstory is often hard to find for archival collections, leaving invisible the complicated material and historical processes by which documents are initially collected or acquired by institutions. Particularly crucial in this case is the complex history of the collaboration between the Mazer and UCLA, including the care taken to honor and preserve the archive's community connections and independent status. The results of the delicate and ongoing negotiations about permissions, access, and the Mazer's future remain open, as is the outcome of the archive's availability at UCLA, which is only just beginning to unfold. The story in the resource guide is necessarily incomplete and partial, as indicated by the multiple voices and positions from which it is told, but it is nonetheless crucial to understanding the significance of the collections.

In addition to providing a history of the project, the resource guide also includes a list, with brief descriptions, of each of the collections at UCLA, affording a comprehensive overview that might not have been available from the Mazer itself, where visitors must often rely on the knowledge of staff or volunteers to know what's there. Although one of the pleasures of research in a grassroots collection can be the personal connections with longtime volunteers who know the collections intimately, the transfer of this knowledge into a written database also has its advantages. Moreover, although the same information is available through the UCLA catalogue, it is convenient to have all of the descriptions in the finding aids redacted and gathered in one place in the resource guide. The list of names and organizations in the table of contents, combined with the brief descriptions that follow, constitutes a synthetic text in its own right, making it easier to get a broad overview of what the collection includes. Since many of the names are not well known, the brief biographies also function cumulatively to indicate the collective significance of the Mazer as an archive of West Coast lesbian feminisms. Moreover, they encourage the study of the collection itself as a historical artifact, in addition to the use of it for research on specific individuals and organizations.

As access to collections, including the Mazer, becomes increasingly digital, there is also something historically appropriate, and literally touching, about having a print artifact that holds them together materially. With its large format, the visual design of the book is reminiscent of classic 1970s activist publications, such as *Our Bodies, Ourselves* and *Our Right to Love*, that aimed to share grassroots knowledge and create community. The brief descriptions of the collections are accompanied by many images that give a quick but vivid sense of the actual contents—allowing for a preview that can be so valuable when working only more remotely with the descriptions of the objects. Although called a resource guide, it's actually more like a curated exhibition in book form, and by making items from the collection readily available for browsing, it helps to replicate the experience of visiting the Mazer's home base, which functions not just as an archive but a museum.[20]

The resource guide also makes good on its title by making visible the often invisible labor that enabled the transfer of the Mazer Archives to their new home at UCLA, which has entailed scanning paper documents, organizing and cataloging collections, creating metadata and finding aids, interviewing Mazer volunteers to create an oral history, and more. Whether one is aware of it or not, research in special collections depends on the labor of others, and not just more visible trained experts, such as archivists and librarians, but others behind the scenes, often hired on contract as grants and funds for specific projects permit, who provide cheap or casual labor (and some of whom, such as library and archive students, may be quite knowledgeable). Many students participated in processing the Mazer for UCLA and by contributing their labor became part of an activist and educational project. The research guide acknowledges this work by featuring their voices in short essays on processing the collections, which contain important critical insights.[21] By giving those who processed the collections a chance to share their stories about what they learned through their contact with the materials, the resource guide also challenges conventional divisions between archivists and researchers. The students' excitement about the work, even when it is tedious, is evident, whether learning more about a person or an artifact or about technologies of preservation. Indeed, as Mike Stone suggests in his brief essay "A Curse as Blessing," "digitizing in real time is slow and time consuming, but it gave the student staff—all of whom had been chosen because of their special interest in the collections or in related fields of study—the time to listen and to watch, thereby putting their knowledge and skills to work."[22] Even the painstaking work of digitization enables a familiarity with the materials that would be the envy of many researchers, and cataloguers also often know more about a collection than anyone else because they have handled every piece of it.

In recognition of that fact, part of my ethnographic research process has involved conversations with those involved in the collections. It has been especially useful to talk to Stacy Wood, who catalogued many of the collections I perused and was able to provide additional information about them, including her failed search for Tyger-Womon, and her careful organization and reassembly of June Mazer's materials from a jumble of boxes. I was drawn to her unusually detailed finding aids, which are such a crucial tool for archival research and can become a textual genre in their own right, as evidenced by the use of the collection descriptions as text for the resource guide.[23] Although it can be a skeletal and abstract version of what's in the boxes and folders, any kind of list is helpful, especially when trying to decide whether a particular collection holds items of interest or where to start with a long list of boxes. But for the queer researcher who is on the prowl for unusual archives or for what doesn't fit, the finding aid's technical and abstract descriptions can leave much unsaid. One searches for clues of various kinds in the brief notations, and Wood's descriptions of objects, such as the June Mazer ephemera, were very suggestive, a kind of poetry of collage in their own right. Although cataloguing often aims to provide only the most neutral or flattest description so as to leave analysis and interpretation to the researcher, Wood uses the conventions of the finding aid to provide an account of her subjects and their materials; the biographical notes, which in some cases required considerable research, endow the ordinary lives of social workers and activists with significance even when confined to factual information. The descriptions of the boxes also suggestively highlight and juxtapose the personal and professional aspects of lesbian lives: June Mazer's astrology reading gets its own folder, and the content lists of Ester Bentley's boxes range from poetry to organizational records, from prayers to sports events. Physical descriptions leave intriguing markers of a materiality that extends beyond paper, such as boxes of ephemera composed of "cotton, wood, plastic." Wood makes strategic use of "content and scope" notes to highlight the significance of what might otherwise be ordinary objects in, for example, the inclusion of Michelle Johnston's reference to ordinary lesbians or the following account of June L. Mazer's personal journal, which is highly evocative without straying from the task of description: "The book was a gift from Linda Wineland and chronicles June's experiences with cancer, her relationship with Bunny, financial and work related anxieties. There are very few entries." Although these notes could be construed as merely descriptive, they bring into view out lesbian lives and artifacts that might not generally warrant description, validating the ordinary by naming it.[24] "There are very few entries" may be flat description, but it also evokes the trailing off of daily documentation that is the sign that a life is coming to an end. The use of the term *lesbian* is itself a strategic choice, given both the historic absence of that category in many finding aids and catalogues, and its renewed disappearance or waning as many people disidentify with the category, including some of those in the collections. (Wood thus had to decide in some cases between *lesbian* and *transgender* as ways of naming those in the collection, another reminder that description is never a simple or transparent task.)

Because of the special circumstances surrounding the Mazer acquisition, many of the UCLA people involved in cataloguing, digitizing, and interviewing understood the importance of what they were doing, and there are traces of their affective investment in the putatively objective documents and metadata that surround the collections. There is a pulse not just in the collections themselves but in the labor that, even as it removes the material objects from the more direct access often possible in a community-based archive and surrounds them with bureaucratic mediation, also makes them available as research collections. In the give-and-take of archival processing, which distances records from direct contact but also brings them closer, traces of the flesh and blood pulse of both the people in the archives and the cataloguers are also encoded in documents such as the finding aids. It is my hope that the collections will continue to retain the personal touch of the cataloguers, as well as their subjects, although I was surprised to discover over the course of my research on the Ester Bentley Papers that Stacy Wood's work had been replaced by that of a later cataloguer who reordered the collections to make them more uniform, including redistributing the box of boxes with which I began my research.[25]

In working with the Mazer collections at UCLA, I came over time to the realization that what I thought might take away from the intimacy of contact with the archives in a more grassroots setting can actually add affective power and value. The care with which humble materials have been filed, boxed, and described can be a form of love and has in many cases enhanced my appreciation for what's there. I would not have known this had I not actually sat there in the Special Collections reading room, marveling sometimes that June Mazer, or Michelle Johnston, or Tyger-Womon now sit alongside, for example, Susan Sontag, perhaps one of the most famous lesbians in the UCLA collections, although she herself might not want to think of it in those terms. In one of my research trips to UCLA, I took some time to look at Sontag's early journals, in order to compare the original artifacts against their recently published versions and was startled by their resemblance to the notes, fragments, and drawings of the Mazer's lesbians.[26] Sontag's lists of books she read and films she saw, as well as the San Francisco gay bars she visited and the girls she kissed, are the archival records not just of a precocious intellectual but of an ordinary lesbian life. In their published print form, the handwritten lists appear more substantive than in the original journals, which include many more fragmentary notations and thus start to resemble the ephemeral evidence of the Mazer's lesbians. In one early notebook, Sontag's outline drawing of her hand demonstrates her own propensity toward self-archiving and resonates alongside June Mazer's sketches and Tyger-Womon's notebooks. I hope juxtapositions like these will produce innovative scholarship, as well as exhibitions and programming, as UCLA continues to take advantage of the Mazer's presence as one of its special collections.

Archival Collections Cited

Ester F. Bentley Papers (Collection 1981), June L. Mazer Lesbian Archives, UCLA Library Special Collections, Charles E. Young Research Library, University of California, Los Angeles.

Martha Foster Papers (Collection 1990), June L. Mazer Lesbian Archives, UCLA Library Special Collections, Charles E. Young Research Library, University of California, Los Angeles.

Michelle Johnston Papers (Collection 2200), June L. Mazer Lesbian Archives, UCLA Library Special Collections, Charles E. Young Research Library, University of California, Los Angeles.

June L. Mazer Papers (Collection 2136), June L. Mazer Lesbian Archives, UCLA Library Special Collections, Charles E. Young Research Library, University of California, Los Angeles.

Tyger-Womon Papers (Collection 1943), June L. Mazer Lesbian Archives, UCLA Library Special Collections, Charles E. Young Research Library, University of California, Los Angeles.

Notes

For the opportunity to learn about the Mazer-UCLA collaboration as it was unfolding, I thank Kathleen McHugh, Angela Brinskele, Sharon Farb, Stacy Wood, and Marika Cifor, among many others at UCLA and the June L. Mazer Lesbian Archives whose labor made my research possible. An earlier version of the section on June Mazer appeared as "Ephemera" in *Lexicon for an Affective Archive*, edited by Palladini and Pustianaz.

1 See Cvetkovich, *Archive of Feelings*, and on the more recent collaboration between the Mazer and UCLA, see Cvetkovich, "Queer Archival Futures," which draws from a 2009 symposium at UCLA showcasing the collaboration.

2 The occasion was marked by an exhibition in Doheny Memorial Library, USC's main library, a material marker of the inclusion and insertion of queer archives in the university. ONE has been able to both consolidate and expand their collections; for example, an NEH grant to catalogue their art collections led to a series of exhibitions called *Cruising the Archive* that were part of the extensive 2011–12 *Pacific Coast Time* exhibitions that showcased art in Los Angeles from 1945 to 1980. For background on the history of the ONE Archives, including its connections to the transgender activist Reed Erickson and his EEF (Erickson Educational Foundation) organization, see Devor and Matte, "One Inc." and Frantz and Locks, *Cruising the Archive*.

3 My understanding of postcustodial archives is indebted to the work of T-Kay Sangwand, the inaugural archivist for the University of Texas's Human Rights Digital Initiative. Before arriving at UT, Sangwand worked on the Mazer/UCLA digitization project while completing her MLIS degree at UCLA, thus linking these two ostensibly distinct collections. For an overview of the HRDI's postcustodial mission, see Kent Norsworthy and T-Kay Sangwand, "From Custody to Collaboration: The Post-Custodial Archival Model at the University of Texas Libraries," which includes citations for many of Sangwand's presentations. University of Texas at Austin, 2013, https://library.stanford.edu /sites/default/files/Univ%20of%20Texas.pdf.

4 See Orazem, "'Violent Nostalgia.'"

5 See Sheffield, *Documenting Rebellions*. I first encountered this work through Sheffield's dissertation, "The Emergence, Development and Survival of Four Lesbian and Gay Archives." My conversations with Sheffield have been invaluable for this project.

6 Access to the Mazer's history might be contrasted to that of LHA, where the ongoing involvement of the original founders, including Joan Nestle and Deborah Edel, allows for more direct and continuous access to its earliest history, however subject to interpretation. Multigenerational histories of lesbian feminist institutions present an interesting methodological challenge, as younger scholars and activists rely on institutional records and other archival materials that stand alongside direct testimony or oral history interviews from those who were there. See, for example, the collaborative work on the history of LHA at its fortieth anniversary, Smith-Cruz et al., "Getting from Then to Now," as well as Joan Nestle's work in progress on the history of LHA, "Who Were We to Do Such a Thing?" in *Radical History Review* and in this volume.

7 The UCLA cataloguer for Tyger-Womon's papers, Stacy Wood, tried to trace her and was unsuccessful, although the finding aid updated by Jessica Tai in 2017 identifies Tyger-Womon as V. L. Adams. The story of her connections to the Mazer and how her collections came to be there thus remain unknown. Conversation with Stacy Wood, November 2014. There is more information available on Hanh Thi Pham, including Machida, *Unsettled Visions*, 167–86, but none of the sources I could find mention the Mazer materials.

8 From "Of Heart and Herstory," 1993, Box 1, Folder 6, Tyger-Womon Papers.

9 On the Xerox and copy shop as representative of a specific moment in the history of the document and print culture, see Gitelman, *Paper Knowledge*, and Eichhorn, *Adjusted Margin*.

10 From "Collected Writings," 1975–1993. Box 1, Folder 5, Tyger-Womon Papers. Tyger-Womon uses her writing as a way to seek connection with others: "As for me, I am still

seeking and growing . . . although no one to share shamanic consciousness with." Those connections include ancestral ones: "My power explodes with the force of a volcano in spirit-song the bones of generations past; all the peoples of this earth rise and beckon me through hallways of various dimensions. I smell the cedar and sage, as my feet pound the pavement in urban nightmare continuing." Depositing her writing in an archive offers another way to extend its outreach.

11 See "A Day in the Life" (1993, Box 1, Folder 4); "Lesbian Lovers Explore Their Sexual Energy," a 1992 interview in PT newspaper that includes discussion of race and gender (Box 1, Folder 2); and the self-published "The Typical and the Transgendered" (1993, Box 1, Folder 8). The article focuses on Pham and further suggests that Tyger-Womon's archival visibility owes much to this relationship.

12 See Wood, "Collective Intimacies," in McHugh, Johnson-Grau, and Raphael Sher, *The June L. Mazer Lesbian Archives*, 50–51.

13 See Micir, *Passion Projects*.

14 See D'Emilio, *Sexual Politics*.

15 For more on this, see Hogan, *Feminist Bookstore Movement*; Beins, *Liberation in Print*; and McKinney, *Information Activism*.

16 See Box 10, Folder 3, Martha Foster material, 1963–1991, Ester Bentley Papers. The Ester Bentley Papers were originally cataloged by Stacy Wood in 2014, and were later reorganized by Jessica Tai in 2017, who produced a new finding aid. When I first encountered them, the letters were listed in the finding aid as Box 18, Folder 12, Correspondence, 1943–1978, with no indication that the materials were related to Martha Foster.

17 The collection includes the transcript (and audiotapes) of an oral history interview, which provides a comprehensive overview of Ester's life, for a 1997 MA thesis for which she and her late-life partner Gayle Scott were interviewed as older lesbians (Box 18, Folder 6 in the 2014 finding aid, Box 11, Folders 2–3 in the 2017 finding aid). This oral history provides an important narrative frame for the personal papers and other archival documents and raises questions about the relative merits of these different forms of archival biography.

18 See, especially, Dinshaw, *Getting Medieval* and *How Soon Is Now?*

19 McHugh, Johnson-Grau, and Raphael Sher, *The June L. Mazer Lesbian Archives*. Also available for digital download through UCLA Center for the Study of Women website.

20 Other examples of books that constitute the public exhibition of archival materials in print form include Devor, *The Transgender Archives*, and Darms, *Fales Riotgrrrl Collection*.

21 See, for example, Archna Patel, "Scanning," 46–47; Ben Raphael Sher, "Stories," 47–50; Stacy Wood, "Collective Intimacies," 50–51, on Ester Bentley's screen; Mike Stone, "A Curse as Blessing," 57, on the value of the labor of digitizing; and Marika Cifor, "Home," 61–63, on oral history interviews, all in McHugh, Johnson-Grau, and Raphael Sher, *The June L. Mazer Lesbian Archives*.

22 McHugh, Johnson-Grau, and Raphael Sher, *The June L. Mazer Lesbian Archives*, 57. "They could identify materials of historical interest that a casual worker might not have been able to spot. This collection of descriptive information, more than any special technical innovation inherent in the digitization, is what is most important for a project such as this."

23 One of my inspirations for this insight is the use of the inventory list for the LHA's T-shirt collection as source for Ulrike Mueller's collective drawing project, *Herstory Inventory*. See Mueller, *Herstory Inventory*, and Cvetkovich, "*Herstory Inventory*."

24 For more on the methodological implications of description, see Marcus, Love, and Best, "Description across Disciplines." My experience with finding aids confirms the special issue's account of how description constitutes a complex method and form of knowledge, rather than merely being the raw material for theory or analysis.

25 The new organization, completed by Jessica Tai in 2017, grouped materials together in similar categories—books, photos, letters, and so on—and also repackaged the ephemeral items for better preservation. This is standard archival practice but also "straightens" out the more random assortments that were likely closer to how they were originally stored.

26 The earliest notebooks have been published as Sontag, *Reborn: Journals and Notebooks*, and were also adapted and performed as a theatrical production by Moe Angelos as *Sontag: Reborn* for the Builders Association in 2013.

Works Cited

Beins, Agatha. *Liberation in Print: Feminist Periodicals and Social Movement Identity*. Athens: University of Georgia Press, 2017.

Cvetkovich, Ann. *An Archive of Feelings: Trauma, Sexuality, and Lesbian Public Cultures*. Durham, NC: Duke University Press, 2003.

Cvetkovich, Ann. "Ephemera." In *Lexicon for an Affective Archive*, edited by Giulia Palladini and Marco Pustianaz, 179–83. Bristol, UK: Intellect, 2017.

Cvetkovich, Ann. "*Herstory Inventory*: Artists in the Lesbian Herstory Archives." *GLQ*, forthcoming.

Cvetkovich, Ann. "Queer Archival Futures: Case Study Los Angeles." *e-misferica* 9, nos. 1–2 (2012). https://hemi.nyu.edu/hemi/es/e-misferica-91/cvetkovich.

Darms, Lisa. *The Fales Riotgrrrl Collection*. New York: Feminist Press, 2013.

D'Emilio, John. *Sexual Politics, Sexual Communities: The Making of a Homosexual Minority in the United States*. Chicago: University of Chicago Press, 1983.

Devor, Aaron H. *The Transgender Archives: Foundations for the Future*. Victoria: University of Victoria Libraries, 2014.

Devor, Aaron H., and Nicholas Matte. "One Inc. and Reed Erickson: The Uneasy Collaboration of Gay and Trans Activism, 1964–2003." *GLQ* 10, no. 2 (2004): 179–209.

Dinshaw, Carolyn. *Getting Medieval: Sexualities Pre- and Post-Modern*. Durham, NC: Duke University Press, 1999.

Dinshaw, Carolyn. *How Soon Is Now? Medieval Texts, Amateur Readers, and the Queerness of Time*. Durham, NC: Duke University Press, 2012.

Eichhorn, Kate. *Adjusted Margin: Xerography, Art and Activism in the Late Twentieth Century*. Cambridge, MA: MIT Press, 2016.

Frantz, David Evans, and Mia Locks, eds. *Cruising the Archive: Queer Art and Culture in Los Angeles, 1945–1980*. Los Angeles: ONE National Gay and Lesbian Archives, 2011.

Gitelman, Lisa. *Paper Knowledge: Toward a Media History of Documents*. Durham, NC: Duke University Press, 2014.

Hogan, Kristen. *The Feminist Bookstore Movement: Lesbian Antiracism and Feminist Accountability*. Durham, NC: Duke University Press, 2016.

Machida, Margo. *Unsettled Visions: Contemporary Asian American Artists and the Social Imaginary*. Durham, NC: Duke University Press, 2009.

Marcus, Sharon, Heather Love, and Steven Best, eds. "Introduction: Building a Better Description." Description Across Disciplines special issue of *Representations*, no. 135 (Summer 2016): 1–21.

McHugh, Kathleen A., Brenda Johnson-Grau, and Ben Raphael Sher, eds. *The June L. Mazer Lesbian Archives: Making Invisible Histories Visible: A Resource Guide to the Collections*. Los Angeles: UCLA Center for the Study of Women, 2014.

McKinney, Cait. *Information Activism: A Queer History of Lesbian Media Technologies*. Durham, NC: Duke University Press: 2020.

Micir, Melanie. *The Passion Projects: Modernist Women, Intimate Archives, Unfinished Lives*. Princeton, NJ: Princeton University Press, 2019.

Mueller, Ulrike. *Herstory Inventory: 100 Drawings by 100 Feminist Artists*. Brooklyn: Dancing Foxes Press, 2014.

Nestle, Joan. "Who Were We to Do Such a Thing? Grassroots Necessities, Grassroots Dreaming: The LHA in Its Early Years." *Radical History Review* no. 122 (May 2015): 233–42.

Orazem, Kate. "'Violent Nostalgia': White Women, Power, and Affect in the Archival Romance." MA/MS thesis, University of Texas at Austin, 2019.

Palladini, Giulia, and Marco Pustianaz, eds. *Lexicon for an Affective Archive*. Bristol: Intellect Books, 2017. Originally published in Polish as *Lekyskon Archiwum Afektywnego*. Gdansk, Warszawa: Narodowy Instytut Audiowizualny, 2015.

Sheffield, Rebecka Taves. *Documenting Rebellions: A Study of Four Lesbian and Gay Archives in Queer Times*. Sacramento, CA: Litwin Books, 2020.

Sheffield, Rebecka Taves. "The Emergence, Development and Survival of Four Lesbian and Gay Archives." PhD diss., University of Toronto, 2015.

Smith-Cruz, Shawn(ta), Flavia Rando, Rachel Corbman, Deborah Edel, Morgan Gwenwald, Joan Nestle, and Polly Thistlethwaite. "Getting from Then to Now: Sustaining the Lesbian Herstory Archives as a Lesbian Organization." *Journal of Lesbian Studies*, 20, no. 2 (2016): 213–33.

Sontag, Susan. *Reborn: Journals and Notebooks, 1947–63*. Edited by David Rieff. New York: Picador, 2009.

5. PERFORMING QUEER ARCHIVES
Argentine and Spanish Policing Files for Unintended Audiences (1950s–1970s)

JAVIER FERNÁNDEZ-GALEANO

On the morning of November 4, 2016, two staff members of the Buenos Aires province prison system were seated at their desks as I, sitting in front of them, began to read aloud the criminological file on an inmate who had been accused of having sex with multiple young men in his apartment in 1970. The staff at this archive—the Museo Penitenciario Argentino Antonio Ballvé, which holds the records of the Instituto de Clasificación (hereafter, the Instituto)—dependent on and managed by the prison system, sat unperturbed. This was indeed a typical morning for *them*, as they had been expecting this performance. The prison archive had devised a method to allow visiting researchers to transcribe prisoners' files without using cameras: by recording themselves reading the documents. In this way, researchers make better use of the mere three days that they are generally granted to access this archive. Given this constraint, recording myself performing a "cold read" for my small audience did indeed save me some much-needed time. However, I could not help now hearing my own voice among those of queer individuals and their state interlocutors. By the same token—as Iván Ramos discusses in his chapter of this volume—"the act of liveness" in this performance *turned* the audience (i.e., the museum staff) into "witnesses" of the inmates' strategies, against all odds, to participate in the interviews with criminologists in their own terms.

The requirement to read files aloud gives rise to a rather unique engagement with the archive. By performing the voices of *both* examiners and inmates, I created audio files that I could later reproduce, time and time again, looking for new inflections of meaning. Yet also by reading these aloud I have added my inflection—each of my minute modulations of pitch and tone carries meaning, layers on context: my own judgments, guilt, shame, desires. This "emotional movement" informs—as Marshall and Tortorici indicate in the introduction—my *turning* to the archive. The "messiness" of this movement, on its turn, means that inmates' recorded testimonies "resists straight interpretation in linear, definitive terms," as I will elaborate on in this chapter by focusing on their productive *ambivalence*.

Similarly, when we transcribe our reading of a photograph, our impression of background, foreground, lighting, and our reactions to its subject or the intent of the photographer, we have created more than a facsimile. The situation in the consultation room made me imagine an era when radio soap operas were an omnipresent soundscape of homes and offices. This time, though, while the museum staffers looked down and continued their cataloguing work, the background sound was my radio play, my voice performing the roles of inmates who between the 1950s and 1970s were suspected of sexually nonconforming practices, and those of police and prison officers alike. In fact, Santiago Joaquín Insausti, a historian and dear friend of mine who also worked in this archive, shared with me that sometimes while reading aloud depositions that were particularly explicit in their erotic content, he felt taken by the moment and adopted a more passionate tone to convey the bodily pleasures captured in these records. As Marshall and Tortorici argue in the introduction, there is no way of understanding the "queer archival turn" without acknowledging that people feel "turned on" by the archive. I would add that people's reactions to this feeling also shapes the archival *turn*. In my case, for instance, I often caught myself lowering my voice or nervously rushing through the words when I encountered, for instance, explicit narrations of group sex, detailed sequences of foreplay and anal penetration, orgasm and ejaculation. In the unique audio records that I produced, my own prudery thus filters the sources, as the quality of the recordings (alas, my "notes" on the files) varied in correlation with the explicitness of their content. The performance became, then, an act of inception of a new archival voice—a record of my subjectivity and of my own sense of sexual shame as much as an intermediate step in the standard procedure of transcribing historical files into computer-readable notes. Thus, *turning archival* transforms the historian into a recorded subject by virtue of the multidirectionality that is intrinsic to this process according to Marshall and Tortorici.

The contraposition of visibility and shame has been a driving narrative for the LGBTQ movement since at least the 1960s. However, in this instance, my investment as a historian in giving visibility to the experiences of nonconforming individuals (even though visibility itself is a problematic concept insofar as it entails legibility) led me to realize how shame continues informing my scholarly archival practice. The distance between scholar and "evidence" that informs the "noble dream" of the historian's objectivity—in Peter Novick's famed phrase—vanished in front of my eyes as the inflections of my voice captured my unintended identification with inmates while I performed their responses to psychological tests.[1] In this chapter I discuss how the productive tensions between shame and bodily pleasure, experienced both by me and by the historical actors I researched, translate into historical records and thereby shape their legibility for different audiences. One of my core arguments is that a performative approach to archival repositories shifts meaning-making endeavors into a focus on ambivalent representations of the self that destabilized the mechanisms of state surveillance. In other words, responding to Marshall and Tortorici's formulation of the problematics of "evidence" (considering the long trajectory of deployment of evidence to subjugate and erase queer people), here I pay attention to how reenactment and embodiment can contribute to *turn* evidence against itself.

The records that I analyze originated in multiple locations and times, but all of them stemmed from the interwoven trends of increasing authoritarianism and homophobia that marked the lives of queer people in both Spain and much of Latin America in the second half of the twentieth century. In particular, I look at the Argentine and Spanish state machines of repression. Part of the rationale for this particular focus is that—between the 1950s and 1970s—both societies were deeply impacted by military interventionism and by the positivist criminological school, which established that homosexuality, as any other anti-social behavior, could be measured and prevented before its occurrence (with the particular archival effect of classifying and cataloging *potentialities* as much as realities). In the case of Spain, the fascist regime of Francisco Franco reigned uncontested throughout this period. In Argentina, military and civilian governments succeeded each other, both of which worked to exclude working-class mass movements, eventually giving way to the state terrorism implemented by the Argentine military between the mid-1970s and early 1980s. The sources that I present here—prison and judicial records—suggest that even as political violence was on the rise and positivism led to an intensification of policing, prosecuted individuals performed their gender and sexuality in ways that perplexed authorities.

These sources also have in common the fact that performance is integral to their recording and deciphering. The parallelism between these performances of *sources* and of *gender* calls into question the notion that both "historian" and "archive" are coherent, stable entities whose existence precedes the moment when the former enters the latter. In this line, I draw from Ian Russell's notion of *ekphrasis* as a performance that materializes "the other in the self and the poet in the reader."[2] In the archival experiences I describe, the historical subject is the other that the historian feels materializing in his performance, while trying to share this experience with the reader ("turning outwards as a way of turning in"). This approach would account for historians' common feeling that, in the words of Judith Butler, "the act that one performs is, in a sense, an act that's been going on before one arrived on the scene."[3] As if they were just impersonating the characters of a play that was written in the document before they entered the archive, while at the same time adding their own inflections of voice.

In the following sections, I trace how multiple kinds of documents produce different kinds of performances. First, I delve into a file from the Instituto in which a prisoner from Buenos Aires was reported to be a danger to society on account of her shamelessness, while she claimed to be a "serious marica." In this section, I theorize dissonance and ambivalence as central components of her interview with criminologists. Then, I describe my encounter with psychological tests—also undergone by Argentine prisoners at the Instituto—and the subtle ways in which these prisoners balanced the performance of conformity and the protection of their intimacy. Among other tests, some prisoners had to draw images of themselves and other objects, which I tried to memorize in lieu of taking photographs of them. As I analyze the implications of this methodology, I transition into the records of the Spanish Vagrancy Courts, where the same "social danger" theory implemented in the Argentine Instituto was used to police the effects of gay tourism and modernization in the country. As I situate the photographs and materials confiscated by Spanish police officers in this context, I emphasize the ambiguity of the metaphors that defendants used to *turn* traditional Catholic icons into homoerotic symbols. In the last section, I weave together the materiality and the performance of these different sources to emphasize the limitations of conventional academic languages in capturing both our pleasures as historians/readers and those of historical actors.

Shame and Pleasure in Reading the Instituto's Files

Private, consensual relationships between adult same-sex individuals were not a crime in Argentina, given that legal codes drew from the Napoleonic penal tradition of decriminalization since Argentina's independence from Spain in the nineteenth century. However, the Instituto's criminologists, who examined prisoners and produced reports for authorities' consideration of their probation and parole requests, saw homosexuality as a "criminal-genetic" factor that indicated an increased potential of a prisoner becoming a danger to society. Homosexuality, in criminologists' view, could become "fixated" through noxious influences (and externalized then in gender "inversion," i.e., men's "effeminacy") or sublimated into heterosexuality by conforming to gender norms.

While performing the interviews between inmates and criminologist at the archive, I was particularly drawn to those prisoners who brazenly described their sexual life. Sometimes, as in the case of a prisoner examined in 1940, I perceived a tone at once challenging and coquettish. I must confess that I experienced a guilty, uncanny pleasure in declaiming some of the prisoners' responses. While meaning-making was my primary endeavor in reading these sources, the pleasure that I found in reciting them emanated from something more elusive than that.[4] As poet John Ashbery once put it:

> The pleasure one gets from reading poetry comes from something else than the idea or story in a poem, which is just a kind of armature for the poet to drape with many-colored rags. These are what one really enjoys but can't admit it, since there is this underlying urge to analyze and make sense of everything. But what is "making sense," anyway?[5]

Brian Glavey has connected Ashbery's poetry with queer performativity in ways that shed light over the pleasure that I myself experienced while reading the file.[6] Reading the criminological files in front of other people made my sense of shame more acute, but it was also emboldening. Like the child who covers his face but peeks through his fingers, while I performed the voice of the inmate my shame was channeled into the production of queerness through the rerecording of the inmate's words in my own voice. I derived a particular kind of pleasure when performing a self-assured sexuality that I felt I lacked. In this sense, not only meaning-making, but also the pleasures of inverse identification, drove my engagement with the sources, as I found an opportunity to declaim responses to authoritarian figures beyond my own perceived capacity for open rebellion. As Roland Barthes suggests, when a text "manages to make itself heard indirectly," leading the reader "to listen to something else," then the reader experiences the most intense pleasure.[7] When reading archival sources, the something else that resonated the most in me was shame, both in its excess and in its lack. I felt the most sympathy for either those individuals who were overwhelmed by shame or for those who expressed their unwillingness to perform being ashamed, even though that was their interlocutors' expectation. Thus not only meaning-making, but also the dynamics of (inverse) identification, drove my historical research.

For instance, when I read a transcript of a 1940 interview between a prisoner and a criminologist, I was particularly drawn to the prisoner referring to her meeting men in public spaces and sleeping with them as "going out to pray."[8] This metaphor suggests an enthralling parallelism between eroticism and ecstatic religions, which share, as Kate Chedgzoy argues, "a flickering of subjectivity," namely, "the sublime dialectic in which the self flickers between affirmation and dissolution."[9] Moreover, the use of religious metaphors to convey the sublime pleasures of public sex called my attention because of my own associations between Catholic upbringing and internalized shame. Reading the responses of someone who subverted this association by parodying the sacredness of sex made me want to know more about how she came to articulate her views.

The sex of the prisoner who uttered the phrase was classified as male at birth and she was aware of this when interacting with state agents. She told the criminologist that from the age of eight she had learned to use makeup and clothing to interact with potential sexual partners. According to the report, homosexual intercourse cemented the prisoner's feminine psyche; since her sexual encounters with a classmate, her life "continued at an identical pace, [she] was a woman, felt like a woman, and acted as such."[10] While she had tried to work with her father in the countryside, she soon realized that she was not made for that life: "I had the same needs as any other woman does, and you can't do anything in the countryside because people talk . . . I am a serious *marica*, and it disgusts me when people point their fingers at me. Therefore, I decided to come to Buenos Aires, where I could get what I sought without calling anyone's attention."[11] In contrast to the criminologist's insistence that a "depraved" environment had induced the prisoner into "perversion," she expressed a yearning to fulfill her sexual needs in the capital without being subjected to public scrutiny. The prisoner shocked the criminologist by subverting the relationship that he had expected to establish, where the prisoner submissively becomes the *object* of study. Instead, according to his report, the criminologist found himself the *object* of the prisoner's sexual attentions, as she coquettishly wiggled her hips when walking and blushed when crossing looks with the criminologist. The prisoner confessed her sexuality "brazenly and with pride," defying the criminologist's expectation that she would show herself to be ashamed or apologetic.[12] As María Elena Martínez demonstrates in her chapter of this volume, official documents can allow us to *turn* a medical expert "into the object of the gaze" when we subvert his "claim to enlightened reason and objectivity, and his presence in the archive as the normal, ideal, and unmarked body" by paying attention to his anxieties when confronted with an assertive sexual *Other*. In their chapter of this volume, Emmett Harsin Drager also approaches medical files "with an intention of inverting, subverting, and returning the gaze upon the gender clinic doctors and psychiatrists." Together, our works suggest that the queer epistemological *return* to medical files aims at inverting the directionality of the empiricist gaze by examining the examiner's subjectivity.

While I read the responses of someone who was described as shameless, I noticed that the sentence "I am a serious *marica*" (in Spanish, "soy una marica seria") was a purposeful statement that condensed the prisoner's grounding of her sense of self-worth on certain norms of behavior. The prisoner did not see her actions as less decent or "serious" than those of any other woman because she followed strict rules of gender complementarity that defined masculinity as penetrating/genital and femininity as receptive/nongenital. She clarified that she would get an erection and ejaculate while being penetrated by another man. However, she would never allow her sexual partners to touch her genitals because a man drawn to male genitalia "is not a man."[13] The prisoner acknowledged that these were flexible rules. For instance, while she emphasized that she had never engaged in transactional sex, she admitted that once she aged, she might be willing to pay for sex.

After the interview, the criminologist wrote a very negative report on the prisoner, so she had to serve her full sentence of three years for theft. In fact, the last traces of her in the file refer to her behavior while in prison between 1939 and 1941, including one sanction for hiding a love letter and another one for possessing soap (which prison officers assumed she had obtained as a present from another prisoner, "given [her] condition of passive pederast").[14] Absent in the file is any information about her life after leaving prison and—equally important—any photograph of her that would allow us to imagine how she used the "technologies of the body" of *maricas*—makeup, clothing, and demeanor—to entice men and express her femininity.[15] We are only left with a few sentences on a piece of paper, but in reading these we encounter different intonations and meanings. If we assume that meaning-making requires imposing a self-evident coherence on the sources, then the prisoner statements about her subjectivity—describing at the same time her playful sexuality and her seriousness—present a challenge. Alternatively, we can let ourselves be taken by the performance of dissonant voices so that we can better appreciate ambivalence in the face of surveillance. Even psychological tests—which in Argentine prisons were meant to surveil the most hidden facets of the soul—became an opportunity for performing ambiguity.

Performing Psychological Tests

When I read Argentine inmates' performances on a battery of psychological projective tests, I had an acute feeling that there were different voices in the same text, each overpowering the other at different moments. This was a double performance, or a performance of a performance, as I re-created in my own voice the actions that inmates were forced to undertake—reading the beginning of a sentence and then completing it with their own words with the aim of revealing their deepest thoughts and feelings. Reading these tests out loud highlighted the difference between the typed words (part of the standardized test) and inmates' responses, which varied greatly from person to person. These responses reveal inmates' balancing acts between criminologists' expectations and their own desires to be released from prison. That was the case in the file of one individual imprisoned sometime between the late 1960s and early 1970s in Buenos Aires. He came from a poor family and spent his childhood and adolescence in a boarding school where, according to an acquaintance, he was forced into homosexual relationships for the first time.[16]

Although the inmate only admitted to heterosexual relationships, the criminologist examining him trusted instead his own impressions of the prisoner's gender performance. Below the prisoner's typed statement, the criminologist handwrote and underlined "*[he] is a homosexual*" ("*es homosexual*"), so the *formality* of the interview was contraposed to and undermined by the *informality* of gendered body readings. In this instance, the contraposition between typed and handwritten words became a testament to experts' reliance on their own subjective reading of inmates' personae to establish their "dangerousness."[17] My voice could not capture my reaction to this document. As I glided through thousands of pages of files and stumbled upon this brief sentence at the bottom of a page, I made a note to myself below my recording to highlight the stark contraposition between the inmate's responses and the criminologist's reading of him. I was producing a new set of correlations and dichotomies between different means of communication and formats. Voice recordings had to be limited to what the documents said word for word (its textual elements), while my written notes' role was to assist my own flawed memory in reproducing an image in my mind of what each document looked like (its visual elements). Strangely enough, this inverted the assumed correlation between written sources and factuality, on the one hand, and oral sources and subjectivity, on the other. In this case, my voice was to remain closer to the original source and my written notes to my own impressions, which has unexpected implications that I explore in more detail next.

Despite the informality of the criminologist's reading of the inmate's sexuality, this factor became central in the evaluation of his social dangerousness. Hence, the prisoner's acquaintances also focused on his sexualized femininity. A former employer claimed that the prisoner once visited him "wearing makeup and very tight clothes." The prisoner's body-conscious fashion and "effeminate speech" did not prevent some neighbors from caring for his well-being and supporting him. However, another former employer focused on the prisoner's eccentric spirituality, describing how when he was younger he had built in his room a "grotto where he placed many religious images." This inmate had built a space, *both* physical and metaphorical, to cultivate an autonomous spirituality that did not require institutional approval. According to the same employer, beyond his spirituality the prisoner also exhibited the "rebellion towards normal people" that characterized youth cultures in the late 1960s.[18]

The prisoner's performance on psychological tests also suggests that he had developed a strong sense of independence from society. As mentioned before, one of the projective tests consisted of asking inmates to complete short sentences. Performing the inmate's responses to this test provoked conflicted reactions in me. First of all, I felt an uncanny parallelism between the context in which this source was produced and my own performance of its content. With the test at the table in front of me, I was reading it sequentially, each prompt followed by the inmate's response, but with a brief stop to say the word *respuesta* (answer) in between each to mark beginning and end. Although this performance was meant to re-create as closely as possible the original source—since the test was written down in poetry-like stanzas—it also mimicked a particular dynamic of the test, in which the subject takes a couple of seconds to come up with a reflex response that logically completes the sentence. As a result of me trying to reproduce the inmate's test performance in an audio format, every time I relistened to the audio file, it felt as if I were listening to a recording of my own replies. This inadvertently led me to identify with the inmate's words as they were pronounced and enunciated in my own voice. At the same time, I was trying to apply an analytical lens to understand how the inmate's responses might reveal his strategies for negotiating criminologists' expectations of social conformity with his own longing for privacy. In this line, for instance, there are responses that pinpoint the prisoner's *apparent* conformity:

I need . . . some help;

Marriage . . . is the most important and sacred thing;

My only concern . . . is coming back to society;

Most girls . . . are cute.[19]

In other answers, the prisoner showed himself unwilling to share his intimacy:

The best thing . . . I never say;

What hurts me . . . I don't show;

In secret . . . nothing.[20]

Lo mejor . . . nunca lo digo

Lo que me duele . . . no lo demuestro

En secreto . . . nada

Other answers suggest a self-asserted attitude:

My mind . . . works well;

I want to . . . be happy in life.[21]

Mi cabeza . . . anda bien

Deseo . . . ser feliz en la vida.

And most of the answers expressed the prisoner's longing for privacy:

When I come back home . . .

I want to be at peace;

What bothers me . . . is company;

People . . . talk too much.[22]

Al regresar a mi casa . . .

quiero estar tranquilo

Lo que me molesta . . . la compañía

La gente . . . habla mucho.

As a historian, I have been trained to read sources so that they "make sense" as part of an overarching historical narrative of change over time. However, as I re-read my interpretation of this text, I wonder whether in that pursuit of meaning I was driven by a desire to amplify that "something else" which Barthes heard in the texts. As Ramos puts it in his chapter, "subjects who must improvise ways of surviving in turn invite us to improvise ways to look and understand their experiences," in this case by listening to the different, dissonant voices from this inmate. Among these, the voice that resonated the most in me as I performed the test was that of the inmate expressing his desire to be left alone. I stand by my interpretation that this desire came across in his responses. Moreover, none of these responses really amounted to the inmate stating his intention to mend his ways by adopting a heterosexual behavior. For instance, to say that "most girls . . . are cute" ("la mayor parte de las chicas . . . son lindas") does not mean that one wants to have sex exclusively with women. If anything, he uttered *ambivalent* phrases that were open to multiple interpretations. Similar to Juana Aguilar's archival presence as Tortorici describes it in his chapter; as this inmate repeatedly turned away from his examiners he became "suspended in a constant state of turning archival," simultaneously constituted and unfixed as an archival subject.

The inmate's performance worked toward its goal of leading to a positive report. The psychologist administering these tests concluded that the prisoner was willing to repress his instincts in order to be socially adjusted.[23] Since criminologists judged the prisoner's homosexuality as playing a significant role in his criminality, and the prisoner had convinced them that he intended to inhibit himself sexually, he was classified as "adjustable" ("adaptable") and posing a "medium social danger."[24] Still, the prisoner was not released, probably because he had homosexual relationships and challenged officers while in prison. In this case, the inmate's performance on psychological tests gave way to the production of texts which communicated a persuasive message to the examiners. However, in other cases, inmates draw images instead as part of their psychological tests. These images represent particular challenges to researchers who have to paint different layers of visual meaning with their voice, while trying to capture the image in their mind for future reference.

One inmate's drawing of himself immediately captured my attention for several reasons—though given the Instituto's restrictions, it cannot be reproduced here or properly conveyed. First of all, it came off to me as less mediated by criminologists than other sources. This was not a transcript of the inmate's words, but rather a trace of his own pencil on the page (or pen, I can't remember). Yet the fact that he had produced this drawing for the psychologists examining him illustrates how power shapes the minds and bodies of surveilled subjects, as the latter try to infer what do "experts" expect. In Argentina by the mid-1960s, criminologists were assessing the dangerousness of young inmates by focusing on whether they were willing to leave behind immediate gratifications (including transactional sex with other men) in exchange for uncertain prospects of upward social mobility. The intertwined ideals of middle-class consumerism and heterosexual familism informing the government's rhetoric shaped criminologists' scrutiny of disgruntled youngsters. Hence, conventional business attire became this prisoner's way of communicating his willingness to sacrifice the rewards of transactional sex. In 1964, an Instituto psychologist argued that the prisoner had learned how to use his genitals as a kind of "Aladdin's Lamp," which allowed him to instantly get anything he wanted—referring to the prisoner's previous involvement in transactional sex by performing the "active" (penetrating) role with men whom he met in cinemas or in the street.[25] The prisoner was diagnosed as suffering from psychopathy on account of his "hedonistic" and "over-excitable" sexuality, among other factors, but the psychologist noted that he had been attracted to a "cultured" male partner who treated him tenderly.[26] In addition, when asked to draw himself, the prisoner portrayed his ideal self as wearing the business attire of a middle-class professional, wearing a tie and a hat, and carrying a suitcase.

The trace of the inmate's pencil is as much a direct result of his bodily actions as a drawing of his mental mapping of social conformity. The image that I analyze when I write about this file is not the drawing itself, but rather my own mental image of it, described in a few words by me (and for me). In this solipsistic process, there is no escaping the realization that the mental images we manage as historians are filtered by our own sociocultural background. From what I remember, the drawing itself was a simple portrayal of a male body with very few attributes, and this simplicity highlighted the importance of the outfit. All the elements of this outfit came together to represent a middle-class professional in my mental image of the drawing, as much if not more than in the page itself. I gave the last touches to this image so that it made sense in relationship with my own knowledge of the period and experiences with fashion codes. By the same token, I analyzed the relationship between the drawing and the prognosis issued by the criminologists being aware that the outcome of the examination had benefited the inmate. The Instituto recommended the inmate's release, considering—among other factors—that the prisoner's aspirations of upward social mobility and appreciation of culture diminished the threats posed by his sexuality.[27] This was not the only time that I had to rely on my memory to analyze images. Indeed, while I conducted research in the Spanish archives that hold the records of individuals accused of homosexuality and tried in the vagrancy courts, this became a common occurrence, with multiple implications for my approach to the relationship between eroticism and power dynamics.

Visual Performances and "Exotic Lubrications" in Spain

In the summer of 2016, I encountered a file, dated in 1963 at the Juzgado Especial de Vagos y Maleantes of Málaga (Special Court of the Idle and Miscreants, or the Vagrancy Court), which was unusually voluminous compared to others I had examined in both Spain and Argentina. Upon further inspection I found that the folder, along with the typical judicial documents, included photographs of black men and a white man having sex. The photos, taken by an amateur, had at some point in time been torn into pieces, and then at another point in time, like a jigsaw puzzle, someone had skillfully reassembled and taped the pieces back together.[28] Reading the file, I discovered that the photographs had been painstakingly reconstructed by, or under the supervision of, police officers. Since I was consulting the file among other historians—most of whom were working on notary records from the early modern period—I felt once again the acute effects of shame on my dealing with the sources, as I looked around while I turned each photograph to make sure that no one noticed the materials that I had in my hands. In consultation with the archivists, it was decided that I would not request photocopies of these images. Therefore, I once again had to draw mental images of these photographs by describing them in a few words that would later allow me to bring these images to life. This was a perturbing experience which entailed fixing in my mind scenes that I interpreted as taking place in a violent colonial context.

These photos had been kept by a British subject who had been deployed in Africa (most likely Nigeria, where he returned after being expelled from Spain). At some indefinite moment after Nigeria gained its independence from the United Kingdom in 1960, he had moved to Spain. There, he established a relationship with a Moroccan subject. Given that Spain colonially occupied part of Morocco until 1958 (under the guise of a protectorate), this subject's status is inscribed in the postcolonial relationship between Spain and Morocco. The Moroccan's vulnerability to arbitrary policing became evident in December 1963, when he was arrested on a train and his suitcase was confiscated. In his suitcase, police officers found an English gay porn magazine and the amateur erotic photographs. He was arrested and charged with homosexuality. When he was placed in a cell, he took the opportunity to rip up the photographs and tear them into pieces. Eventually, however, police officers uncovered his attempt to destroy evidence, and subsequently reassembled them. One can imagine them holding up, examining, and trying to fit each minute photographic trace back together into a coherent image. The reassembled images were of black men exhibiting their genitals to the camera, performing oral sex on each other, and penetrating a middle-aged white man whose face is out of frame.[29] By synecdochally foregrounding the black subjects' genitals, these photographs erased their individuality and objectified their bodies in an almost ethnopornographic vein.[30] Spanish state agents, for their part, not only censored and eradicated pornography or prevented its circulation, but also in some instances reconstructed it—thereby producing it, both materially and discursively—in order to trace the effects of gay tourism in the country and in order to seek out and punish homosexuality in its myriad instantiations. This case shows that in order to fully understand the power dynamics inscribed in the archive, historians must "reembrace a materialism that had been abandoned under poststructuralism," as Kate Eichhorn indicates in her chapter in this volume.

The context for this case was one of contradictions between the Franco regime's rhetoric and policies. In 1939, General Francisco Franco—leading a multifarious coalition of conservative and fascist forces—had defeated the middle-class progressives and socialist, communist, and anarchist workers who supported the Spanish Second Republic. Franco's victory gave way to a systematic campaign of extermination of political opponents, through summary executions and labor camps. In the aftermath of the war, the international community censured the Franco regime and the population suffered from conditions of political repression and food shortages.[31] By the mid-1950s, Francoist policies of economic autarchy had proven to be a failure. At the same time, the United States and its Cold War allies demonstrated interest in Spain's strategic position as the gateway to the Mediterranean. Hence, liberal democracies suspended their condemnation of Franco's fascist ideology and offered his regime a path of "normalization" through a military alliance that opened Spain to international investment and tourism.[32] Through a series of legal reforms, the Franco regime rebuilt its institutional framework in the mid- to late 1950s, which in the 1960s allowed it to consolidate a model of economic development based on mass tourism, cheap labor, and state propaganda and repression to contain workers' discontent.[33] A double moral standard was at the root of this economic model: international tourists would be allowed greater sexual freedoms than Spanish citizens, all the while Catholicism remained the state's official religion and the Catholic clergy maintained its monopoly over education, censorship, and public morality.[34] In this context, the regime revised the Vagrancy Law in 1954 to codify homosexuality as a danger to society, asserting its authority and capacity to reconcile the agendas of socioeconomic modernization and Catholic-nationalist indoctrination. Homosexual individuals were to be interned in "special institutions" (most often prisons), displaced from their hometowns, and surveilled.[35] Under a political system that enshrined masculinity as a nationalistic duty, the Vagrancy Law became an instrument for enforcing gender and sexual normativity among the disenfranchised poor.

This ideological milieu informed queer people's experiences, as well as the debris, traces, and remains left in the archives. The very archival classification of these files within the legal framework of vagrancy ("Vagos y Maleantes," in the language of archival classification and categories) points to the state's focus on the sexuality of "nonproductive" social sectors, namely, domestic migrants who had been excluded from the expansion of the formal economy. However, state policies are inscribed in historical records in a distorted way. While police officers could be bribed or instructed to not harass affluent tourists, they did not leave written evidence of this practice.[36] Instead, they occasionally arrested some tourists whose violations were particularly visible to maintain the façade of law enforcement. The following 1960 report by the Torremolinos police department (shown in Figure 5.1) shows their *stated*, more than practical, commitment to prevent the spread of gay tourism:

> Torremolinos has an acquired fame, not just within the country but also abroad, due not only to its fantastic geographic location and benevolent climate, but also due to the creation of an environment of libertinage, vice, corruption and immorality... Foreigners—sexual inverts—have been identified who had chosen young men as the object of their preference, inducing them into *exotic lubrications* ["lubricaciones exóticas," a euphemism for homosexual behavior, italics added]. These recurring events and the contact between local people and foreigners have produced a psychological phenomenon: specifically, the vanishing of the sense of morality.[37]

Exotic lubrications communicated the idea that foreign currency was a powerful social lubricant, one that would make young men convivial and lower their defenses against the penetration of international visitors' "depraved" morality, emasculating Spanish young men. The language used in this report, including the verb "inducing" and the adjective "exotic," explicitly situates homosexuality as a "foreign" influence, alien to Spanish customs. Yet the report also reveals officers' limited trust in the capacity of Spanish young men to resist the temptations of transactional sex with other (foreign) men. While this report was a significant piece of nationalistic rhetoric through performative moral panic, it did not prevent police officers from looking the other way when it was convenient for the local and national economies. Such tacit tolerance directly influenced the contours of the archives in the present, insofar as young Spanish men who engaged in transactional sex with foreign tourists are overrepresented in the judicial records in comparison with their clients. Moreover, those carrying out the law excluded foreign nationals sentenced as dangers to society from some security measures (internment in a prison or work camp, and surveillance) that were standard for Spanish citizens, forcing them instead to leave Spain, a comparatively bearable penalty.

The class discrimination at the core of the Franco regime also became evident in the differential treatments of Spanish nationals of different socioeconomic

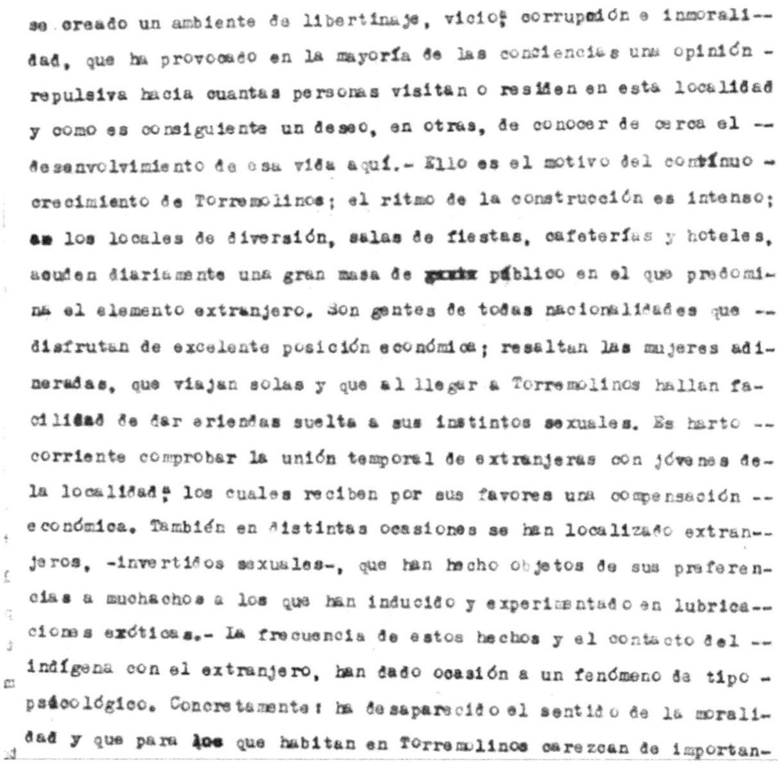

se creado un ambiente de libertinaje, vicio, corrupción e inmorali--
dad, que ha provocado en la mayoría de las conciencias una opinión -
repulsiva hacia cuantas personas visitan o residen en esta localidad
y como es consiguiente un deseo, en otras, de conocer de cerca el --
desenvolvimiento de esa vida aquí.- Ello es el motivo del contínuo -
crecimiento de Torremolinos; el ritmo de la construcción es intenso;
a los locales de diversión, salas de fiestas, cafeterías y hoteles,
acuden diariamente una gran masa de públio en el que predomi-
na el elemento extranjero. Son gentes de todas nacionalidades que --
disfrutan de excelente posición económica; resaltan las mujeres adi-
neradas, que viajan solas y que al llegar a Torremolinos hallan fa-
cilidad de dar rienda suelta a sus instintos sexuales. Es harto --
corriente comprobar la unión temporal de extranjeras con jóvenes de-
la localidad, los cuales reciben por sus favores una compensación --
económica. También en distintas ocasiones se han localizado extran--
jeros, -invertidos sexuales-, que han hecho objetos de sus preferen-
cias a muchachos a los que han inducido y experimentado en lubrica--
ciones exóticas.- La frecuencia de estos hechos y el contacto del --
indígena con el extranjero, han dado ocasión a un fenómeno de tipo -
psícológico. Concretamente: ha desaparecido el sentido de la morali-
dad y que para los que habitan en Torremolinos carezcan de importan-

FIGURE 5.1. Police report on Torremolinos issued in 1960, included in File 10/1960, Juzgado Especial de Vagos y Maleantes de Málaga (AHPSE).

background. For instance, in the case of a love affair between a factory owner and a younger mechanic, the former was allowed to return to his hometown after serving his prison sentence so that he could take care of his business, while the latter was forced to leave the city.[38] During the trial, the mechanic had handed over to the police a series of intimate materials, including photographs, letters, and even a holy card, which usually depicts a saint and a popular prayer. The photographs that I discuss henceforth are preserved in the judicial archives of Barcelona. And while I was eventually allowed to take photographs of many of these images for my own reference, for the sake of protecting defendants' privacy I do not reproduce here any photographs of them. These memora-bilia show how these two individuals had used the ambivalent language of "friendship" to code their relationship. Two years prior, the factory owner had conveyed in a letter to his lover how precious their intimacy was for him: "I can't get you out of my imagination for an instant . . . You are my only friend. I should rather say [that I feel] closer to you than to my own brothers, since I can share any concern with you."[39] The concept of friendship veiledly referred in this letter to the "queer" kinship that they had built together. Their photographs also capture their kinship practices; they pose with the family of the mechanic, sitting together informally, standing in formal wear at a lookout over the city, and holding arms as they stroll in a park.

These sources betray how archival voyeurism often informs our approaches to the lived experiences of queer people. State agents engaged with sexual subcultures by trying to establish their scope and cyphered meanings, but also betraying voyeurism as a guiding principle in the state policing of homosexuality. As Zeb Tortorici emphasizes, archival voyeurism is a virtually inescapable component of historical inquiry into non-normative sexual desires.[40] The most illuminating sources are often those that capture authorities' violent intrusion into the intimate aspects of such individuals' relationality. As state agents tried to erase homoerotic representations from the public sphere, they paradoxically inscribed them into state records (and the archives) where they were supposed to preserve the stigmatization of homosexual subjects. However, as Elliot James suggests in their chapter, part of the connecting tissue of this volume is the collective aim to *turn* "both toward and away from government archives," reading official sources in a way that confronts the epistemological violence of their own creation.

In this line, deciphering these sources requires a contextual awareness of the ways in which such individuals kept sight of and navigated different mechanisms of control. As the Spanish homosexual author Juan Gil Albert put it in 1955, "Speaking in a low voice is still speaking, but only to those who have an alert ear."[41] Accessing the voices of queer desires entails deciphering the veiled homoerotic and affectionate messages found in personal materials. For example, one undated photograph dedicated by the factory owner in English illustrates the strategies of silence and double meaning that informed these relationships. He initially wrote "to my good friend, for always you [*sic*] [the author's nickname]."[42] He probably meant "always yours" but being aware that this romantic formula revealed too much, he crossed out his nickname and wrote "friends" on top of it, so it reads "for always friends."[43] This performance of friendship preserved in its archival sediment a semiexplicit statement of forbidden affection, of the author surrendering himself to another man.

Similarly, by *turning around* a holy card, the factory owner challenged the Catholic doctrine on the guilty and depraved nature of same-sex desires. The mechanic kept a holy card depicting Saint Roque with a printed prayer, as shown

FIGURES 5.2 AND
5.3. Holy card in-
cluded in File 454/1959,
Juzgado Especial de
Vagos y Maleantes
de Barcelona, Arxiu
Central dels Jutjats de
la Ciutat de la Justícia.
Photographs taken by
the author in February
2018.

98 —Curad, gran San Roque, las llagas
que en el alma produce el pecado.

in Figure 5.2: "Heal, great Saint Roque, the wounds that sin leaves in the soul."[44] This prayer encapsulates the Catholic doctrine that believers ought to atone in front of the saints to redeem themselves from the intrinsic sinfulness of the flesh. However, on the back of this card, shown in Figure 5.3, the factory owner wrote in Spanish: "Let's try healing our sins with the best medicine, which is love. That is the only way we make God happy: loving each other truly. The Almighty helps us to reach what we desire, *always* [in English in the original]."[45] In this way, he articulated the view that same-sex love, and not atonement and guilt, redeemed homosexual lovers from their sins so that they can invoke the "Almighty" to fulfil their desires. While the front of this card echoes the Catholic condemnation of the flesh, by flipping it we encounter a vindication of

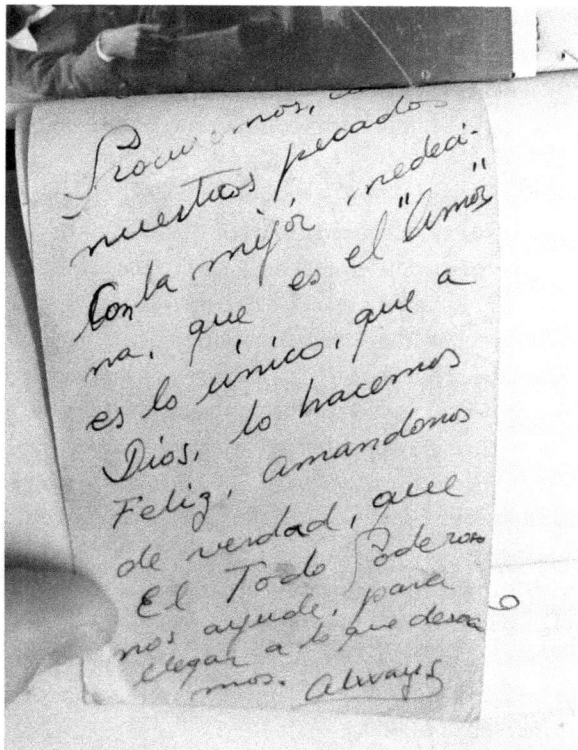

homosexual love as a sacrament. *Turning* here becomes a metaphor for the operationalizing of Catholic ideologies to maintain the view that same-sex desires are transcendental.

Archival Twists and Turns

"But what is 'making sense,' anyway?"—Ashbery interpellates us, questioning the routinization of this endeavor in the shape of academic disciplinary methods, and calling attention to the "many-colored rags" that incite us to read and perform (historical) texts. In the previous pages, I have looked closely at the textures and shades of color of these rags: at the different inflections of meaning in the adjective "serious" when used by an Argentine prisoner in 1940 to describe herself in dissonant ways (for instance, as unattracted to transactional sex but willing to engage in it later in life); at the ambivalence of another Argentine prisoner's responses to psychological tests, as he uttered sentences that hid more of his intimacy than they exposed; at the paste tape that revealed police officers' intervention in creating images of interracial sex; at my own mental re-creations of a prisoner's pencil's traces on the page; and at the experience of turning traditional Catholic holy cards to find cyphered homoerotic messages.

The conditions of access and reproducibility set by different archives shape the relationship between the historian and the materiality of the sources. In the case of the Instituto, performing the transcripts of interviews and tests contributed to highlight for me the different intonations that the declamation of prisoners' responses required, depending on how they navigated criminologists' expectations. The pleasure that I experienced in performing these responses stemmed from impersonating prisoners' ways of playing with ambiguity, flirting with criminologists, and reclaiming their privacy. Contrary to my own expectation that prisoners would do anything necessary to perform conformity, their responses were not univocal but rather complexly ambivalent. I hardly could surrender control by letting myself be taken by the performance (as Santiago Joaquín Insausti shared with me he did), but instead I experienced full-fledged the tension between shame and desire that informs the historical experiences that I study. One of my mentors told me once that my work deals with the space between *guilt* and *desire*, as well as with the intense pleasures that take place in that space but escape verbalization.[46]

That pleasure is a driving force of my scholarship—and, I would argue, of much historical research—as is the guilt that I feel for using sources that are the direct result of state violence does not extinguish my desire to access the stories that they contain. Moreover, as the multiple examples in this chapter show, the engagement with the archive entails not just a transcription of sources for their subsequent study, but a re-creation of them in which the historian becomes an archival agent, along the lines of Marshall and Tortorici's suggestion that the view of archives as agentic is particularly relevant in the case of queer archives. For instance, in my recollecting the images from the Instituto and the Vagrancy Court of Sevilla which I could not take photographs of, I was fixing my first impressions of them, as well as the violent contexts in which they were taken. The sense of distance with the sources was difficult to maintain in these circumstances. However, by relying on my memory and my voice for the (re-)creation of these sources, I became more aware of their unsettledness; of the ways in which conventional language fails to convey the pleasures between guilt and desire and—therefore—of the centrality of ambivalent metaphors to express them. Both in the case of the Argentine prisoner who went out "to pray" in Buenos Aires in the late 1930s, and in the case of the two Spanish lovers who exchanged holy cards in the 1950s, Catholic sacraments provided the most powerful metaphor to convey those pleasures. Not in vain, the communion with the sublime has traditionally been conceived as an inerrable experience. *Turning archival* entails then to go beyond conventional academic languages to relate meaning-making with the materiality and the performance of the sources—not as opposite to each other, but as mutually interdependent—so that we can fully feel the connections between the desires of historical actors and ours.

Notes

My work is part of the research groups "Memorias de las masculinidades disidentes en España e Hispanoamérica" (PID2019-106083GB-100); "La clínica de la subjetividad: Historia, teoría y práctica de la psicopatología estructural" (PID2020-113356GB-100); and "El problema de la alteridad en el mundo actual" (HUM536). I want to acknowledge the Museo Penitenciario Argentino Antonio Ballvé, the Archivo Historico Provincial de Sevilla, and the Arxiu Central dels Jutjats de la Ciutat de la Justícia for their assistance in accessing the sources incorporated in this chapter. Finally, I want to thank the editors of the volume, Daniel Marshall and Zeb Tortorici, and my colleague Santiago Joaquín Insausti, for their valuable comments.

1   Novick, *That Noble Dream.*
2   Russell, "Temporalities of Desire," 91.
3   Butler, "Performative Acts," 526.
4   Lehman, "The Pleasures of Poetry."
5   Ashbery, cited in Lehman, "The Pleasures of Poetry."
6   Glavey, *The Wallflower Avant-Garde,* 132.
7   Barthes, *The Pleasure of the Text,* 24.
8   "Antecedentes individuales," File 2531, Instituto de Clasificación, Museo Penitenciario Argentino Antonio Ballvé, Buenos Aires, Argentina (MPAAB). Since the prisoner commonly identified herself as female in the transcripts of her interview, I will use the pronouns she/her/hers.
9   Chedgzoy, "Region, Religion and Sexuality," 53.
10 "Antecedentes individuales."
11 "Antecedentes individuales."
12 "Pronostico social provisorio," File 2531.
13 "Pronostico social provisorio," File 2531.
14 Prison Report issued on March 11, 1940, File 2531.
15 I borrow this concept from Guerrero, *Tecnologías del cuerpo.*
16 "Relaciones sociales"; "Información social," File 48836, MPAAB.
17 "Vida sexual," File 48836.
18 "Información Social."
19 Test administered by the Applied Psychology Department, File 48836.
20 Applied Psychology Department, File 48836.
21 Applied Psychology Department, File 48836.

22 Applied Psychology Department, File 48836.

23 Report by the Applied Psychology Department, File 48836.

24 "Síntesis diagnostica," File 48836.

25 Report on the psychological exam signed on February 18, 1964, File 39023, MPAAB.

26 Report on the psychological exam signed on February 18, 1964, File 39023, MPAAB.

27 Report by the Classification Institute in February 1964, File 39023.

28 File 93/1963, Box 8935, Juzgado Especial de Vagos y Maleantes de Málaga, Archivo Histórico Provincial de Sevilla, Sevilla, Spain (AHPS).

29 File 93/1963.

30 Sigal, Tortorici, and Whitehead, *Ethnopornography*.

31 Radcliff, *Modern Spain*, 214–18.

32 Casanova and Gil Andrés, *Twentieth-Century Spain*, 250–52.

33 Casanova and Gil Andrés, *Twentieth-Century Spain*, 256–62.

34 Casanova and Gil Andrés, *Twentieth-Century Spain*, 239–43.

35 "LEY DE 15 DE JULIO DE 1954 por la que se modifican los artículos 2° y 6° de la Ley de Vagos y Maleantes, de 4 de agosto de 1933," *Boletín Oficial del Estado*, July 17, 1954, 4862.

36 Fernández Rodríguez, email message.

37 "Informative note" submitted by the police department, n.d., File 10/1960, Box 8937, Juzgado Especial de Vagos y Maleantes de Málaga, AHPSE.

38 Sentence issued on December 4, 1959, File 447/1959, Juzgado Especial de Vagos y Maleantes de Barcelona, Arxiu Central dels Jutjats de la Ciutat de la Justícia, Hospitalet de Llobregat, Spain (ACCJB); Sentence issued on December 27, 1959, File 454/1959, ACCJB.

39 Letter signed on May 10, 1957, File 454/1959.

40 Tortorici, *Sins against Nature*, 3.

41 Gil Albert, *Heracles*, 11.

42 Photograph number 1, File 454/1959.

43 Photograph number 1, File 454/1959.

44 Document number 3, File 454/1959.

45 Document number 3, File 454/1959.

46 In this line, this chapter builds on Daniel Marshall's recognition in his chapter here in *Turning Archival* that "reflections on the private pleasures of the self so often turn to explorations of the public pleasures of the archive."

Works Cited

Barthes, Roland. *The Pleasure of the Text*. New York: Hill and Wang, 1998.

Butler, Judith. "Performative Acts and Gender Constitution: An Essay in Phenomenology and Feminist Theory." *Theatre Journal* 40, no. 4 (1988): 519–31.

Casanova, Julián, and Carlos Gil Andrés. *Twentieth-Century Spain: A History*. Cambridge: Cambridge University Press, 2014.

Chedgzoy, Kate. "Region, Religion and Sexuality: Pilgrim through this Barren Land." In *De-Centering Sexualities: Politics and Representations Beyond the Metropolis*, edited by Richard Phillips, David Shuttleton, and Diane Watt, 47–62. London: Routledge, 1999.

Fernández Rodríguez, Serafín. Email message to the author. June 29, 2015.

Gil Albert, Juan. *Heracles: sobre una manera de ser.* Madrid: Josefina Betancor, 1975.

Glavey, Brian. *The Wallflower Avant-Garde: Modernism, Sexuality, and Queer Ekphrasis.* New York: Oxford University Press, 2015.

Guerrero, Javier. *Tecnologías del cuerpo: exhibicionismo y visualidad en América Latina.* Madrid: Iberoamericana, 2014.

Lehman, David. "The Pleasures of Poetry." *New York Times,* December 16, 1984.

Novick, Peter. *That Noble Dream: The "Objectivity Question" and the American Historical Profession.* Cambridge: Cambridge University Press, 1988.

Radcliff, Pamela Beth. *Modern Spain: 1808 to the Present.* Hoboken, NJ: John Wiley & Sons, 2017.

Russell, Ian Matthew. "Temporalities of Desire: Queer Relations across the Spanish Atlantic." PhD diss., Brown University, 2019.

Sigal, Pete, Zeb Tortorici, and Neil L. Whitehead, eds. *Ethnopornography: Sexuality, Colonialism, and Archival Knowledge.* Durham, NC: Duke University Press, 2020.

Tortorici, Zeb. *Sins against Nature: Sex and Archives in Colonial New Spain.* Durham, NC: Duke University Press, 2018.

6. LOOKING AFTER MRS. G

Approaches and Methods for Reading Transsexual Clinical Case Files

EMMETT HARSIN DRAGER

What would convince a biologically normal woman that she had a penis? How does one go about finding out? How reliable is the information one collects?—DR. ROBERT J. STOLLER, *Splitting*

Looking for Trans History

I came across Mrs. G's file in September 2016 in the Robert J. Stoller Papers at UCLA Special Collections.[1] I was in the archive because, after my own encounter with the web of private surgeons and complicated insurance classifications that make up the trans medical complex, I wanted to understand more about the history of trans therapeutics in the United States. As a trans studies scholar,[2] my archival and historical research is always entangled with questions about the possibilities and limits of searching for trans in the past. "Trans" holds a variety of meanings. It is an identity, a descriptor of certain kinds of bodies, an umbrella term for gender variance, an analytic, and a movement of crossing. Because of the relatively recent emergence of "transgender" in the early 1990s and "transsexual" only a few decades before that, the project of looking for trans in the past requires us, as scholars, to be self-reflexive about what exactly we are looking for.[3] K. J. Rawson explains: "In the context of historical research, this very recent and geographically specific emergence of *transgender* means that we must always be mindful of how we are imposing an identity category onto pasts in which that identity is anachronistic and onto places where that identity is foreign."[4] I recognize the impulse of trans scholars to search for people in the past who may have looked and lived like us; however, in this impulse to excavate trans pasts, we must remain cognizant of the fact that this project of looking is always about looking for ourselves. We look in order to be found.

In 1957, Dr. Robert J. Stoller and Dr. Robert Geertsma, both professors of psychiatry at the University of California Los Angeles (UCLA), walked into the L.A. County Hospital to film interviews with psychiatric patients to use for medical students' clinical evaluations.[5] One of the patients they would interview was a young, twenty-something woman with an already thick medical and legal case file that included check fraud, car theft, homicidal thoughts, and armed robbery. In addition to her run-ins with the law, her gender appearance and comportment—men's clothes, a short haircut, and an insistence that she possessed both a penis and a vagina—interested the doctors. The clinical relationship between Stoller and this woman, sometimes referred to as "Mrs. B" and other times as "Mrs. G," would continue for the next fourteen years, with Mrs. G's history providing the "evidence" for many of Stoller's theories on female masculinity, female transsexualism, and gender identity.[6]

After meeting Mrs. G, Stoller would go on to found the UCLA Gender Identity Research Clinic (GIRC) in 1962 with his colleagues Ralph Greenson and Richard Green.[7] This clinic, along with many other university-based gender clinics, operated throughout the 1960s and 1970s, an era that trans historian Susan Stryker refers to as the "big science period of transgender history."[8] The GIRC generally did not recommend or approve surgical interventions, except in rare cases, often when the clinicians (falsely) believed the patient to have an intersex condition.[9] Using a psychiatric approach, the GIRC was focused on reforming non-normative gender expressions in childhood in order to prevent transsexuality in adulthood. While the majority of the clinic's patients were effeminate young boys, UCLA was unique in the fact that the GIRC was interested in female-to-male (FTM) transsexuals, or as Stoller referred to them, "female transsexuals." In Joanne Meyerowitz's history of transsexuality in the United States, *How Sex Changed*, she writes about the uniqueness of UCLA's interest in FTMs:

> At the end of the 1960s, doctors at UCLA's Gender Identity Research Clinic debated privately as to whether FTMs even qualified as transsexuals. From 1968 to 1970 they held at least fifteen meetings devoted to FTMs. Stoller wondered "whether there should be such a diagnosis as transsexualism for females." After twelve years of treating FTMs, he could not find "etiological events which hold from case to case or even a very consistent clinical picture, other than the raging desire to become a male."[10]

Mrs. G was one of the primary case histories that shaped Stoller's scholarship on female transsexualism.[11] During this time period, from 1968 to 1970, he was working on a manuscript that would become his book *Splitting: A Very Masculine Woman*. Mrs. G is the central character of that book.

Mrs. G came to me, quite by accident, on one of the many sunny Saturday afternoons I spent in the windowless basement of UCLA's Charles E. Young Research Library. The Stoller Papers comprises 90 linear feet of materials that span the thirty-plus years Robert Stoller worked in the department of psychiatry at UCLA. Because of the untimeliness of Stoller's death, he was not involved in organizing his materials into an official archive, which is evident in this unredacted collection's abundance and disorganization.[12] The sheer size of the archive, paired with the scarcity of information provided on the finding aid, left me randomly selecting boxes from the library storage facility. One afternoon, while sifting through a cardboard box full of unfiled papers, I came across one of Stoller's drafts of *Splitting*. As I pored over the recalcitrant transcripts of Mrs. G's therapy sessions, I felt like I had found pieces of myself—of my masculinity and my gender certainty and my defiance. I spent the next few months reading every file I could on Mrs. G. I wanted to make a timeline out of the bits and pieces of her life that I could gather from the transcripts. However, the more time I spent with the transcripts, the further away from Mrs. G I felt. This is an essay about looking for someone, getting lost, and finding something else entirely. It is an attempt to understand the layers of translation, restriction, and secrecy in the transsexual case file archives. Ultimately, it is a reflection on the limits of writing trans history.

The Case File

As we see a surge of institutionally supported trans scholarship, trans studies is at a pivotal moment of shaping its epistemological investments. As trans studies orients itself in the academy, I ask, what will be its relationship to transsexuality and the history of trans medicalization? Trans studies emerged in relation to queer theory. Queer theory, as a field of thought, is based in the anti-binary, and non-normative gender has been the central analytic and object for queer scholars. The terms "transgender" and "genderqueer" have been taken up by queer theory for their perceived anti-binary modes of being, while experiences of transsexual FTMs and MTFs have been largely ignored because of the ways that medicalized transition has been interpreted as reifying the gender binary. Through this lens, the figure of the transsexual is seen as retrograde, untimely, or a relic of the past.

This chapter considers how a turn to the archive requires trans studies to contend with the category of transsexuality—how it emerged, who it was made to encompass, and how it manifests in the present. To write about those who self-identified as transsexual or were diagnosed/classified as such requires a more nuanced understanding of trans medicalization than has usually been afforded in queer studies. Grappling with the transsexual as a figure with a complex set of desires, motivations, political or apolitical investments, life circumstances, and transition stories pushes back against the notion that sex reassignment surgery, hormone replacement therapy, and "passing" exist under the hegemonic and colonial rubric of the gender binary.[13] While gender performance and the elasticity of identity are useful for interrogating gender, a focus on transsexuality demands a rigorous investment in understanding norms, materiality, desire, and the embodied. At this crossroads, it is imperative that trans studies critically engages with transsexual archives. How, then, should trans studies approach transsexual and clinical case files?

The case file as a genre symbolizes the intervention of institutions and the state in the lives of people "with the purpose of supervising, treating, punishing, servicing, and/or reforming individuals or groups deemed in some way deviants or victims."[14] The modern clinical case file emerged during the eighteenth century, in tandem with European state-formation and population growth.[15] The need to discipline and regulate the population led to an increase in record-keeping.[16] This record-keeping occurred not only on an institutional level, but also on an individual level through the case file. As Mike Featherstone writes: "This was a new form of power, based not on the ideology of individualism, but the actuality of individuation, as whole populations, their bodies and life histories became documented, differentiated and recorded in the archive."[17] For trans studies scholars, the medical case file is one of the main avenues for finding out information about trans pasts.

Lauren Berlant has argued that the case file is the primary tool of biopower.[18] For Berlant, the case file as a genre takes the singular and makes it the general in order to establish the normative: "It is a genre that organizes singularities into exemplary, intelligible patterns, enmeshing realist claims (x really is exemplary in this way) with analytic aims (if we make a pattern from x set of singularities we can derive y conclusions) and makes claims for why it should be thus."[19] For Berlant, scholarship on case files should raise questions about the ability of a single object to be spun into an explanation of something bigger. Berlant operates under the rubric that the case file *must* be reworked, and because the case file operates through claims to realism, we must rework not only the case file, but also realism itself.

However, in the context of psychiatric clinics like GIRC, these case files are not like the bureaucratic collection of data that one might see in juridical or governmental contexts (e.g., census reports, arrest records, and population data); rather they are case *studies*, what Warwick Anderson would refer to as "modernist short stories."[20] For Anderson, it is important to distinguish between the case file and the case study. While the case file systematically measures and records information about individuals for bureaucratic administrations, the case study operates differently—it emphasizes the clinical encounter. By providing a narrative of the interaction between patient and analyst, the case study has the potential to operate as a counterdiscourse. Anderson writes: "Indeed, these ideographic case studies convey the impression of resisting, perhaps even subverting, the bureaucratically serviceable, and hence nomothetic, case file."[21] Case studies are lengthy, subjective, and full of narrative. They expand the scope of the file beyond the individual in question, as case studies interpolate an(other): the author/narrator.

This essay focuses on some of the complications and issues that emerge when working with transsexual clinical case studies, specifically in relation to Mrs. G and the UCLA GIRC. Knowing the power dynamics that are present when institutions intervene in and regulate individual lives, is it possible for us to reroute these power dynamics by reading against the grain of the case study? What methodological approaches might allow us to read through or across the layers of mediation? Can a case study such as Mrs. G's be read as a counterdiscourse? I contend with these questions in order to address some of the main issues—translation, restriction, and secrecy—that come about when reading a case study. My aim is to consider how trans studies, as a field, should engage with the clinical case studies from the university-based gender clinics of the 1960s and 1970s.

A Trans Archive

The Stoller Papers raise interesting questions about how an archive can turn a set of objects into something new. A group of documents and ephemera take on different meaning when they are placed together, organized, named, and maintained as a cohesive collection. Institutional and organizational power deem which voices and people are heard or seen. The majority of UCLA's gender clinic patients were effeminate young boys brought to the GIRC by their parents. They most likely did not identify as transsexuals at the time they received treatment, and perhaps they never did (the same is true of Mrs. G). What does it mean then to read the Stoller Papers collection as a trans(sexual) archive? Of the ninety boxes in the archive, only two of them are restricted due to patient–physician privilege. These restricted boxes undoubtedly contain personal information about Mrs. G—her full name, address, date of birth—along with that of countless other patients who were seen by Stoller during his decades at UCLA. The information in these boxes may very well reveal that the majority of these patients were never transsexuals. However, I argue that the Stoller Papers at UCLA are undoubtedly a transsexual archive for two specific reasons: their collection of transsexual life writings and Stoller's influence on the establishment of trans(sexual) therapeutics.

First, while the GIRC did not perform sex reassignment surgery, this did not stop countless transsexuals across the country from contacting the clinic in the hope that they would. Before the emergence of university-based gender programs in the United States, trans people had to seek medical treatment abroad, limiting access of such therapeutic options to individuals who had money, the means to travel, and the knowledge of where to go. The development of clinics like the GIRC opened a floodgate of people who, after years of waiting, thought surgery might finally be within reach. The Stoller Papers provide a rich repository of letters written by just such people, all asking Dr. Stoller for advice and help.

Similarly, scattered throughout the boxes of Stoller's conference schedules and gender publications are a collection of transsexual autobiographies, some handwritten in epistolary format, others typed and stapled into pamphlets. These autobiographies, mailed from all over the country, speak to the heterogeneity of transsexual experiences. It is unclear why all of these autobiographies were sent to Stoller, but one can assume that since they are not contained in the restricted boxes, the authors never became patients. Perhaps the autobiographies were sent to Stoller in attempts to influence or add to his research on transsexuality or, like the letters, they were sent as individual appeals for surgery. As Chase Joynt and Kristen Schilt have written about the collection: "A tension exists between the redacted files of those of patients who received treatment from Stoller—and the nonredacted files of those patients who were not able to receive care. The people who were denied services are now rendered more available for future finding than those afforded institutional services and protections."[22] While transsexuals may not have been the majority of patients at the GIRC, transsexual life narratives are what animate the Stoller Papers collection, a testament to how archives produce their own histories.

Second, despite the fact that much of Stoller's research on transsexuality was conducted on people who did not then and perhaps never did identify as transsexual, Stoller's books, papers, and presentations deeply shaped the trajectory of trans therapeutics in the United States. In trans studies and trans healthcare, we continue to experience the afterlives of Stoller's transsexual research. Indeed, the very concept of "gender identity"—which is central to both vernacular and medical descriptions of transness—was developed by Dr. Stoller during the course of his research with individuals like Mrs. G. Being attentive to his work allows for a more complex understanding of the trans pasts that shape trans presents.

Mediation and Translation

Archives obscure. They produce stories that may or may not capture what actually happened (assuming there is an originary event to be captured in the first place). Archivist and scholar Verne Harris refers to this as the "archival sliver," writing, "the documentary record provides just a sliver of a window into the event."[23] Like a game of telephone, each step of recording, preserving, and organizing serves to distort. The event, person, moment, or story being captured in the archive is irretrievable. Instead, the information has been passed along from person to person, only being preserved if someone found it necessary to record and save. Archivists, in the process of developing and organizing a collection, add their own layer of mediation and meaning, changing the already-skewed message yet again. The final product only slightly resembles the original.

In the case of Mrs. G, everything that we know about her comes through Stoller. Even then, we are limited to the moments, conversations, and interactions that he decided to keep a record of *and* we are only capable of knowing those *if* they made it into the Stoller Papers collection. In her essay "Pulp Fictions and Problem Girls," Regina Kunzel argues that the case file is a reflection of the questions asked, who was asking, and what was actually recorded. She states, "case records often reveal as much, if not more, about those conducting the interview as they do about those interviewed."[24] From the transcripts of Mrs. G's therapy sessions, we are able to see the questions Stoller asked, the ways in which he responded to her, and how he directed or reoriented the conversations.

Despite the fact that Stoller claims to have recorded or taken notes on all of his sessions with Mrs. G, there is no trace of this in the Stoller Papers. We only "hear" Mrs. G in the edited transcripts published in *Splitting*. Aside from Stoller and Mrs. G's first interview in 1957, which is printed in its entirety, the therapy transcripts published in *Splitting* have been severely pared down in scope and size. The archive contains various drafts of the book, with different transcripts included, but no direct notes from therapy sessions. Stoller is explicit about the editing of the transcripts and his rules for deciding what to eliminate and what to include:

> I simply cannot publish all the typescripts on Mrs. G. No one would read them. So what can be deleted without distorting the data? The only answer is that I must use my judgement. Which immediately removes my findings from the realm of science. The best I can hope is that if the editing is proper, the end result will adequately approximate the original data-collecting experience, the treatment.[25]

The transcripts that remain are a heavily curated version of the original. Years of treatment have been collapsed into one chunk of text with no indication where one therapy session ends and a new one begins. Stoller continues, "Although I have not indicated how much time has passed between quotations—it may have been days or years—the reader will know that, within each chapter, there is always a progression of time."[26]

In conversations between Robert Stoller and his book editor, Emanuel Geltman, we can see a tension about how to use the transcripts in the book. In Geltman's prepublication correspondence with Stoller, he is overly preoccupied with Mrs. G. His letters of editorial suggestions and book publicity information are littered with tangential questions about Mrs. G's masculinity and sexuality. In one letter, dated June 11, 1971, Geltman writes to Stoller about the publishing company's concerns as to whether Mrs. G would criticize the book publicly.[27] In the middle of this discussion, he writes, "I couldn't help but wonder, now that the penis is gone, whether she permits women to touch her," followed by, "Back to the manuscript, an important point that I almost forgot."[28] This voyeuristic preoccupation with Mrs. G shapes Geltman's vision for the book. In his comments to Stoller, Geltman suggests that the book needs to be more centrally focused on the transcripts and less on the psychoanalytic theory. Geltman wants to cut the theory that relates to transsexuality, telling Stoller that his long explanation on transsexualism at the end of the manuscript "hardly belongs" since "transsexualism is only a hint of Mrs. B's case."[29] Stoller replies:

> I know you have felt enthused about Mrs. B's history (and I have been most grateful to you for the support your interest has given me), but to me this is not primarily an interesting case report. I would not want the book accepted on that basis. The case report is the vehicle for presenting issues about psychodynamic theory, psychoanalytic practice, but most important of all, it represents a struggle to elaborate ideas concerning early personality development, especially gender identity. While I do not see how

this can properly be done without case material, I also do not feel that the book should be edited in order to give the world a fascinating script.[30]

Despite Stoller's resistance, he accepts Geltman's vision for the book. In fact, the exact format of the book, with each chapter based on a different "theme" that arose in treatment (e.g., "homosexuality," "homicide," "mothering"), is Geltman's suggestion. Stoller's theorization of different types of masculine females and transsexual females is moved to the appendix. From Stoller's correspondences with his editor, we can see how the book is mediated not only through Stoller but also through Geltman.

There are countless layers, then, of translation between Mrs. G and us, readers of the archive or Stoller's publications. If we think about these layers of mediation and translation as steps away from Mrs. G, we can begin to imagine the distance that exists between her and ourselves. I want to highlight this distance as a prompt to pause and consider whose story the Stoller Papers are actually telling. As Warwick Anderson says, case histories are "modernist short stories in which the author becomes the central character."[31] I quote this as a means to suggest that in this case history, perhaps we are reading the story of Stoller just as much as that of Mrs. G. By understanding Stoller's omnipresence in the archives, how can we turn our gaze away from Mrs. G and instead focus our attention on him? Redirecting the gaze to Stoller is not only about shifting the power dynamics at play, but is also an opportunity to consider how looking at Mrs. G might recommit a kind of violence she was subjected to under the clinical gaze.[32] I wonder, what can this redirection of the gaze teach us about transsexuality and gender research that we don't learn from the salacious details of Mrs. G's life story? Rather than attempting to understand exactly how Mrs. G identified, what does it mean that her life was enlisted by the GIRC for their project of naming, defining, and classifying types of transsexuality? This provides rich opportunities for critically analyzing transsexual medical history without becoming myopically preoccupied with recuperating and exposing already-exposed patients.

Lack versus Abundance

While Harris's concept of the "archival sliver" is useful for understanding the limitations and impossibilities of archives, I want to be careful to not think of the Stoller Papers as solely a space of lack. Indeed, for researchers, the Stoller Papers often produce feelings of abundance. In the reading room of the Young Research Library, I have seen other historians and researchers with slim magazine folders or single files. I, on the other hand, have been working with foot-long cardboard boxes overflowing with pamphlets, papers, binders, and newspaper clippings. One can visually register the excess of this process. Without folders or a proper organizing system, I carry handfuls of papers back to my desk. This feeling of abundance is unique not only in comparison to the other archives housed in UCLA's special collections, but also because, as a trans scholar, I have been led to believe that queer and trans archives are typically characterized by lack and erasure.

In his article "I Am 64 and Paul McCartney Doesn't Care about Me," Abram Lewis offers a compelling critique of queer and sexuality studies' foundational belief in queer erasure. Because I view Lewis's claim as essential to my arguments regarding trans history and methodologies of inquiry into transsexual pasts, I will quote from him at length:

> Scholars have not only maintained but also actively investigated the political and psychic costs of historical loss which continues to be rendered a primary site of queer injury and impetus for reparative historical production . . . Especially in recent years, this problem of historical loss has been engaged increasingly as a problem of archivization. The archive emerges recurrently as an original cause of historical deprivation and the ultimate mechanism by which queer history may be secured or extinguished . . . In fact, historiographical claims about queer absence would seem to have begotten an ontology of the archive that recapitulates a kind of repressive hypothesis: this logic posits the queer archive as always impoverished and fractured, distinguished by power's erasures and disavowals.[33]

While we could undoubtedly offer an account of the materials that are absent from the Stoller Papers archive, focusing on gaps and erasure can prevent us from seeing what is right in front of us.

This pervasive paradigm of queer archival absence has already made an imprint in trans studies scholarship. In November 2015, *Transgender Studies Quarterly* released a groundbreaking special issue, "Archives and Archiving," geared directly at questions of archival absence. The general editors caution that in contending with the "fragmentary nature of surviving [transgender] documentation" we must be careful to avoid treating existing pieces of the archive as constituting any kind of whole or complete picture.[34] All archives, by nature, both capture and fail to capture. They collect some materials and leave others out. What the editors describe is the archival sliver, the ontological impossibility of Borges's Library of Babel in which all things written and thought are captured. There is no whole trans archive because there is no whole archive. Through a framework of archival lack, we are trapped in a constant cycle of recuperation and recovery. As Anjali Arondekar writes, "This movement from archival secrecy to disclosure echoes what Eve Kosofsky Sedgwick has famously called the 'epistemology of the closet.' Such a movement relies upon the maintenance within the epistemological system of the hidden, secret term, keeping all binaries intact."[35] If transness is about defying binaristic thinking and being, how can we better enact this in our approaches to trans archives?

Daniel Marshall and Zeb Tortorici suggest in the introduction to this anthology that as we turn to archives, we must remember that the act of turning or rotating implies a proliferation of directions. The dynamic, multidirectional way that archives turn an assortment of materials, paper, and ephemera into a collection and into a body of knowledge also allows for a proliferation of interpretations. We must not approach archives through a binary of whole versus fragmentary, or absent versus present, but rather with the knowledge that trans life abounds in front of us if only we find creative ways of looking and reading.

Secrets

In "Secret and Spectral: Torture and Secrecy in the Archives of Slave Conspiracies," Greg Childs differentiates between that which is silent in the archive and that which is secret.[36] Childs challenges us to consider the fact that many enslaved and colonized people made intentional decisions to keep secrets from authorities, and thus from the archive. Such absences are not accidental but, rather, intentional. Childs says that he is concerned with "the production of secrets that were deliberately not spoken or written into the record by historical actors."[37] He argues that secrets were fundamental to Black political life and survival.

It is important to distinguish between silences and secrets in the archive in relation to transsexual clinical case files. For many transsexuals seeking surgery, university gender clinics were the only avenue to access such medical interventions. As Sandy Stone writes in "The 'Empire' Strikes Back: A Posttranssexual Manifesto," many transsexual patients at the gender clinics were well versed in the criteria for a transsexual diagnosis and knew how to reveal or conceal the correct information in order to get the operations they so desperately wanted.[38] After the 1966 publication of Dr. Harry Benjamin's book *The Transsexual Phenomenon*, the differential diagnosis of transsexualism began streamlining at clinics across the country. At the time, applicants far outnumbered clinic capacity. Only transsexuals who perfectly matched the differential diagnosis were considered for surgery. To increase their chances of being selected, prospective patients would circulate Benjamin's book as a kind of "how-to" for being approved for treatment. Because doctors and medical professionals would not operate on patients with genders outside of the male/female binary or on homosexual-identified patients, transsexuals at these gender clinics learned to access care through strategic secret-keeping.

In the case of Mrs. G, to speculate about the secrets she may have kept, we have to understand the trajectory of her treatment. Mrs. G voluntarily became a patient at UCLA after her interview with Stoller in the County Hospital in 1957. According to Stoller, "She asked if she could be transferred to UCLA Hospital for treatment; she feared her path from the county hospital would lead back to the hospital from which she had run away and to the unavailing experiences she had had in the past with state hospitals."[39] After being transferred to UCLA, she worked with various psychologists for seven years before Stoller took her on as his patient. During those first seven years, Mrs. G corresponded regularly with Stoller. In 1964, following a string of concerning letters, Stoller set up a series of appointments with Mrs. G, nearly all of which she canceled. She began to consistently see Stoller only after she was arrested for a traffic violation while on probation and was court-ordered to attend psychiatric treatment.

The letters that sparked Stoller's concern were about Mrs. G's son Chris. Chris was born blind and albino, and he was later diagnosed with autism. At the time of the letters, he was three years old and having severe behavioral issues along with skin rashes. Mrs. G was desperate to find some sort of treatment; however, doing so would require her to be honest about Chris—he was not her biological son, but rather a neighbor's child that she had cared for since birth. One of her letters to Stoller reads, "I have no legal rights . . . I'm afraid to tell anyone for fear they'll take him away from me and, Dr. Stoller, Chris is my life . . . I could never imagine the welfare department allowing me to adopt him, with my background they might even take all three boys from me. I can't take that chance . . . Maybe you can help me to help him."[40] Stoller helped Mrs. G get Chris into the UCLA hospital, but after receiving advice that she needed to send him away to a "mental retardation hospital," Mrs. G had a mental health crisis and threatened to kill both Chris and herself. This led to a long hospitalization at UCLA, which was the true beginning of Stoller and Mrs. G's clinical relationship. During this time, they met six days a week.

When Stoller began to treat Mrs. G in approximately 1964, the GIRC was only two years old, and Stoller was busy working on what would be his most popular and acclaimed book, *Sex and Gender: On The Development of Masculinity and Femininity*.[41] While the narrative in *Splitting* makes it seem like

Stoller took Mrs. G on as a patient out of a genuine concern for her well-being and that of her son, at the time, his research on transsexuality was focused on mother-son relationships. He took Mrs. G on as a patient because he wanted to test his theory that boys with bisexual mothers were more likely to be transsexual.[42] Mrs. G was a "masculine woman" with three sons between the ages of approximately three and thirteen years old. She was, in many ways, a perfect test case for Stoller's theories. Indeed, she does appear in the 1968 book *Sex and Gender* in chapter 15: "A Bisexual Mother: A Control Case."[43]

This distills the exact conflict that would play out during Mrs. G's time with Dr. Stoller: She was motivated to see him out of concern for her children, and he was motivated to take her on as a patient to further develop his theories about gender identity, motherhood, and female transsexualism. Mrs. G was seeking treatment because she did not want her children to be impacted by her legal and mental health troubles, but Stoller was most interested in Mrs. G's claim to have a penis. As Stoller sought to make her into a "normal female," Mrs. G resisted. In the archival documents, she continues to insist that her masculinity and her penis are not the problem: "Why worry about this one little thing? I am not hurting anybody. I'm not hurting anybody with it. And it's not hurting me. It's not a delusion. It's inside of me. This is something I've always known, and I've always felt; and it's there, and it's real, and it's mine; and you can't take it away from me."[44] Mrs. G made it very clear that her penis had been her protection and survival strategy through childhood sexual abuse, incarceration, addiction, and sterilization. In one of her objections to Stoller's poking and prodding, she forcefully declared her right to secrecy: "If you knew everything about me, you would be taking from me the things that have made it possible for me to survive."[45] Mrs. G wanted to be a better mother, but she was not interested in having Stoller "fix" her gender.

Mrs. G's case history highlights the fact that she was a mother who was deeply invested in her children and fearful of losing them. Her case history also indicates that at the age of twenty, after five "illegitimate" pregnancies, she was nonconsensually sterilized at "R State Hospital."[46] As Stoller writes, "Her greatest sense of having been cheated came whenever she recalled her sterilization."[47] During Mrs. G's hospitalization at UCLA and her daily meetings with Stoller, she asked to have a tubal ligation reversal. Stoller forcefully objected. Her reproductive rights were in his hands. Eventually, she would convince him that she wanted the tubal ligation reversal not because she wanted to have another baby, but because she wanted to be "intact as a female."[48] Her request for having her reproductive capacities restored, which she framed as a means to regain proper femininity, appealed to Stoller's desire to reform her into a "normal female." After years of insisting that she was a woman with a penis (invisible to others, but felt by her), Mrs. G conceded: "I am a woman; I can't have a penis."[49] Finally, Mrs. G got her tubal ligation reversal at the UCLA hospital.

A Methodology of Care

In Childs's essay, he warns against enacting violence through searching for the secrets of archival actors: "By choosing to agonize over secrets that we cannot know, we may be close to replicating the violence that some subjects were attempting to avoid in the first place when they kept secrets from colonial officials."[50] Rather than embrace narratives of recovery, he argues that we should honor the secrets for how they may have "aided future subaltern political formations."[51] This problem of recommitting the violence of the gender clinic gaze feels most apparent to me in my quest to know *who* Mrs. G truly was or is.

As mentioned earlier, throughout the Stoller Papers, Mrs. G is given multiple pseudonyms. One day, as I was reading through Stoller's personal correspondence, I stumbled across her legal name. This was due to an error in the archive—a small moment in which something slipped through the cracks. I have a lead on Mrs. G's identity. With this name, along with an approximation of Mrs. G's date of birth and city of residence, I feel confident that I could find her in LA County juridical records. A part of me wants to find Mrs. G, to give us one more name, one more story to tell. Another part of me hesitates— what becomes of a life turned lesson? I am reminded of Kara Keeling's article, "Looking for M—: Queer Temporality, Black Political Possibility, and Poetry from the Future," in which Keeling urges us against looking for the disappeared black, trans protagonist of Daniel Peddle's film *The Aggressives*. She insists that M's disappearance from the film and the public eye is a form of resistance and survival. She asks, "What are the ethical implications of looking for hir?"[52] Keeling insists, "The first question that must be asked of M— is not where is s/he but when might s/he be."[53] Keeling urges us to consider a queer ethics of looking *after* rather than looking *for*. What would it mean to look after Mrs. G?

Lisa Lowe also urges us to consider the motivation behind the impetus for recovery. In "History Hesitant," Lowe provides us with a methodological approach for resisting the desire to recuperate.[54] She probes the question of whether archival recovery is motivated by an ontological desire for reparation. How does recovery conceive of the relationship between the past and present? Drawing from African American social critique, Lowe challenges the ways that recovery frames the present as a place of freedom and the past as a place of unfreedom. How do we reckon with the fact that unfreedom is still here in the present? Lowe states, "This critique acknowledges not only that history and historical knowledge fix and structure the relationship of the past to the present but also that the meaning it attributes to the past determines what might be imagined as possible, just, or desirable, now and in the future."[55] Lowe's methodological approach is one of hesitation. Rather than rushing to recovery and perhaps reproducing the violence of the archive, Lowe proposes pausing and attending to the meaning of our critical approaches. Hesitation allows us to tarry in a space of uncertainty, in order to "reckon with the connections that could have been but were lost and are thus not yet—before we conceive of freedoms yet to come."[56] This hesitation requires us to slow down.[57] It necessitates attention, patience, tenderness, and care.

Transsexual case files demand a differentiated reading practice.[58] The various layers of mediation, translation, and secrecy require us to slow down and sift through not only what is visibly present in the file, but also what is missing, what is secret, and what cannot be understood from our present time and place. To look after our trancestors, we must be careful to not subject transsexual patients to the same kind of scrutiny they experienced at the hands of gender clinic doctors. Transsexual case histories showcase multidimensional moments of encounter. What would it mean for us to approach these files with an intention of inverting, subverting, and returning the gaze upon the gender clinic doctors and psychiatrists? A methodological approach of returning the gaze moves emphasis away from recovering individual subjects and their secrets.

To read transsexual case files with a hesitation to recuperate furnishes a methodological approach that responsibly attends to the complexity of the gender clinic archives. It answers K. J. Rawson's call for "the need for thoughtfully conceived and ethically executed trans archival practices."[59] Rather than projecting ourselves onto the subjects we find in the archive and deem to be *like us*, hesitation respects the fugitivity of trans pasts. To read transsexual clinical case files with an understanding that patients and prospective patients kept intentional secrets from the medical authorities, and thus from the archives, allows for a more nuanced view of transsexual narratives. Rather than assume the heterogeneity of trans experience was flattened by medicalized transness, we can understand that transsexual patients found creative ways of revealing, concealing, and fashioning their life stories to strategically access resources. It extends a kind of critical generosity, or as Avery Gordon describes it, "a right to complex personhood." As Gordon explains, "Complex personhood means that all people (albeit in specific forms whose specificity is sometimes everything) remember and forget, are beset by contradiction, and recognize and misrecognize themselves and others."[60]

Mrs. G was not a woman who set out to change the course of transsexual medicine. She was not a radical nor a gender warrior, but she also was not a cog in the transsexual medical matrix. She was a person who was entangled with various systems of power, trying to navigate a way forward that would preserve not only her life and personhood but also that of her children. She told lies, and she also told the truth. Her life was made into an example, and her life also resisted capture in Stoller's theories, in diagnostic criteria, and in the archive. As trans studies engages with transsexual pasts, it is imperative that we enact a methodology of care in which we look after our transcestors rather than looking for their secrets in the name of recovery and recuperation.

Notes

1   Robert J. Stoller Papers (Collection 373), Library Special Collections, Charles E. Young Research Library, UCLA.
2   Throughout this chapter I will be using "trans" as an umbrella term to encompass genders that exceed the colonial, cisheteropatriarchal, two-gender binary system (e.g., trans studies, trans scholars). Terms like "transgender," "transsexual," or "genderqueer" are used to refer to specific identity categories with their own sets of meanings. I use "transsexual" to refer to individuals who seek medical forms of transition (e.g., sex reassignment surgery, hormone replacement therapy, and facial feminization surgery).
3   Williams, "Transgender," 232.
4   Rawson, "Introduction."
5   Stoller, *Splitting*, 1.
6   When writing about Mrs. G, I have struggled to decide which pronouns and gender descriptors to use. From Mrs. G's therapy transcripts, it seems like she *most* identified as a woman with a penis. For this reason, I will be using the pronouns she/her/hers throughout.
7   Meyerowitz, *How Sex Changed*, 126.
8   Stryker, *Transgender History*, 93.
9   In the early days of gender clinics, aspiring patients would often mislead doctors to believe that there was a biological (e.g., hormonal or gonadal) reason for their cross-gender identification. By claiming intersex status, their cross-gender identity was framed as an error of nature rather than a personal pathology.
10 Meyerowitz, *How Sex Changed*, 149.
11 The great paradox of Mrs. G is that she was likely not a transsexual, in the sense that there are no indications that she pursued sex-reassignment surgery, wished to live full time as a man, or self-identified with the term. However, her case study was highly influential for Stoller's theories of both MTF and FTM transsexuality. Over the years, Stoller referred to Mrs. G in many different ways: "a very masculine woman," "a bisexual mother," "a female transsexual." The identity of "woman with a penis" defied and exceeded researchers' understandings of sex and gender.
12 Joynt and Schilt, "Anxiety at the Archive," 639.

13 Here, I am not arguing that the figure of the transsexual is *more* non-normative or radical than other trans identity categories—following the lead of thinkers such as Nikki Sullivan, my argument is not based in a binary of "good" versus "bad" body modification. Rather, my argument is simply that transsexuality has historically been dismissed as "bad" body modification and/or as "false consciousness" and that it should not be. Sullivan, "Transmogrification."

14 Iacovetta and Mitchinson, *On the Case*, 3.

15 Featherstone, "Archive," 591.

16 Foucault, *History of Sexuality, Volume 1*; Foucault, "17 March 1976."

17 Featherstone, "Archive," 592.

18 Berlant, "On the Case."

19 Berlant, "On the Case," 670.

20 Anderson, "The Case of the Archive."

21 Anderson, "The Case of the Archive," 535.

22 Joynt and Schilt, "Anxiety at the Archive," 643.

23 Harris, "The Archival Sliver," 64.

24 Kunzel, "Pulp Fictions," 1468.

25 Stoller, *Splitting*, xvii.

26 Stoller, *Splitting*, xviii.

27 Emanuel Geltman to Robert Stoller, June 11, 1971, Box 32, Robert J. Stoller Papers, Library Special Collections, Charles E. Young Research Library, UCLA.

28 Emanuel Geltman to Robert Stoller, June 11, 1971, Box 32, Robert J. Stoller Papers, Library Special Collections, Charles E. Young Research Library, UCLA.

29 Emanuel Geltman to Robert Stoller, June 11, 1971, Box 32, Robert J. Stoller Papers, Library Special Collections, Charles E. Young Research Library, UCLA.

30 Robert Stoller to Emanuel Geltman, August 25, 1971, Box 32, Robert J. Stoller Papers, Library Special Collections, Charles E. Young Research Library, UCLA.

31 Anderson, "The Case of the Archive," 535.

32 My concerns about the ethics of historical representation and the dual violence of the clinical gaze and the historian's gaze have been highly influenced by Saidiya Hartman. She asks: "How does one revisit the scene of subjection without replicating the grammar of violence?" Hartman, "Venus in Two Acts," 4.

33 Lewis, "I Am 64," 15–16.

34 Stryker and Currah, "General Editors' Introduction," 541.

35 Arondekar, "Without a Trace," 16.

36 Childs, "Secret and Spectral," 35–57.

37 Childs, "Secret and Spectral," 37.

38 Stone, "The 'Empire' Strikes Back," 161.

39 Stoller, *Splitting*, 12.

40 Stoller, *Splitting*, 98–99.

41 Stoller, *Sex and Gender*.

42 In this context, "bisexuality" refers not to a sexual interest in both males and females, but rather to an individual who embodies the two sexes of male and female. It is a gender-related, not sexuality-based, term.

43 Stoller, *Sex and Gender*, 170–75.
44 Stoller, *Splitting*, 15.
45 Stoller, *Splitting*, 36.
46 Stoller, *Splitting*, 50.
47 Stoller, *Splitting*, 71.
48 Stoller, *Splitting*, 72.
49 Stoller, *Splitting*, 28.
50 Childs, "Secret and Spectral," 38.
51 Childs, "Secret and Spectral," 51–52.
52 Keeling, "Looking for M—," 575.
53 Keeling, "Looking for M—," 577.
54 Lowe, "History Hesitant."
55 Lowe, "History Hesitant," 97.
56 Lowe, "History Hesitant," 98.
57 Lowe's concept of "hesitation" and Keeling's question of "when" both gesture to a future- (rather than past-) oriented temporality of historical inquiry.
58 Baik, "Sensing through Slowness."
59 Rawson, "Introduction," 544.
60 Gordon, *Ghostly Matters*, 4.

Works Cited

Anderson, Warwick. "The Case of the Archive." *Critical Inquiry* 39, no. 3 (2013): 532–47.
Arondekar, Anjali. "Without a Trace: Sexuality and the Colonial Archive." *Journal of the History of Sexuality* 14, no. 1/2 (2005): 10–27.
Baik, Crystal Mun-hye. "Sensing through Slowness: Korean Americans and the Un/Making of the Home Film Archive." *American Studies* 56, no. 3/4 (2018): 5–30.
Berlant, Lauren. "On the Case." *Critical Inquiry* 33, no. 4 (2007): 663–72.
Childs, Greg L. "Secret and Spectral: Torture and Secrecy in the Archives of Slave Conspiracies." *Social Text* 33, no. 4 (2015): 35–57.
Featherstone, Mike. "Archive." *Theory, Culture & Society* 23, nos. 2–3 (2006): 591–96.
Foucault, Michel. *History of Sexuality, Volume 1*. New York: Vintage Books, 1978.
Foucault, Michel. "17 March 1976." In *"Society Must Be Defended": Lectures at the Collège De France 1975–1976*, 239–64. New York: Picador, 2003.
Gordon, Avery. *Ghostly Matters: Haunting and the Sociological Imagination*. Minneapolis: University of Minnesota Press, 2008.
Harris, Verne. "The Archival Sliver: Power, Memory, and Archives in South Africa." *Archival Science* 2, no. 1 (2002): 63–86.
Hartman, Saidiya. "Venus in Two Acts." *Small Axe* 12, no. 2 (2008): 1–14.
Iacovetta, Franca, and Wendy Mitchinson. *On the Case: Explorations in Social History*. Toronto: University of Toronto Press, 1998.
Joynt, Chase, and Kristen Schilt. "Anxiety at the Archive." *Transgender Studies Quarterly* 2, no. 4 (2015): 635–44.
Keeling, Kara. "Looking for M—: Queer Temporality, Black Political Possibility, and Poetry from the Future." *GLQ: A Journal of Lesbian and Gay Studies* 15, no. 4 (2009): 565–82.

Kunzel, Regina G. "Pulp Fictions and Problem Girls: Reading and Rewriting Single Pregnancy in the Postwar United States." *American Historical Review* 100, no. 5 (1995): 1465–87.

Lewis, Abram. "I Am 64 and Paul McCartney Doesn't Care about Me: The Haunting of the Transgender Archive and the Challenges of Queer History." *Radical History Review* 2014, no. 120 (2014): 13–34.

Lowe, Lisa. "History Hesitant." *Social Text* 33, no. 4 (2015): 85–107.

Meyerowitz, Joanne. *How Sex Changed: A History of Transsexuality in the United States.* Cambridge, MA: Harvard University Press, 2002.

Rawson, K. J. "Introduction: An Inevitably Political Craft." *Transgender Studies Quarterly* 2, no. 4 (2015): 544–52.

Robert J. Stoller Papers (Collection 373). Library Special Collections, Charles E. Young Research Library, University of California, Los Angeles.

Stoller, Robert J. *Sex and Gender: On the Development of Masculinity and Femininity.* New York: Science House, 1968.

Stoller, Robert J. *Splitting: A Case of Female Masculinity.* New Haven, CT: Yale University Press, 1997.

Stone, Sandy. "The 'Empire' Strikes Back: A Posttranssexual Manifesto." *Camera Obscura: A Journal of Feminism, Culture, and Media Studies* 29, no. 29 (1992): 151–76.

Stryker, Susan. *Transgender History.* Berkeley, CA: Seal Press, 2008.

Stryker, Susan, and Paisley Currah. "General Editors' Introduction." *Transgender Studies Quarterly* 2, no. 4 (2015): 539–43.

Sullivan, Nikki. "Transmogrification: (Un)Becoming Other(s)." In *The Transgender Studies Reader*, edited by Susan Stryker and Stephen Whittle, 552–64. New York: Routledge, 2006.

Williams, Cristan. "Transgender." *Transgender Studies Quarterly* 1, nos. 1–2 (2014): 232–34.

7. NAMING AFRIKA'S ARCHIVE "QUEER PAN-AFRICANISM"

ELLIOT JAMES

Don't you know the meanings of names are fulfilled?—THAT MOUNTAIN WOMAN in *Ways of Dying*

And in our community, the glory of your name is everything.—BLANCA EVANGELISTA in *Pose*

Coming Apart, by Way of Introduction

The first archival collection I worked with was a box ironically labeled "A Better Chance" (ABC). Named after the 1960s–present nonprofit committed to desegregation and the education of young people of color in the United States, the boxes of letters, newspaper clippings, and photographs, when mined, illuminated the lives of urban black teenagers living in nonblack homestays and attending high school in Northfield—the rural, predominantly white community in the Midwest where I went to college. The ABC students' lives in the 1990s very much resembled my own in the early 2000s. Like them, I left the community that raised me for the promise of a liberal arts education and reversing the cycle of poverty in my family. It was 2004—exactly fifty years after the landmark *Brown v. Board of Education* made "separate but equal" schools unconstitutional—and archival work was required for my history major. The visit to the archives also preceded a summer flight to South Africa and the first time I would stand on soil outside the United States. South Africa had seen *de jure* apartheid end only a decade prior, and I—an unincarcerated, black-male-presenting, queer, nonbinary person—would study history and isiXhosa (one of the country's indigenous black languages), and live with black, brown, and white homestay families.

Today, I am struck by the overlapping "A Better Chance" narratives that co-alesced the day a couple of white archivists at the Northfield Historical Society (NHS) directed me to the ABC box. All of NHS's collections were preserved in a nineteenth-century building downtown and stewarded by community volunteers and staff. Originally Northfield's First National Bank, the structure doubles as an archive and open-air theater for the annual Defeat of Jesse James Days celebration.[1] Only a couple months after the town's 2004 festivities—which featured a live-action gunfight between Jesse James's gang and a militia of white settlers—I experienced what cultural historian Saidiya Hartman calls "scenes of subjection" in the archives.[2] In the ABC box, two classmates and I discovered that a nameless gang of Northfielders or some surrounding community members burned a cross in front of one of the black ABC teenagers' homestays. Perhaps it was because the Ku Klux Klan was not explicitly named in the ABC box materials, I now wonder why learning about my college town's history of racial violence not long before my own arrival did not immediately dissuade me from believing that archives—from the nations that commission them to the workers that receive and direct researchers—could do anything but also terrorize marginalized students of history. Fifteen years have since passed and, believing there was little more I needed to learn about Northfield's history of bandits, klansmen, and settlers, I have not returned to the NHS archives.

Revisiting this archive story today recalls queer, Africa-based literary the-orist Keguro Macharia's retelling of a proverb about the frog and scorpion.[3] Somewhere along the edges of a water source, a scorpion asks a frog if it could hitch a ride on the frog's back across because the scorpion could not swim. The frog agreed, the scorpion mounted the frog, the frog swam halfway across the stream, and, in return, the scorpion stung the frog to death. Con-fused, the frog asked why the scorpion stung it. Right before the frog's dying breath, the scorpion replied, "I'm a scorpion! That's what I do." On the one hand, the story of the frog and scorpion is like the colonial encounter. Like the explorer in uncharted waters, the scorpion took advantage of the frog's knowledge to navigate the environment. The scorpion's exploit, however, doomed them both.

In environments where universities build reputations on the backs of black, indigenous, and queer people of color scholarship, yet fail to fully fund them, Macharia's proverb reminds black queer Africa-based scholars that scorpions are everywhere in area studies, no frog can ever escape, and the "area-studied" subject may in fact witness its fate in institutions of power such as archives. Within the proverb's framework, Macharia explains that the question burden-ing the black queer Africa-based scholar is, "How does one choose to die?"[4] What both figures did not choose, however, were the identities embedded in how the proverb named them: frog and scorpion. For me, their names signaled their ends of life in the context of crossing the waterway, as well as the origins of study for black queer Africanists such as Macharia and myself. As Macharia described in a blog post—a piece of writing—following an African queer studies conference we both attended exactly a decade after my first visit to the NHS archives, "the problem, as always, is where to start."[5]

This chapter pieces together a selection of public events I attended in South Africa and the United States between 2010 and 2019 to conceptualize a buildingless space I name Queer Pan-Africanism (QPA). Within communities experiencing change, I explain, the power to name gave marginalized subjects the power to make their own future through their relationship with junior relatives. In the fifteen years following my experience with the ABC box, I witnessed names invoke ancestors across geographically distinct bloodlines. By bringing together narratives of live events in a collection on power and the construction of history, I follow Sara Ahmed's lead in *Living a Feminist Life*, "that women of color are already ethnographers of universities . . . participating [and] also observing, often because we are assumed not to belong or reside in the places we end up."[6] Black queer Africanist scholars invested in diaspora and transnational research methods have an uneasy relationship with institutional archives because they are often doing their work in environments they are continuously (re)making and (re)naming—a constant process of always *turning archival*, yet never fully arriving at archival completion. Rather than having commissioned communities emerge in space, like archives, with established finding aids, dedicated research staff, and common work areas—black queer Africa-based scholars, Macharia lamented, "find each other, when [they] do, by accident, coincidence, [and] luck."[7] My attempts to overcome impasses in translating archival knowledges to understand queer mobilities connected me to networks that were also asking questions about how to work in archives.

How do marginalized researchers use archives and other institutions of state power to, within Daniel Marshall, Kevin P. Murphy, and Zeb Tortorici's formulation, "put themselves together as historical subjects" after being torn asunder by their own workplaces?[8] The following recounts my journey between the years 2010–2020.

Piecing Myself Back Together

Through my engagements with black queer Africa-based scholars across the Atlantic Ocean, I traveled between Minnesota and South Africa to understand my place in the history profession and working with archives more specifically.

I traveled with the concern that the galleries, NGOs/nonprofits, and universities would be too disconnected from the urgent politics of our time to protect myself from unraveling further in their archives. The concern built on Keguro Macharia's, who, in a 2014 piece, meditated over the challenges of doing work on queer Africa. Here, I quote Macharia at length:

> I worry about ongoing schisms between activists and intellectuals, and how those schisms are exploited by funding agencies which continue to promote research methods that are indifferent to African intellectual production and methodological innovation. I worry that those of us invested in Queer African intellectual production lack the resources— space, time, institutional support—to think collectively and ethically about how we can imagine and inhabit livable spaces. I worry that we do not have any established Queer Studies programmes in Africa, that we find each other, when we do, by accident, coincidence, luck. I worry that we do not have the luxury to assemble together for a semester or longer to read and think collectively about the shape and future of Queer African Studies. I worry that we speak past each other because the urgencies of our geo-locations demand attention, and we can't spare the time to listen properly, with care and attention.[9]

Precisely because building resources and making space for black queer Africa-based scholars to work in tandem requires significant emotional labor, what are some ways marginalized researchers working in archives can use the materials they find to heal, build community, and develop critical theories of black queer Africanness across borders?

Galvanized around activist efforts to free feminist scholar Stella Nyanzi (2019), remember queer activist David Kato Kisule (2011), lift up the persons in photographer Zanele Muholi's *Only Half the Picture* (2006) and *Faces and Phases* (2009–ongoing), and resurrect performance artist Area Scatter (2014) in Nigeria's archives, I witnessed black queer Africa-based artists and scholars actively bringing back old names from the archives and the countryside, refiguring them for contemporary moments, and creating new ones to chart unexplored directions of inquiry. Importantly, Zethu Matebeni and Jabu Pereira described this space of engagement as "Afrika"—a name that stands in for a global community of queer and gender nonconforming persons across the African continent.

In *Refiguring the Archives*, South Africa–based historian Carolyn Hamilton and coeditors understand archives as "but one facet of a range of institutions . . . designed to create a particular vision of society."[10] As institutions of power, therefore, archives play a fundamental role in marking the limits of belonging in local communities.[11] As a name, Afrika directly challenged the specter of the 1884–1885 Berlin Conference in African politics a century after. "As sexual and gender nonconforming or queer persons, we have been alienated in Africa. We have been stripped of our belonging and our connectedness," they explain.[12] "For these reasons, we have created our own version of Afrika [with a 'k']—a space that cuts across the rigid borders and boundaries that have for so many years made us feel disconnected and fractured."[13]

Desiring to know what that space might feel like for me, I traveled by airplane and automobile from Minnesota Mni Sota Makoce ("the Land Where Waters Reflect the Clouds" in Dakota) to South Africa to attend my first queer studies conference on the continent. The trip followed two months of teaching US history on colonized Dakota land and sixteen months of conducting fieldwork on queer mobility in postapartheid Cape Town and Johannesburg, and I was still drafting a plan to process all the archival materials I had gathered. Funded by the University of Minnesota, I crossed former Middle Passage waterways and previously colonized lands of Middle America again to the Institute for Humanities in Africa's (HUMA) offices at the University of Cape Town (UCT), a historically white university overlooking the city. While UCT's HUMA sponsored "Queer in Africa: Confronting the Crisis," it was a cohort of black queer Africa-based scholars whose hard work organizing brought activists, scholars, and artists across Africa and the world to do what seemed impossible: to create, understand, and teach in the context of pervasive gender- and sex-based violence, and to uplift queer and trans people there at the same time.

The conference also launched a text (*Reclaiming Afrikan: Queer Perspectives on Sexual and Gender Identities*) and a corresponding art exhibition (*Critically Queer*). Hoping both to add to my home university's library collection and promote books published in Africa, I purchased an additional copy and resolved to use *Reclaiming Afrikan* in the classroom. *Critically Queer* included artwork from *Reclaiming Afrikan*, and both pieces' inclusion in the official "Queer in Africa" proceedings revealed the conference's multimedia and interdisciplinary nature. Combining the book and exhibition also signaled how such events could be preserved for people who could not attend and scholars interested in looking back to the conference for answers about queer organizing after 2014. No book alone could capture the energy of the event, however. While the conference featured formal papers from *Reclaiming Afrikan* contributors and commentators, the event prioritized participatory events like concerts and poetry readings. And while centered in Cape Town, the conference drew authors and artists with identity documents from Europe, Turtle Island North America, the Caribbean, and Africa outside South Africa's borders, mostly Anglophone countries like Nigeria and Kenya. It would only be through spending time with the participants that I was able to envision the rationale behind Matebeni and Pereira's preface to *Reclaiming Afrikan*, which I would only read months after the conference. Together, the book and exhibition brought together different queer and trans Afrikan observations on Africanness and belonging to imagine the African continent and the African diaspora anew: as Afrika. As the conference proceeded, it became even clearer that "Queer in Africa's" aim was not simply about affirming sexual and genderqueer bodies on the continent. The conference's constituent parts reproduced Pan-Africanism's method of convergence, joining "Queer in Africa" with the continent's decolonization project.

The year 2020 marked the 120-year anniversary of the first Pan-African Conference (PAC) in London, yet it is unclear how queer and trans people were able to truly show up at the Global Pan-African Conference in The Gambia, for example, considering that homosexual behavior goes against section 144 of the Gambia Criminal Code. The original conferencing of representatives from across the African diaspora directly confronted the Berlin Conference 1884–1885. Fifteen years after the Berlin conference representatives divided various ports of entry into the African interior among Leopold of Belgium and the British, French, German, Portuguese, and Spanish, Turtle Island–born W. E. B. Du Bois joined Trinidadian organizer Henry Sylvester Williams and dozens of delegates at the center of the British empire to make a statement. In his address "to the nations of the world," Du Bois made the famous claim that "the problem of the twentieth century is the problem of the color line."[14] While the Cotton States' International Exposition in Atlanta (1895) and Paris's Exposition Universelle (1900) extolled the technologies of the late nineteenth-century colonial era in building agriculture and industry all around the world, Du Bois dissented. At the dawn of the twentieth century, race, Du Bois argued, became "the basis of denying to over half the world the right of sharing to utmost ability the opportunities and privileges of modern civilization."[15] While the conference at Berlin and the following expositions across the Atlantic Ocean brought powerful minorities together to exploit the world's human and natural resources, the Pan-African conference convened a global black educated class to help plan a revolution for the marginalized.

The *Critically Queer* exhibition, *Reclaiming Afrikan* book, and "Queer in Africa" conference created, named, and performed Afrika through the less-well-cited materiality of the body, which was central in Du Bois's critique and also raises questions about the place of gender and sexuality in the various Pan-Africanist movements around the world. While the color line divided global haves and have-nots structurally, the problems of the color line in the everyday "show[ed] themselves chiefly in the color of the skin and the texture of the hair," Du Bois explained in the address.[16] And like the ways Europe's empires drew lines on the map of Africa to mark access to the continent's natural resources, apartheid South Africa famously used skin color and hair texture differences to criminalize non-normative gender identities and sexual orientation through policing who black and white bodies could be around.[17] Today, Afrikans across Africa are exercising rights to be in each other's presence in public and private spaces in a historical moment, in which a third of the world's national laws criminalizing same-gender sex and relationships, according to the International Lesbian, Gay, Bisexual, Trans and Intersex Association, are in Africa alone. While activists and legislators debate Botswana's penal code, the Gambia's criminal code, and Nigeria's anti-homosexuality act, among others,[18] Afrikans are conferencing in South Africa and around the world, "in open rebellion," to borrow from Saidiya Hartman's understanding of urban black women and girls at the dawn of the twentieth century in the United States.[19]

Considering the "Queer in Africa" and PAC conferences alongside each other highlights the ways in which gender and sexuality join race and class to mark the lines of national, continental, and human citizenship and belonging in Africa. Rethinking gender and sexuality from Matebeni, Pereira, and the "Queer in Africa" conference's vantage points poses a challenge to the contemporary pan-African movement to erase the divides colonialism created and bring formerly colonized people together across difference. By viewing the color line as inextricably linked with the lines drawn on the map of the African continent in the immediate aftermath of the 1884–1885 Berlin Conference, Matebeni, Pereira, and the "Queer in Africa" conferences, I observed, were bringing Du Bois's critique and method into the twenty-first century. It was via these connections in 2014—twenty years after the end of *de jure* apartheid (1948–1994) and sixty after the overturning of *Plessy v. Ferguson* (1896–1954)—that I was beginning to conceptualize and name queer pan-Africanism as such.

The morning after the *Critically Queer* exhibition opening, Macharia reflected on the conference's participatory format to advance preliminary methods for building Afrikan archives on the African continent. In a roundtable discussion on the timeliness of burgeoning scholarship in African queer studies, Macharia discussed a South African archival document concerning male-gendered homosexuality in the 1960s. The 1960s marked several important moments at the intersections of African history, queer history, and US history. The 1960s saw Africa's rapid decolonization and queer and trans people of color discontent leading up to the Stonewall riots of 1969. Challenging the idea that male homosexuals should not have appeared in South Africa's archival collection, particularly ones preserved by churches, Macharia urged Afrikan scholars to take note of "disposable" figures in colonial documents.[20] I began to ask myself what spaces could be potentially used to flip the logic of apartheid in global society on its head and rather foster queer inclusion. Archives centered on queer experiences in Africa like the Gay and Lesbian Memory in Action's (GALA) in Johannesburg struck me as one such place. Graeme Reid identifies GALA archives in Johannesburg, South Africa, as a site of preserving and excavating "existing records and documents relating to lesbian and gay experience."[21] What might black lesbian or trans women researchers find when they comb through the boxes? Does the space help black queer Africa-based scholars grow, I wondered?[22]

I took Macharia's call back to the United States, and in the fall semester of 2014 I went to see US-based writer, trans activist, and television director/producer Janet Mock speak at Macalester College in Minnesota, and witnessed a connection between both events that would prove foundational for my theorizing of QPA. The talk was part of Mock's book tour, though I would be unable to read the memoir cover to cover until five years later. *Redefining Realness* takes Mock's coming-of-age story as a mixed-race, black trans woman to illuminate black, indigenous queer and trans people of color's confrontations with discourses about authenticity and imposter syndrome. For Mock, these challenges are embedded in the ballroom category of "realness." In a realness category, ballroom contestants dress and perform experiences of going to work and school "in the real world," and compete by embodying specific gender identities while catwalking and showing off their looks in front of judges.

Though performance played important roles in the "Queer in Africa" conference and the ballroom scene, I want to draw attention to Mock's book tour performance at the elite private liberal arts college that evening. Before introducing her book and life story, Mock paid homage to Sylvia Rivera and Marsha P. Johnson, invoking their names to call the audience to witness the trans women of color in an ancestral pantheon of womanhood. In the book, Mock expanded that ancestry beyond Rivera and Johnson, to women of color across historical and geographic spaces:

> *I exist* because of the women who came before me, whose work, lives, and struggles I've greatly benefitted from. Whether it was 1966's Compton's Cafeteria riots or the Stonewall uprisings of 1969 or the daily battles against policing, exiling, violence, and erasure, trans women—specifically those from the streets with nothing to lose—always resisted. My foremothers

have role modeled, through their lives and work, the brilliance of anchoring yourself in marginalized womanhood.[23]

Invoking Rivera and Johnson's names at events centered around QTPoC in community evokes histories of resistance and erasure during and after the Stonewall uprising. Only in the decade leading up to the fiftieth anniversary of Stonewall has the US press centered racial and gender equity in commemorating the event. The She Built NYC campaign to install statues of transgender women of color Marsha P. Johnson and Sylvia Rivera near the Stonewall Bar site was one example. While Rivera and Johnson are now routinely commemorated as some of the firsts to stand their ground and fight back against the police when they raided the Stonewall Bar in 1969, their stories have gained new currency in popular culture. While these Stonewall Riots mark the beginning of the modern gay rights movement in the United States, popular narratives often ignored Rivera and Johnson's contribution, which are now only coming to light with the increased visibility of trans women in youth and popular culture.[24] By invoking their names, Mock confronted Johnson and Rivera's exclusion from the nation's origin story of the various rights movements for the protection of queer and trans people. For Mock, claiming ancestry to Johnson and Rivera reminded Mock's audience that trans women of color were at the forefront of gay rights: "They started Stonewall!" While Johnson, Rivera, and Mock descended from different genealogical trees, they each remain firmly rooted in a genealogy of transgender people of color revolutionaries.

In Andrea Jenkins's poem "eighteen," naming black queer and trans life came in the form of shout-outs: "S/O [shout-out] TO 18 TRANS SISTAS OUT THERE DOING THE DAMN THING," Jenkins exclaimed, in all caps. "CHERNO BIKO, LOURDES ASHLEY HUNTER, ARIANNA LINT, CECILIA CHUNG, VALERIE SPENCER, ASHLEY LOVE, ANGELICA ROSS, ARYKAH CARTER, MONICA ROBERTS, MISS MAJOR!, JANET MOCK, LAVERNE COX, TRACEE MCDANIEL, REINA GOSSETT, CECE MCDONALD, PARADISE LASHAY, REHEMA MERTINEZ, JUNE REMUS."[25] Jenkins—the United States' first black transgender elected official, serving her first term as vice president of the Minneapolis City Council in 2018—premiered the poem at Minneapolis's first Transgender Equity Summit in the fall of 2014. When the queer student leaders at my undergraduate college in Northfield invited me to recognize graduating seniors at the queer student programs banquet, I distributed copies of Jenkins's poem beforehand so the attendees could see the names as they heard me say them. Since I was becoming increasingly aware that the problem of the twenty-first century in Africa and across the diaspora may very well be the murders of trans women and femmes who are black, indigenous, and people of color, I shared Jenkins's poem to connect the students in rural Minnesota to the world beyond.[26] In the ten years between Jenkins's watershed victory and when she and I sat on a roundtable and used our names to speak and write into existence "Queer People of Color Histories in the Twin Cities" in document form,[27] I began sharing names as signals to build queer and trans solidarities across the Atlantic.

I learned that organizing what I had seen and heard across the Atlantic could fit under the African queer studies (AQS) I encountered after becoming more familiar with Macharia's interventions at the "Queer in Africa" conference. However, several structural and institutional roadblocks embedded in naming and timing made organizing across the disciplinary boundaries difficult and expensive. In spring 2016, for example, I helped host a conference at the University of Minnesota with fellow graduate students in African history. I learned closer to the conference's start date that our "Faultlines: Rethinking Temporal and Disciplinary Traditions in African Studies" would run over the same time period as another conference: "Learning to Breathe: Black Feminism, Performative Pedagogies, and Creative Praxis." As both events approached, I realized that I could not attend either because the postcolonial theory and black feminism conferences conflicted with a class I was teaching at the University of Minnesota's public liberal arts campus in Morris, which was a three-hour drive away from the conference site in Minneapolis. The experience illuminated the spatial and logistic faultlines that overlapped with the temporal and disciplinary ones we wanted to expose in the African studies conference. The overlapping events also reflected tensions between African studies and queer studies, and AQS and African feminism, and research and teaching in the neoliberal university.[28] Despite these roadblocks, I was able to find funding to invite AQS and African feminist scholars from the United States, Canada, and South Africa to join me on a roundtable at "Faultlines." Naming the roundtable after AQS, I incorporated the roundtable into my course syllabus and brought my students with me over 170 miles to attend. Midway through the African studies conference day, I brought my students to the "We Levitate: Making Music to Save Our Lives & Hear Our Truths" workshop at the black feminism conference. Moving across the different spaces and disciplines convinced me and my students that decolonial work must be multisited to exist in any shape or form. Moreover, the work must move, as the title "We Levitate" suggested, if only to save lives and hear truths.

In the fall of the same year, the Canadian colleague on the AQS roundtable, Taiwo Adetunji Osinubi, invited me to "Directions in African Queer Studies:

Agendas, Epistemologies, Practices," a conference at the University of Western Ontario in Canada. Every conference participant discussed work in progress, making it an intimate event, but we also felt more Afrikan work needed to be done on the African continent. At "Directions," conference participants discussed AQS's intellectual rootedness in area studies and queer studies.[29] Conferences usually take place in North America, Europe, or South Africa, and AQS scholars are oftentimes based there. I also considered what it meant to locate an AQS conference on colonial, contested land. While neighboring Canadian Indigenous studies departments actively promote ways to indigenize universities, our "Directions" conference took place on probably one of the whitest and wealthiest of Canada's universities. How many of us found it odd that no presentations began with land recognitions. Despite the problems embedded in our refusals to name the indigenous land on which we conferenced, our conversations were often redirected to *Reclaiming Afrikan*. In so doing, many of us saw our Afrikan scholarship as a corollary to Canada's ongoing decolonization project. At "Directions," Afrika clearly stood beside the liberation of Canada's indigenous populations.

Several controversies around naming involving religious minority and people of color communities in the United States, indigenous South Africans, and black cisgender and trans women all over the world transpired in the years following. #SayHerName became a rallying cry for the Black Lives Matter movement after Sandra Bland was found deceased in a Texas jail cell in the summer of 2015. Black students at Rhodes University began questioning their alma mater's namesake after comrades at the University of Cape Town successfully petitioned to remove Cecil Rhodes's statue from its prominent location on campus two months prior. #SandraBland and #RhodesMustFall would precede an exhibition at the University of Minnesota titled "A Campus Divided: Progressives, Anticommunism, Racism and Antisemitism at the University of Minnesota 1930–1942," which sowed the seeds for a movement to rename buildings on campus named after administrators who signed off on segregationist policies.

In 2017, famed Nigerian feminist novelist Chimamanda Ngozi Adichie told Cathy Newman in an interview for the United Kingdom's Channel 4 News that she did not believe the issues transgender women and cisgender women faced were one and the same. Newman asked if Adichie considered trans women to be "women." Adichie replied, "'trans women' are 'trans women.'"[30] Adichie's reply revealed a faultline in African feminism and trans feminism around gender identity, and trans women of color in the United States, the United Kingdom, and South Africa responded to Adichie's contention with harsh criticism: "If your feminism does not respect trans women in their full womanhood," black trans woman activist and essayist Raquel Willis wrote, "it's not truly intersectional."[31] Willis continued, sending the same message to activists in other communities: "If you don't advocate for the liberation of trans people, you aren't truly invested in equality. And if you don't advocate on behalf of black trans women, then you aren't truly invested in black liberation."[32] Other black trans women personalities including actor/activist Laverne Cox—who Jenkins invoked in "eighteen"—followed suit, calling out Adichie's particular brand of African feminism as dangerous for trans women of color everywhere.[33] The exchange illuminated the invisibility of all sorts of "women" in the archive when gendered subjects are rendered as such but not named.

While not emphasized in the 2014 book talk, Mock explained in *Redefining Realness* that naming ancestors in places that experienced settler colonial rule like Hawaii recalls important indigenous names and naming traditions. Mock explained it was important for her to name her ancestors before speaking about herself because contemporaries always stand on the shoulders of those who came before them. In the book *Redefining Realness*, Mock taught readers about *mahu*, for example. "Similar to the *mahu vahine* in Tahiti, *fa'afafine* in Samoa, and *fakaletti* in Tonga, which comes from the Tongan word *faka* (meaning 'to have the way of') and *leiti* (meaning 'lady')," *mahu* helped Hawaiians name femmes of all genders, though the term could help trans women and girls make sense of their identity as much as it could be used as an epithet to bully them in schools.[34]

Because the Adichie controversy transpired over my university's spring break, I asked my undergraduate Gender and Sexuality in African History students to follow the debate while they read historian Marc Epprecht's *Hungochani* for homework. Epprecht's book importantly advocated for the use of indigenous African terms for gender and sexuality, and used Southern Africa as a case study. In addition to paying close attention to the book's narrative, I assigned *Hungochani*'s glossary of terms and asked them to see whether or not "trans women" appeared. If they could not find the word, I asked students to judge whether or not the omission was justified. In our class discussion, students identified the Zulu word *isikhesana* and the Shona word *muremukadzi* as the book's best examples of trans women. According to the glossary, *isikhesana* translated to "female-gendered person or homosexual wife" and *muremukadzi* to "a male who lives as a female-gendered person" or a "Woman-man," which has a more derogatory connotation.[35] When my students returned from the break, I asked students why Adichie did not respond to Newman with an Igbo term. In conversation, we came to the conclusion that the debate restricted every argument to the English colonial language, making anything else tangential. The debate could only be settled, students concluded, when a variety of indigenous African terms defining sexual minorities and gender-nonconforming people were read alongside English terms.[36] It also became clear to them, as it is for me, that transnational debates over gender identity need to undertake the difficult project of translation to be decolonial.[37]

Bringing Shona and Zulu words into my Minnesota classroom helped my students think more closely with names in the readings I assigned that they found too challenging to say out loud—Tiwonge Chimbalanga, for example. One of the few faces of 2010s transgender rights in Africa, my predominantly white and Native American students only became aware of her story in Sibusiso Kheswa's "Negotiating Personhood—What It's Like Being Transgender in South Africa." Part of the *Reclaiming Afrikan* collection, Kheswa's article revealed the limits of the South African state's recognition of transgender individuals.

Even though South Africa's Alteration of Sex Description and Sex Status Act 49 of 2003 allows preop transgender citizens and asylum-seekers to list their gender identity in government documents, Tiwonge—a trans woman refugee escaping gender-based persecution in nearby Malawi—was initially unable to secure a government ID because of the country's strict immigration laws. With Act 49 and a constitutional definition of equality under the law as being protected from discrimination based on "race, gender, sex, pregnancy, marital status, ethnic or social origin, colour, sexual orientation, age, disability, religion, conscience, belief, culture, language and birth," students became more aware of how the words on an identity document could prevent transgender women from accessing neccesary medical care. Chimbalanga's story also illuminated the ways segregationist apartheid policies continue to exist de facto for gender and sexual minorities.

Naming Some Beyond

By way of conclusion, I invoke Tyna Adebowale, Rafeeat Aliyu, Jennifer Shinta Ayebazibwe, Unoma Azuah, Dineo Seshee Bopape, Amatesiro Dore, Pamella Dlungwana, Sokari Ekine, Yvonne Fly Onakeme Etaghene, Pumla Dineo Gqola, Charles Gueboguo, Milumbe Haimbe, Jessie Kabwila, Sibusiso Kheswa, Happy Mwende Kinyili, David Kato Kisule, Idza L, Thato Magano, Zandile Makahamadze, Makgano Mamabolo, Selogadi Ngwanangwato Mampane, Wamuwi Mbao, T. O. Molefe, Wame Molefhe, Audrey Mbugua, Bishara Mohamed, H. W. Mukami, Danai Mupotsa, Kagendo Murungi, Neo S. Musangi, Mphati Mutloane, Makau Mutua, Kenne Mwikya, Sibongile Ndashe, Lindiwe Nkutha, Kelebogile Ntladi, Stella Nyanzi, Awino Okech, Olakunle Ologunro,

Ola Osaze, Diriye Osman, Davina Owombre, Jabulani Chen Pereira, Olumide Popoola, Busisiwe Sigasa, Matshepo Thafeng, Dolar Vasani, Queenie, and Zukolwenkosi Zikalala to unsettle the silences around racial violence I encountered in the white community-based archives I trained with to learn the practice of history nearly twenty years ago.[38]

Many more need human lips to say their names across the black diaspora. Living anxiously in democracies and under constitutionally upheld laws that do not protect free gender and sexual expression, the Afrikans above and unnamed say each other's names to claim radical existence across and beyond Europe's maps of Africa and the world. The black queer Africa-based names I invoked in this chapter have pushed up against homophobic and transphobic laws and prevailing attitudes with their activist, artistic, and scholarly praxis, turning both toward and away from government archives. "A decolonial archival praxis begins from this understanding," for J. J. Ghaddar and Michelle Caswell explain "that western colonialism, empire and race are much more pervasive aspects of our field than is usually considered."[39] Building on Ghaddar and Caswell's method, this chapter has made the case for thinking with names as archival material to make sense of histories that oppose institutions of power as they create, preserve, organize, and recall histories of anti-colonialism in the era after colonialism.

Each event I recounted convinced me of the simple yet powerful truth that, in archives, names alone are already material enough. Names adorning archives matter just as much as the materials destroyed and preserved.[40] Recent debates over the renaming of buildings and bodies of water, and the removals of statues honoring slavedrivers, reveal the dynamic nature of space lawmakers and the constituents fix in place with names. The stakes of thinking with names in documents and on (and throughout) buildings are high for the black queer nonbinary historian because each one holds the potential to either heal or reproduce the state violence embedded in historical practice before they turn archival. I endeavor to think with and read aloud names as material for self-making.

Moving forward, queer pan-Africanism will name a practice and space that preserves the collaborative, dynamic spirit W. E. B. Du Bois and others brought to London in 1920, while also pushing back against settler colonial nativisms, which view citizens who do not conform to heterosexual gender binaries as pariahs undeserving of lives and afterlives. While not comprehensive in the least, the names invoked in this space bring me in conversation with the ancestors and relatives.[41] Therefore I offer up this document to shed a light on a network of folks who deserve their own houses. That the names they inherited, created, and abandoned will continue to live on, I say, "Viva!"

And in so doing, together, we dismiss "divide and rule," and we invoke the Afrika where our lives belong.

Notes

1 See Defeat of Jesse James Days, http://djjd.org (last accessed July 6, 2020).
2 Hartman, *Scenes of Subjection.*
3 Antoinette Burton defines "archive stories" as "self-conscious ethnographies" and "narratives about how archives are created, drawn upon, and experienced by those who use them to write history." Burton, *Archive Stories,* 6.
4 Macharia, "On Being Area-Studied," 188.
5 Macharia, "Archive & Method." To see the fruits of a queer African studies method, see Macharia, *Frottage.*
6 Ahmed, *Living a Feminist Life,* 90.
7 Macharia, "Archive and Method in Queer African Studies."
8 Marshall, Murphy, and Tortorici, "Editors' Introduction," 2.
9 Macharia, "Archive and Method in Queer African Studies."
10 Hamilton et al., *Refiguring the Archive,* 15.
11 Anderson, *Imagined Communities.*
12 Matebeni and Pereira, "Preface," in Matebeni, *Reclaiming Afrikan,* 7.
13 Matebeni and Pereira, "Preface," in Matebeni, *Reclaiming Afrikan,* 7.
14 Du Bois, "To the Nations of the World."
15 Du Bois, "To the Nations of the World."
16 Du Bois, "To the Nations of the World."
17 Zanele Muholi explored the tensions black and white lesbian skin and hair touching in South Africa raises in three triptych series of photographs: *Caitlin & I, Boston, USA* (2009); *ZaVa I, II, and III, Paris* (2013); and *ZaVa I, II, and III, Venice* (2013). For more on these politics within the context of postapartheid South Africa, see Thomas, "Zanele Muholi's Intimate Archive."
18 The criminalization of gender and sexual nonconformers pervades the formerly colonized Global South, not least in India. As gathered from Gayatri Gopinath's reading of the film *Fire,* Arnaldo Cruz-Malavé and Martin F. Manalansan IV remind us, "queer sexualities and cultures have often been deployed negatively to allay anxieties about 'authentic' national belonging." Cruz-Malavé and Manalansan, *Queer Globalization,* 2.
19 Hartman, *Wayward Lives,* xiii.
20 Macharia, "African Queer Studies."
21 Reid, "'The History of the Past,'" 194.
22 James, "Screwing the Assembly Line."
23 Mock, *Redefining Realness,* xvi.
24 Rivera and Johnson's histories are often invoked in times of crisis for trans people of color. See, for example, Pelaez Lopez, "17 Trans-of-Color Leaders."
25 Caps also prompts readers to reread the women's names and say them aloud and bring them to life, especially today, when trans women's lives and names face everyday precarity. Jenkins, *The T Is Not Silent,* 29–31.

26 The original title of the poem "eighteen" was "'loving a trans woman of color is a revolutionary act,' Laverne Cox," and inspired by the *Orange Is the New Black* television star's keynote address at the 2014 Creating Change conference in Houston, Texas. For Cox's full address, see National LGBTQ Task Force, "Laverne Cox at Creating Change 2014."

27 Albrecht, Campos, and Giusti, "Myth of the Great White North."

28 The African/queer studies divide is discussed at length in Currier and Migraine-Georges, "Queer Studies/African Studies." The AQS and African feminism divide is discussed in Nyanzi, "Queering Queer Africa." The challenges facing scholar-teacher-activists in the neoliberal university is discussed in Ferguson, *The Reorder of Things*.

29 Again, see Nyanzi, "Queering Queer Africa."

30 Newman, "Chimamanda Ngozi Adichie on Feminism."

31 Willis, "Trans Women Are Women."

32 Willis, "Trans Women Are Women."

33 Adichie, *We Should All Be Feminists*.

34 Mock, *Redefining Realness*, 103.

35 Epprecht, *Hungochani*.

36 The same was proposed for isiXhosa in Lwando Scott, "'South Africa.'"

37 The method of translation was proposed in Arondekar and Patel, "Area Impossible."

38 These names were behind written contributions to the following works, which I consider as part of a growing archive of queer pan-Africanism: Ekine and Abbas, *Queer African Reader*; Matebeni, *Reclaiming Afrikan*; Tamale, *African Sexualities*; and Xaba and Martin, *Queer Africa 2*.

39 Ghaddar and Caswell, "To Go Beyond," 78.

40 For Achille Mbembe, archives and buildings are connected. Here, I understand names as the critical symbol that connects archives and buildings. This interpretation riffs off the following passage: "The term 'archives' first refers to a building, a symbol of a public institution, which is one of the organs of a constituted state." Mbembe, "The Power of the Archive," 19.

41 Macharia, *Frottage*.

Works Cited

Adichie, Chimamanda Ngozi. *We Should All Be Feminists*. New York: Anchor Books, 2015.

Ahmed, Sara. *Living a Feminist Life*. Durham, NC: Duke University Press, 2017.

Albrecht, Charlotte Karem, Brandon Lacy Campos, and Jessica Giusti. "The Myth of the Great White North: Claiming Queer People of Color Histories in the Twin Cities (a Roundtable Discussion)." In *Queer Twin Cities*, edited by Kevin P. Murphy, Jennifer L. Pierce, and Larry Knopp, 90–118. Minneapolis: University of Minnesota Press, 2010.

Anderson, Benedict. *Imagined Communities*. London: Verso, 1991.

Arondekar, Anjali, and Geeta Patel. "Area Impossible: Notes Toward an Introduction." *GLQ: A Journal of Lesbian and Gay Studies* 22, no. 2 (2016): 151–71.

Burton, Antoinette, ed. *Archive Stories: Facts, Fictions, and the Writing of History*. Durham, NC: Duke University Press, 2005.

Cruz-Malavé, Arnaldo, and Martin F. Manalansan IV, eds. *Queer Globalizations: Citizenship and the Afterlife of Colonialism*. New York: NYU Press, 2002.

Currier, Ashley, and Thérèse Migraine-Georges. "Queer Studies/African Studies: An (Im)possible Transaction?" *GLQ: A Journal of Lesbian and Gay Studies* 22, no. 2 (2016): 281–305.

Du Bois, W. E. B. "To the Nations of the World." https://www.blackpast.org/african-american-history/1900-w-e-b-du-bois-nations-world/ (last accessed August 21, 2019).

Ekine, Sokari, and Hakima Abbas, eds. *Queer African Reader*. Dakar: Pambazuka Press, 2013.

Epprecht, Marc. *Hungochani: The History of a Dissident Sexuality in Southern Africa*. Montreal: McGill-Queen's University Press, 2005.

Ferguson, Roderick. *The Reorder of Things: The University and its Pedagogy of Minority Difference*. Minneapolis: University of Minnesota Press, 2012.

Ghaddar, J. J., and Michelle Caswell. "'To Go Beyond': Towards a Decolonial Archival Praxis." *Archival Science* 19, no. 2 (2019): 71–85.

Hamilton, Carolyn, Verne Harris, Jane Taylor, Michele Pickover, Graeme Reid, and Raxia Saleh, eds. *Refiguring the Archive*. Berlin: Springer-Science+Business Media, 2002.

Hartman, Saidiya V. *Scenes of Subjection: Terror, Slavery, and Self-Making in Nineteenth-Century America*. New York: Oxford University Press, 1997.

Hartman, Saidiya V. *Wayward Lives, Beautiful Experiments: Intimate Histories of Social Upheaval*. New York: Norton, 2019.

James, Elliot. "Screwing the Assembly Line: Queerness, Art-Making and Mandela's Mercedes-Benz." *Kronos: Southern African Histories* 42, no. 1 (2016): 56–70.

Jenkins, Andrea. *The T Is Not Silent: New and Selected Poems*. Minneapolis: Trio Bookworks, 2015.

Macharia, Keguro. "African Queer Studies." Gukira, August 24, 2014. https://gukira.wordpress.com/2014/08/24/african-queer-studies/.

Macharia, Keguro. "Archive & Method: Toward a Queer African Studies." Gukira, June 6, 2014. http://gukira.wordpress.com/2014/06/06/archive-method-toward-a-queer-african-studies.

Macharia, Keguro. "Archive and Method in Queer African Studies." *Agenda: Empowering Women for Gender Equity* 29, no. 1 (2015): 140–46.

Macharia, Keguro. *Frottage: Frictions of Intimacy across the Black Diaspora*. New York: NYU Press, 2019.

Macharia, Keguro. "On Being Area-Studied: A Litany of Complaint." *GLQ: A Journal of Lesbian and Gay Studies* 22, no. 2 (2016): 183–90.

Marshall, Daniel, Kevin P. Murphy, and Zeb Tortorici. "Editors' Introduction: Queering Archives: Historical Unravelings." *Radical History Review* no. 120 (Fall 2014): 1–11.

Matebeni, Zethu, ed. *Reclaiming Afrikan: Queer Perspectives on Sexual and Gender Identities*. Athlone: Modjaji Books, 2014.

Mbembe, Achille. "The Power of the Archive and Its Limits." In *Refiguring the Archive*, edited by Carolyn Hamilton et al., 19–26. Berlin: Spring-Science+Business Media, 2002.

Mda, Zakes. *Ways of Dying*. Cape Town: Oxford University Press South Africa, 1995.

Mock, Janet. *Redefining Realness: My Path to Womanhood, Identity, Love and So Much More*. New York: Atria Books, 2014.

Murphy, Ryan, Brad Falchuk, and Steven Canals. "Pilot." *Pose*. FX Network. First aired: June 3, 2018.

National LGBTQ Task Force. "Laverne Cox at Creating Change 2014." February 5, 2014.

Newman, Cathy. "Chimamanda Ngozi Adichie on Feminism." Channel 4 News, March 10, 2017. https://www.channel4.com/news/chimamanda-ngozi-adichie-on-feminism.

Nyanzi, Stella. "Queering Queer Africa." In *Reclaiming Afrikan*, edited by Zethu Matebeni, 65–69. Athlone: Modjaji Books, 2014.

Pelaez Lopez, Alan. "17 Trans-of-Color Leaders Resisting, Inspiring, and Keeping It Real in 2017." Everyday Feminism, July 21, 2017. https://everydayfeminism.com/2017/07/trans-of-color-leaders-inspiring/ (last accessed August 21, 2019).

Reid, Graeme. "'The History of the Past Is the Trust of the Present': Preservation and Excavation in the Gay and Lesbian Archives of Southern Africa." In *Refiguring the Archive*, edited by Carolyn Hamilton et al., 193–207. Berlin: Spring-Science+Business Media, 2002.

Scott, Lwando. "'South Africa Needs to Find a New Way to Talk About Being Gay.'" *The Guardian*, January 27, 2015.

Tamale, Sylvia, ed. *African Sexualities: A Reader*. Cape Town: Pambazuka Press, 2011.

Thomas, Kylie. "Zanele Muholi's Intimate Archive: Photography and Post-Apartheid Lesbian Lives." *Safundi: The Journal of South African and American Studies* 11, no. 4 (2010): 421–36.

Willis, Raquel. "Trans Women Are Women. This Isn't a Debate." The Root, March 13, 2017. http://www.theroot.com/trans-women-are-women-this-isn-t-a-debate-1793202635.

Xaba, Makhosazana, and Karen Martin, eds. *Queer Africa 2: New Stories*. Braamfontein: MaThoko's Books, 2017.

8. SECONDHAND CULTURES, EPHEMERAL EROTICS, AND QUEER REPRODUCTION
Notes on Collecting David Bowie Records

DANIEL MARSHALL

The erotic cannot be felt secondhand.—AUDRE LORDE, "Uses of the Erotic: The Erotic as Power"

. . . Again and again
Want to be here, and I want to be there
Living just like you, living just like me
Forever . . . —DAVID BOWIE, "Never Get Old"

"People used to make records," as Ani DiFranco reminds us, "as in a record of an event, the event of people playing music in a room."[1] And while archival records are ordinarily secured in place—the catalogued folder, the compactus, the archive-suitable building—so that people can access them, LPs have been, in my experience growing up with secondhand albums, records that have traveled. At first, I would listen to my parent's records—Dusty Springfield, Elvis, Black Sabbath, rock and roll collections, Jimmy Little; later I would buy my own secondhand records, as cheap purchases in charity stores and garage sales in the 1990s. Of course, radio, music videos on television, cassettes, and later, compact discs all played important roles in how I accessed music before the internet, but these uses of vinyl records meant that my earliest thinking about music was shaped by my embodied interactions with the ephemerality of the record as object. In terms of both the materials from which they were made and the equipment required to play them, vinyl records demanded a (this) child's keen concentration. From the textual detail of album covers' often icon-style photography and their sometimes elaborate design and discursive text, to the feel and smell of the aging cardboard and plastic, records distinguished themselves by their sensory presence as objects. And in the handling of a record, this materiality disciplined a kind of informal, embodied ceremony: with the small hands of my childhood, removing the record from its sleeve, lowering it onto the turntable and maneuvering the needle into place without smudging or scratching required a kind of care and reverence which meant, at least, that my training to be a good altar boy who did not drop the bells or spill the wine had not all been in vain.

Of course, vinyl records have been foundational to the theorization of ephemerality within queer studies, at least since José Esteban Muñoz's pathfinding work in his 1996 essay "Ephemera as Evidence: Introductory Notes to Queer Acts." Here, Muñoz draws inspiration from Paul Gilroy, especially "Gilroy's reading of vintage soul, R & B, and funk album covers as part of the exchange of ephemera that connects and makes concert a community like the Black Atlantic."[2] Building on Gilroy's emphasis on the cultural productivity of the circulation of ephemera, Muñoz theorizes the study of queer ephemerality as an examination of the performative circulation of objects—objects in action—rather than straight textual analyses of the objects as discrete things themselves. The study of queer ephemerality is, for Muñoz, a study of "what a queer act does, performatively and, in turn, socially." "By focusing on what acts and objects do in a social matrix," argues Muñoz, we can develop our understanding of the roles objects play in "*doing* queerness," in "perhaps, *making* queer worlds."[3]

"Ephemera" in archive studies is generally taken to refer to a collection of materials that were thought to only have a use in the short term, but have nevertheless been preserved for the longer term (a distinction this chapter will consider in more detail in terms of a distinction between firsthand experience and secondhand use). Typically in LGBTQ archives emerging over the past fifty years, ephemera has come to encompass a broad range of materials and objects including, in the case of the Australian Queer Archives, "flyers, brochures, circular letters, postcards, stickers, sales catalogues and theatre programs," and "2500 files documenting organisations, events, individuals and subjects from across Australia."[4] Muñoz of course famously expands the definition of ephemera to include "traces of lived experience and performances of lived experience, maintaining experiential politics and urgencies long after these structures of feeling have been lived."[5] This emphasis on the "trace" is important for Muñoz as it reflects the shift away from a focus on the object itself and a move toward a focus on the object's circulation. The vintage badge in the queer archive carries significance for Muñoz, one could argue, less because of the historical moment that it might evidence and more because of the queer life and knowledge suggested and enacted by the historical movement of the object.

In this chapter I lean on a capacious and loose definition of the queer archive (as exemplified in Muñoz's theorization of the ephemeral) in the context of my arguments about secondhand record collecting as a site for the circulation of ephemeral materials that can help us think about queer reproduction via archival encounter. As others have argued (e.g., Eichhorn in this volume), such definitions of the queer archive risk obscuring the material practices of work upon which institutional or physical archives rely. I'm wagering that a diffuse concept of the archive in discussions of secondhand relations can be politically useful, taking the critique by Eichhorn and others into account, as this focus on the secondhand draws attention to questions of labor and the materialist economics of exchange and circulation that Eichhorn argues have often been obscured by poststructuralist definitions of the archive (although Eichhorn focuses the discussion about labor and economics on the material practices of archival collection management). I am deploying this queer understanding of the archive in the service of an argument that seeks to be attentive to questions of materiality and labor in an effort to contribute to work by Eichhorn and others to think across those old false dichotomies of theory and practice.

The shift away from a positivist interpretation of historical evidence that characterizes the turn to the archives in queer studies since the 1990s is based in large measure on the historically controversial role of evidence in queer life and culture. This is principally due to the ways in which evidence has historically been used to police or deny queer life. There is also, Muñoz suggests, a kind of temporal lag structuring much of the archival endeavor, which means that archival evidence struggles to speak to contemporary gender and sexual difference because such evidence has been collected, catalogued, and preserved according to historical knowledges and not present realities: "Evidence's limit becomes clearly visible when we attempt to describe and imagine contemporary identities that do not fit into a single preestablished archive of evidence."[6] Because, in Muñoz's analysis, "proof" of queer life has often been ignored (because queers can't "count") or defaced (because leaving a trace can be too dangerous), queerness has come to be associated with subcultural modes of expression and replication:

> Queerness is often transmitted covertly. This has everything to do with the fact that leaving too much of a trace has often meant that the queer subject has left herself open for attack. Instead of being clearly available as visible evidence, queerness has instead existed as innuendo, gossip, fleeting moments, and performances that are meant to be interacted with by those within its epistemological sphere—while evaporating at the touch of those who would eliminate queer possibility.[7]

Muñoz describes queer ephemera as a type of "invisible evidence," shaped by a "fundamental indeterminacy," which he situates within a cultural technology of "queer worldmaking" where queerness is understood as "a possibility, a sense of self-knowing, a mode of sociality and relationality."[8] The question of how ephemeral objects function within broader "mode[s] of sociality and relationality" to "transmit" queerness is the key starting point for this chapter, prompted in part by the way in which queer understandings of ephemera can help provide accounts for the ways in which people's experiences of queerness often have sticky relationships to objects.

In particular, this chapter considers the secondhand record as a queer object and its material circulation as a practice of queer reproduction partly because of the way in which queer definitions of ephemera invoke ideas about secondhand records and their circulation. As a "record of an event," LPs are among "those things that remain after a performance, a kind of evidence of what has transpired but certainly not the thing itself."[9] And as a particular type of remnant, a materialization of what remains after the event, the record as a residualized object necessarily prompts us to understand its significance as linked to the processes of production and circulation through which this residualization, and thus the object itself, is made possible. Therefore, the record materializes the distance—in time, space, experience, and epistemological framings—between the moment of its production and its subsequent moments of use. It is in an attempt to think in a more detailed way about this *distance* that this chapter arrives at its central preoccupation with notions of firsthand, secondhand. In particular, this chapter takes up Muñoz's interest in the role of ephemera—all those "traces, glimmers, residues, and specks of things"—in the transmission of queerness by exploring ideas about firsthand, secondhand in the context of ephemeral record circulation.[10] As a nonbiological "modality" or "transmission" of "queer sociality and relationality" (to use Muñoz's words), this chapter argues that in secondhand record circulation we can find a cultural account of queer reproduction that deepens understandings of how "ephemeral objects in part constitute . . . queerness" (see Muñoz's discussion of Michael Moon).[11]

Insofar as queerness is understood by Muñoz as a "shared structure of feeling" (drawing on the work of Raymond Williams), this structure is composed then of objects and their patterns of circulation. If queerness is "shared," it clearly relies on mechanisms through which this sharing occurs. For Muñoz, these practices of sharing—practices of queer transmission—have been shaped by antagonism to sexual and gender difference ("since queerness has not been let to stand, unassailed, in the mass public sphere") and thus pressed into ephemeral forms, specific kinds of "invisible evidence."[12] The transmission of queerness via objects has been shaped, then, by a kind of stealth behavior, materializing queerly but "evaporating at the touch of those who would eliminate queer possibility."[13] In Muñoz's analysis, ephemeral objects are pregnant with "queer possibility," and circulate in anticipation of a queer reception.

But what kind of terms can we use to deepen a discussion of the ways in which queerness as a "feeling" is fostered by queer users' encounters with objects? Following Williams, Muñoz emphasizes the importance of a social and cultural understanding of the function of ephemera—"ephemera, and especially the ephemeral work of structures of feeling, is firmly anchored *within* the social"—and his essay is a clear call for the development of more detailed social and cultural accounts of queer transmission via objects.[14] Because, for Muñoz as for Williams, ephemera are shaped by "culture's particularities"—what are described as culture's "specific dealings, specific rhythms"—the study of the cultural work of ephemera requires methods which privilege nongeneralized critical vantage points: "ephemera is always about specificity."[15] In sum, the study of ephemera is always by necessity a study of the user, either by explicit or implicit disclosure.

So to develop this discussion about secondhand record circulation as a technology of queer reproduction, this chapter is also instigated in some respects by the specifics of my own experience with records as queer ephemera (largely in Australia over the past couple of decades, but in North America and Europe too), and as someone situated within a broader cultural economy of secondhand record circulation. The subtitle for this chapter, "Notes on Collecting David Bowie Records," is a kind of unfortunate misdirection because the idea of collecting records has become so freighted with a problematic politics of hipster social capital that it distracts from what this subtitle is attempting to designate. What I am trying to reference here are my experiences, in the 1990s, when I started more actively buying secondhand records as cheap alternatives. The late 1980s and early 1990s had seen vinyl albums largely replaced by cassettes and compact discs, and I started buying secondhand records because they enabled me to access more music. As a teenager, I had pored over my *Bowie The Singles Collection 1* and *2* CDs, but in secondhand record format I could afford to dig deeper into Bowie's back catalogue with *Hunky Dory, Ziggy Stardust, Aladdin Sane, The Man Who Sold The World*, and more—all secondhand records that I understood as queer objects and that, once I had them in my own collection, made me feel as if I were connected, in some inchoate way, to a broader cultural experience of queerness.

There are, then, three main reasons for focusing on secondhand Bowie records in this chapter. First, our earlier discussion of Muñoz's adaptation of

Williams demonstrated that the study of queer ephemeral specificity requires a methodology which privileges nongeneralized critical vantage points (that is, a critical reflection on ephemera by critically reflecting on their uses and users). Second, and following on from the first, it has been, for me, my own experiences handling secondhand Bowie records that have in many ways generated these questions about erotic ephemerality and queer reproduction, and I'm working on the presumption that the popular legibility of Bowie as a queer cultural figure makes the queerness of secondhand record circulation more explicit and functional as an illustrative case for the purposes of this chapter if the records I am discussing are Bowie's. The third reason, and this in turn is an extension of the second, is that as this chapter will demonstrate, the queerness of Bowie has been produced through a range of different cultural forms—film parodies (*Velvet Goldmine*), the traveling Bowie archive, and the events marking his death—that provide further illustration of the queer reproductive effects of secondhand relations which this chapter centrally discusses in relation to used records but are evident across so many different sites of what we might call "Bowie culture." This chapter is largely a response to some key questions I have asked myself as I have variously searched for, bought, played, and organized Bowie records in my collection: If I describe my experience with secondhand Bowie records as queer, what does that actually mean? And, while queerness itself necessarily resists demands to explain itself, if we are to deepen our shared discussions about cultural histories of queer transmissions, then on what terms might these experiences of secondhand records as queer be further discussed?

A central issue here is a consideration of the way in which queerness as a diffuse erotics of gender and sexual dissidence is experienced ephemerally or archivally—that is, via ephemeral objects. Recalling Muñoz's argument about the compression of queer transmission into stealth maneuvers and "invisible evidence," secondhand records present us, within the terms of our analysis here, with an opportunity to think about how they—and the distributive rhythms of firsthand, secondhand characterizing archival ephemera—constitute queerness by "doing" queer erotics. This shift to focus on what archival objects "do" rather than what they "mean" is a central characteristic of Muñoz's queer deconstruction of the archive, and it provides a key way to theorize queer archival encounters as technologies of queer reproduction.[16] A study of secondhand Bowie records circulation provides one way to think about the active archive performatively doing queerness through actions of circulation and use—archival or ephemeral objects in motion—and by expressing erotics in ephemeral form. By focusing on secondhand exchange, this discussion can deepen understandings of the erotics of using things used by others, and the intimate connections thus fostered by accessing archival collections.

Ephemeral Erotics

In queer archive and museum studies and practices, the relationship between the erotic and the ephemeral has historically been understood in a number of ways. Often the relationship is understood in what could be described quite literally as a self-evident manner, where the archive or museum holds ephemeral objects which are said to evidence queerness in one way or another in and of themselves (e.g., the inclusion of "queer ephemera" at the 2017 Tate Britain show *Queer British Art 1861–1967* is one enactment of this understanding).[17] This *repository* relationship, where institutions are understood to hold objects in which a queer erotics somehow naturally (or at least "self-evidently") inheres, is in contrast to a more explicitly conceptual or *metaphorical* understanding of the relationship between queer erotics and ephemerality, where the structures of the latter—including a critical indeterminacy and a fleeting temporality or liveness—are interpreted as mirroring the undulations of the former. As Jennifer Tyburczy writes:

> Ephemera, like queerness, are elusive and indefinable, gritty and fragmented. So often policed into silence and shadows, queerness has historically shared with ephemera a marginalized relationship to the archive, a lingering status as detritus, an unworthiness of being saved. For scholars and archivists in search of queer histories, ephemera's evocative relationship to remains and traces mirrors the ongoing struggle to cope with the loss and mourning that characterized the height of the HIV/AIDS crisis.[18]

Influentially, the relationship between the study of erotics and ephemera in LGBTQ archives has been shaped by analyses privileging what Muñoz called "the tyranny of identity."[19] While critiques of essentialist interpretations of erotics in the archive have been a staple of queer archive studies since the field's inception, with a focus on the erotic truths that ephemeral materials may or may not reveal, less attention has been given to the way in which the circulation of such ephemeral objects constitute an erotics through the terms of their object circulation.

The circulation of ephemeral objects constitutes a queer erotics—and perform a kind of queer transmission or reproduction—through a distributive rhythm of firsthand, secondhand. A central feature of the wave of gay and lesbian archiving that swept through the 1970s was a focus on preserving "traces" (to recall Muñoz's term) of homosexual erotics. Love letters, photographs, and memoirs were some of the ephemeral forms generated and archived to preserve evidence of "firsthand" experiences of dissident erotic desire and activity. For many people, Gay Liberation's injunction to "come out" was taken as a call to produce (and then reproduce in the form of publication and archival preservation) evidence or proof of the realities of sexual and gender difference by creating records which documented their own firsthand erotic experiences. In "Uses of the Erotic: The Erotic as Power," Audre Lorde provides a succinct summation of this cultural affirmation, grounded in her lesbian literary poetics of the self: "The erotic cannot be felt secondhand."[20] Curiously, however, this affirmation of sexual and gender difference as unequivocally defined by personal firsthand experience begins to unravel as soon as a reader encounters eroticism in Lorde's work or, as I will argue, in any archival or ephemeral encounter. Indeed, no reader of Lorde can make their way through much of her work without experiencing Lorde's eroticism "secondhand."[21] Her account of her "first time," with Ginger on the creaking "old brass bed" at Walker Road in *Zami: A New Spelling of My Name* is an evocative example of how, through recollection and circulation, the erotic is received on secondhand terms: it is a "queer transmission," to use Muñoz's term, from firsthand experience to secondhand reader:

> I reached out and put an arm around Ginger, and through the scents of powder and soap and hand cream I could smell the rising flush of her own spicy heat. I took her into my arms, and she became precious beyond compare. I kissed her on her mouth ... Ginger's breath warmed my neck and started to quicken.[22]

The reader inherits Lorde's eroticism through her reproduction of it in language and its circulation through circuits of reading practices, interpretation, and publication economies. This recollection of eroticism—in literature as in archives—explicitly conveys eroticism as a secondhand experience. Erotics, then, is shaped by practices of secondhand circulation and is consequently inseparable from the diverse types of ephemera—books, diaries, photos, fabrics, case notes, and so forth—that carry expressions of eroticism through their many varied routes of circulation. This strong emphasis on the public expression and interpretation of the erotic via the ephemeral underlines eroticism's strongly social character and, alongside an expansive understanding of archives as social spaces in which interpretive moments are convened in relation to ephemera, it provides an explanation as to why reflections on the private pleasures of the self so often turn to explorations of the public pleasures of the archive.

There is no firsthand experience of the erotic in the archive—it's all second-hand: all of the pleasures described or depicted, and all of the documents scuffed and darkened, or kept pristine and organized, evidence the social histories of the many hands, eyes, and countless keen hopes that have brought that document to its current resting place with you, as reader, in the archive. A potential caveat: one *could*, perhaps, mount an argument that one could experience the erotic "firsthand" in the archive if one asserted that the ephemeral stimuli was not an expression of the erotic in the first place. The logic of this argument would then rest on one's assertion that it is one's engagement with the otherwise innocent ephemeral object that is the primal scene of eroticism. This could be an argument for a firsthand erotic encounter in the archive—one sparked by, and impossible without, one's own insertion into the archive. However, this argument that an ephemeral object becomes eroticized through encounter does rely on there being something stimulating in the ephemeral object in the first place, so insisting on the capacity to experience a firsthand erotics in the archive seems to require an obfuscation of the material presence of what functions as erotic stimuli in the ephemeral object (and the archival space), and of the labor practices of preservation that have enabled one to access the object. I contend that erotic encounters in the archive are structured by secondhand relations. The expression of eroticism through the social circulation of ephemeral materials means, then, that eroticism and ephemera are bound together by crucial questions of movement. Here we recall Muñoz's emphasis on the social life of the ephemeral—queerness resides less in private markers indicating difference to the self, but as pulsing, circulating signals to others: queer ephemera "*are meant to be interacted with*."[23]

In the discussion of the motion from the first hand to the second—from a personal, privatized felt experience (as in Lorde's account) to the inevitably social and shared experience of interpreting expressions of such firsthand experience (as enacted by Lorde's readers)—what comes into focus is the centrality of a broad cultural politics of circulation that glues erotics and ephemera together and asks us to think more deeply on the contours of this cultural politics of how sexuality and gender get handed on through things. The movement of used David Bowie records provides us with one specific example of how ephemeral erotics circulate within a queer cultural economy of firsthand, secondhand, and how this structure of circulation materializes cultural practices of queer reproduction, transmission, or inheritance in particular ways. Moreover, by thinking about secondhand record collection as a practice through which people mark and recirculate cultural products, we can diversify cultural accounts of Bowie as a queer figure, and people's experiences of queerness via the cultural consumption of Bowie, by elaborating the queer effects and relations enabled by the unsteady practices of accumulation and distribution that characterize secondhand record collecting. Unmoored, critically, from "the tyranny of identity" and interpretive practices that seek to identify the queerness in Bowie as text—from his lyrics to his imagery to his celebrity and beyond—this focus on secondhand cultures and queer reproduction as practices illustrates not what archives *mean* but instead what they *do*. Indeed, the practice of collecting used David Bowie records can be seen as an enacted elaboration of queer textual preoccupations that are often read into the records themselves but one that requires us to acknowledge the ephemerality of the circulating objects. Reading used Bowie records as objects that accrue significance not only as records of queer textuality but *as records of queer relations*, secondhand record collecting materializes a specific form of queer reproduction, evidenced by the ephemeral transmission of queerness from hand to hand, user to user.

Crate-Digging

Let's picture a secondhand record store—one that is perhaps familiar to you, or perhaps one that you like the most. Crates, dust, vinyl, music posters, music playing. Maybe there's a general studied silence, people cruising the shelves, cruising each other. Someone—generally, a bloke—is behind the counter, and he's doing something important or looking bored; maybe he's helpful and you end up talking for twenty minutes about that record that's hard to find; or maybe he doesn't like the record you pick and so it's all a kind of disheveled, arch aloofness. This is a familiar scene and an increasingly romantic one: an image of the secondhand record store as the place where we might find ourselves, and others like us. Famously, to the point of parody, secondhand record stores have historically provided a portal to an otherwise hard-to-access musical past and, along with it, the opportunity to curate your own cultural lineage through the choices you make therein. The romance of the record store lies, no doubt, in the way in which it has historically provided a material location for people to actively assemble their sense of their own tailored cultural space and genealogy, both of which are stepped out according to the particular routes one cuts through the store and its holdings based on taste and desire and the limits of the store's stock and the money in one's pocket.

Of course, buying secondhand records isn't what it used to be. The revival of vinyl consumption over the past decade in the context of the electronic distribution of music, which has dramatically reshaped the cultural and social role of the record store, reveals a revitalized commodification of the cultural experience of secondhand record collecting. Expensive vinyl reissues, online auctions for rare pressings, record stores that are fitted out with their own fashionable cafés, the absorption of records and record paraphernalia within the highbrow market of art galleries and museums, and the marketing of record store merchandise by famous record stores that have effectively become brands themselves all illustrate how buying new and used records has changed markedly since the growth of the public market for vinyl in the twentieth century.[24] Incorporated now within a widening capitalist hipster economy, contemporary cultures of secondhand record collecting that value rarity and sponsor the cashed-up collector are set against the recent past of the 1980s and 1990s when vinyl was willfully abandoned by many for the affordances offered by the new media of the cassette and compact disc. Where buying secondhand records might once have been the thrifty option, often it is now pitched to consumers at the other end of the retail market.

We could talk more about the details of these transitions, including the way in which nostalgia is working all over the place here—both in terms of how the resurgence in vinyl consumption can be read as an effective commodification of nostalgia for the past that the records (whether secondhand or reissued) materialize as well as in terms of my nostalgia for a time when secondhand records were, well, cheaper, and when purchasing them was, perhaps, more social. In the wake of Bowie's death, there have been a variety of Bowie vinyl products hitting the market. One example was the special release of "Space Oddity 50th Anniversary Box Set"—two 7-inch records—for around $60 (AUD).[25] And the contrast between this consumption opportunity and my memories of digging through crates to come across Bowie titles I'd been looking for that were priced at a third or a sixth of that price is not only cast in monetary terms. The perseverance of crate-digging, of getting my hands dirty digging through all those records, a literal kind of ephemeral dirtiness of dust and cardboard flakes, alongside a successful feeling of thrift when a record was found mean that the experience of digging out secondhand records is culturally different than buying a reissue online, even when you could buy more or less the same record both ways. Coming upon a desired used record in the crates felt like I was participating in something other than just capitalist consumption because someone had put that record into the stream of circulation and here I was picking it up, if only for a while.

While "limited deluxe" box sets and rereleases cultivate an aura of prestige by presenting themselves as rare and tightly held in a few hands (thus justifying their expense), the thrifty secondhand record purchase somehow made me feel like I was joining in a larger cultural experience suggested by the many hands that had moved that record my way. In secondhand exchange, the profits of the large record companies are subordinated to different logics of value and exchange. I was always reminded of this by the little stickers you would sometimes see on records which declared "Not for commercial sale! Promotional use only!" or words to that effect; nevertheless, these records blithely made their way through the stream of secondhand circulation, moving on the current of a differently configured market. All of which is to say that the shifting social and economic conditions of buying and selling vinyl, as marked out in this little sketch, demonstrate that used record collecting has not been a static set of cultural practices with a self-evident set of cultural meanings across time and place. Understood as a cultural practice with shifting meanings and effects, secondhand record collecting can be understood, similar to sexuality and gender, as a set of actions whose significance is in motion, performatively enacted and diffusely brought into life.

The question of why people buy secondhand records is one that invites, then, many possible responses. Prosaic explanations might suggest to us that people buy used records simply because they like the music, or because there is some form of profit to be made. Perhaps the record is very cheap—cheaper than accessing the music in alternative ways—and perhaps the consumer believes they are investing in an asset that will increase in value over time, whether that is cashed out in terms of monetary return or accumulated in terms of acquired cultural capital. I would suggest, though, that neither of these accounts sufficiently explains the particular significance of vinyl records in queer culture. Examples of this significance are easy to locate across a variety of diverse data sources, including oral history, fictional biography (including film), and conducted and imagined ethnographies (by which I mean to refer to lived knowledges—things we know and infer anecdotally based on the lives we live and the lives we observe). For instance, I have written elsewhere about British singer Tom Robinson and his oral history recollections of the deep impact of discovering *Hunky Dory* (1971) as a young person in the early 1970s, and how that record went on to shape the Tom Robinson Band's pathfinding contribution to the gay music scene later in that decade (best demonstrated by the fame of the band's signature anthem, "Glad to Be Gay" [1978]).[26] We can find another vivid illustration of the potent relationship between Bowie records and queer youth life in Todd Haynes's David Bowie fantasy film, *Velvet Goldmine* (1998). In this film, Brian Slade (played by Jonathan Rhys Meyers) stands in as Bowie's proxy, and Haynes presents us with a relationship between an adolescent Arthur Stuart (played by Christian Bale) and the proxy Bowie record which goes beyond Stuart simply liking the music, offering instead a depiction of some of the intensities driving historical queer fandom and queer attachments to records as objects.

The link between the record and Stuart's teenage queer desire is made explicit across a set of scenes that bridge together two key moments in the film. In the first scene Stuart is shown embarrassedly buying a copy of Brian Slade's *The Ballad of Maxwell Demon*—a proxy Bowie album replete with an explicit, homoerotic cover which clearly references the covers of *Diamond Dogs*, the dress cover of *The Man Who Sold the World*, and the interior fold-out image of *Aladdin Sane*. Later, in the second key moment, this record is referenced again when Stuart is caught by his parents masturbating in his bedroom to the queer prospects visually and aurally fostered by the proxy Bowie. The film tells us that Stuart's relationship to the record and the erotic promise of the proxy Bowie that it brings into his bedroom is homosexual because of the way in which humiliation frames its recognition: the boys in the record store mock Stuart calling the Bowie proxy a "pansy rocker" and a "fucking poof";[27] and his father, having walked in on his son, yells at him for bringing "shame to this house" by doing such "filthy" things, leaving his son hunched over, shaking and weeping, thoroughly disgraced.[28]

That these scenes are presented to the viewer as retrospective glances by Stuart as a now more solidly and self-assuredly queer adult, encourages us to situate the value of that record within a cultural economy of queer youth life: it lit a spark, nurtured a desire, and contributed in some patchwork way to giving some form to those dissident gendered and erotic prospects in life which Stuart might yet have desired but not so far had such a clear vision of.

Across the film, the adult Stuart pursues the Bowie proxy, the sponsor of his adolescent queer desire, and the queerness of his teenage reception of the record is presented causally as a seed that grows into the queer things Stuart grows up to do. Like Oscar Wilde's badge that a queer child (a character called Jack Fairy, no less) finds in the opening sequence of the film—a sequence which links queer children a century apart by the possession of this object—the record as object is depicted as holding some kind of magical power: a power to foster within the queer youth the capacity to more vividly imagine a queer future by offering that young person tangible, explicit sounds and images that give audible and visual form to otherwise amorphous queer feelings. The object instantiates far more than an advantageous interpretive moment—it provides orienting matter for sensory experience and thus a materialization of the queer possibilities referenced. A hallmark of recollections of queer youth life is the extent to which queer prospects materialize through encounters with creative cultural textual resources. As the teenage Stuart excitedly exclaims to his disapproving parents when the Bowie proxy appears in sexualized, live interview on the television screen in the family's living room: "That's me! That, that, that is me!"[29] (Indeed the ways in which both the record cover and the television screen invoke the idea of the framed portrait, the mirror and the window perhaps helps us to understand how Stuart's reading of the proxy Bowie on vinyl covers and on television can inspire such simultaneous identification and projected visioning.) As a film based on the substitution of Slade for Bowie, and Stuart as a double for queer youths everywhere, *Velvet Goldmine* is a film of magical transferrals, and one that suggests that precious properties reside in the proxy Bowie record, the discovery of which is depicted as a revelation for Stuart. Finally, he is able to see his own queer self by seeing the queerness in the Bowie proxy. Through this process of transferred identification, the Bowie proxy reveals the queer youth to himself with sounds and visions that, naturally enough, Stuart takes on then as his own. (And we see this expressed visually in the wardrobe choices that develop in the film where Stuart begins to dress more like his idol, echoing the now familiar cultural practices of fan mimicry which are not limited to Bowie fan cultures but were immortalized in the vivid depiction of Bowie fans in the classic concert film, *Ziggy Stardust and The Spiders from Mars* [1973/1979].)

While insights regarding these practices of identification, celebrity emulation, and identity confirmation have long been a feature of fandom and celebrity studies, what I want to focus on here is how we might think about records as objects fitting in to all of this. If *Velvet Goldmine* is a film about magical transferrals, it is also surely one about fantasy origins, opening as it does with its queer sci-fi mash-up of the Oscar Wilde and Moses nativity stories (the film opens with a spaceship depositing an infant Oscar Wilde on the doorstep of an Irish home). The infant Wilde is wearing an identifying brooch which, as previously discussed, the queer child (Jack Fairy) picks out of the dirt, a century or so after Wilde's time, after being pushed to the ground by schoolyard bullies. The film invites the audience to think about how queerness is transferred across generations. Insofar as the record functions within a technology of queer recognition for Stuart, the film draws parallels between Wilde's brooch and the proxy Bowie record: they are both presented as material objects in which a kind of transgenerational queerness inheres and where the discovery and possession of the object works to confirm the recognition of the subject as a queer one, to themselves and to us as we look on.[30] A central theme within what we might call "Bowie studies" is to approach, in more or less formal ways, Bowie ephemera—records, costumes, photographs, and so on—as queer objects. To conduct queer readings of the sleeve photography, song lyrics, sexual and gendered personae, and so forth has become, ironically, routine. However, a focus on the materiality of the record rather than its textuality provides a critical opening for examining queerness in the context of Bowie's work. Taking up Todd Haynes's popular presentation of the circulation of Bowie records in queer lives, we can use this creative depiction of the enduring significance of Bowie records to queer life and the capacity of queer objects to transfer queerness through the transfer of the object as a generative site for thinking about the effects of such in terms of *queer reproduction*.

On Queer Reproduction

I am using the term *queer reproduction* to refer to the eventuation of queer people—that there are queer people in the world—and the relationships these people have with queer people and cultural materials preceding and coming after them. The eventuation of queer people has routinely been framed as an error in reproduction (children have historically been expected to grow up heterosexual and gender normative). Relatedly, queer people rarely have straightforward relationships to their queer antecedents (detached from biology and blood lines the "straight" lines of genealogy and inheritance are replaced by diverse ways to experience connections to the past). For these reasons, the notion of "queer reproduction" is used here to suggest the range of non-normative modes of generation, growth, and development that accrue around the event of queer life. A key focus within queer temporality studies has been the theorization of divergent patterns of growth which deviate from standard reproduction within normal gendered and sexualized time. For example, Jack Halberstam famously marked out subcultural practices, including archival endurances, that index forms of life that are not the product of heteronormative temporal arrangements in some of the early work theorizing "queer time":[31]

> Queer subcultures afford us a perfect opportunity to depart from a normative model of youth cultures as stages on the way to adulthood; this allows us to map out different forms of adulthood, or the refusal of adulthood and new modes of deliberate deviance. Queers participate in subcultures for far longer than their heterosexual counterparts . . . Just as homosexuality itself has been theorized by psychoanalysis as a stage of development, a phase, that the adolescent will hopefully pass through quickly and painlessly, so subcultural involvement has been theorized as a life stage rather than a lifelong commitment. For queers the separation between youth and adulthood quite simply does not hold.[32]

Lee Edelman has also advanced theoretical arguments for an understanding of what we might call queer reproduction as diverging from the straight, linear reproductivity of a model of futurity that preserves prevailing gender and sexual arrangements.[33] Mikko Tuhkanen has critically engaged the work of Guy Hocquenghem to theorize queer reproduction (or "queer breeding") as a mode of generation marked by "non-limitative horizontal relations" and a "model of horizontal proliferation" that dispute the "hierarchical succession" associated with heterosexuality.[34] This "model of horizontal proliferation" offers a useful way to think about queer reproduction because it also underlines how queer reproduction incites anxieties about time as well as sexuality and gender. As is made clear in Tuhkanen's reading of Hocquenghem, this anxiety about time centers on the mystery of homosexual genesis and aetiology:

> [Hocquenghem] suggests that homosexuality does not only represent the eugenic fear/hope of extinction, but also the eugenic nightmare of uncontrolled breeding, asexual parturition, contagion, and infection . . . [arguing that] "the transmission of homosexuality has something faintly mysterious about it . . ." (109) and [Hocquenghem] quotes a member of the Parisian police force who . . . refers to homosexuals as "people who, though not procreating, have a marked tendency to multiply" (qtd. in Hocquenghem 109).[35]

That is, the "mystery" of homosexuality draws from anxieties about how homosexuals emerge from heterosexual couplings. The question of how queer subjects develop over time despite ostensibly heterosexual origins has helped motor a whole field of queer studies which has taken as its focus the intersection between queerness and temporality. From observations about the essentially productive nature of time and historical conditions by foundational social constructionists including Gayle Rubin, Jeffrey Weeks, and Jonathan Ned Katz, through to the emphasis on time in Foucauldian discourse analysis, to queer emphases on repetition and durationality in theories of performativity, queer studies has wedded queerness itself to concerns about temporal structures. Scholars such as Elspeth Probyn, Angus Gordon, and Kathryn Bond Stockton have theorized how queerness can be understood as a set of experiences, subject positions, and knowledges produced through retrospection, anticipation, and "sideways" growth.[36]

Because of the enduring mystery of homosexuality, the question of queer reproduction hangs like a loose thread, like a recurring question. While working on this chapter, I attended a family reunion, and pasted high across one of the long-plastered walls in the church hall were genealogical diagrams of family trees. Little boxes of children descended from little linked-up boxes of relatives and spouses—until they didn't. Here and there a little box would find no part-ner and yield no other little boxes—it just hung there, winking its questions. An irony of the way in which the lack of children has worked as a historical sign of queerness is that it raises questions not only about the childless person's lack of children but also about their own upbringing. Is this person queer, and if so, how did they become that way? The family tree works as a diagrammati-cal way of understanding cascading, generational hereditary relations until the lives contained within such diagrams fail to yield the requisite information to keep the diagram in function. These lives become abrupt full-stops. And by bringing to an abrupt dead-end a straightforwardly reproductive way of un-derstanding generation, these lives call on us to find other sources of infor-mation—to dig deeper. Queer life has a naturalized relationship to archival retrieval work because the histories of intimacy recorded in charts of births, deaths, and marriages explain so little. We are compelled to seek out signs of life in more diverse ephemera.

This imperative to identify traces of queer life has bound together a queer-affirmative politics with the technologies and scholarship of archives—it is part of the glue sticking together erotics and ephemera. The question of how queerness can be identified through things is thus a live question in critical reflections on the interpretation of evidence and on the recognition of di-verse sexual and gender practices over time. In *For the Record: On Sexual-ity and the Colonial Archive in India*, Anjali Arondekar asks, "What does it mean for the material history of objects to provide a genealogy for a history of sexuality?"[37] Through the story of the india-rubber dildo, Arondekar raises questions about the implications of instrumentalizing objects to help tell particular stories about sexuality. Archival objects, Arondekar reminds us, are often freighted with extra significance because their materiality is often taken to signify the kind of evidentiary or epistemological "presence" which is, for Arondekar, "the plangent predicate for any archival logic, despite concessions to the fact that this meaning is always under erasure and in need of recon-struction."[38] Arondekar's recourse to an aural characterization—"the plangent predicate"—is especially evocative in the context of this chapter's meditations on used records. From this perspective, the playing of used records this chap-ter conjures up could be interpreted as literally enacting the kind of mournful sound of archival "recovery" which Arondekar's critique identifies—second-hand record use as an enactment of queer loss and lamentation—where the "something missing" being added to "the archive" of used records is a cultural theory of queer reproduction, its own kind of technique of archival recovery.[39] Agreeing with Arondekar's critique of an archival hermeneutics which falsely promises "recovery and repleteness," this chapter's situation of a material history of used records within cultural ideas about histories of queerness is not, then, for the purposes of stitching together a more complete history—where lost parts of some queer family tree can be revealed and remembered—but to contribute to developing a critical language for queer proliferations or "plenitude," as Arondekar might say.[40] Building on Stoler's critique of Foucault, Arondekar engages Foucault's theorization of the "perverse implantation,"

> whereby sexual perversions . . . have to be "replanted" . . . not in the circuits of "reproductive" activity but rather in the ends of bourgeois profit or knowledge. "Let them take their infernal mischief *elsewhere*," Foucault reasons, pointing out that it is only in the safely "elsewhere" that the illegitimate avatars of sexuality and untrammeled sex have "a right to [safely insularized] forms of reality."[41]

Arondekar goes on to describe "Foucault's diagnosis of an elsewhere, [as] a space where aberrant ('infernal') sexual matters can be shepherded into profitable service."[42] As an interpretive approach to a cultural practice and not a historical method, queer reproduction builds on Arondekar's identification of the false binary established between sanctioned reproduction and the queer "elsewhere" to think about queerness in terms of cultural practices of reproduction, and ones that are made legible through histories of uses of material objects.

While records circulate in many ways, the notion of the secondhand record binds our understanding of the object to a particular set of practices of exchange. If we can regard a record like *Hunky Dory* as a queer object from the moment of its public reception in 1971, through queer readings of its signs, values, and qualities, then finding an old copy of that LP in a record store in 2001 or 2071 invites us to think about this record as an object of exchange in an economy of transferring used records, and the relationship between such practices of exchange and the queerness of the object. The record's histories of circulation invite us to reflect on the queer significance of secondhand exchange. If a Bowie record holds particular significance as a queer object to Tom Robinson or Todd Haynes's Stuart in the 1970s, then does it make sense to think of the circulation of records like *Hunky Dory* in a used records economy as practices of handing around or handing down, through time, textual sites for the recognition of queerness? And if this contention holds, then can we say that the secondhand circulation of Bowie records compounds—or multiplies (recalling Hocquenghem's "model of horizontal proliferation")—the queerness that is already associated with the album by merit of its lyrics, image, musicality, and celebrity? And if we are prepared to read secondhand record exchange as a technology of ephemeral queer multiplication, then I think we can develop a more detailed understanding of how queer reproduction works through the shared distribution of Bowie records by briefly discussing two features of buying secondhand records.

The first feature characterizing secondhand records is prior ownership. Each used record has a previous user—someone who has presumably listened to it, handled it, made it their own in some way—thus the secondhand record inevitably becomes a sign of a particular social history of use, and this history often vividly marks albums, through creases, stains, damage, additions, and annotations. The scratched record, for instance, becomes a physical and often visible and audible marking that alters the record, making that historical social relation something the next user can see and hear and sometimes feel. These interventions in the record invite the latest user to be curious about the historical markings; how and why did they happen, what occurred to mark the records in these ways, what kinds of hands have been here before?[43] Through its "secondhand" character, a used vinyl copy of *Hunky Dory* invokes for its new owner a cross-generational history of users of the queer object that simply did not exist for those people buying the record new and experiencing it firsthand when it was first released. Thus, the used record builds a sense of queer life by retrospectively providing the secondhand buyer with a sense of history which is pregnant with possibility to the extent that the specific details of that history cannot be fully known. We see this especially when records are marked with people's names, or with annotations next to the songs they like best, and so on. This retrospective installation of a queer history works like reproduction in reverse, giving the secondhand user already in existence a sense of the firsthand owner of the record, and of all the imagined hands on the record in between. Here, predecessors are not conjured up as ancestors in a hereditary line of transhistorical homosexuality but as guarantors of the prospects of living a life structured, in part, by queer tastes and attachments. (The question of what constitutes "queer tastes and attachments" is, of course, an unsettled question, and one which can only be posed within shifting interpretive contexts. This means that accounts of what queer tastes and attachments are will necessarily vary among people, and their accounts will be shaped, in part, by the ephemeral objects, like secondhand records, they use, and by the ways they share them.) The imagined queer social history which the used record materializes might be seen as securing the possibility of future queer life (again, however, that is understood within the context of the interpretive moment).

Through participation in this economy of exchange, the used record collector can enter into this imagined queer social history. Is it too much to suggest that through possession of used records record collectors might come to imagine themselves as sharing a kind of social space with the shadows of all those other users across time and place? And if these records materialize spectral queer kin, might that be one explanation for the ways in which records can be understood as keeping us company? And if they help make queer life more imaginable not only through their textual queerness but through the ways in which their histories of exchange suggest the prospect of living in a world where others might share our queer affinities, do the records themselves—demanding as they do so much physical space in people's private spaces—come to stand in as proxies for all those lost queer users the secondhand user can never know? As the singer sings, "sometimes it gets so lonely."[44] Could this be one explanation for the vinyl revival—that ephemeral materials comfort us through their material accumulation? Might the sheer volume and materiality of archival objects perform a role of signification that the textual knowledge carried and conveyed by each discrete object cannot? Could this be, recalling Muñoz, because the objects materialize a way of doing queer life instead of simply suggesting some kind of LGBTQ "meaning"?

If buying used records can be understood as an active process of situating the self within an imagined nest of social relations, then these relationships are also structured by the economic terms under which the queer object is exchanged. While there is a thriving market in expensive used records, the second feature of secondhand record distribution that I want to note is the significance of the remaindered record. An inspiration for this chapter was my curiosity at finding a copy of *Aladdin Sane* in a secondhand record store, somewhere in Melbourne I think, with its corner cut off. Apparently, albums have been historically marked and defaced not only by previous users but also by stores that would cut into album covers to mark remaindered stock. This could be done by cutting off the corner off the album, slicing into the album sleeve, or puncturing a hole through it. And far from being incidental, these markings are crucial to the ways in which these objects accrue significance within cultural practices of queer reproduction because they materialize their histories of having been handled. In his reflections on archives, bodies, and violence, Zeb Tortorici theorizes "archival misinscription," expanding on a Derridean notion of archival inscriptions, to explore "the body and its desires to enter the historical record":

> In Derridean terms, "inscription" can perhaps be best understood as "the processes through which traces of a lived past life are 'archived' by individuals or societies in ways that make the place of uncovering—the archive—a point of intersection between the actual and the imagined,

lived experience and its remembered (or forgotten) image." Archival misinscription—working alongside, and not necessarily in opposition to, archival inscription—goes one step further, showing how misrepresentation becomes a necessary precondition for (representations of) the body and its desires to enter the historical record in the first place. It participates in, and thus pushes on, what Marisa Fuentes has called *mutilated historicity*.[45]

While Tortorici's theorization of archival misinscriptions of the body references a particular set of concerns distinct from those of this chapter, the emphasis on the role of violence in the shaping of archival materials and the role of this violence in assisting them to "to enter the historical record" provides a useful way to approach the archival significance of the damage and literal inscription work which so often characterizes used records. Described sometimes as "cut outs,"[46] these markings often reference slow or failed circulations of the product within the capitalist economy of consumption at the time of its original release. As the "remaindered," these records are circulating not just via the queer modality of the secondhand but also through the modality of the discount sale, a modality we might also retrieve as queer insofar as it materializes a failure or frustration of its maximal incorporation within a capitalist economy of profit-based exchange. Insofar as cut outs materially mark records as remainder or surplus stock, they allegorize queer life: as referencing that which is left over, historical homosexuality is perhaps a classic illustration of remaindered life, an illustration brought to life by vernacular historical descriptions of lesbians as having been "left on the shelf" and gay men as being "such a waste." Secondhand record exchange, of course, is at its base a process of adding value, insofar as the object continues to attract monetary expenditure and cultural interest, and we can see this in the way in which that damaged, remaindered secondhand copy of *Aladdin Sane* continues to float between an unfinished sequence of secondhands. Marked by queer social histories of prior users and queer economic histories of allocating value to previously devalued stock, the secondhand Bowie record provides a material site for inheriting a historical sense of queer attachments to objects and fostering an imagination of a queer social life.

The Afterlives of the Secondhand

This chapter began as a response to Bowie's traveling archive—"David Bowie Is" was exhibited at ACMI in Melbourne as part of the city's Winter Masterpieces suite of artistic and curatorial programming across the city's major galleries and exhibition spaces, after opening at the Victoria and Albert Museum in London in 2013.[47] Featuring materials from Bowie's own archive in New York (a "75,000-piece collection that an archivist had spent several years organizing"[48]), the exhibition includes illustrative displays of toys Bowie likely played with as a child through to handwritten lyrics and iconic costumes which signal key moments in his long recording career. In both its place-based and virtual incarnations (the exhibition toured globally and is now available in smartphone app form as an "official augmented reality adaptation of the legendary exhibition," and as an online collection at the Victoria & Albert), this exhibition formalized secondhand encounters with Bowie ephemera in an unprecedented way.[49] Turning the Bowie Archive into a blockbuster traveling art exhibition which is then turned into an app blurs lines between archives, museums, galleries, and virtual spaces, mirroring in some ways the transformation of ephemera that occurs when archival collections are turned into institutional repositories (see, for example, Cvetkovich in this volume). As a hybrid show—archives-as-exhibition—"David Bowie Is" accentuates the secondhand character of experiencing Bowie's ephemera. A world away from *Velvet Goldmine* and the private queer moment which Stuart enjoys with the record in his teenage bedroom, "David Bowie Is" knocks the private walls down and visitors mill about together as if the whole exhibition is something like a teenage fan's bedroom, fantastically supercharged. From (personal) object to (institutionalized) object, visitors are called to a particular form of historical witnessing. The intense repetition of Bowie material only serves to emphasize Bowie's absence, underlining how the visitor's experience of the archive-as-gallery is not a firsthand experience with Bowie himself but encounters at another remove. Suddenly, the attendants become the show: "David Bowie Is" convenes a historical witnessing, less of Bowie himself and more of the social spectacle of the fans themselves.

Bowie died six months later. In many ways, the "David Bowie Is" show had institutionalized the idiom for reproducing Bowie and the queerness associated with him after his death through its careful curation of opportunities for secondhand relations through which firsthand, personal encounters with the man himself are subordinated to engagements with what he signifies via archival encounters with Bowie ephemera. This cultivation of secondhand relations is made more explicit in what we might call the *Lazarus* suite of legacy works across which Bowie's death was publicly staged.

In the wake of Bowie's death, I put this chapter away for some time because the international outpouring of grief dramatically changed the scale of my reflections on Bowie, secondhand relations, and queer reproduction. Across multiple media platforms, what was observable was a scaled-up version of the social spectacle of fan engagement with Bowie ephemera which I had witnessed in a more curated way at the "David Bowie Is" exhibition. Mourning his passing, fans painted murals, assembled shrines, dressed up like Bowie, performed his songs, watched his screen performances, and wrote about him. In so many ways, these efforts to achieve proximity to Bowie represented a spectacularized mode of the secondhand experience, echoing Bowie across globalized media markets. In many respects, these cultural practices of remembrance and legacy generation themselves demanded to be considered as forms of queer reproduction.

Far from incidental, these practices of secondhand relations and queer reproduction are observable in the body of work which accompanied Bowie's death. This is made most explicit by the thematic emphasis in these works on the biblical story of Lazarus—a story of resurrection that is used as a metaphor for Bowie's endurance, after death. Insofar as metaphors are always devices of secondhand relations—where the designation of one thing is achieved by the designation of something else—the *Lazarus* poetics of Bowie's late works reveal this emphasis on reproducing himself through others. On December 6, 2015, a musical, *Lazarus*, cowritten by Bowie and featuring his songs, opened at the New York Theater Workshop.[50] This production provides a sequel to the 1976 film *The Man Who Fell to Earth*, with Michael C. Hall playing the character Bowie had played in the film. A couple of weeks later, Hall sang the title track on Stephen Colbert's *Late Show*,[51] introducing his performance this way:

Hello, it's me, David Bowie. Ziggy Stardust, The Thin White Duke, and now, in my most outlandish persona yet, acclaimed actor Michael C. Hall. Don't recognise me?[52]

"Look up here, I'm in heaven," Hall sings, "I've got scars that can't be seen / I've got drama, can't be stolen / Everybody knows me now."[53] The single and its accompanying video were released less than a month later, on Bowie's birthday, and two days prior to his death.[54] The day after his death, the cast of the musical recorded the soundtrack, which was subsequently released.[55] Across those final months, Bowie manages the transition from life to death by managing the transition of performing Bowie from himself to others. Through these things, Bowie—who popularized the idiomatic presentation of the pop star as a series of diverse personae—ends his life by staging the presentation of himself as a person performed by others.[56] He is reproduced through others—the character in the musical, the impersonation by Michael C. Hall, the life of the music video postmortem and the emulative activities accompanying so many of the commemorations that occurred in the wake of his death. Through these *Lazarus* legacy works, Bowie becomes a performance of himself back to himself, and then to the rest of us. Performed by someone else, he is collapsed into a secondhand relation. This "horizontal proliferation" of so many Bowies underlines how Bowie's reproduction of himself, postdeath, is enabled by the collapsing of being Bowie into acts of secondhand impersonation and engagement. Secondhand cultures facilitate his queer reproduction. For his 2014 retrospective compilation *Nothing Has Changed*, Bowie released three different versions with three different covers—each featuring an image of Bowie staring into a mirror. The photographs are taken years apart from each other.[57] As the singer sings, "And nothing has changed, everything has changed."[58] Recalling Stuart's use of the record sleeve as screen, window, and mirror, these portraits bring into relief the mutability at the heart of Bowie's artistic presentation. "Don't you recognise me?" asks Hall as Bowie—Bowie continues, but in changed form. In these ways, these portraits prefigure the queer proliferations that take center stage at Bowie's death. Through the many performances of Bowie by others, these legacy works present a kind of staged secular resurrection, a second coming that keeps coming "again and again" as Bowie sings in "Never Get Old," illustrating how the secondhand circulation of ephemeral fragments can be put to work in queerly reproductive ways.

As is so often the case, death is lucrative for the archive. Bowie's practices of postdeath queer reproduction, as we have seen through this brief discussion of his *Lazarus* poetics, have yielded so many more objects for attachment and accumulation—ephemera that have been so centrally incorporated into the secondhand lives that Bowie has enjoyed since dying. Vinyl copies of Bowie's final album, *Blackstar*, released two days prior to his death, sold out in a matter of days, with secondhand copies subsequently listed for sale for close to a thousand pounds.[59] Similarly, vinyl releases of the *Lazarus* soundtrack and other posthumous titles have gone into circulation, generating more and more ephemeral possibilities for users as yet unknown.

This returns us to where we began: a reflection on how theorizing the secondhand and queer reproduction can help us think about our engagements with things like records, and how the accumulation of these things can help us think about the social lives of archives. In this chapter I have argued that queer reproduction is a generative conceptual approach to the archive because we need to develop more theoretical resources for thinking about how sexual and gender difference—queerness—gets reproduced through ephemeral encounters. Here, I have suggested that thinking about the routes of circulation and exchange which constitute archives in terms of secondhand relations can be a useful way for conceptualizing relationships between ephemera, firsthand producers, and subsequent "handlers" of such ephemera. I have suggested that this conceptualization provides a way of recognizing the social character of the archival encounter which then provides a conceptual grounding to appreciate how people use ephemera to shape and inform their own sense of themselves and the social that exists beyond the archive (that is, it can help them produce new understandings of ways to be queer). In this sense, while it may seem more reasonable to call these archival and ephemeral engagements practices of queer *production* rather than queer *reproduction* (because the reader in the archive is hardly reproducing a facsimile of the queerness or eroticism depicted in the ephemeral object), I have stuck with queer reproduction as a term because what we are theorizing here is not a straight, hierarchical replicant model of reproduction (à la the cascading little boxes of the family tree) but, recalling Hocquenghem, a queer model of reproduction as "horizontal proliferation," as nonhierarchical difference. Like the rows and rows of crates filled with used records that present the secondhand record store as a neat visual metaphor for this kind of horizontal proliferation, secondhand erotics circulate ephemerally, close at hand, inviting the next hand. Queer ephemera call us into life. By paying attention to the ways in which the archive yields life we can deepen our understanding of what is at stake in the attachments that adhere between queerness and its things and find more readily, in the remnants of what has been used and discarded, resources for more queer life.

Notes

An earlier version of this chapter was presented at the Bowie Symposium accompanying the tour of the Bowie Archives to ACMI (Melbourne) in 2015. I thank the conference organizers and audience for their engagement with this work. I am especially grateful to Zeb Tortorici for his generous and detailed feedback; thanks also to Valda Marshall, Kevin P. Murphy, Joan Nestle, and my fellow volunteers at the Australian Queer Archives who have inspired so much of my thinking about queer archiving.

1 DiFranco, "Fuel."
2 "Muñoz, "Ephemera as Evidence," 11. See also Cvetkovich, *An Archive of Feelings*.
3 Muñoz, "Ephemera as Evidence," 12.
4 "Ephemera", March 11, 2022, https://queerarchives.org.au/collections/ephemera/.
5 Muñoz, "Ephemera as Evidence," 10–11.
6 Muñoz, "Ephemera as Evidence," 9.
7 Muñoz, "Ephemera as Evidence," 6.
8 Muñoz, "Ephemera as Evidence," 6.
9 Muñoz, "Ephemera as Evidence," 10.
10 Muñoz, "Ephemera as Evidence," 10.
11 Muñoz, "Ephemera as Evidence," 11.
12 Muñoz, "Ephemera as Evidence," 11; see also 6.

13 Muñoz, "Ephemera as Evidence," 6.

14 Muñoz, "Ephemera as Evidence," 10.

15 Muñoz, "Ephemera as Evidence," 10.

16 Muñoz, "Ephemera as Evidence," 11–12, 14.

17 See "Queer British Art 1861–1967," press release, December 9, 2016, http://www
.showonshow.com/tate/2017/queer_british_art/pressdocs/press_release.pdf.

18 Tyburczy, "Queer Acts of Recovery and Uncovering," 4.

19 Muñoz, "Ephemera as Evidence, " 14.

20 Lorde, "Uses of the Erotic," 59.

21 The Oxford/Lexico dictionary defines "secondhand" as, among other things, referring to "(of goods) having had a previous owner; not new" and "(of information or
experience) accepted on another's authority and not from original investigation" (see
"second-hand," March 13, 2022, https://www.lexico.com/definition/second-hand).

22 Lorde, *Zami*, 138–39.

23 Muñoz, "Ephemera as Evidence," 6.

24 For some discussions of the history of vinyl records, see Richard Osborne's chapter
"Vinyl" in *Vinyl: A History of the Analogue Record*. For other examples of telling histories of vinyl, see "A Fascinating Look Back into the History of Vinyl Records,"
November 8, 2020, https://phonostage.co.uk/blog/a-brief-history-of/the-history
-of-vinyl-records/; and Matt Davenport, "Groovy Chemistry: The Materials Science
Behind Records," *Chemical and Engineering News*, June 13, 2016, https://cen.acs.org
/articles/94/i24/Groovy-chemistry-materials-science-behind.html.

25 "Space Oddity 50th Anniversary Box Set," Warner Music Australia, March 11, 2022,
https://store.warnermusic.com.au/collections/david-bowie/space-oddity-50th
-anniversary-box-set. On record collectors see Shuker, "Beyond the 'High Fidelity'
Stereotype."

26 Marshall, "Queer Breeding."

27 *Velvet Goldmine*, at about the 18-minute mark.

28 *Velvet Goldmine*, at about the 70-minute mark.

29 This is a reference to Bowie's legendary performance of "Starman" on *Top of the Pops*
in 1972. See David Hepworth, "How Performing Starman on Top of the Pops Sent
Bowie into the Stratosphere," *Guardian*, January 15, 2016, https://www.theguardian
.com/music/musicblog/2016/jan/15/david-bowie-starman-top-of-the-pops.

30 For a related discussion about the ways in which ephemeral objects can be understood
to confer or transmit queerness, please see Leah DeVun and Michael Jay McClure's discussion of unruly archival objects, like *Womanist Pin*, which, reframed through artistic
redeployment refuse to be "stilled in the past." Rather than being subsumed within "a
catalog of dead objects" such ephemera "may foster an afterlife" recognizable through
their "recirculat[ions]." See DeVun and McClure, "Archives Behaving Badly," 122. For
some related discussions of *Velvet Goldmine*, see Fontenot, "The Dandy Diva"; Luciano,
"Nostalgia for an Age Yet to Come"; and O'Neill, "Traumatic Postmodern Histories."
On Bowie and fandom, see Cinque and Redmond, "Introduction."

31 Halberstam, "What's That Smell?"; also see Halberstam, *In a Queer Time and Place*.

32 Halberstam, "What's That Smell?," 44.

33 Edelman, *No Future*.

34 Tuhkanen, "Breeding (and) Reading," 1001; and Tuhkanen, "Mestiza Metaphysics," 281. See also Hocquenghem, *Homosexual Desire*, 109; and Marshall, "Queer Breeding."

35 Tuhkanen, "Breeding (and) Reading," 1002; see also 1022.

36 Gordon, "Turning Back"; Probyn, "Suspended Beginnings"; Stockton, "Growing Sideways"; and Stockton, *The Queer Child*.

37 Arondekar, *For the Record*, 98.

38 Arondekar, *For the Record*, 102.

39 Arondekar, *For the Record*, 102.

40 Arondekar, *For the Record*, 102; 99.

41 Arondekar, *For the Record*, 105.

42 Arondekar, *For the Record*, 105.

43 For a related discussion of archival or ephemeral "liveliness," please see Cifor, "Stains and Remains." I thank Zeb Tortorici for encouraging me to think more about stains and scratches. For a discussion of secondhand markets see Appelgren and Bohlin, "Growing in Motion," and Hansen and Le Zotte, "Changing Secondhand Economies."

44 Bowie, "Be My Wife."

45 Tortorici, *Sins against Nature*, 49–50.

46 For some thoughts on "cut outs"/defacement see "Record Sleeve Corners Cut—Why?," November 2003, http://boards.straightdope.com/sdmb/showthread.php?t=224198 and "Cut-out (recording industry)," February 13, 2022. https://en.m.wikipedia.org /wiki/Cut-out (recording_industry).

47 Please see "David Bowie Is," March 11, 2022, https://www.acmi.net.au/whats-on/past -exhibitions-david-bowie-is/ and "David Bowie Exhibition Breaks V&A Record," BBC, November 8, 2016, https://www.bbc.com/news/entertainment-arts-37907055.

48 Please see Roslyn Sulcas, "Ch-Ch-Ch Changes of David Bowie," *New York Times*, March 22, 2013, https://www.nytimes.com/2013/03/23/arts/music/david-bowie-is -opens-at-the-victoria-and-albert-in-london.html.

49 See "David Bowie Is Virtual," July 16, 2018, https://www.davidbowie.com/blog/2018 /7/16/david-bowie-is-virtual-press-release; "David Bowie Is: The AR Exhibition," March 12, 2022, https://davidbowieisreal.com/; and "David Bowie," March 12, 2022, https://www.vam.ac.uk/collections/david-bowie.

50 See Ben Brantley, "Review: David Bowie Songs and a Familiar Alien in 'Lazarus,'" *New York Times*, December 7, 2015, https://www.nytimes.com/2015/12/08/theater/review -david-bowie-songs-and-a-familiar-alien-in-lazarus.html.

51 See Alex Young, "David Bowie, as Michael C. Hall, Performs 'Lazarus' on Colbert— Watch," *Consequence*, December 19, 2015, https://consequence.net/2015/12/david -bowie-as-michael-c-hall-performs-lazarus-on-colbert-watch/; for the performance also see Messi Begh, "Michael C. Hall, Lazarus CBS Performance," YouTube, March 17, 2016, https://www.youtube.com/watch?v=hKBUc4yW2bo.

52 See Young, "David Bowie, as Michael C. Hall, Performs 'Lazarus' on Colbert."

53 See "Lazarus Lyrics in Full," December 16, 2015, https://www.davidbowie.com/2015 /2015/12/17/lazarus-lyrics-in-full.

54 See Hannah Furness, "David Bowie's Last Release, Lazarus, Was 'Parting Gift' for Fans in Carefully Planned Finale," *Telegraph*, January 13, 2016, https://www.telegraph.co.uk /news/2016/03/16/david-bowies-last-release-lazarus-was-parting-gift-for-fans-in-c/.

55 See "David Bowie's Lazarus Musical Records Cast Album," *Playbill*, January 11, 2016, https://www.playbill.com/article/david-bowies-lazarus-musical-records-cast-album -com-378935.

56 Which is not to say such transitions and impersonations only featured in Bowie's final months. Kate Moss, for example, appeared as Bowie's proxy at the 2014 Brit Awards (see Jamie Feldman, "Kate Moss as David Bowie at the Brit Awards Is the Coolest Thing You'll See Today," *HuffPost*, February 20, 2014, https://www.huffpost .com/entry/kate-moss-david-bowie-brit-awards_n_4822738; see also Linda Sharkey, "Kate Moss Pays Tribute to David Bowie through Her Outfit Choice," *Independent*, January 12, 2016, https://www.independent.co.uk/life-style/fashion/features/kate -moss-pays-tribute-to-david-bowie-a6807891.html). Given the integral role, in Bowie's work, of slipping between "selves"—of dissolving a solid sense of the "first person" through the proliferation of so many "secondary" expressions—the presentation of himself as just one other persona that could be handed on to others to perform is not an artistic departure. The event of his death does, however, underline the centrality of secondhand relations and queer reproduction to thinking about Bowie because his death makes emphatic the loss of any future prospect of a "firsthand" experience of Bowie. The endurance—indeed the proliferation—of Bowie beyond the grave demonstrates the need to develop a way of thinking about reproduction that extends beyond a linear progression from birth terminating at death. Reflecting on Moss's performance as Bowie's proxy, like the Bowie proxy in Haynes's film, helps us observe how these exchanges, like metaphors, convey one thing by presenting another, helping us to understand the generative effects of ephemeral traces and how they reside in practices of signification like archival collections, language and celebrity.

57 See Dan Stubbs, "David Bowie Reveals Sleeves for 'Nothing Has Changed' Compilation," NME, October 8, 2014, https://www.nme.com/news/music/david-bowie-198-1242232.

58 Bowie, "Sunday."

59 See Luke Morgan Britton, "David Bowie's 'Blackstar' Album Sells Out on Vinyl as Copies Listed Online for £800," NME, January 13, 2016, https://www.nme.com/news /music/david-bowie-134-1195215.

Works Cited

Appelgren, Staffan, and Anna Bohlin. "Growing in Motion: The Circulation of Used Things on Secondhand Markets." *Culture Unbound* 7 (2015): 143–68.

Arondekar, Anjali. *For the Record: On Sexuality and the Colonial Archive in India*. Durham, NC: Duke University Press, 2009.

Bowie, David. "Be My Wife." Side One Track 6 on *Low*. RCA, 1977, LP.

Bowie, David. "Sunday." Track 1 on *Heathen*. ISO Columbia, 2002, CD.

Bowie, David. "Never Get Old." Track 3 on *Reality*. ISO Columbia, 2003, CD.

Cifor, Marika. "Stains and Remains: Liveliness, Materiality, and the Archival Lives of Queer Bodies." *Australian Feminist Studies* 32, nos. 91–92 (2017): 5–21.

Cinque, Toija, and Sean Redmond. "Introduction: 'We're Just the Space Cadets, and He's the Commander.'" In *The Fandom of David Bowie: Everyone Says "Hi,"* 1–16. Cham, Switzerland: Palgrave Macmillan, 2019.

Cvetkovich, Ann. *An Archive of Feelings: Trauma, Sexuality, and Lesbian Public Cultures.* Durham, NC: Duke University Press, 2003.

DeVun, Leah, and Michael Jay McClure, "Archives Behaving Badly." *Radical History Review* no. 120 (Fall 2014): 121–30.

DiFranco, Ani. "Fuel." Track 2 on *Little Plastic Castle.* Righteous Babe, 1998, CD.

Edelman, Lee. *No Future: Queer Theory and the Death Drive.* Durham, NC: Duke University Press, 2004.

"Ephemera." Australian Queer Archives. March 11, 2022. https://queerarchives.org.au /collections/ephemera/.

Fontenot, Andrea. "The Dandy Diva." *Camera Obscura* 23, no. 1 (2008): 165–71.

"A Fascinating Look Back into the History of Vinyl Records." Phonostage Audio. November 8, 2020. https://phonostage.co.uk/blog/a-brief-history-of/the-history-of-vinyl -records/.

Gordon, Angus. "Turning Back: Adolescence, Narrative, and Queer Theory." *GLQ: A Journal of Lesbian and Gay Studies* 5, no. 1 (1999): 1–24.

Halberstam, Jack. *In a Queer Time and Place: Transgender Bodies, Subcultural Lives.* New York: NYU Press, 2005.

Halberstam, Jack. "What's That Smell?: Queer Temporalities and Subcultural Lives." In *Queer Youth Cultures,* edited by Susan Driver, 27–50 Albany: State University of New York Press, 2008.

Hansen, Karen Tranberg, and Jennifer Le Zotte. "Changing Secondhand Economies." *Business History* 61, no. 1 (2019): 1–16.

Haynes, Todd, dir. *Velvet Goldmine.* Zenith Productions, Killer Films, Single Cell Pictures, Newmarket Capital Group, Goldwyn Films International and Film 4, 1998.

Hocquenghem, Guy. *Homosexual Desire.* Durham, NC: Duke University Press, 1993.

Lorde, Audre. "Uses of the Erotic: The Erotic as Power." In *Sister Outsider: Essays and Speeches by Audre Lorde,* 53–59. New York: Crossing Press, 2007.

Lorde, Audre. *Zami: A New Spelling of My Name: A Biomythography by Audre Lorde.* New York: Crossing Press, 1982.

Luciano, Dana. "Nostalgia for an Age Yet to Come: *Velvet Goldmine*'s Queer Archive." In *Queer Times, Queer Becomings,* edited by E. L. McCallum and Mikko Tuhkanen, 121–55. Albany: State University of New York Press, 2011.

Marshall, Daniel. "Queer Breeding: Historicising Popular Culture, Homosexuality and Informal Sex Education." *Sex Education: Sexuality, Society and Learning* 13, no. 5 (2013): 597–610.

Muñoz, José Esteban. "Ephemera as Evidence: Introductory Notes to Queer Acts." *Women & Performance: a journal of feminist theory* 8, no. 2 (1996): 5–16.

O'Neill, Edward R. "Traumatic Postmodern Histories: *Velvet Goldmine*'s Phantasmatic Testimonies." *Camera Obscura* 19, no. 3 (2004): 157–85.

Osborne, Richard. *Vinyl: A History of the Analogue Record.* London: Routledge, 2016.

Pennebaker, D. A., dir. *Ziggy Stardust and The Spiders From Mars.* Mainman and Pennebaker, 1979.

Probyn, Elspeth. "Suspended Beginnings: Of Childhood and Nostalgia." *GLQ: A Journal of Lesbian and Gay Studies* 2, no. 4 (1995): 439–65.

"Queer British Art 1861–1967." Tate Britain [press release]. December 9, 2016. http://www .showonshow.com/tate/2017/queer_british_art/pressdocs/press_release.pdf.

Shuker, Roy. "Beyond the 'High Fidelity' Stereotype: Defining the (Contemporary) Record Collector." *Popular Music* 23, no. 3 (2004): 311-30.

Stockton, Kathryn Bond. "Growing Sideways, or Versions of the Queer Child: The Ghost, the Homosexual, the Freudian, the Innocent, and the Interval of Animal." In *Curiouser: On the Queerness of Children*, edited by Steven Bruhm and Natasha Hurley, 277–315. Minneapolis: University of Minnesota Press, 2004.

Stockton, Kathryn Bond. *The Queer Child, or Growing Sideways in the Twentieth Century*. Durham, NC: Duke University Press, 2009.

Tortorici, Zeb. *Sins against Nature: Sex and Archives in Colonial New Spain*. Durham, NC: Duke University Press, 2018.

Tuhkanen, Mikko. "Breeding (and) Reading: Lesbian Knowledge, Eugenic Discipline, and *The Children's Hour*." MFS: *Modern Fiction Studies* 48, no. 4 (2002): 1001–40.

Tuhkanen, Mikko. "Mestiza Metaphysics." In *Queer Times, Queer Becomings*, edited by E. L. McCallum and Mikko Tuhkanen, 259–94. Albany: State University of New York Press, 2011.

Tyburczy, Jennifer. "Queer Acts of Recovery and Uncovering: Deciphering Mexico through Archival Ephemera in David Wojnarowicz's *A Fire in My Belly*." *Text and Performance Quarterly* 35, no. 1 (2015): 4–23.

Bootlegs, Archives, and Performance in Mexico City

IVÁN A. RAMOS

I begin with perhaps a curious piece to think queerly about the archive: *Remake*, a 10-minute video from 1994 by Mexican artists Luis Felipe Ortega and Daniel Guzmán. The piece consists of a series of short reperformances of works made in the late 1960s and 1970s by male North American performance artists, including Terry Fox's *Corner Push*, Paul McCarthy's *Press* and *Face Painting*, and Bruce Nauman's *Self Portrait*, among others. Ortega and Guzmán, however, re-create these performances unfaithfully. The artists completed these reenactments using photographs, film and video stills, and descriptions they had found in art books. *Remake* restages the original pieces from conjecture, as Ortega and Guzmán imagine these performances capturing only the fragments they had encountered. I most recently rewatched *Remake* at the Museo Universitario del Chopo in Mexico City, where it was exhibited in the show *Punk: Sus Rastros en el Arte Contemporáneo* (Punk: Traces in Contemporary Art). The exhibit label contextualized the piece's inclusion because of its "use of appropriation and the citation of referent works of art common to punk's traces, but it also uses a 'do-it-yourself' aesthetic that links remaking with copying in a Mexican context, where piracy is another element of the scope of the national economy." This description is not simply coincidental. Young Mexican artists working during the early 1990s had learned many lessons from the punk subcultures that emerged in the outskirts of Mexico City during the 1980s. Indeed, a new generation of Mexican artists who began making work during this period had crossed with the punk scene, sharing not only aesthetic concerns but also venues and audiences. This intersection was particularly important for emerging artists in Mexico, and perhaps across Latin America, for whom the question of access has been a major concern. As the editors of the volume *The*

Age of Discrepancy, a text devoted to aesthetic production in Mexico from the 1960s until the present, make clear, remakes and reappropriations in Mexican contemporary art of the late 1980s and early 1990s were a recurring theme and formal preoccupation.[1] The authors explain that Latin American critics and artists have often had to make do with a lack of direct access to canonical works of modern and contemporary art. Yet in the histories of Mexican cultural production, the lack of access to cultural objects made outside of the country has rarely stopped artists or musicians from engaging and producing their own interpretations. This spirit of making-do, its DIY ethos, has served as a lifeline for these subcultures. In other words, punk provided musicians, artists, and audiences expansive ways of engaging with archives defined by lack and absence. Yet the punk scenes that gave way to these aesthetic emergences left their own traces in fragments, wayward stories, incomplete objects, and what we might think of as otherwise "thin" archives. In the context of Mexican contemporary art, punk was the drive that allowed artists to turn away from the archival certainty of documentation and engage it instead through the possibility of speculation.

I use punk both as an actual subcultural scene and as an aesthetic concern, to propose a notion of the bootleg as an archival practice enacted by those at a temporal or geographic distance from the locations, times, and class strata of official histories. Conceiving the archive as bootleg, as a pirated copy, and thus as something that has already made use of appropriation, shows how subjects who share the space of the underground reframe and expand the epistemological authority of the archive and its contribution to shaping alternative ways of knowing. I suggest a notion of archival practice that relies on improvisation, welcomes unknowing, and attempts to leave its own traces scattered as unfaithful remnants of what once was. In other words, punk invites us onto an archival turn that embraces a lack of fidelity that allows artists and punks to improvise, to come up with something new from the absence, or incompleteness, of the known archive. Central to my argument is what I call the sense of *not having been there*, experienced by subjects at a distance from official canons, in this case the historical relationship between punk and a contemporary art scene in Mexico City during the late 1980s and early 1990s. This in turn speaks to the kinds of imaginative yet rigorous leaps that chroniclers of punk subcultures and art scenes outside of Western narratives have had to make do with in order to reconstruct these histories. Indeed, what first drew me to *Remake* was the recognizable experience of rendering an aesthetic history through fragmentary re-creations of the past in books, films, records, and other objects. This encounter invites viewers in the present to re-create such moments as an incomplete "perhaps."

This chapter explores the sense of not having been there through two different, but related, approaches. The first corresponds to *Remake*, which I locate as an attempt by Ortega and Guzmán to insert themselves into art history canons by appropriating an archive to which they had limited access. Their attempts at restaging pieces that helped define performance art create an alternative archive not only for themselves but for other audiences left outside of these art historical narratives. The second takes up my own relationship to not having been there through my attempts to locate the archive and reconstruct the short-lived history of a feminist punk band briefly active during the 1980s, Susy's Peleoneras Punk. Ever since learning of their existence, I have tried to find traces of their short-lived reality, having only the certainty of the fact that they once existed, but being rebuffed each time by a band that refuses to be found. I approach these two examples in order to develop an idea of how the bootleg might offer an alternative way to insert minoritarian subjects into the archive. I must admit that by the end of this chapter the reader may find that my two case studies fail to insufficiently come together. This is partly because I have chosen to present these two examples against chronological order, and because the first example attempts an intervention into how we understand aesthetic genealogies, whereas the second is engaged with my own experience of trying to locate what seems like an archive that simply does not exist. There are other ways in which I could frame this discussion, following a logic that argues that Susy's Peleoneras Punk's incomplete traces provided a blueprint that artists adopted by embracing incompleteness and uncertainty. And although I believe that this is indeed the case, it is not the point of this chapter. But allow me to leave the rigor of academic detachment for a moment to admit that my investment in reading Ortega and Guzmán's relationship to an archive of performance and my own search for Susy's Peleoneras Punk together through a notion of the bootleg are ultimately inseparable for me. As someone working in the recent past, with objects that may for some lack the more immediate legibility and importance afforded by time, and writing from performance studies, a discipline (or interdiscipline) so often concerned with the value of the ephemeral and the live, I want to use this chapter and the case studies in it to make an argument for the ways in which something like the archive remains an essential framework.

However, even if the two objects discussed here fail to completely cohere into a single discernible argument, my attachment to engaging both of them comes from my own shared relationship to each, a relationship I see emerging from my own queer desires to bring them together. In *Why Karen Carpenter Matters*, Karen Tongson argues for the kinds of queer attachments that define our connection to objects that perhaps were never meant to belong to us. She suggests that these attachments exceed the limits of the evidentiary, that they "may appear to be fashioned entirely from fantasy and projection. We queers are really good at that sort of thing, as Oscar Wilde implies in *The Art of Lying*, which he describes as 'the telling of beautiful untrue things.'"[2] Yet Tongson continues, "I want to insist here and now that our fantasies are forged as much from the facts of our shared intelligence, which are far from being untrue even if they aren't always grounded in what is verifiable fact."[3] These queer archival speculations drive my own relationship to both *Remake* and Susy's Peleoneras Punk. On the one hand, Ortega and Guzmán as well as La Zappa Punk make use of scarce resources to insert themselves into canons, genres, histories, and archives that were never meant to include them. At the same time, my proposal here to decipher this as their original drive is born out of my own relationship to both. It might also appear curious to use queer attachment to examine objects that might otherwise never necessarily be read as particularly queer. Yet as Tongson reminds us, Carpenter and her legacy especially might also resist being interpreted as "queer," yet such is the seduction of encountering objects that find ways to speak to us beyond sexual taxonomies.

Zeb Tortorici has explained how critical evaluations of archival knowledge cannot help but be suspicious of the perils of seduction and desire that draw scholars to their objects. He writes, "the notion of seduction intimates the archive as a source of temptation, both dangerous and disingenuous. From the 'seductions of access' and 'seductions of historical recovery' to the 'epistemological seduction' of the archive and the archive's penchant for 'seducing us by its appearance of the real,' archival seduction comes off largely as something that we must guard ourselves against—at least if we want to be good, methodologically rigorous scholars."[4] Indeed, to become seduced by an archive implies the inevitable risk of letting one's desires take precedence over the work of faithfulness, no matter how certain we are by now that such a thing is ultimately impossible. But Tortorici proposes that giving in to the archive's seduction "is most valuable when it causes us to articulate our own desires in relation to the archive as an institution, a system of classification, and as a physical space, each with its own peculiar history. Archival seduction thus should force us to examine and analyze the ways in which we understand the past, as well as our relationship to it."[5] But here I want to ask, what happens when we become seduced by archives that might refuse us even as we fall for their siren call? I engage two different modes of archival refusal. Ortega and Guzmán are perhaps refused from an aesthetic archive that fails to see them as its intended audience, while concrete evidence that would allow me to re-create Susy's Peleoneras Punk's existence refuses my desire to find them. I hope, however, that in bringing these two objects together, the contributions that the bootleg can bring to the archive will become clear.

In the introduction to their anthology *Curatorial Dreams*, editors Shelley Ruth Butler and Erica Lehrer advocate for "dreaming" as a methodology that might fill the gaps and insufficiencies created by the often limited scope of the global art market. Their project encourages scholars to devise, or curate, impossible exhibitions and museum and gallery shows that may never come to be either because of institutional limitations or because of the absence of particular works or objects in the archive. Butler and Lehrer are particularly mindful of the kinds of suspicions the scholar-critic brings when engaging with the museum, suspicions that resonate with the scholar's ambivalences around the archive. They write, "museums and critics are often viewed as monolithic structures, removed from the complex intra-institutional workings and the broader web of forces that shape their final forms."[6] With this context in mind, the exercise of dreaming offers the possibility of expanding upon institutional constraints while still making productive use of their offerings. As Roger Simon explains in *Curatorial Dreams*, the work of dreaming need not be necessarily tethered to the impossibility of utopian longings, instead "daydreaming ventures beyond what is, beyond existing norms and conventions in concrete plans directed at achieving something new. In this, daydreams can embody the seriousness of laying out conditions of possibility. They offer an incisive critique of the present, and a prescient, possible movement toward something better."[7]

I maintain that the bootleg might be an expression or a methodology by which daydreaming can offer productive ways to approach archives that refuse us. I take this mode of daydreaming, which I propose also as a kind of archival infidelity, as a practice that understands that for those who must survive at the margins of History and culture, the work of imagining and piecing together one's place in larger narratives might arise from what José Esteban Muñoz once called "ephemera as evidence." In this influential essay, Muñoz argues that the power of queer ephemerality rests in our ability to recognize and decipher the lingering traces left in the afterburn of queer relations. From the spatiality of public sex to subtle descriptions of romantic (or sexual) relationships, the sense of recognition, of our ability to find some sense of truth, no matter how uncertain, becomes central to our explorations of archives often maintained outside of the purview of official institutions.[8] Indeed, there is always a sense of excitement, not to mention achievement, when one encounters evidence of one's queer hunches, as the archive opens up to transform our suspicions into truth. And yet even in searching for traces, I argue, there cannot help but be a certain act of betrayal from us to these hidden queer pasts. Is not making an act of public recognition from a previously underground history still bringing its anonymity into view in order to fulfill our desires in the present? In other words, if queer theory has insisted that the cloaking of queer lives has been essential to their dissident potential, are we not then endangering their contrarian power by making them knowable to spectators in the present? Or, as Heather Love makes clear in *Feeling Backward*, our desires for a queer past remain tied to our desires to explain or justify or even challenge the present in which we live.[9]

The bootleg, as an archival practice, welcomes the evanescence of the past and dares us to leave it unreconstructed, cognizant of its uncertainties, yet open to the possibilities of daydreaming about it. The two case studies here allow me to conceptualize the bootleg's contribution to the archive, developing a sense of its modalities, its potential shapes, and the demands that it may have for us as scholars invested in locating the wayward trajectories of subjects who have been historically defined by social and cultural marginality. My analysis of *Remake* shows how its restagings challenge concepts central to the documentation and archiving of performance art history through a method of unreliable recreation. I turn toward theories of documentation and liveness in performance studies to discuss notions that have been essential to the field's conception, rooted on an idea of ephemerality which in turns suggests the impossibility of ever knowing the true effect of a performance. I then move away from the analysis of an object to engage my own experiences over the past few years researching the history of Mexican feminist punk. I focus on the case of Susy's Peleoneras Punk, a band headed by the legendary *punkera* La Zappa Punk, and their material, if not narrative, absence in the archives of Mexican punk, a material absence that I have been unable to fill because of the group's fleeting and minor existence. In both cases, artists and musicians had to fill the gaps of official circulation through piracy, bootlegs, infidelity, and speculation. By turning to these alternative modes of approach, I want to highlight the improvisational methods that dispossessed subjects make use of in order to, even if fleetingly, record their traces. In particular, I am interested in how perhaps subjects who must improvise ways of surviving in turn invite us to improvise ways to look and understand their experiences. This is a practice that I then undertake most fully in the second part of the chapter, as I create my own bootleg archives from the sense of (me) not having been there. I am responding here to scholarship deeply engaged with pushing the boundaries of the institutional power of something like "the Archive" and toward fragmentary forms of knowledge that break down the distinction between the archival and the ephemeral. These critical engagements with the archive allow me to propose a way of knowing where uncertainty provides the ability to reframe our relationship to a past that we never belonged to.

Punk is perhaps a particularly appropriate genre to encounter *Remake* and Susy's Peleoneras Punk. As mentioned earlier, a work like *Remake* not only resonates with an earlier and contemporaneous punk scene in Mexico, but La Zappa Punk's contribution to the formation of such a scene was essential for the emergence of a new generation of contemporary artists. Although the origins of punk are usually attributed to England and New York around the year 1977, mostly to white musicians, a number of musicians, journalists, curators, archivists, and scholars have located alternative geographies of punk in places like Los Angeles, Latin America, Eastern Europe, and other sites that expand our understanding of its histories and geographic circulations. As Shane Greene writes, "more than a collection of musical sounds, punk is a conglomeration of bands and shows, fanzines and fliers, social relations and political statements held together loosely by desires to subvert mainstream cultural production with a gritty aesthetic and a do-it-yourself ethic."[10] Greene points in particular to Peruvian punk's synonymous moniker as "rock subterráneo" to highlight its relation to "underground" sensibilities, which he contends "presumes an exchange that takes place across and below the surface of the borders of language, nation, culture, and global commerce."[11] This relation to the underground, Greene continues, "intends to intervene in [the] arena of aesthetic overproduction by de-fetishizing the cultural industry norms and processes that surround creative production via whatever DIY strategies are available to it."[12]

Greene's articulation of the subterranean and underproduction are especially helpful to situate my own discussion of punk. Although I do not provide here a comprehensive history for the context of punk's appearance in the Mexican underground of the 1980s, it is worth mentioning that the very emergence of punk (alongside metal and other rock genres) was in part the result of the Mexican government's prohibition of rock music recordings, live performance, and other forms of dissemination in 1971, following the aftermath of the Avándaro festival, otherwise known as the "Mexican Woodstock." This massive gathering was particularly notable for drawing working-class youth who had up to this point been mostly excluded from a rock and roll scene that seemed to appeal primarily to middle- and upper-middle-class youth. Upon realizing the kinds of interclass contact that Avándaro revealed were possible, Luis Echeverría's government moved to ban all forms of such potential gatherings.[13] Yet rather than disappear, rock moved to the undergrounds of Mexico City, to sites that had already been excluded from mainstream culture. Here rock's edges only grew rougher, giving way to the punk ethos personified by La Zappa Punk and many others. During this period these genres circulated not via official avenues but through bootlegs that became the bedrock for Mexico's own punk subcultures. I want to emphasize that in this context, the underground spaces where rock's harder cousins thrived were the result of class alienation that made these locales particularly receptive to punk's DIY ethos. This resonates especially with the Peruvian context that Greene explores, in which, as he writes, "the particular political dialogue into which Peruvian punks inserted their subterranean message was one not merely about mass culture and its discontents. It was about life and death, struggles for social liberation and the realities of political imprisonment, a country's repressive past and its uncertain future."[14]

However, rather than remaining on punk's social and historical context in Mexico, I want to linger on what I argue was an essential archival and aesthetic mode that emerged in the midst of the underground and the underproduced: the bootleg. Curiously, the bootleg as an object and as a practice has been for the most part undertheorized by scholars working at the queer intersections of performance, art history, archives, and punk. Indeed, most studies of bootlegs have belonged to media studies and adjacent fields where they have been examined in relation to transnational markets, piracy, and copyright laws.[15] However, the fact that a majority of this research has centered on markets outside of the West, in places like Asia and Africa, shows that bootlegs thrive in spaces that frame them in resistant collusion to the legal reach of Western copyright laws. If bootlegs have been largely left out of discussions in queer studies it is partly because there might be an implicit trust in the originality in the objects that the field engages in. However, even in approaches to fakes, bootlegs, and pirated reproductions found in fields such as art history, the presumed logic of copyright law remains undisturbed, partly because there is an assumption that the distance between the original and its bastardized copies will always be apparent to us, the authoritative scholar and consumer. Scholars and others working in archives that exceed official, mainstream, or state narratives have had to rely on artifacts and documents that attempt to smuggle themselves into history as unofficial, dubious, or bootleg documents as essential tools for reconstruction. In other words, we may come to question the official narratives that the archive might attempt to offer, but the originality and integrity of the objects housed within it still holds the lure of authenticity. Of course, scholars invested in recuperating and finding ways to understand the histories of those who have at one time or another been silenced or lost to the archive are familiar with the methodological inventiveness that looking for this past requires. Looking for stories and lives that had to sustain themselves besides "official" or mainstream

History requires excavating at times surprising sources, always aware that any attempt at "reconstruction" can never help but be woefully incomplete. As I will discuss in the first section, for many of us who work in the queer past and its attendant aesthetics, it is through the unfaithful reproduction of a video, a photograph, or even the retelling of an experience, where we may first gain access to our objects of study.

My own turn toward the bootleg as a queer practice rests precisely on the premise that those invested in finding "invisible" objects in the past have made us keenly aware of the limits of reconstructing histories which draw exclusively from documentary evidence in favor, for example, of affective relations to forms of knowledge that remain outside the realm of mainstream narratives. I suggest that these improvisations might illuminate how the intersection of punk subcultures and contemporary art was made possible by their shared contestation of a notion of fidelity and instead by favoring the bootleg. I draw from Lucas Hilderbrand's essential *Inherent Vice: Bootleg Histories of Videotape and Copyright*, where he conceives of video bootlegs as "a set of practices and textual relationships that open up alternative conceptions of access, aesthetics, and affect. Perhaps a sexier way of saying the same thing is that this book is about desire—the desire for access—and about the aesthetics and ethics related to access."[16] Hilderbrand's formulation is especially useful considering that he ties the notion of desire to that of access, a desire to have access to objects and histories, and thus the desire to *be a part* of objects and histories that might remain otherwise foreclosed. I follow his definition of bootlegging as a set of noncommercial practices that can function to "fill in the gaps of market failure (when something has not been commercially distributed), archival omissions (when something has not been preserved for historical study), and personal collections (when something has not been accumulated or cannot be afforded)."[17] This approach is especially relevant when considering my own objects of study here. Anyone who has traveled in Mexico has invariably encountered markets structured around bootleg copies, from films and music recordings to other goods such as designer clothing and toys. In the case of *Remake*, the video itself becomes the bootleg reproduction of the original performances, and in the case of Susy's Peleoneras Punk it becomes a relation to a band that refuses to be archived. I return to Hilderbrand's definition of the bootleg one more time and the aim "to reclaim its productively illicit meanings, its intoxicating pleasures, and its amorous relationships between texts and audiences."[18] Indeed, how else could we read then the relation between bootlegs and its consumers than as one steeped in queer modes of attachment to subjects and objects? And yet taking the bootleg as the structuring force of such attachments and relations allows us to expand how we think about access and fidelity, pointing instead to one of the ways in which the contradictions inherent in any archive allow for queer inventions.

It is also worth mentioning that the bootleg becomes especially essential in spaces in the Global South where access to technologies and archives might prove challenging. As Laura U. Marks writes, "Images have a life cycle that is material, social, and imaginative. Images' materiality constitutes an everyday problem in poorly infrastructured countries,"[19] even if these issues are not exclusive to them. She continues, "Analog demagnetization and lossy digital compression; glitch, error, and artifacts introduced by compression; and layers of formatting draw attention to the trajectories and life cycles of images."[20] Yet as she points out, these challenges might prove aesthetically useful to artists and audiences working within these contexts. She explains that "like others in places where official image archives are difficult to access, artists value glitch, error, and loss of resolution not only for their own aesthetic interest but also as indications of the labor of love required to access the past."[21] With this in mind, the fragment appears throughout the chapter in various ways. First, throughout Remake, which stages the actions it reperforms not as a continuous narrative, but as a series of fragments that in some way reproduce the limited encounter with the archive that these artists had access to. I extend the fragment to frame my own encounters with Susy's Peleoneras Punk, which have taken place mostly in the shape of fragmentary recollections that resist being arranged into a complete and legible narrative. But as Marks argues in her essay, the bootleg has been essential not only in the circulation of objects but also in the possibilities opened by turning to the bootleg as a formal element itself. She explains that "it enables more people to participate in image circulation,"[22] in this case not only the artists but also the audiences who find their own entries to histories of contemporary art and punk.

Indeed, the bootleg and the works I discuss here are even connected through Ortega's own history. As the artist relayed to me over email, he supported his university studies in the 1980s by selling bootleg rock and punk cassettes in a street market in San Felipe during the latter part of the decade. Ortega would play the tapes at the Sunday market, attracting punks curious about the new sounds he would play each week. This punk spirit extends to Ortega and Guzmán's practice, which they can trace to this earlier moment. Indeed, their relationship to the art world was established from this kind of DIY spirit, as Ortega never formally trained in art (he abandoned a philosophy master's program in 1992, and Guzmán dropped out of art school in 1988).[23] Thus, as I write about the piece's relationship to a thriving culture of piracy in the city, Remake also embodies the work of two artists who came to their practice beyond the bounds of formal training.

Ostensibly, the protagonist here is Mexico City and a genealogy of counter-archival knowledges I argue may be situated by understanding the particular relation to the bootleg that its inhabitants have needed to rely upon. In my discussions, I favor the bootleg instead of appropriation to understand the challenges that my objects posed to the state's attempt to scrub what they saw as the potential dangers posed by rock music. Although in recent years Mexico City has become a global destination for hip tourists seeking cultural currency, during much of the 1980s and 1990s, the city was mostly seen as a dangerous place that was in turn also a key example of globalization's failures. The bootleg enables, for me, a queer reading practice that resists the State's longing for order.

Remake

My first desire to find a queer past, before I could even conceive of such a thing as the archive, just as I was beginning to grasp what queerness could be, was borne out of my encounter with Andy Warhol's Factory. The back cover of *The Velvet Underground and Nico*, an album that had altered my entire existence, featured several images of their live touring show, the Exploding Plastic Inevitable, and on the front cover the name of the person who had organized these spectacles, the creator of the banana on the cover, Andy Warhol. This encounter would introduce me to a new and expansive imaginary that going forward I would place under the umbrella of "queer." I collected art catalogs, biographies, and any objects I could find for a personal reconstruction of the Factory, and Warhol himself. I watched Mary Harron's 1996 film *I Shot Andy Warhol*, which I had taped on a blank VHS during a broadcast on PBS, over and over, caught in its dramatization of Valerie Solanas's shooting of the artist, looking to its re-creations for clues that might place me in the moment when these events happened. My teenage bedroom became a bootleg monument, its walls plastered with cheap and rudimentary printed reproductions of Warhol's paintings, images of the Factory, and even printouts of the front pages of newspapers from the day after Solanas shot Warhol.

I provide what might seem like an amusing anecdote partly because as I encountered *Remake* for the first time, I couldn't help finding myself in a moment of recognition after reading the methods the artists had used to reproduce the canonical performances in the video. My own access to an aesthetic world that wasn't my own had been rendered in unfaithful and even grainy reproductions of Warhol's paintings and films, which I had begun collecting in the only format I could find them in, as pirated copies. As I returned to the video, it recalled my own familiarity with the original performances the piece (mis)re-creates, caught in my own fragmented memories of incomplete reconstructions. There was almost a stunning yet purposeful lack of *fidelity* to the video's re-creations, while at the same time incompletely and excitedly undertaking this performative task. Yet this refusal to reproduce the pieces with exactitude is what provides *Remake* its aesthetic pulse, as Marks might suggest. The settings were different, the architecture of Mexico City serving as a counterpoint to the galleries that originally hosted these actions. The brown bodies also seemed markedly different from the composure of the originating artists, as in the movement of a body pushing itself repeatedly against a wall, as is the case with Bruce Nauman's *Bouncing in the Corner No. 1* and the reappropriation of a Mexican artist in the video.

Recounting the artist's intentions for *Remake,* Barbara Clausen writes that "Ortega recalls his and Guzmán's motivation to generate their own version of performance history, through the appropriation of what was in fact only available to them as traces and fragments."[24] The piece consists of a single channel video which plays on a television monitor. The description also names the works that the artists reperform, in the following order: Action 1, Tom Morioni, *Pissing*, 1970; action 2, Terry Fox, *Corner Push*, 1970; action 3, Chris Burden, *Deadman*, 1972; action 4, Paul McCarthy, *Press*, 1972; action 5, Paul McCarthy, *Face Painting*, 1972; action 6, Bruce Nauman, *Self Portrait*, 1967; action 7, Stephen Laub, *Smile Support*, 1969; action 8, Daniel Guzmán, *Boca*, 1992; action 9, Luis F. Ortega, *Informe Sanitario*, 1992. Out of these performances, actions 1, 3, and 9 appear to be missing from the final version, and one unmentioned piece, Bruce Nauman's *Bouncing in the Corner No. 1* from 1968, is included.

Remake opens with a wide shot of a white plastic chair illuminated by the natural light coming from an arched window. The following shot shows a blank corner wall, as Guzmán walks up to the space and places his body against it, his back toward the camera. He wriggles, cutting to a close up of the back of his head moving against the wall. The camera pulls back slowly, revealing his body once again. This is action 2, which is a reperformance of Terry Fox's *Corner Push* (Figure 9.1). The following action is number 6, Bruce Nauman's *Self Portrait*, as Ortega, framed from the chest up, shirtless, spits out a stream of water. The frame freezes, leaving the action suspended for a few seconds, although the sound continues playing (Figure 9.2). The following action fades up on an empty floor, action number 5, Paul McCarthy's *Face Painting*. Guzmán appears on the frame, back against the camera, and places a small bucket of white paint on the floor, which he begins to empty out as he gets on his knees,

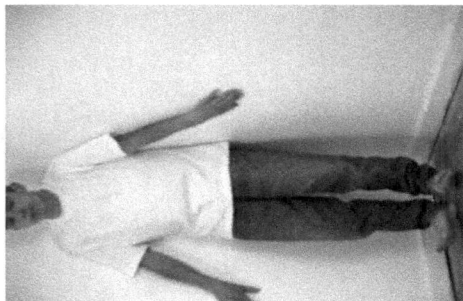

FIGURE 9.1. Still from *Remake*. Luis Felipe Ortega and Daniel Guzmán, 1994, 10 min.

FIGURE 9.2. Still from *Remake*. Luis Felipe Ortega and Daniel Guzmán, 1994, 10 min.

back turned to the viewer. He crawls face down, pushing the bucket of paint, creating a puddle as he advances, and leaving a white trail with his body (Figure 9.3). Next, we see a shot of the empty bucket against a wall at the far end of the space, emptied out, as the camera backs away capturing the trail of white paint on the floor. This is followed by Guzman's face planted firmly against a glass plate, an iteration of Paul McCarthy's *Press*. Guzmán's face twitches and distorts as he pushes against the glass, giving him a nearly grotesque appearance. This is the only action that is not accompanied by ambient sound (Figure 9.4). Next is Bruce Nauman's *Bouncing in the Corner No. 1*, in which the image is tilted at a 90-degree angle, as Ortega, his body framed from his feet up to his chin, bounces repeatedly against a corner. We see the contortions of his body as it presses against the surface, bouncing back and forth against the walls. This action lasts for a couple of minutes, as the exhaustion of Ortega's body becomes more and more apparent to the viewer. The final action in the video shows a close-up of Guzmán's right side, as he inserts a finger into his mouth, moving it around in an almost brushing motion. The camera zooms in on his mouth, which cuts to a frontal close-up of his fingers exploring his mouth. This is the only action by one of the artists in the piece, Guzmán's previous *Boca*, made

Pirates and Punks · 245

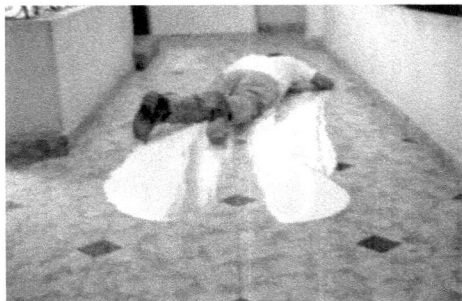

FIGURE 9.3. Still from *Remake*. Luis Felipe Ortega and Daniel Guzmán, 1994, 10 min.

two years earlier. The video closes by returning to the opening shot of the white plastic chair, as the screen fades to black.

In a way, the video enacts two forms of temporal and geographic distance: first is the aforementioned distance between object and spectator, but the second is the form of reenactment as a video. In *Remake*, the reperformed actions are done for the camera, with no audience present. However, in reproducing the fragments that the artists had available, Ortega and Guzmán retained fidelity to the originals by reproducing the camera angles of the photographs they had. The sound of the recording itself highlights the absence of an audience, the supposed bodies that activate the power of any given performance. Although not all of the actions by these artists were performed before an audience, most were, and it was this generation of artists that first provided art critics with a particular vocabulary of performance practice different from the theatrical.

In *Performing Remains*, Rebecca Schneider argues that "if the twentieth century was famous for, among other things, criticizing the concept of historical facticity, such criticism has not resulted in the end of our particular investment in the logic of the archive. Rather, we have broadened our range of documents to include that which we might have overlooked and included the stockpiling of recorded speech, image, gesture."[25] Schneider is particularly invested in questioning the appearance of a divide between the materiality of the archive and the ephemerality of performance. Her aim is to "[trouble] the prevalence of presentism, immediacy, and linear time in most thinking about live performance."[26] Instead, she favors "a more porous approach to time and to art—time as full of holes or gaps . . . in the curious inadequacies of the copy, and *what inadequacy gets right* about our faulty steps backwards, and forward, and to the side."[27] I want to argue that the video exemplifies Schneider's attempt to rescue performance from the weight of liveness, instead favoring a sense of bootleg aesthetics provided by the medium the artists use. After all, as Hilderbrand points out in *Inherent Vice*, video technology has been favored by contemporary artists because it provides *access*. The fact that video, unlike film, did not require prohibitive costs has historically allowed projects that use the very quality of video as form and content.

In his analysis of Chris Burden's works from the 1970s, Patrick Anderson has written about the shift spectators experienced in relationship to performance. Reflecting upon Burden's acts of potential self-harm, Anderson writes, "such moves did not, in the idealized language of theatrical realism, attempt to facilitate emphatic exchange; on the contrary, they represented an indictment of passive looking that characterizes the most conventional understanding of the gallery."[28] At this time, the very way in which spectators conceived of their role as such went through a deep transformation. Anderson continues, "Burden's explicit deployment of the look in such works did not operate as single allegories for the techniques and technologies of looking that conventionally define the gallery; nor did they function as enhancements of the spectator's ability to empathize with him by seeing as and thus feeling as the artist. Rather Burden incorporated the look, and thus the looker, directly into the act itself: the spectator became a witness."[29] This tendency to question the passivity of the audience in the gallery space became an ongoing tendency in performance art of the 1970s, although in various intensities. For example, Bruce Nauman's *Body Pressure* (1974) consists of a text that instructs the viewer to press their body against a gallery wall to focus on the sensation, which as the text describes, could become quite erotic. Other canonical pieces by artists like Yoko Ono and Marina Abramović invited the audience to become a part of the performance, who often took this as the opportunity to enact various intensities of abuse on the performer's bodies.

Yet although notions of witnessing and participation remain in the analysis of these texts, the role of the audience as witness comes into question when considering both geographic and temporal distance. In *Remake*, the video turns the perception of an original audience on its head by filtering the meaning of these performances through the interpretation of an audience member who has encountered these works in books and pictures. If the ability of performance to turn the audience into a witness relies in large part on the act of liveness itself, video from its very inception is tasked with *documenting*, an archival impulse built into its formal mechanisms. The graininess and quality of video creates a stark distinction to the original pieces. Most of them were captured using early video technology or photographed using high-quality film stock. Further, although artists during the 1970s aimed to expand space (whether the gallery or another site), most of the pieces were performed within sanctioned locations. *Remake*, on the other hand, has a dirtier quality. Particularly significant is the contrast between the galleries where the originals were performed and the spaces that Guzmán and Ortega use. The sites in *Remake* bear the recognizable textures of buildings for anyone familiar with the architectural character of Mexico City. This spatial element of the piece creates another break, as we experience two artists working outside the bourgeois cleanliness of the gallery space.[30] But as the video's unstable quality and spatial specificity come together, the viewer does not experience loss but an aesthetic encounter that renders these materialities vivid, or as Laura Marks suggests, although "it's a poor comfort to someone watching a bad bootleg, or downloading lo-res media bristling with unintended artifacts . . . that they are more in touch with the materiality of the infrastructure. They may lose meaning; but they might make poetry of the distorted original."[31] The use of sound in the video heightens this, as it captures dead air, a blankness that sticks to the ear. We, as the video's audience in the present, become even more removed as we take in these elements, separating any possibility of fidelity to the originals. Barbara Clausen suggests, however, that by reproducing the performances in this new form, Ortega and Guzmán imbue the originary works with new feeling and meaning that encourages us to reconsider the originals' own place in performance history, revealing "the representational politics of performance as a dense net of relations, in which the restaging of a document allows the work to circulate from multiple points of authorship."[32]

I want to suggest that the performances in the video commit to the act of bootlegging the performances it re-creates by giving access to viewers who may have never encountered the history of performance art in the 1960s and 1970s. Yet as Clausen remarks, there is something radical in the kinds of accessibility that *Remake* makes available. She writes, "The fine line between mimicry and critique, when it comes to claims of authenticity and authorship, becomes evident when one considers the fact that *Remake* can be viewed as a video on Ortega's site."[33] This access, however, is always already mediated by the distances I have outlined throughout the chapter. Even for an audience member with knowledge of these original performances, one must access them through the mediation of the video screen, itself a mediation of the archival encounters of the artists as they encountered these works. The kind of access that *Remake* gives is not faithful either, but part of a series of interactions that may now include the viewer.

A person in a gallery encountering *Remake* is faced with a mechanism of documentation in which the work exists as its own object but also as the bastard of the original performances, their bootleg, placing the viewer at an archi-

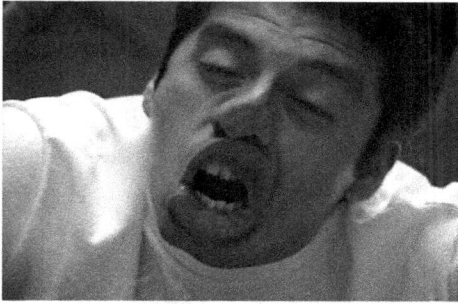

FIGURE 9.4. Still from *Remake*. Luis Felipe Ortega and Daniel Guzmán, 1994, 10 min.

val distance twice removed. The Mexican context is especially significant, as neither Mexican performance nor video art feature prominently in the canonical histories of these genres. Encountering the video in Mexico City, a spectator may or may not be familiar with the original works, and depending on the contextualization given in the work's description, she may never become fully aware of the pieces from which *Remake* is not only derived but which it radically reimagines, queerly mimics, and performs with a renewed political and artistic potential. In re-creating these works, the artists both place themselves within this larger history of performance that might grant them a different form of access to it. It is this sense of distance from my queer adolescence to these artists' reperformances that offers me a queer method and approach by which to theorize archival tendencies that structure knowledge of pasts that never belonged to us.[34]

Punk and Mexico

The absence of Mexican and Latina punks in the archive has been remarked upon by scholars like Michelle Habell-Pallán, who writes, "although these women helped shape the sounds and concerns of the local independent music community, with a few notable exceptions almost no scholarly documentation of their participation exists."[35] Other scholars working in Latina/o sound and music studies such as Deborah R. Vargas, Alexandra Vazquez, and Licia Fiol-Matta have additionally suggested that encountering the sonic transnational Latina/o archive demands looking for alternative pathways of creating knowledge, listening beyond the official record and to stories, gossip, and other forms of distribution that exceed the official.[36]

I listen to these scholars in order to locate a notion of the punk archive that includes not only material objects, including recordings, fliers, photographs, zines, and others, but also one that is attentive to the ways in which these objects allow us to reconstruct a sense of the ways in which punk made certain kinds of survival possible for those at the social and cultural margins. I also follow Nancy Mirabal's attempts to reconstruct the traces of the Black Cuban diaspora, of which she writes, "Often these periods have gone without study because the assumption is that 'nothing really happened' . . . But to my way of thinking, there are always fragments of experiences, of histories that lead to those moments where something supposedly 'happened.' Nothing occurs in a vacuum. There are hints, signposts, and clues that ultimately prove to be the most interesting and provocative."[37] Even as interest in global punk undergrounds has increased significantly over the past few years, there is still often a need to justify the reasons for studying such seemingly minor subcultures, particularly in relation to much larger national frameworks. As Greene explains at the beginning of *Punk and Revolution*, writing and research on punk and other similar subcultures often faces multiple challenges when circulating within academic spaces, an experience I have encountered firsthand. But Mirabal reminds us of the imperative to try and reconstruct these histories, no matter how fragmented, in the face of a "history that leaves us." As history slips away, Mirabal writes, "it both haunts and forces me to understand the power and urgency of historical work and the precariousness and ephemerality of a history that doesn't always fit traditional historical narratives. What [does] it mean to write a history so shaped by impending death, fragmented collective memories, and dissoluble archives that could 'leave us'?"[38] However, the punk archive, and perhaps any good punk, whether person, band, or scene, proposes an act of refusal to be documented, committed to memory. Lest we forget, this is partly because punk scenes outside of the United States and Western Europe often emerged in the shadows of oppressive regimes to which they had to remain illegible. It is from this context that I approach my own archival searches for Susy's Peleoneras Punk.

Patricia Moreno Rodríguez adopted the moniker of La Zappa Punk partly as a tribute to Frank Zappa, but also because her family had "worked with shoes and leather," *zapato* being the Spanish word for "shoe." She was a part of bands like Secta Suicida Siglo Veinte (Twentieth-Century Suicide Sect) and Virginidad Sacudida (Discarded Virginity). La Zappa Punk, of course, is not the only woman central to the punk scene in Mexico, and although these bands managed to record and perform at a modest scale, it is another one of La Zappa Punk's bands that drew my attention. In an interview with Julia Palacios and Tere Estrada, La Zappa Punk describes one of her acts, Susy's Peleoneras Punk, named after the Ramones' song "Suzy Is a Headbanger." According to her recollections, the band was made up of women and girls she had met on the streets, up to thirty-two of them at a time, and the group functioned more like a women's collective than a traditional band. She describes them in the following way: "The band was like family; we were very close. Some were single mothers from the street, others came from neighborhood families. The *chavas* [Spanish slang for 'girls'] who ended up pregnant were helped according to whatever they decided. It was a form of resistance against marginalization and repression in a system as rotten as ours."[39]

My first encounter with the group was in Estrada's magnificent history of women in rock music in Mexico, *Sirenas al ataque*.[40] I immediately became fascinated and drawn by the description of the band in Estrada's recollection of La Zappa Punk's memories. On subsequent research trips to Mexico City, I set out to find out more about Susy's Peleoneras Punk in an attempt to know more about them, to understand more of their rebellious spirit. However, I found almost nothing about the band other than the particularly seductive story that La Zappa Punk had already provided. After pursuing many attempts to find evidence of Susy's Peleoneras Punk's short life, I returned to La Zappa Punk's description for hints. But her recollections of the band, and Estrada's own findings, provide the very reasons they refuse to be fully discovered. Members of the group were most likely women attempting to escape from dangerous situations, not wanting to be found, hiding in the then-present as well as in the future-to-be (in which I myself was researching them through their own largely untraceable pasts). We might also assume that in the spirit of great punk, many of the band's members did not know how to play instruments, playing a few shows here and there but never achieving even the rough virtuosity to record an album, most likely not even having access to a recording studio. Indeed, even the number of women in the collective means that only a handful of them ever played their live shows at a time, a self-generating rotating lineup. There seem to be no video recordings of the band, and as with most punk of the period in Mexico City, there was probably little access to video equipment to begin with. Even La Zappa Punk's memory of the group is by now incomplete. In video interviews with the singer, she bears the comportment of many other punks, her memories distorted by the roughness of a life devoted to punk.

As I was revising this chapter, however, I decided to do yet another search to see if any new information about the band had appeared. To my surprise, I encountered a text that had escaped the archives and bibliographies of Mexican punk I was so familiar with before this moment, José Manuel Valenzuela's *A La Brava Ese!* Originally published in 1988, the book chronicles two major youth subcultures, cholos and punks. The book is organized as a Marxist/Gramscian analysis of these groups, supported by a series of fragmentary anonymous ethnographic interviews which run anywhere from a sentence to a page long. Valenzuela gives little information about the interviewees, using their stories as the evidence of his larger argument. One of the primary themes of the book is the ways in which young people adopt these styles to protest against systems of inequality, and it is particularly attentive to the specific struggles that women face in these subcultures. Although the book primarily chronicles the emergence of these subcultures in the border city of Tijuana, Valenzuela devotes one large section to punk in Mexico City. The interviewees describe feelings of social dispossession, and several women highlight the fact that in addition to feeling distanced from society as a whole, their adoption of punk comes from more immediate alienation from their families and the patriarchy, detailing how often they are labeled as "whores" for adopting punk. But amid the stories I found a fragment that is perhaps the closest I have gotten to the immediate existence of Susy's Peleoneras Punk. The anonymous interviewee says:

> When we started to come out there was a band playing, and they played "Susy is a Headbanger" (peleonera), and the girls liked it. We are not from the same place, some are from Ixtapalapa, some are from San Felipe. Right now the majority of the Susys are from San Felipe, but we all get together. Then we started getting together, to talk, and everything started. No pues que onda, let's start a band, no pues let's call ourselves Susys Punk, the Susys ended up sticking. When we go to a show we all wear skirts and on our shirts it says Susys Punk.[41]

This, of course, immediately interrupts several assumptions that I had been working under when looking for the band. For one, the name is different, omitting the Peleoneras moniker La Zappa Punk had mentioned in the interview with Estrada. Other details emerge as well: for example, the idea that the band members all adopted the Susy moniker, creating a sense of collectivity that in some ways displaced their everyday identities. It provides an entirely new way of referring to the band and its members as Las Susys, a name by which they were probably referred to during their short heyday. I had also originally assumed the members of the band were mostly in punk attire, but this was the first evidence that the band members maintained an explicitly "girly" aesthetic in their adoption of skirts. It also reveals that even if these women were marginalized, they still maintained a social world in the larger punk scene. The following fragment in the book gives a description of gangs of girls fighting among each other. However, given the lack of names or any other biographical information, I am unsure whether this statement was given by one of Las Susys or by another girl who found herself confronted by them.

And yet rather than attempt to authoritatively correct the archival absences of Las Susys, or any other countless Mexican punk bands of the period, I am instead moved to interrogate my own desires to find them. This impulse comes from perhaps a certain sense of queer Mexican solidarity with a group of women who so fully elided and resisted the potentially oppressive cultures of their surroundings. I cannot help but read not only the sense of feminist collectivity but also the alternate forms of queer relationality the band practiced. In this sense, Susy's Peleoneras Punk could be said to embody what theorists Stefano Harney and Fred Moten have called the Undercommons.[42] But this is an undercommons that, in its punk ethos, refuses to be integrated into the tenets of proper political and historical remembering. They remain encapsulated in fragments, recollections that can never be anything more than elusive for a listener that will never get to hear them.

So what remains? One might ask, what is the point of attempting to write them into existence? To reveal them against the archival opacities that occlude their existence? But I return to the pages of books that will give us, the readers who were never there, a slight glimpse into how things *might have been*. Other traces remain. Although there might be no video of Las Susys, other videos and music recordings show the ferocity of La Zappa Punk's presence, her aggressively powerful scream, her ability to command the stage. There are other documents, for example, Sarah Minter's 1991 feature-length video *Alma Punk*, which chronicles the everyday life of Alma, a teenage punk girl who sleeps around, goes to shows, smokes weed, and eventually makes her escape from Mexico City to Tijuana and across the border. The video is set against the backdrop of these punk scenes, capturing their messy sociality in the background and in the story itself.[43] Like I once did with the Velvet Underground and scenes from the Factory, I can plug in Susy's Peleoneras Punk as a band in one of the video's scenes, allowing for the soundtrack to remain silent, perhaps filling it in with what I could only imagine as sloppy punk standards being performed by a band that prized its roughness around the edges. The practice I want to propose here then is one in which the very notion of recollecting becomes a mode made possible by the bootleg as incomplete, productively corrupted by my own distances. This is an attempt to reconstruct a sense of punk existence through its very evanescence, which by doing so still might give me an understanding of what feminist punk meant for women who had been so near the edge of dispossession.

Conclusion

In her book *Into the Archive*, Kathryn Burns explains that in approaching the archive, scholars must be especially attentive to "the archives that aren't." Looking at the construction of the archive in colonial Peru, she writes, "examined closely, the archives of colonial Cuzco are full of small inconsistencies that hint at a productive tension between *teoría* and *práctica*: between the way documents were supposed to be made and the ways they were made in practice."[44] Like other scholars who over the past few decades have questioned the claims toward authorative knowledge the archive might afford us, she compels us "to read the archive's silences . . . to understand, as much as possible, who collaborated with whom, what was 'customarily' done, and what the record was built to exclude."[45] Throughout this chapter I have argued that the bootleg might provide a useful framework to approach not only how archives gain meaning, but perhaps also how we come to give meaning to them. Although the examples I have provided here might seem somewhat distant, they are both in the end joined by an attempt to find, and place, oneself in historical relations from which we are out of time. In the case of *Remake*, Ortega and Guzmán approach the art historical archive by unfaithfully reproducing a series of performances via incomplete fragments, thus creating a bootleg object that gives the artists, as well as us, an alternative way to access the canons of performance art. The second example has centered my own encounters with incomplete fragments throughout my attempts to find a feminist punk band that left no recording, photographs, fliers, or any other materials, only recollections and other anecdotes to be found. However, although I have hinted at modes of writing the archive that must rely on imagination, dreaming, and risking fiction, perhaps what Saidiya Hartman has recently developed as "critical fabulation,"[46] I choose to refrain from imagining or critically fabulating the life span of Las Susys. If I have sprinkled my own queer desires throughout these pages, I will withhold, at least for now, my own bootleg fabulation of what a Susy's Peleoneras Punk show might have been like, who would have been there, what it would have sounded like.

In the end, *Remake* and Las Susys were the product of a Mexico City where artists, musicians, and their publics had to make do with what they had. Removed from the consumer cultures of the United States, they had to reimagine their relationship to the history of contemporary art and punk from the absences of an archive they would perhaps never be able to fully access. Like other subjects placed outside of the West's cultural imaginary, they had to appropriate and bootleg what little they knew in order to make do. That Mexico City's contemporary art and punk rock scenes thrived under these conditions shows how the insufficiency of their archives could still produce works and life-forms that even now invite us to linger in our own unfaithful desires.

Notes

1 See Debrose and Medina, *Era de la discrepancia.*
2 Tongson, *Why Karen Carpenter Matters*, 93.
3 Tongson, *Why Karen Carpenter Matters*, 93.
4 Tortorici, *Sins against Nature*, 241.
5 Tortorici, *Sins against Nature*, 242.
6 Butler and Lehrer, *Curatorial Dreams*, 7.
7 Simon, "The Terrible Gift," 175–76.
8 See Muñoz, "Ephemera as Evidence."
9 See Love, *Feeling Backward.*
10 Greene, *Punk and Revolution*, 7.
11 Greene, *Punk and Revolution*, 10.
12 Greene, *Punk and Revolution*, 12.
13 See Zolov, *Refried Elvis.*
14 Greene, *Punk and Revolution*, 16.
15 See for example, De Kosnik, *Rogue Archives*; Heylin, *Bootleg*; Manuel, *Cassette Culture*; Marshall, *Bootlegging*; Mertha, *The Politics of Piracy.*
16 Hilderbrand, *Inherent Vice*, 5–6.
17 Hilderbrand, *Inherent Vice*, 22.
18 Hilderbrand, *Inherent Vice*, 23.
19 Marks, "Archival Romances," 30.
20 Marks, "Archival Romances," 30.
21 Marks, "Archival Romances," 30.
22 Marks, "Archival Romances," 35.
23 Ortega, "Re: Fotografias de *Remake*."
24 Clausen, "Archives of Inspiration."
25 Schneider, *Performing Remains*, 7.
26 Schneider, *Performing Remains*, 6.
27 Schneider, *Performing Remains*, 6.
28 Anderson, *So Much Wasted*, 77.
29 Anderson, *So Much Wasted*, 77.
30 I am thinking of "grain" here both as a formal and material quality in concert with Ann Laura Stoler's invitation to grasp the "feel" of the archive. See Stoler, *Along the Archival Grain.*
31 Marks, "Archival Romances," 34.
32 Clausen, "Archives of Inspiration."
33 Clausen, "Archives of Inspiration."
34 However, we might think of Ortega and Guzmán's intervention in *Remake* as being particularly successful, since it has been collected by various institutions, most notably the Centre Pompidou in Paris.

35 Habell-Pallán, *Loca-Motion*, 152–53.
36 See Fiol-Matta, *Great Woman Singer*; Vargas, *Dissonant Divas*; Vazquez, *Listening in Detail*.
37 Mirabal, *Suspect Freedoms*, 10.
38 Mirabal, *Suspect Freedoms*, 2.
39 Palacios and Estrada, "'A contra corriente,'" 155–56.
40 See Estrada, *Sirenas al ataque*.
41 Valenzuela, *¡A la brava ese!*, 203, translation mine.
42 See Harney and Moten, *The Undercommons*.
43 I have written elsewhere about the ways in which Sarah Minter's *Alma Punk* might provide an invaluable bootleg archive of the otherwise uncaptured punk scene in Mexico. See Ramos, "Aimless Lives."
44 Burns, *Into the Archive*, 124.
45 Burns, *Into the Archive*, 132.
46 See Hartman, *Wayward Lives*.

Works Cited

Anderson, Patrick. *So Much Wasted: Hunger, Performance, and the Morbidity of Resistance*. Durham, NC: Duke University Press, 2010.

Burns, Kathryn. *Into the Archive: Writing and Power in Colonial Peru*. Durham, NC: Duke University Press, 2010.

Butler, Shelley Ruth, and Erica Lehrer, eds. *Curatorial Dreams: Critics Imagine Exhibitions*. Montreal: McGill-Queen's University Press, 2016.

Clausen, Barbara. "Archives of Inspiration." *Ciel Variable*, no. 86 (Fall 2010): 17–24. http://cielvariable.ca/numeros/ciel-variable-86-performance/les-archives-de-linspiration-barbara-clausen/.

De Kosnik, Abigail. *Rogue Archives: Digital Cultural Memory and Media Fandom*. Cambridge, MA: MIT Press, 2016.

Debrose, Olivier, and Cuauhtémoc Medina. *La era de la discrepancia: Arte y cultura visual en México, 1968–1997*. 2nd ed. Mexico: Museo Universitario de Ciencias y Artes, 2014.

Estrada, Tere. *Sirenas al ataque: Historia de las mujeres rockeras mexicanas*. Mexico City: Editorial Océano, 2001.

Fiol-Matta, Licia. *The Great Woman Singer: Gender and Voice in Puerto Rican Music*. Durham, NC: Duke University Press, 2017.

Greene, Shane. *Punk and Revolution: Seven More Interpretations of Peruvian Reality*. Durham, NC: Duke University Press, 2016.

Habell-Pallán, Michelle. *Loca-Motion: The Travels of Chicana and Latina Popular Culture*. New York: NYU Press, 2005.

Harney, Stefano, and Fred Moten, *The Undercommons: Fugitive Planning and Black Study*. Chico, CA: Minor Compositions, 2013.

Hartman, Saidiya. *Wayward Lives, Beautiful Experiments: Intimate Histories of Social Upheaval*. New York: Norton, 2019.

Heylin, Clinton. *Bootleg: The Secret History of the Other Recording Industry*. New York: St. Martin's Press, 1994.

Hilderbrand, Lucas. *Inherent Vice: Bootleg Histories of Videotape and Copyright*. Durham, NC: Duke University Press, 2009.

Love, Heather. *Feeling Backward: Loss and the Politics of Queer History*. Cambridge, MA: Harvard University Press, 2007.

Manuel, Peter. *Cassette Culture: Popular Music and Technology in North India*. Chicago: University of Chicago Press, 1993.

Marks, Laura U. "Archival Romances: Found, Compressed and Loved Again." *FKW Zeitschrift für Geschlechterforschung und Visuelle Kultur* 61 (February 2017): 30–41.

Marshall, Lee. *Bootlegging: Romanticism and Copyright in the Music Industry*. London: Sage, 2005.

Mertha, Andrew. *The Politics of Piracy: Intellectual Property in Contemporary China*. Ithaca, NY: Cornell University Press, 2005.

Mirabal, Nancy. *Suspect Freedoms: The Racial and Sexual Politics of Cubanidad in New York, 1823–1957*. New York: NYU Press, 2017.

Muñoz, José Esteban. "Ephemera as Evidence: Introductory Notes to Queer Acts." *Women & Performance: A Journal of Feminist Theory* 8, no. 2 (1996): 5–16.

Ortega, Luis Felipe. "Re: Fotografías de Remake para publicación." Email interview received by Iván A. Ramos, December 13, 2020.

Palacios, Julia, and Tere Estrada. "'A contra corriente': A History of Women Rockers in Mexico." In *Rockin' Las Américas: The Global Politics of Rock in Latin/o America*, edited by Deborah Pacini Hernandez, Héctor Fernández L'Hoeste, and Eric Zolov, 142–59. Pittsburgh: University of Pittsburgh Press, 2004.

Ramos, Iván A. "Aimless Lives: Amateur Aesthetics, Mexican Contemporary Art, and Sarah Minter's Alma Punk." *Third Text* 34, no. 1 (2020): 190–205.

Schneider, Rebecca. *Performing Remains: Art and War in Times of Theatrical Reenactment*. London: Routledge, 2011.

Simon, Roger I. "The Terrible Gift: Difficult Memories for the Twenty-First Century." In *Curatorial Dreams: Critics Imagine Exhibitions*, edited by Shelley Ruth Butler and Erica Lehrer, 172–86. Montreal: McGill-Queen's University Press, 2016.

Stoler, Ann Laura. *Along the Archival Grain: Epistemic Anxieties and Colonial Commonsense*. Princeton, NJ: Princeton University Press, 2009.

Tongson, Karen. *Why Karen Carpenter Matters*. Austin: University of Texas Press, 2019.

Tortorici, Zeb. *Sins against Nature: Sex and Archives in Colonial New Spain*. Durham, NC: Duke University Press, 2018.

Valenzuela, José Manuel. *¡A la brava ese!: Cholos, punks, chavos banda*. Tijuana: Colegio de la Frontera Norte, 1988.

Vargas, Deborah R. *Dissonant Divas in Chicana Music: The Limits of La Onda*. Minneapolis: University of Minnesota Press, 2012.

Vazquez, Alexandra T. *Listening in Detail: Performances of Cuban Music*. Durham, NC: Duke University Press, 2013.

Zolov, Eric. *Refried Elvis: The Rise of the Mexican Counterculture*. Berkeley: University of California Press, 1999.

10. UNFIXED

Materializing Disability and Queerness in Three Objects

KATE CLARK AND DAVID SERLIN

In late summer 2016, Historic England, a government-sponsored group tasked with recommending architectural sites of national or cultural significance for legal protection, announced six buildings around Great Britain that qualified as sites of "queer history."[1] What made these sites historically "queer"—a term plastered across their online promotional materials—was their identification with LGBTQ figures from British history. These included both the well-known, such as Benjamin Britten and Oscar Wilde, as well as those whose profiles deserve greater recognition, such as Amelia Edwards, one of the founders of Egyptology. Perhaps the most intriguing of the "queer" sites named by Historic England was the modernist house added to St. Anne's Court, a sprawling estate in Chertsey, Surrey. A rounded turret cast in steel, crisp white concrete, and glass to evoke the nautical lines of an ocean liner, the house was codesigned in 1936 by British architect Raymond McGrath and his client, Christopher Tunnard, an influential avatar of modern garden landscape design.[2]

Tunnard contributed to the house a plan for a massive master bedroom suite, which he intended to share with his longtime partner, Gerald Schlesinger, featuring two wedge-shaped "wings" on the far sides of the central sleeping space (see Figure 10.1). The design ensured that, during public events when their private lives might be called into view, the couple's double bed, which occupied the center of the suite, could be separated in half and moved on casters into two single day beds. Anchoring supports and separating walls built into each of the wings enabled the two men to preserve the notion that they lived as bachelors in separate (though proximate) sleeping quarters.

What, exactly, qualifies this site as a "queer" site, and in particular Tunnard's bedroom as a historic example of a "queer" space? Is it the bedroom? The bed?

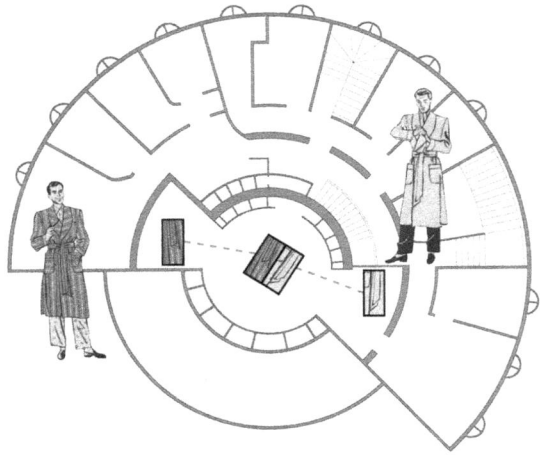

FIGURE 10.1. Schematic plan of the master bedroom suite in the McGrath-Tunnard House (1936), on the estate at St. Anne's Court, Chertsey, Surrey, UK. Illustration by Per Brekke and Kate Clark and reprinted with their permission.

The wings? Certainly, for Tunnard and Schlesinger, to be publicly open about their relationship in the years before the decriminalization of homosexuality in 1967 with the lifting of the Sexual Offences Act would have been an act of bravery that few men of their generation were willing to risk life and liberty to promote.[3] But what, then, makes this a "queer" space as opposed to, say, a "gay" space? Is its queerness indexed by the space's association with early twentieth-century same-sex eroticism as practiced, however surreptitiously, by Tunnard and Schlesinger? Or is it indexed by the implicit invitation to visitors to conjure two men, at the end of a long night entertaining houseguests, deciding whether or not to go to opposite sides of their sleeping chamber?

In his history of the closet as a material and metaphorical space, Henry Urbach has argued for the linkage between the words "closet" and "disclosure."[4] So is Tunnard's bedroom "queer" because of its dual complicity with and resistance to disclosure—the bedroom's spatial layout, the beds, and the ephemeral gestures of separation and reconnection deployed to disguise the couple's sexual intimacy? Such seemingly unresolved, and unresolvable, contradictions bring to mind what John Paul Ricco has called a "disappeared aesthetics," a form of queerness that is "neither a matter of the visible nor the invisible, but of the imperceptible . . . a refusal of either/or logics, a non-dialectical double refusal that is 'no-longer-being' and 'not-yet-being,' at once."[5] Ricco goes on to associate a disappeared aesthetics with what Michel Foucault once described as "not in showing the invisible, but in showing the extent to which the invisibility of the visible is invisible."[6]

In this chapter, we examine the lives of three distinct archival objects—a piece of concrete sidewalk, a polyurethane mannequin, and a cotton bandage—that suggest the critical implications of a disappeared aesthetics for both disability history and queer history. The artifacts presented are not ordered chronologically or spatially; they cut across both time and space, thereby sustaining challenges to normative notions of temporality or privileges of geography.[7] In doing so, we endeavor to highlight the ways in which approaches to the archive often do not inhere necessarily to the provenance of the objects per se, but instead to their dispositions within LGBTQ history and disability history, where they are often "fixed" according to the orientations and demands of those disciplines. Ultimately, however, we hope to demonstrate the implications of "unfixing" archival objects, especially those that are typically "fixed" not only by their disciplines but also by their association with archival or curatorial practices and normative regimes of meaning-making.

Scholars of disability history have only begun to revisit the role that various objects have had in coproducing forms of disabled subjectivity.[8] This shift marks a dramatic transformation in sensibility and emphasis. Beginning in the 1970s, activists and academics insisted on what is called the social model of disability that would challenge legal and environmental barriers to participation and citizenship, replacing the conventional medical model that associated disability with the perceived limitations of the individual body. Over the past decade, however, developments in disability studies and in the emergent area of crip theory have facilitated a kind of rapprochement with the medical model in order to explore the coproduction of disabled subjectivity as mediated by the objects that currently constitute disability's material archive.[9] As Katherine Ott and Richard Sandell have argued in their respective work on exhibiting objects of disability history in museum settings, there is more to the relationship between the disabled body and medical technology—a prosthetic leg; a wheelchair used by a famous person; a hypodermic needle that delivers "the cure"—than highlighting the controlling and often triumphalist narratives of medical science.[10] Individual artifacts of disability history are now routinely exhibited within networks of domestic and personal artifacts through which people engage the built environment and also help to foster forms of identification beyond those of the pathological subject.

Yet it is instructive for scholars of disability to think about assessing the significance of queerness as part of the lived experiences of bodies and objects, just as it is instructive for scholars of LGBTQ history and culture to think about assessing the significance of disability as part of the lived experiences of bodies and objects. Sandell, for instance, has enumerated some of the curatorial interventions by both small and large museums in the United Kingdom over the past two decades. In 2007, for example, the Northampton Museum and Art Gallery, which holds the largest collection of historical footwear in the world, mounted *I Stand Corrected?*, an exhibition that paired objects identifiable with disability history, such as early twentieth-century orthopedic shoes, with counter-cultural and queer objects such as glam rock platforms, drag queen heels, and dominatrix stilettos.[11] Similarly, the value and meaning of such objects that are handled, worn, inserted, breathed through, and even pissed in and shat on contrasts enormously with the value and meaning attributed by archivists and curators that treat them as indexical of sickness, imperfection, or lack. One thinks of, for example, the pioneering performance art work of "supermasoch-ist" Bob Flanagan, or the use of catheters in sex play, both of which cut across both queer and disability histories without reducing either to its "proper" place in hierarchies of knowledge.[12] And in a parallel with queer theory's engage-ment with such once reviled social topics as shame, loss, failure, and abjection, the goal of such projects is neither to reduce disability history to a positivist history of assistive technologies nor to align the legislative triumphs of the dis-ability rights movement with unchecked narratives of humanitarian progress.[13] As Robert McRuer has argued, objects associated with fixed understandings of LGBTQ public history—the display of the AIDS Memorial Quilt on the Mall in Washington, DC—cut across both disability and queer histories as ob-jects that make visible the intertwined histories of pathology and stigma, as well as forms of resistance to them, that sexual minorities and people with disabilities have long encountered and in which they have long participated.[14] The AIDS Quilt, as well as the NAMES Project organized in 1987 to assist in its admin-istration and exhibition, are examples of monumental artifacts that emerged from within the sweep of queer and crip histories, long before such histories even had those eponymous designations. There are countless other artifacts and histories from the domestic realm that trace the same contours of queer and disabled intersectionality.

Taking a cue from recent archaeological research that emphasizes not just the import of the artifact but the very soil and site conditions in which the object was excavated, we argue that by considering the broader environmental condi-tions and contexts out of which, or into which, the object emerged may give clues to other users and communities to which the object "belongs."[15] By "un-fixing" an artifact from its commonly perceived place and social orientation, the interpreter/curator is then required to take a more open perspective, con-sidering other site conditions that may have woven through the archival object's place of origin. This "unfixing" gives way to finding cross sections between constituencies previously designated as separate. This is a process particularly crucial to the interpretation and curation of objects connected to individuals who have been marginalized, medicalized, and considered as subhuman through modernity's flattening stare. The three archival objects discussed in the following sections are intended to resonate with historians of disability as well as historians of queerness, serving as mediums for innovating both curatorial practice and interpretive method.

Material Manifestoes: The Atlantis Community Curb Cut (Denver, Colorado, 1980)

Wielding sledgehammers, disability activists hammered concrete chunks from the curbs of East Colfax and Colorado avenues in Denver.[16] July 7, 1980, was not the first day that activists George Roberts and Les Hubbard took to East Colfax and Colorado to demonstrate against inaccessible space. Roberts and Hubbard were members of Denver's Atlantis Community, formed in 1974 as one of the earliest advocacy centers for people with disabilities in the United States. Atlantis, like its counterparts in US cities like Berkeley and Seattle and Urbana-Champaign, subscribed to the principles of the Independent Living Movement, which originated in Berkeley in the early 1970s to foster physical, social, and economic autonomy among people with disabilities who were more accustomed to being treated as objects of medical intervention rather than subjects of their own self-determination.

The streetside moment of radical resistance for wheelchair users and blind pedestrians has made the Atlantis curb cut one of the featured artifacts of the disability rights movement and is one of the cornerstones of *Every Body: An Artifact History of Disability in America.* Curated by Katherine Ott, this traveling and online exhibition of the US disability rights movement honors the twenty-fifth anniversary of the Americans with Disabilities Act (hereafter ADA), signed into law in 1990 by President George H. W. Bush (see Figure 10.2).[17] The Atlantis Community curb cut exemplifies what Barbara Kirshenblatt-Gimblett has called an "ethnographic fragment," a piece of material evidence surgically cut from a historical incident or cultural practice.[18] Among other things, the curb cut is an ethnographic fragment of mid-twentieth-century aesthetics cast in the Fordist sensibility of regular, interchangeable forms of the modern (and able-bodied) cityscape. The corner of East Colfax and Colorado is the site of National Jewish Health, a hospital that once housed generations of people with disabilities deposited there by family members. Two years earlier in July 1978, members of the Atlantis Community had staged a similar grassroots protest

FIGURE 10.2.
Sidewalk fragment
removed, via sledge-
hammer, by local
disability rights activ-
ists from the Atlantis
Community, Denver,
Colorado, dated July 7,
1980. Accessioned in
2004 by the National
Museum of American
History, Smithsonian
Institution. Photo-
graph by Kate Clark
and reprinted with her
permission.

nearby to demand that public buses were wheelchair accessible. As Christina Cogdell has argued in her study of streamline design in the 1930s and 1940s, such forms become witting participants in an aesthetics of eugenics, dimin-ishing or eliminating use by undesirable subjects whose shapes or orientations make them unruly cogs in an imaginary machine of urban civility and utility.[19] Many US municipalities, as Susan Schweik has shown, invoked the power of "ugly laws" to discourage and regulate the public exhibition of these asym-metrical or abnormal bodies of the disabled or queer (or both).[20] Even in the post-ADA era, the appeal of the Fordist aesthetic among urban planners and architects remains a seductive force of presumptive neutrality that continues to be the basis for designing and building environments for nondisabled users in order to maximize efficiency and impact. This often necessitates the involvement of legal advocates and grassroots disability activists in order to ensure ADA compliance.

While the Smithsonian's exhibition of the Atlantis Community curb cut could be considered a disruptive unfixing of able-bodied social attitudes beyond legislative demands, the geographical and material specificity of the Atlantis Community curb cut might be better situated within local and national histories of queerness and disability. Following Kirshenblatt-Gimblett's cue, if considering the curb cut as a surgical cut from a historic moment, this chunk of concrete wasn't only hammered from a corner of Denver's urban sprawl, but also from a terrain freighted with disability and LGBTQ histories. Indeed, this chunk of object removed from East Colfax—a twenty-six-mile stretch that connects Denver with the city of Aurora—holds multiple queer histories in its concrete.[21] A historic thoroughfare once lined with elegant mansions and high-end commercial pleasures, by the mid-twentieth century, the eastern part of Colfax became a contested terrain of public safety and hygiene, a perfect example of what Kevin Mumford has called an "interzone" of sexual and racial minorities brokering often-marginal commercial interests that might appeal to thrill-seeking clients.[22] By the early 1970s Colfax's overflow of strip clubs, pawn brokers, head shops, and liquor stores and its intersections of sex workers, hustlers, junkies, and homeless and disabled populations in public view allegedly inspired no less a cultural arbiter than Hugh Hefner to observe Colfax to be the "longest, wickedest street in America."[23]

That Colfax Avenue is historically relevant for not only disability history but queer urban history—it became, in the 1970s, a central cruising corridor for Denver's emergent gay ghetto, and since 1976 has been the site of the Center on Colfax, Denver's LGBTQ community center—suggests that the interpretive possibilities of the Atlantis Community curb cut remain undervalued (see Figure 10.3). How, then, might the presence, and absence, of forms of LGBTQ and disability history and activism be brought into productive alignment by the curb cut? Reclamations of the street by both sexual rights activists and disability rights activists are a neglected point of interpretive overlap—consider, for instance, the surge of public demonstrations on the steps of San Francisco City Hall in 1977 and 1978 by disability activists, gay activists, and their allies in social justice.[24] Even in the era of more well-known gay activism, the 1980 Atlantis Community curb cut remains a kind of manifesto for action, a performance of disability rights activism brought into being by its excision from the sidewalk and its accession at the Smithsonian. Three years later, in 1983, Atlantis became ground zero for the organization of Americans Disabled for

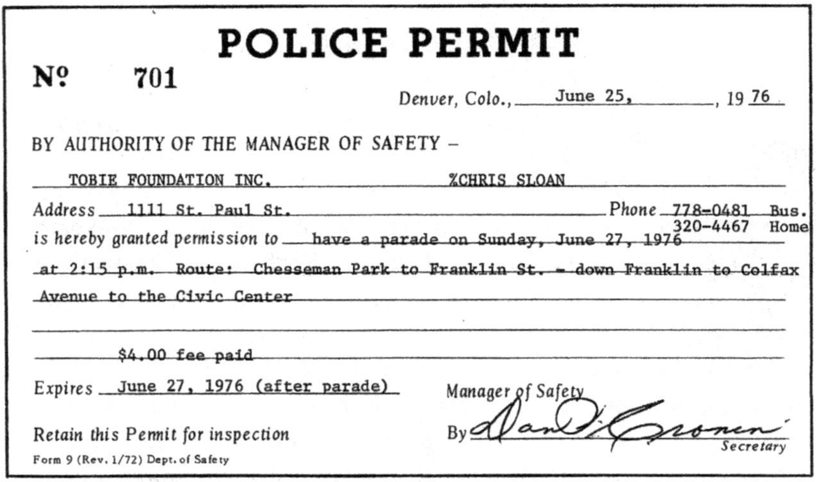

POLICE PERMIT

Nº 701

Denver, Colo., ___June 25,___ , 19 76

BY AUTHORITY OF THE MANAGER OF SAFETY –

___TOBIE FOUNDATION INC.___   ___%CHRIS SLOAN___

Address ___1111 St. Paul St.___ _____ Phone ___778-0481___ Bus.
320-4467 Home
is hereby granted permission to ___have a parade on Sunday, June 27, 1976___
at 2:15 p.m. Route: Chesseman Park to Franklin St. – down Franklin to Colfax
Avenue to the Civic Center _____

_____

_____$4.00 fee paid_____

Expires ___June 27, 1976 (after parade)___   Manager of Safety

Retain this Permit for inspection   By _____
Secretary
Form 9 (Rev. 1/72) Dept. of Safety

FIGURE 10.3. Police permit issued to "Chris Sloan" (pseudonym for local activist Christi Layne) for Denver's first gay pride parade, held on June 27, 1976. Note Colfax Avenue's role in the conclusion of the parade route. Photograph reprinted courtesy of The Center on Colfax (https://lgbtqcolorado.org/).

Accessible Public Transportation (ADAPT), the first advocacy group of its kind that was responsible for dozens of disruptive public actions across the United States. During the same year, Denver became one of the first locations of AIDS activism, galvanizing gay health activists from San Francisco and New York to meet and generate a manifesto known as the Denver Principles.[25] Drafted by Bobbi Campbell and Michael Callen, the 1983 document is often referred to as "the Magna Carta of AIDS activism" for its emphasis on empowering gay men with AIDS (and, indeed, coining the phrase "people with AIDS") and encouraging patient autonomy and community networks of care in the face of government neglect and institutional hostility. The curb cut thus opens up shared ontologies of stigma and shared strategies of resistance that not only make the necessary historical linkages between people with disabilities and people with AIDS in the early 1980s, but also provide the basis for linking histories of disability rights activism to histories of AIDS activism.

The Atlantis Community curb cut does not merely metaphorize access. Rather, it materializes the process by which an artifact enters into a system of intelligibility by simultaneously marking the presence of physical struggle (inability to ascend to the curb) as well as the absence of that struggle. In this sense, the curb cut is like the double bed at the center of Christopher Tunnard's master suite; it enacts a disappeared aesthetics that neither affirms nor denies the presence of queerness but instead makes its residual traces—rather than, say, its unique aura, as Walter Benjamin might have described it—central to how its meaning is publicly communicated. This is why the significance of the Atlantis Community curb cut to histories of disability as well as histories of queerness is concretized not only in the materiality of its presence but in the immateriality of its gesture.

"Get Closer": The Pro Infirmis Campaign (Zurich, Switzerland, 2013)

The Atlantis Community curb cut, transformed into an artifact through necessity, helped both symbolically and materially reimagine disability in the US public sphere. Grassroots efforts like those of the Atlantis Community and the National Organization of People with AIDS might be productively contextualized with other efforts at disability legislation or advocacy, such as the Chronically Sick and Disabled Persons Act (Great Britain, 1970), the Declaration of the Rights of Handicapped Persons (France, 1975), and Disabled Peoples International (Canada, 1981), before the symbolic capstone of the Americans with Disabilities Act of 1990.[26] Broader lawmaking efforts by the European Union followed, and after years of ad hoc committee assemblies, the United Nations Convention on the Rights of Persons with Disabilities was adopted in 2006. Individual European nations, such as Switzerland, responded with a variety of local and national projects.

In 2013, for instance, the Swiss disability advocacy organization Pro Infirmis launched an activist campaign, "Because Who Is Perfect? Get Closer," less than two months after the UN Convention was adopted by the Swiss Council of States. On December 3, marked as the International Day of Disability, the street-level windows of the Modissa department store—located on Zurich's Bahnhofstrasse, one of the world's most expensive and exclusive shopping promenades—were transformed for one day into a temporary exhibition space. In the Pro Infirmis campaign, contemporary fashion garments were draped on mannequins shaped to replicate the bodies of five Swiss personalities: Jasmin Rechsteiner, winner of Miss Handicap 2010; radio presenter and film critic Alex Oberholzer; Paralympic track and field athlete Urs Kolly; blogger Nadja Schmidt; and actor Erwin Aljukic (see Figure 10.4).

Polyurethane mannequins molded directly from the bodies of runway models, often displaying exaggerated morphologies that are seven sizes smaller than their average onlooker, are only the latest iterations of a much older historical

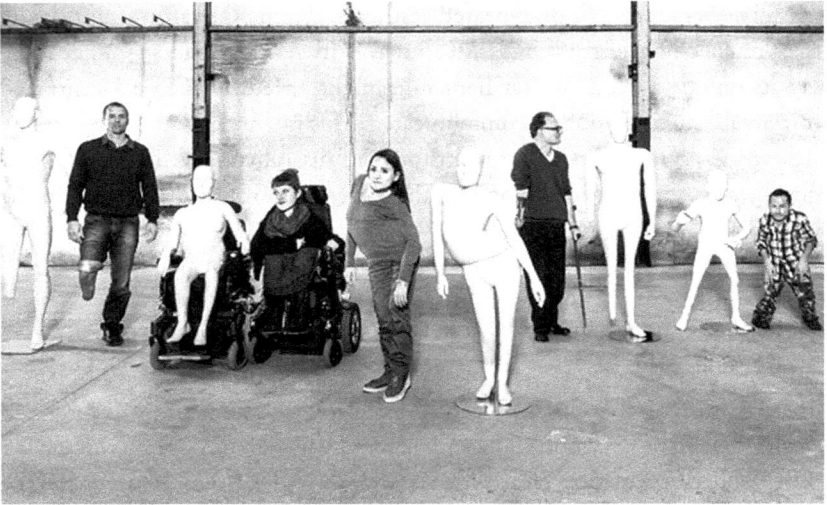

FIGURE 10.4. Swiss celebrities, all of whom identify publicly as people with disabilities, posing with their polyurethane counterparts. From the 2013 exhibition and film project "Because Who Is Perfect? Get Closer," available at https://www.youtube.com/watch?v =E8umFV69fNg&t=12s. Reprinted with permission of Pro Infirmis.

tradition of curated display. Since the early nineteenth century, the manne-quin form has affirmed aspirational ideals: during the early 1930s, for instance, plump and elegantly styled (and phenotypically "white") wax figures installed in shop windows fed an impossible vision of recuperative health for an impoverished public.[27] Yet beyond modeling impossible ideals of individual embodiment, the Pro Infirmis mannequins are unique in that they reveal how few artifacts of disability have been materialized deliberately through art-historical production. As Andrew Marcum has argued, sculptures of famous historical figures such as Franklin Delano Roosevelt and Helen Keller, cast in bronze and installed in symbolic public spaces, distort historical complexity by turning them into physical objects that, ironically, lack any dimensionality.[28]

Most artifacts of disability history, however, are not deliberately forged. Instead, they are hewn retrospectively (and, one could argue, inadvertently) from what Eyal Weizman has described as "political plastic—social forces slowing into form."[29] Only in hindsight, as objects of political plastic that have been slowed into material form, do we recognize them to be worthy as artifacts of disability history that constitute what Svetlana Alpers has called "the museum effect," the process by which otherwise ordinary objects become meaningful.[30]

This explains how the same institution that maintains the mythical Hope Diamond and Dorothy's magical ruby slippers from *The Wizard of Oz* also holds a chunk of industrial concrete from a busy intersection in Denver. It is only the detritus of these political gestures that ends up landing in the archives of the Smithsonian Institution, ferried by the ministrations of a sympathetic curator. As Jani Scandura writes, these objects are "expendable material that . . . may be recuperated into existent systems of value, even as a symptom of what has gone wrong."[31]

The polyurethane Pro Infirmis mannequins are anything but detritus, of course, as indicated by the curator's choice of the windows of Modissa, the upscale department store, over a museum or gallery space (see Figure 10.5). These disabled mannequins are noteworthy not because of *who* they represent but because of *where* and *how* they are situated—in particular, the resistant (though invisible) gestures inscribed *onto* them as a result of their mass-produced origins and their relationship to larger histories of display and consumerism. Some of the most accessible spaces found in contemporary urban cityscapes are its shopping areas, even those shopping boulevards cut centuries before sidewalks or questions of access entered the planning vocabulary. Curbs, those legacies of the early twentieth-century transition from cobblestones to sidewalks, are often nonexistent in contemporary shopping promenades that provide seamless transitions between busy thoroughfares and browsing zones. Elevators and escalators convey equally those with mobility impairments and those burdened by parcels and prams. By controlling sizable street footprints and street corner entrances and exits, pedestrian corridors protect shoppers from vehicles and offer ample seating and toilet facilities. Yet despite these aspects of heightened or expanded public access, the Pro Infirmis "Because Who Is Perfect? Get Closer" campaign created a level of pageantry that, ironically, follows the contours of the same modernist aesthetic that figured in the original normative mannequins and the bourgeois concept of the shopping street or arcade. By lauding a famous Paralympic athlete or a Miss Handicap winner as people appointed as spokesmodels for a routinely marginalized community, they declare that they are molding from only "the best." The affective dimensions of feel-good calculation emerge from a day-long action based in self-congratulatory symbolism. This seems to demonstrate, as Marta Russell has argued, the mandate among contemporary designers of urban public space to increasingly "accept signs and images of contact as more natural and desirable than contact itself."[32]

Although the Pro Infirmis exhibition was accessible in material form for only one day, the exhibition continues to exist as a short promotional documentary on YouTube and Vimeo. In the film, the smooth, elongated mannequins in

FIGURE 10.5. Jasmin Rechsteiner, Miss Handicap 2010, the model for the mannequin *(center)* visible in the window, stops in front of Zurich's upscale Modissa department store to view herself. From the 2013 exhibition and film project "Because Who Is Perfect? Get Closer," available at https://www.youtube.com/watch?v=E8umFV69fNg&t=12s. Reprinted with permission of Pro Infirmis.

Modissa's windows become deliberately provocative objects of the pedestrian gaze. We observe the public's quizzical response, pausing briefly amid the hubbub to examine the torqued and uncanny forms. Crisp, well-lit footage tracks the reverse engineering of mass-produced department store manne-quins, showing each model for the project undergoing the meticulous process of manufacturing disability for public consumption: from measuring the stump below Kolly's left knee, the "S" curve of Schmidt's back, and the slender calves of Aljukic, to the production of each mannequin as it is cut, bent, sanded, and lacquered in austere white polyurethane. At the end of the production pro-cess, the human models are shown standing alongside their inert doppelgang-ers, running their fingers against the mannequins' smooth surfaces in slowed moments designed to mirror their emotional processing. The video concludes with the Pro Infirmis logo shown with gentle guitar chords and inspirational ascending crescendos and the eponymous question, "Because Who Is Perfect? Get Closer."

Although the Pro Infirmis video focuses its documentary gaze on galva-nizing normative modes of empathy among those who passed in front of the Modissa shop window on the day of exhibition, YouTube viewers can linger on the behind-the-scenes images of production through the intimate interactions of the camera lens with the bodies of the disabled models. In the vignette featuring the mannequin casting for the Swiss Paralympian Kolly, for instance, the camera wraps around to what can be described as a crip-tease: wearing only briefs, first Kolly removes his prosthetic, then the prosthetic cushion, and finally the sock from the stump that extends below his toned right thigh. Next, we watch Kolly lean against a pole, stretching his body and tilting his head in a saucy pose (see Figure 10.6). What features as B-reel footage in the documentary becomes the main subject in other Pro Infirmis campaign posters, where a statuesque Kolly stands above the viewer holding his prosthetic C-leg, clad only in sports briefs. The languid pose, as well as the sports briefs themselves, arrest the viewer's gaze while stirring the erotic imagination, calling to mind the titillating publicity shots of disabled US veteran and model Alex Minsky in campaigns for Jack Adams athletic underwear taken the following year in 2014.[33]

In the Pro Infirmis video, as in underwear advertisements featuring Minsky, Kolly's crip-tease deliberately blurs the lines of masculinity, desire, and vulnerability that are supposed to distinguish disabled male bodies from their nondisabled counterparts. This is reflected in the thousands of YouTube user comments, some of which invoke problematic associations between modernist ideals of beauty and productivity routinely exploited to assess disabled and queer bodies. As one viewer observes somewhat enigmatically, "There's some

FIGURE 10.6. Urs Kolly *(left)*, the Swiss Paralympic champion, crip-teases for the camera. From the 2013 exhibition and film project "Because Who Is Perfect? Get Closer," available at https://www.youtube.com/watch?v=E8umFV69fNg&t=12s. Reprinted with permission of Pro Infirmis.

really gorgeous people in that selection, wow, it's sad to see disabilities like this ruin someone's appearance (according to modern standards) when you know, without it, they wouldv [*sic*] been extremely attractive."

As an art project, Pro Infirmis's exhibitionary legacy attempts to create a disability object for a new public sphere. The material that constitutes public space, described by Henri Lefebvre as "a never-ending oeuvre in which all of its citizens participate," moves beyond the bounds of brick and mortar, or steel and glass, and dematerializes into the world of YouTube.[34] The campaign thus does not need to rely on the archive or the museum (or, for that matter, the department store) as a necessary final resting place. Rather, it completes itself by treating the production, curation, exhibition, documentation, and archiving as epistemic variations of one-stop shopping. And since this new form of producing and archiving objects for a collective memory vertically integrates process, exhibition, artifact, and spectatorship, no docent is required to interpret the cultural significance of the mannequins, which were fabricated only as a means to an end. With over twenty-five million views on YouTube, the documentary allows us to witness the subtlety and intimacy of someone caressing a replica of themselves for the first time in their life, thereby reinforcing the idea that in the early twenty-first century, the disabled body now can move smoothly across the curb, enter the shopping district, and find itself mirrored and confirmed in sites of consumerist desire.

Performing Triage: The Esmarch Bandage (Berlin, Germany, 1870)

One precedent for the image of Urs Kolly—one likely unknown to the production teams at Pro Infirmis or the Modissa department store, and perhaps unknown even to Kolly or the other disabled models—can be found on a triangular piece of cotton fabric printed in 1870 in Konstanz, Germany, an industrial city only seventy kilometers from Zurich. Measuring four feet at the base, with sides nearly three feet in length, the triangular fabric depicts six men arranged with the formality of a Bethlehem crèche (see Figure 10.7). At each corner of the triangle, a prone man rests against his kneeling counterpart, flanking two men standing at the center. It is unclear if their far-off gazes are channeled from beatific poise or through medical neutrality; regardless, the reasoning for their blissful expressions is further complicated by the fact that they all are naked save for a few bound and draped pieces of fabric. With painstaking detail, the illustrations go beyond medical necessity to softly shade one man's muscled buttocks pulling against fabric as his profile reveals a neatly trimmed mustache. He faces another figure, whose carefully rendered Olympian thighs

FIGURE 10.7. Final design of the triangular triage bandage by Johannes Friedreich von Esmarch, printed in Konstanz ca. 1873. From the collection of David Serlin.

and draped groin presage that of Kolly's crip-tease. The sensuousness of this scene is contrasted by the clinical numbering of the figures. Though none of the young men's bodies show any visible marks of impairment, each model performs the visible conditions of disablement in order to demonstrate the thirty-two distinct ways that the bandage can be knotted, splinted, and draped across, around, and within various configurations of their bodies.

Johannes Friedrich August von Esmarch, a professor of medicine at the University of Kiel and called into service as Germany's surgeon general during the Franco-Prussian War, designed his eponymous bandage to respond to what he perceived as a dearth in resources for field trauma. At the time the bandage was manufactured in 1870, warfare had entered the modern era even though military medicine was still woefully underdeveloped. The newly developed machine gun and rifle made the killing of nearly 115,000 Prussian soldiers far more efficient than technologies used in previous wars. As surgeon general, Esmarch recommended that all soldiers carry his bandage onto the battlefield. He pioneered the idea that by combining triage technology with instructional diagrams, he could devise an object that would be inexpensive to produce, easy to use under stressful conditions, and disposable. Requiring a nationwide undertaking of fabrication, transportation, and distribution—the cotton fabric used in the Esmarch bandage was manufactured in Hilden, in southern Germany, by the Ludwig and Gustav Cramer Company, before being shipped across the country to Konstanz, in the north, where the medical illustrations were printed—the bandage is a model of modern warfare industrialized. With its

Gothic letters at the apex of the triangle, which functions to brand both the author and his namesake bandage at all times, versions of the Esmarch have landed in textiles collections of the Cooper Hewitt Museum in New York City, design collections of the Museum of Applied Arts and Sciences in Sydney, Australia, medical collections of the Wangensteen Historical Library of Biology and Medicine at the University of Minnesota, and in fashion collections of the Fashion Institute for Design and Merchandising in Los Angeles.

Some scholars have analyzed the bandage, situating it both representationally and pedagogically as evidence of the transfer of professional medical expertise to the expediencies of the battlefield.[35] Yet beyond its didactic function, the Esmarch bandage exceeds its singular identity as an artifact of medical technology. Among other things, the Esmarch bandage illustrates (both figuratively and literally) forms of homosocial bonding knotted to understandings of male vulnerability. The original illustrated design, for instance, featured models on the battlefield, but many determined the scenes too graphic and a potential threat to morale (see Figure 10.8). By contrast, the final, and recognizable, version of the bandage features a white background with vague hints of foliage, creating a minimalist environment that foregrounds the bandage's unusual combinations and bindings with the gravitas of a university course in classical art history.

Esmarch's bandage raises compelling questions about the complex relationship between disabling injuries incurred during wartime and expressions of normative nondisabled masculinity. Since triage is only intended as a temporary stopgap measure, the use of the bandage may mark a potential for disability, but it just as likely marks a temporary status wherein one is a visitor to the land of disability but not a permanent resident there. In addition, one could discuss the bandage as an intimate response to industrial modern warfare in which the object is not solely a medical technology but also a medium of interdependent care between soldiers more closely aligned with forms of mutuality and reciprocity than of traditional triage. Esmarch became one of the first medical practitioners to encourage new forms of same-sex intimacy and socialization, training and tasking soldiers on the battlefield in the intimate skills of triage—binding, splinting, and nursing each other—amidst harrowing warscapes. In this sense, the inherent queerness of the Esmarch bandage thus does not depend on connecting its use to the sexual practices of those who may or may not have used it, but instead to the material circulation of the bandage on the battlefield as it moves between the hands of soldiers trained for warfare but not for welfare.

FIGURE 10.8. First (and later rejected) design of the triangular triage bandage by Johannes Friedreich von Esmarch, printed in Kiel for use "on the battlefield" ca. 1869. Originally published in Esmarch, *The Surgeon's Handbook on the Treatment of Wounded in War*, trans. H. H. Clutton (Hanover, Germany: Charles Rümpler, 1878), 23.

The queer dimensions of the Esmarch bandage are even more pronounced, however, when one considers the late nineteenth-century context out of which it emerged. Brian Joseph Martin has identified numerous recorded cases of erotic encounters between soldiers during the Prussian War, at least on the Napoleonic side.[36] But the term *homosexual* was coined by Karl-Maria Kertbeny, who had served for a spell in the Hungarian army but who found the itinerant life of a travel writer, poet, and translator far more to his liking. Upon arriving in Berlin in 1868, Kertbeny found the same stringent laws against same-sex fraternizing as he did in Hungary. Kertbeny shifted his gaze from literary translation to an "anthropological" interest in individuals persecuted as pederasts, all the while burning his own potentially incriminating personal letters. In 1868, under the name "Dr. M," Kertbeny published a treatise that argued against Paragraph 143 of the Prussian Penal Code, which stated that "unnatural fornication, whether between persons of the male sex or of humans with beasts, is punished with imprisonment, with the further punishment of a prompt loss of civil rights."[37] Drawing upon eighteenth-century French botanical terms to describe plants as *unisexuel* and *bisexuel*, Kertbeny pronounced these men were not subjects of depravity, but of *homosexualität*.[38] Historians and sexologists have long championed the significance of Kertbeny's newly coined term, especially its linkage between the "natural" rights of man and the modern sexual subject.

During the same period that Kertbeny released his pamphlet, Esmarch moved to Berlin to develop his sensuously illustrated bandage, which naturally lead to some speculation. Although Esmarch and Kertbeny moved in different social circles, perhaps they would have had more to talk about than expected if they had run into each other. As a medical man, Esmarch would have taken interest in the later written works of "Dr. M," where Kertbeny was the first to posit a medical model of homosexuality, claiming that it was an inborn trait, just like any other congenital disability. Perhaps Kertbeny could have shared with Esmarch the delights associated with the gentle touches and ministrations he had encountered with men in semiprofessional settings, such as the "young barber lad" with whom he was "very much in love."[39] In any case, Kertbeny used a medical model as the basis for establishing a legally acceptable (and remarkably modern) argument for homosexual identity, stating that the law had nothing to do "with this inclination, be it innate or intentional, since the state does not have the right to intervene in anything that occurs between two consenting persons older than fourteen, which does not affect the public sphere."[40] Perhaps a Prussian soldier, confused by the pleasant experience he had when triaging a fellow soldier using Esmarch's bandage, might have discovered a term that described feelings he had had all his life while leafing through one of Kertbeny's pamphlets.

In their own ways, both Kertbeny and Esmarch advanced notions of individual agency and bodily needs that have had profound implications for both queer and disabled subjectivities. Both men transformed their research passions into printed, indispensable matter that, within the context of late nineteenth-century German medical and legal culture, produced medical models that appear less fixed than such terms conventionally imply and more unfixed in terms of their potential to assess bodily difference and advocate for individual rights and protections. By the beginning of World War II, popular use and professional interest in the potential uses of the Esmarch bandage had precipitously declined.[41] And as Esmarch's bandage was reprinted, the design lost its queer tinge of decorative filigrees, supple shadings, and soft poses. During World War I, the US medical and cosmetic supply giant Johnson & Johnson adapted the triangle for the American Red Cross; within a decade, the UK company Vernaid distributed the design to the British Red Cross, depicting the same rigid male figure repeated *ad nauseum* who poses in clothing that would be appropriate to any middle-class male civilian (see Figure 10.9). Still, the fact that the vast majority of bandages were either used or destroyed before they could be preserved carves out a special (non)space for them in the archives; they are literalized examples of a disappeared aesthetics.

FIGURE 10.9. The lamentably de-eroticized version of the Esmarch triangular triage bandage, printed by the UK company Vernaid, ca. 1920. Photograph reprinted courtesy of RudolfH and Wikimedia Commons.

The queerness of detritus—what Jani Scandura has described as the aesthetic of the thrown away or the cast off—can often be more instructive than the officially preserved "texts" of a given historical moment.[42] Unlike Esmarch's famously branded bandages, Kertbeny printed his two pamphlets anonymously; the publication of such a treatise even discussing pederasty could entail corporal punishment or execution. Yet in terms of staying power, only one of these artifacts can be considered a success story for the queer canon. Though Kertbeny died in 1882, purportedly of syphilis or a stroke,[43] four years later Krafft-Ebing published *Psychopathia Sexualis* (1886), which quickly became the preeminent text in describing the homosexual identity and which would later inform Freud's research. In less than two decades, Kertbeny's once incendiary word went through what David Halperin has called the "historical process of accumulation, accretion and overlay," especially since the heroic and virtuous discourses of Victorian masculinity were "largely untouched by the distinction between homo- and heterosexuality."[44] In less than fifty years, two life works of overlapping queer and crip interest whose creators were both temporally and geographically proximate were firmly separated into different interpretive camps.

Conclusion

In this chapter, we have attempted to push seemingly unrelated objects toward one another while always paying attention to the irreducible properties inherent in the objects themselves. In the Denver curb cut, we have tried to show how the history of access for Denver's disability rights activists is bound in concrete to the history of access for Denver's LGBTQ community. The curb cut materializes the sidewalk as a medium of liberated mobility, offering visitors a tangible urban artifact that simultaneously preserves both local disability activism and gay urban cruising culture. Similarly, in the Pro Infirmis project, mannequins made to replicate the bodies of well-known figures from the Swiss disability community are displayed for public contemplation in a chic department store window. But it is through its archival orientation, including its self-conscious behind-the-scenes documentation and its multiple digital afterlives, that the project offers unexpectedly queer variations on disability representation that were not baked into its sleek white polyurethane bodies. And the Esmarch bandage, a medical instruction manual and the medium through which that instruction is practiced, binds histories of disability and homoeroticism together in a Romantic tourniquet. Unlike the curb cut preserved in the Smithsonian or the mannequins memorialized in the Pro Infirmis video, the Esmarch bandage was never intended for survival; it was manufactured to be used and destroyed in the process. Its measure of success was its disappearance. Any examples that survive are thus damned to an austere and bloodless life that is removed from the collision of disability and intimacy that catalyzed the design and production of the bandage in the first place.

In their own ways, however, all three objects demonstrate John Paul Ricco's suggestion of a "disappeared aesthetic" offered at the beginning of this chapter—an approach that we have endeavored to recover or at least make available as a critical strategy that potentially serves a range of archival and curatorial practices relevant to queer history, disability history, and the various interstices between them. Of course, some might argue that declaring any approach as a "strategy" is potentially counterproductive to a queer methodology. David Halperin pointedly notes that it is as impossible to define with precision what constitutes the phenomenon of "homosexuality" as it is to define what its related historical artifacts might be. The same could be said for artifacts related to disability history since its artifacts exceed and even confound the binaries on which, historically, the distinction between disability and nondisability were constructed—including, among other things, the idea that disability and eroticism, or disability and desirability, are irreconcilable states of being. The development of crip theory as a critical intervention has been instrumental in drawing attention to these binaries, insisting that a focus on disability per se often leaves the conventions and privileges of able-bodiedness unquestioned, as unmarked and invisible as heterosexuality or whiteness. In undertaking this chapter, we have been inspired by the promise of crip theory for museum studies and archival practice by considering what it means both to fix an object—to situate it in time, place, and context—as well as to unfix that same object by questioning heuristics of time, place, and context as conventions of practice and habit rather than necessity. The process of unfixing requires us to treat queer and/or disability artifacts with the same steadfastness with which the soldiers treat each other on Esmarch's bandage. One should cultivate a capacity to identify a need in the object and respond to it with intimacy and industriousness: an extrapolation of a single digit from a complex system, a gentle touch to a twist of fabric.

There are countless objects of queer and/or disability history that deserve an exploratory touch: not just because of the identities of the people who used them but because of the wide range of embodied subjectivities that such objects made possible, some of which may well exceed the designations of "queer" or "disabled." Their value as historical objects, in other words, arrives by toggling between the desire to fix them while also endeavoring to unfix them. What many twentieth-century figures like Christopher Tunnard chased after, in the end, was unfixing the meanings attributed to homosexuality as a form of sexual and social deviance while at the very same time fixing the meanings attributed to homosexuality as a form of sexual and social (and some thirty years later, political) freedom. Of course, the daily practice of maintaining that posture in a home with his lover, Gerald Schlesinger, was vexed with complications and the need to dissemble publicly while living privately according to one's own choosing. So what if the present-day owners of the Tunnard House presented the two beds pushed into their recessed nooks as evidence of what it means to live between marked identities or diagnostic categories? What kind of "history" would thus be imparted to the visitor? Perhaps the master stroke of Tunnard's master suite is how much its meaning relies on the proximity of two objects that are forever being pushed together and pulled apart.

Notes

1 Chan, "6 Sites."
2 For an example of Tunnard's work, see his influential *Gardens in the Modern Landscape*, a compilation of articles written for the *Architectural Review* just after he and Schlesinger had taken up residence at St. Anne's Court.
3 See Higgins, *Heterosexual Dictatorship*. See also Houlbrook, *Queer London*.
4 Urbach, "Closets, Clothes, Disclosure."
5 Ricco, *The Logic of the Lure*, 41.
6 Michel Foucault, quoted in Ricco, *The Logic of the Lure*, 41–42.

7   For further elaborations of this concept in its queer and crip iterations, see for example Edelman, *No Future*; Freeman, *Time Binds*; the special issue of *Radical History Review* on "Queer Futures"; Kafer, *Feminist Queer Crip*; and Samuels, "Cripping Anti-Futurity."

8   See, for example, the concept of "cripistemology" in McRuer and Johnson, "Proliferating Cripistemologies."

9   See for example McRuer, *Crip Theory*.

10 See Ott, "Disability," and Sandell, *Museums*, esp. 138–72. See also Serlin, "Making Disability Public."

11 Northampton Museum and Art Gallery, "I Stand Corrected?"

12 See Kirby Dick's *Sick: The Life and Death of Bob Flanagan*. See also McRuer, "Crip Eye."

13 For further elaboration of these concepts, see for example Halperin and Traub, *Gay Shame*; Halberstam, *The Queer Art of Failure*; and Love, *Feeling Backward*.

14 See McRuer, "Disability and the NAMES Project."

15 Linderholm, "The Soil as a Source Material."

16 Hulse, "Handicapped Protest Curbs." See also Scanlon, "Atlantis Members."

17 The online version of the Smithsonian's *Every Body: An Artifact History of Disability in America* can be viewed at https://everybody.si.edu/ (last accessed June 8, 2022).

18 Kirshenblatt-Gimblett, "Objects of Ethnography."

19 Cogdell, *Eugenic Design*.

20 Schweik, *The Ugly Laws*.

21 For a recent assessment of Denver's mid-century queer history, see Moore, "Queen City of the Plains?"

22 Mumford, *Interzones*.

23 Williams, "Return of the Neon."

24 See Johnson, "Mobilizing the Disabled." See also Shapiro, *No Pity*.

25 See Callen and Turner, "A History of the PWA."

26 See Nepveux, "Activism."

27 For an interesting perspective on the gendered and racial dimensions of the mannequin, see Brown, *Work!* See also Gross, *Dream of the Moving Statue*.

28 See Marcum, "Material Embodiments."

29 Eyal Weizman, *Forensic Architecture*, 7.

30 Alpers, "The Museum as a Way of Seeing."

31 Scandura, *Down in the Dumps*, 12.

32 Russell, *Beyond Ramps*, 141.

33 See Serlin, "Introduction."

34 Lefebvre, *The Production of Space*, 73.

35 See Null, "A Beautiful Technology." See also "Mayor to Esmarch."

36 See Martin, *Napoleonic Friendship*.

37 Kertbeny, "Paragraph 143."

38 Norton, "The Term 'Homosexual.'"

39 Takács, "The Double Life of Kertbeny."

40 Takács, "Queering Budapest," 192.

41 See Null, "A Beautiful Technology."

42 See Scandura, *Down in the Dumps.*

43 See Takács, "The Double Life of Kertbeny."

44 Halperin, *How to Do the History of Homosexuality,* 3.

Works Cited

Alpers, Svetlana. "The Museum as a Way of Seeing." In *Exhibiting Cultures: The Poetics and Politics of Museum Display,* edited by Ivan Karp and Steve Lavine, 25–32. Washington, DC: Smithsonian Institution Press, 1991.

Brown, Elspeth. *Work! A Queer History of Modeling.* Durham, NC: Duke University Press, 2019.

Callen, Michael, and Dan Turner. "A History of the PWA Self-Empowerment Movement." In *Surviving and Thriving with AIDS: Collected Wisdom, Vol. 2,* edited by Michael Callen, 288–93. New York: People with AIDS Coalition, 1988. http://michaelcallen.com/mikes -writing/a-history-of-the-pwa-self-empowerment-movement/.

Chan, Sewell. "6 Sites Recognized by Britain for Significance to Gay History." *New York Times,* September 23, 2016.

Cogdell, Christina. *Eugenic Design: Streamlining America in the 1930s.* Philadelphia: University of Pennsylvania Press, 2005.

Dick, Kirby, dir. *Sick: The Life and Death of Bob Flanagan, Supermasochist.* 1997.

Edelman, Lee. *No Future: Queer Theory and the Death Drive.* Durham, NC: Duke University Press, 2004.

Freeman, Elizabeth. *Time Binds: Queer Temporalities, Queer Histories.* Durham, NC: Duke University Press, 2010.

Gross, Kenneth. *The Dream of the Moving Statue.* College Park: Pennsylvania State University Press, 1992.

Halberstam, Jack. *The Queer Art of Failure.* Durham, NC: Duke University Press, 2011.

Halperin, David. *How to Do the History of Homosexuality.* Chicago: University of Chicago Press, 2002.

Halperin, David, and Valerie Traub, eds. *Gay Shame.* Chicago: University of Chicago Press, 2010.

Higgins, Patrick. *Heterosexual Dictatorship: Male Homosexuality in Post-War Britain.* London: Trafalgar Square, 1997.

Houlbrook, Matt. *Queer London: Perils and Pleasures in the Sexual Metropolis, 1918–1957.* Chicago: University of Chicago Press, 2006.

Hulse, Jane. "Handicapped Protest Curbs." *Denver News,* July 8, 1980. http://adaptmuseum .net/gallery/index.php?/category/16.

Johnson, Roberta Ann. "Mobilizing the Disabled" (1983). In *Waves of Protest: Social Movements since the Sixties,* edited by Jo Freeman and Victoria Johnson, 25–45. Lanham, MD: Rowman & Littlefield, 1999.

Kafer, Alison. *Feminist Queer Crip.* Bloomington: Indiana University Press, 2013.

Kertbeny, Karl-Maria. "Paragraph 143 of the Prussian Penal Code." Reprinted in *Sodomites and Urnings: Homosexual Representations in Classical German Journals,* edited by Michael A. Lombardi-Nash, 64. Binghamton: Harrington Park Press, 2006.

Kirshenblatt-Gimblett, Barbara. "Objects of Ethnography." In *Exhibiting Cultures: The Poetics and Politics of Museum Display*, edited by Ivan Karp and Steve Lavine, 386–443. Washington, DC: Smithsonian Institution Press, 1991.

Lefebvre, Henri. *The Production of Space*. Oxford: Blackwell, 1991.

Linderholm, Johan. "The Soil as a Source Material in Archaeology: Theoretical Considerations and Pragmatic Applications." PhD diss., Umeaå University, Sweden, 2010.

Love, Heather. *Feeling Backward: Loss and the Politics of Queer History*. Cambridge, MA: Harvard University Press, 2009.

Marcum, Andrew. "Material Embodiments, Queer Visualities: Presenting Disability in American Public History." PhD diss., University of New Mexico, 2011.

Martin, Brian Joseph. *Napoleonic Friendship: Military Fraternity, Intimacy, and Sexuality in Nineteenth-Century France*. Lebanon: University of New Hampshire Press, 2011.

"Mayor to Esmarch to Johnson: The History of the Triangular Bandage." History & Safety Institute, March 24, 2015. http://www.hsi.com/blog/mayor-to-esmarch-to-johnson-the-history-of-the-triangular-bandage.

McRuer, Robert. "Crip Eye for the Normate Guy: Queer Theory, Bob Flanagan, and the Disciplining of Disability Studies." *PMLA: Publications of the Modern Language Association of America* 120, no. 2 (2005): 586–92.

McRuer, Robert. "Disability and the NAMES Project." *Public Historian* 27, no. 2 (Spring 2005): 53–61.

McRuer, Robert. *Crip Theory: Cultural Signs of Queerness and Disability*. New York: NYU Press, 2006.

McRuer, Robert, and Merri Lisa Johnson. "Proliferating Cripistemologies: A Virtual Roundtable." *Journal of Literary and Cultural Disability Studies* 8, no. 2 (2014): 149–69.

Moore, Keith L. "Queen City of the Plains? Denver's Gay History 1940–1975." MA thesis, University of Colorado, 2014.

Mumford, Kevin. *Interzones: Black/White Sex Districts in Chicago and New York in the Early Twentieth Century*. New York: Columbia University Press, 1997.

Nepveux, Denise. "Activism." In *Keywords for Disability Studies*, edited by Rachel Adams, Benjamin Reiss, and David Serlin, 21–25. New York: NYU Press, 2015.

Northampton Museum and Art Gallery. "I Stand Corrected? New Perspectives on Orthopaedic Footwear." In *Rethinking Disability Representation in Museums and Galleries*, edited by Jocelyn Dodd, Richard Sandell, Debbie Jolly, and Ceri Jones, 44–45. Leicester, UK: RCMG/University of Leicester, 2008.

Norton, Rictor. "The Term 'Homosexual.'" From *A Critique of Social Constructionism and Postmodern Queer Theory*. 2002, updated 2008. http://www.rictornorton.co.uk/social14.htm.

Null, Maria. "A Beautiful Technology: The Lost Art of Triangular Bandaging." *Bulletin of the History of Medicine*, April 19, 2016. https://teachhistmed.com/2016/04/19/a-beautiful-technology-the-lost-art-of-triangular-bandaging/.

Ott, Katherine. "Disability and the Practice of Public History: An Introduction." *Public Historian* 27, no. 2 (Spring 2005): 9–24.

Radical History Review. Special issue on "Queer Futures." No. 100 (Winter 2008).

Ricco, John Paul. *The Logic of the Lure*. Chicago: University of Chicago Press, 2002.

Russell, Marta. *Beyond Ramps: Disability at the End of the Social Contract*. Monroe, ME: Common Courage Press, 1998.

Samuels, Ellen. "Cripping Anti-Futurity: Or, If You Love Queer Theory So Much, Why Don't You Marry It?" Paper presented at the annual meeting of the Society for Disability Studies, San Jose, CA, 2011.

Sandell, Richard. *Museums, Prejudice, and the Reframing of Difference*. New York: Routledge, 2007.

Scandura, Jani. *Down in the Dumps: Place, Modernity, American Depression*. Durham, NC: Duke University Press, 2008.

Scanlon, Bill. "Atlantis Members Bludgeon Curb in Protest." *Denver News*, July 9, 1980. http://adaptmuseum.net/gallery/index.php?/category/16.

Schweik, Susan. *The Ugly Laws: Disability in Public*. New York: NYU Press, 2010.

Serlin, David. "Making Disability Public: An Interview with Katherine Ott." *Radical History Review* 94 (Winter 2006): 197–211.

Serlin, David. "Introduction." In *Phallacies: Historical Intersections of Disability and Masculinity*, edited by Kathleen Brian and James Trent, 1–24. New York: Oxford University Press, 2018.

Shapiro, Joseph P. *No Pity: People with Disabilities Forging a New Civil Rights Movement*. New York: Three Rivers Press, 1993.

Takács, Judit. "The Double Life of Kertbeny." In *Past and Present of Radical Sexual Politics*, edited by Gert Hekma, 26–40. Amsterdam: UvA-Mosse Foundation: 2004.

Takács, Judit. "Queering Budapest." In *Queer Cities, Queer Cultures: Europe since 1945*, edited by Jennifer Evans and Matt Cook, 191–210. London: Bloomsbury, 2014.

Tunnard, Christopher. *Gardens in the Modern Landscape*. London: Architectural Review Press, 1938.

Urbach, Henry. "Closets, Clothes, Disclosure." In *Gender Space Architecture: An Interdisciplinary Introduction*, edited by Jane Rendell, Barbara Penner, and Iain Borden, 342–52. New York: Routledge, 2000.

Weizman, Eyal. *Forensic Architecture: Notes from Fields and Forums: Documenta 13*. Kassel: Documenta und Museum Fridericianum Veranstalungs, 2012.

Williams, M. Perry. "Return of the Neon—The Resurgence of West Colfax." *West Colfax Lately* 1 (2015): 2–15.

11. AN ARCHIVAL LIFE
Unsettling Queer Immigrant Dwellings

MARTIN F. MANALANSAN IV

The idea of an archive has gone beyond being a repository or storage of information and documents or as a legitimizing instrument of power structures and
prevailing authorities. In recent years, feminist scholars have suggested that the
archive is a space for and a process of inhabiting space and time, as well as a
quotidian site for marginalized subjects that generate gendered and erotically
charged energies, meanings, and other bodily practices.[1] Dwelling as habita-
tion and shelter is an important dimension of the archive. Archive as space
and process dwelling is a crucial dimension of everyday life and is involved in
the making of queerness through the composition of recalcitrant lives, the enactment of unruly selves, and in the construction of alternative worlds. Specifically, queer archives are constitutive of the various tactics and strategies and
ways of being in the world by marginalized people, in particular, queer undocumented immigrants as they face the tribulations of xenophobic periods such
as those happening during the present political regime in the United States.
While the insights derived in this chapter are based on fieldwork conducted
between 2003 and 2012, they are strongly resonant, viscerally gripping, and
pedagogically instructive in thinking through the contemporary and ongoing
conditions of fascist populism and anti-immigrant moods across the world.

In this chapter, I offer a capacious queer notion of the archive by focusing
on the exigencies of queer immigrant lives and unraveling the various ways
in which queerness is inhabited by and formed through an unruly coterie of
objects, bodies, and spaces. Following and extending these ideas of feminist
scholars mentioned earlier, I intend to map the queer immigrant archive as
not merely emplaced within the private realm of domesticity but rather as a
shifting, unstable set of practices around and engagements with everyday strug-

gles for survival, pleasure, and pathos. In this regard, I develop a notion of an "archival life," where unofficial minoritarian histories such as those of undocumented queer immigrants are embodied through and constituted by practices around collecting and caring, placement and displacement, acquisition and loss. An archival life focuses on the uncertainty and precariousness of history's materiality, and the messy entangled intimacies between time, spaces, and bodies. An archival life is a form of dwelling where affective events and atmospheres are awash in the fluid and ambivalent forces of modernity, morality, legality, and hygiene. It is also built on minoritarian grit and is intrinsic to the formation of an alternative queer notion of the archive through mess instead of order.

This chapter looks at such "dis-arrangements" that have been devised by undocumented queer immigrants' households in New York City as settings for archival lives. Using ethnographic fieldwork and buoyed by writings in affect theory and material culture studies, this chapter aspires to understand how seeming hoarder-like household material, symbolic, and emotional conditions are arenas for creation of a queer immigrant archive and an archival life that enable the contestations of citizenship, hygiene, and the social order. An archival life, it can be argued, is a turning away from these institutionalized and normalized conditions that are memorialized in hegemonic orderly "brick and mortar" historical collections, widely disseminated texts, and officially sanctioned documents. By foregrounding the un-HGTV dwellings of several undocumented queer households,[2] this theoretical and ethnographic exploration seeks to expand the idea of archive by departing from the planned coherent borders of the "archival" and deploying a sustained focus on the seemingly trashy, dirty, disgusting, and untidy dis-organization of bodies, things, and emotions. In other words, it looks to queerness as mess to be the foundational vantage for articulation of an archival life. This chapter suggests that mess, clutter, and muddled entanglements are the "stuff" of queerness, historical memory, and aberrant desires and therefore of the archive and the archival life. Archives, therefore, are constituted by these atmospheric states of material and affective disarray and the narratives that are spun from threads of survival struggles and episodes of pleasure and suffering.

To lay the groundwork for the argument, I offer an abbreviated and focused thick description of a queer household, emphasizing the narratives about one domicile as a way to "orient" or ground the succeeding discussion and analysis. This ethnographic section is deployed as an instantiation of the idea of "archiving otherwise" or a queer take on "dwelling in the archives" as the quotidian becomes the fuel for animating capacious engagements with queer undocumented immigrants as "impossible subjects" of history.[3]

The Story of an Apartment: Objects, Bodies, Documents

Since 1989, I have conducted fieldwork among Asian queer immigrants in New York City. Since 2004, my ethnographic forays have included Latino and African American queers. For this chapter, I concentrate on my observations around a group of undocumented Asian and Latino queer immigrants who live in several households in the neighborhood of Jackson Heights in the borough of Queens in New York City. Jackson Heights is a gentrifying neighborhood that has seen its transition from being a predominantly Jewish and Italian enclave to a mostly mixed group of post-1965 immigrant community of Latinos (particularly Ecuadorians, Peruvians, and Columbians) and Central Americans, and Asians (Koreans, Chinese, Filipinos, and South Asians—Indians, Pakistanis, Bangladeshis, and Afghanis) in the late twentieth century. In the twenty-first century, the signs of urban renewal have set in with the coming of nonimmigrant white-collar professionals finding refuge in the lower rental and real estate costs in the area. This dramatic shift is the backdrop of the stories that I will relay next.[4]

Considering the constraints of this work, I am only going to discuss one household in particular. This household consists of six immigrants and includes a Filipina trans woman, two South Asian gay men, an Ecuadorian lesbian, and two Colombians, a lesbian and a bisexual man. Note that I use the sexual identity categories loosely and provisionally as these immigrants deploy them rather ambivalently and oftentimes in contradictory ways. The residents are a motley crew of working-class immigrants. They work in various service jobs such as selling clothes, busing tables, occasional sex work, dressmaking, cooking in an ethnic restaurant, and other part-time and seasonal jobs. Each one of them has to cobble together two to four jobs to barely survive and to be able to send money to their families back home. The household members were rarely together in the apartment due to their erratic and divergent work schedules. Part of the reason I focus on this household is that it was the only one among five households that was able to maintain their living arrangement for more than a few months and more importantly, these six queers were more forthcoming and generous with sharing their lives with me. Having said that, I do not claim the same level of intimacy with all of them on the same range of topics. Hence, for this chapter I focus more on detailed conversations with a couple of the residents. I first encountered this household through Imelda,[5] the Filipina trans woman. She was the common denominator in the household—everyone knew her and she was the catalyst for forging this household arrangement. We have known each other casually since the 1990s, since we knew friends in common. I unexpectedly ran into her in a coffee shop in Jackson Heights on a cold spring day in 2003. She looked rather worried as she held a piece of paper in her hand. When I asked her what the problem was, she replied that she was worried about this form that came in the mail. It was a federal census form that was asking for information regarding her household. When I asked her why an innocuous document such as the census questionnaire would upset her, she said that she was afraid that if she did not respond or if she answered the form truthfully, she would get in trouble. I tried to reassure her that her fears were unfounded and that the document was harmless. She then told me that she was worried because as an undocumented immigrant any federal paperwork is a cause for concern. Additionally, she confided that she did not live alone but rather with five other queers who were also undocumented. They lived in a one-bedroom apartment, which she suspected violated several city housing ordinances despite the fact that their landlord had turned a blind eye toward this arrangement. Imelda fretted that their living conditions and immigration status might open themselves up to scrutiny, eventual prosecution, and maybe deportation. After folding the document and finishing her coffee, she invited me to visit her apartment.

The apartment was several blocks from Roosevelt Avenue (the neighborhood's main thoroughfare) and was on the first floor of a three-unit brick apartment building. When I first entered Imelda's apartment, my initial reaction was that of disgust and shock. I was appalled at the conditions of the domicile, where cramped, uncomfortable conditions were the (dis)order of the day. My visceral reaction to the apartment was similar to reactions of people when they enter the homes of hoarders.

The apartment was like a haggard old person, weighed down by the burdens of things and lives. It was dimly lit and somewhat dusty in some corners, and, from my own perspective, dismal all over. The living room and bedroom, if one were to call these demarcated spaces as such, were filled with plastic bags and carton boxes, mostly neatly piled in every available place. With the lack of spatial symmetry and functional clarity, the home seemed to reek of confusion and of the smell of intense human intimacy. Imelda immediately noticed my reaction and immediately pointed out that while it may seem to any visitor that the things in the apartment seemed to have no sense of order in them, each of the six residents have sequestered a portion or corner and placed their belongings. It is not just a jumble of things, she countered. Each of the six residents knew where their possessions belonged. Sleeping arrangements were makeshift—typically a small mattress or pile of blankets on the floor or over boxes and other containers. The kitchen was really a sink, refrigerator, and a gas stove lined up on one side of the living or main room.

When I first visited the apartment there was only one other person there, Natalia, the Colombian woman. Imelda and Natalia both told me that each of the six residents worked three or more jobs and their schedules were so erratic that it was a very rare occasion when all of them were at the apartment at one time. It seemed that they have created an everyday rhythm that was acceptable and enabled them to survive as they pooled their meager incomes to pay for the rent.

Impossible Lives: Queerness and Mess

Having given a short background or context of the household and the neighborhood, two questions remain: What makes this household queer other than the fact that the six immigrants sexually identified as transgender, bisexual, gay, or lesbian? Furthermore, what makes this household an archive? What are the forces at work in an archival life? At the heart of my discussion and analysis is the pivotal idea of mess as constitutive of queerness, a queer immigrant archive, and an archival life.

This household of six queer undocumented immigrants, who I have through the years affectionately nicknamed as the Queer Six, inhabits a queer space of waywardness in terms of its physical, affective, and social arrangements. "Messy" or "mess" is the word that comes up in pejoratively describing this particular immigrant household, but I would argue that "mess" is a word that can creatively illuminate the idea of queerness in general and queer archives in particular. My assertion of queer and queering as mess and messing up comes out of a critical reading of queer theory, popular culture, vernacular language, and everyday life. My use of "queer" and "mess" are not limited to bodies, objects, and desires but also to processes, behaviors, and situations. "Queering" and "messing up" are activities and actions as much as "queer" and "mess" can be about states/status, positions, identities, and orientations. These various formulations of queer and mess are not independent of each other and are relevant to my following discussion. While people may balk at the idea of mess as "constituting" queer, it is precisely the discomfort elicited and provoked by the idea and realities of mess that is at the heart of my formulation and provocation.

The idea of queer as mess takes off from the initial impetus that propelled the contemporary reappropriation of "queer." Michael Warner has famously likened the project of queer theory in terms of a sensorial morass by creating a funky atmosphere in an otherwise staid academia and making it stink of sexual rut.[6]

Such a messing-up mission reverberates in the kinds of queer scholarship that focus on the recognition and centering of underrecognized practices, stances, and situations that deviate from, resist, or run counter to the workings of normality. Far from romanticizing deviance and oppositionality, I intend to locate discomfort, dissonance, and disorder as necessary and grounded experiences in the queer everyday and not as heroic acts of exceptional people. In other words, while mainstream queer studies scholarship has valorized dissident dimensions of disorder, my deployment of mess is about funking-up queerness in a way that retains the mundane, the banal, and the ordinariness of queer experience and its mercurial, often intractable, qualities.

Queer as mess also takes its inspiration from reality television, particularly makeover shows. For example, *What Not to Wear* is a show that purports to ambush unsuspecting "fashion victims" and transform them into chic fashionistas. *Hoarders: Buried Alive* is a different kind of intervention show that seeks to literally and metaphorically clean up the lives of hoarders who inhabit crowded and decrepit abodes. In both shows, the stories revolve around the narrative of normalization. In the fashion makeover TV series, the hosts literally take women who either dress too "butch" or masculine and those who look "slutty" in their everyday garb and reform them into proper female/feminine subjects. Similarly, the hoarder show is a lesson on proper domesticity and the ways in which normative value is held as the key to propelling the movement from pathology to normality.

The Queer Six are not hoarders in any sort of way. I take more than a visceral interest in the *Hoarders* show because it provides indirect yet vital lessons about queer immigrant archives. It would be too cavalier and irresponsible to equate the analogy between hoarders and these queer immigrants to one of simple correspondence. Hoarding carries particular cultural and psychological baggage. I do not intend to place the Queer Six in a category that is always already pathologized. Rather, I juxtapose the queer immigrant and the hoarder in meaningful tension in relation to each other.

To go a bit deeper into the reality show, the story of every *Hoarders* episode almost always start at the point of impossibility and untenability. This impossibility is founded on material conditions that persist in the chaotic, dirty, trashy, disgusting, and crowded living conditions of a hoarder. The typical *Hoarders* plot begins with a friend or relative visiting the hoarder's home and then, in almost scripted horror-filled manner, they exclaim, "How can you [meaning the hoarder] live like this?" This moment of impossibility becomes the catalyst for a planned intervention by a makeover crew including a mental health/social worker, professional organizer, and a team of cleaners and movers. The impossibility of mess, in my view, is not the turning point to normality but is in fact the very stuff of queerness.[7] Mess is not pathology but rather a productive orientation toward bodies, objects, and ideas that do not toe the line of hygiene, "practicality" or functionality, value, and proper space/time coordination.[8]

In several episodes of the show, the hoarder is often asked to evaluate their sense of value by pointing to their erratic (deemed unacceptable) ideas about which object is valuable and needs to be kept for posterity and which one is trash and should be thrown away. The show argues that the capacity to assess normative value or more accurately, the very idea of normative value, is lacking in the hoarder's life and something he or she should learn as part of the therapeutic clean-up. The bifurcation between value-filled/treasures or valueless/trash creates not only binaries but teleologies of value. The movement from pathology to normality, from impossibility to tenability, from mess to order can also be portrayed in terms of the teleological routes of value.[9]

The ethnographic observations I offer engage with and refuse such routes of value. Moreover, these refusals also emphasize the dynamic role of mess in social life. Part of these observations can be gleaned in vernacular and quotidian uses of mess. "So and so is a hot mess!" is a statement that most readers might easily categorize as pejorative and negative. However, popular culture blurs the lines between pathetic, tragic, and sorry states of mess with ones that are admirable, sexy, and attractive. Consider the rather slippery and erratic judgments of entertainment figures such as Amanda Bynes, Lindsay Lohan, and Britney Spears and how such judgments are never static and are in fact mobile in their ascriptions of attractiveness and repulsion, between fabulous disasters and just plain tragic. Oftentimes, the idea of a "hot mess" involves less a clear-cut binary and a highly gendered one, but it interestingly occupies a frictive dimension that runs simultaneously within crisscrossing grids of "positive" and "negative" messes.

Apart from popular culture, other alternative but equally compatible ways of looking at mess are through the lenses of the science of systems management and critical social science research methodology. In these two bodies of literature, mess is seen not as an aberration but rather as constitutive of social realities and systems. Recent literature on the management of systemic crises, especially around those that seek to administer complex circuits of process and relationships like urban transport, emergency/disaster services, and other organizational processes, trenchantly proposes that messes should not be considered as always already bad or negative but rather as an intrinsic part of typical expectations built into the structure.[10] Social science research methodology is another set of lenses that have strongly reconsidered mess as an integral part of understanding social phenomena. John Law submits that instead of creating neat analytical categories and routine regularities, social researchers should look to mess and messiness as a way to more accurately and sensitively portray everyday social interactions and institutions.[11]

Overall, mess provides a vibrant analytical frame and a visceral phenomenological grip on the exigencies of marginalized queers—especially those who do not occupy the valorized homonormative spaces of the contemporary West. Mess, as I demonstrate with a brief ethnographic vignette in the following section, is a route for funking up and mobilizing new understandings of stories, values, objects, and space/time arrangements. As such, mess is a way into a queering of the archive that does not involve a cleaning up, but rather a spoiling and cluttering of the neat normative configurations and patterns that seek to calcify lives and experiences.

Discards, Dishes, and Impossible Domesticity

The story of the Queer Six involves many episodes of quotidian struggles and moments of hilarious interactions. While scholars might just want to render these queers as people living threadbare lives, I aim to give flesh to their experiences and mobilize more than just a concatenation of zombie-like or already dead routines. It is very easy to relegate impossible messy subjects such as hoarders and undocumented immigrants into the realm of the dead/undead. For example, the hoarder show is subtitled "buried alive," and recent scholarship has likened marginalized subjects as inhabiting a space of death using Mbembe and Agamben as the pallbearers of contemporary life. I intend to refrain from these necropolitical/necrophilic accounts and instead focus on the "aliveness" of these queers in terms of their encounters with other bodies and objects. As such, I highlight moments of insignificance and illegibility that hopefully will give rise to a more luminous account of queer immigrant lives. Mess therefore is not always about mere chaos, misery, complete desolation, and abandonment but can also gesture to moments of vitality, pleasure, and fabulousness.[12]

This vignette begins and ends with dishes—implements for food and not objects of sexual desire, but of other kinds of desires and aspirations. Natalia, one of the Queer Six, found a stack of dishes and bowls on the curb, around the corner from the apartment. Such finds are not unusual as the streets are the typical sites for disposing discards and refuse of various city households. The dishes and bowls were made of melamine, a material that is used for dining utensils and occupies a middle ground between china/porcelain and plastic. It has a shiny, slightly heavier feel than plastic and is quite cheap. The set of seven dishes and four bowls that composed Natalia's find were decorated with blue leaves. The dishes and bowls must have been used for a long time, as some of the decoration had faded or chipped.

When Natalia took out her scavenged treasures, Imelda squealed with delight. "Oh my, beautiful dinnerware." Then, both women looked at each other and almost simultaneously said, "Someday." When I asked them what they meant, the women admitted that no one ever really eats regularly at home. Because of the congested apartment and their own fear of having rats and cockroaches, they did not have any communal meals. Cooking was kept to reheating food bought from one of several ethnic restaurants in the neighborhood. Eating was limited to using plastic or take-out containers mostly alone or with another roommate.

Natalia's "treasure" of melamine dishes and bowls soon found their way to one of her Rubbermaid containers that were piled rather haphazardly in her corner of the living room. But before these implements were consigned to some dark corner, Natalia plucked one of the bowls and made sure she did not pack it together with the rest. She said she was going to use it as either a soap dish or for coins, pins, and other small items. Natalia was very much invested in seeing the bowl as a reminder of the treasures that are tucked away in her pile that would eventually find the light of day when the "right time comes." While there was not a lot of room left in the crammed apartment for a stray bowl, both Imelda and Natalia wanted something other than packages, luggage, and other piles of stuff to make up the apartment.

When I asked them whether they thought the bowl was a decorative *objet* (*d'art*), they looked at me as if I had just asked a stupid question. Imelda pointed to the chipped worn condition of the bowl and she asserted that both of them have other more beautiful and functionally decorative items in their possessions. But this bowl was not really about adornment so much as it was a reminder or more specifically a mnemonic trigger for other things hidden and buried amid the chaos of objects, packages, and possessions. I was not really clear about what she was saying. Imelda explained that after living in several dozen apartments, most of them under illegal leases, the precarious and itinerant lives they lead compel them to be always ready to move to another apartment as quickly as possible. In such events, having one's possessions or "stuff" already stored away made such regular occurrences less inconvenient and easier to deal with. Imelda further admitted that even with her own attempts to keep her possessions intact, things break, get lost, or have to be abandoned. In short, her notion of possession is shaped by the persistent possibility of loss and dispossession.

When I asked Natalia whether she thought she would be dining with those plates and bowls in a proper dining room sometime in the future, she shrugged and said that nothing is ever certain. Imelda said that all of them had hopes, aspirations, and dreams of better times ahead but at the same time, she also was clear that those aspirational futures did not hold these women captive to objects and possessions. She implied that one can keep one's possessions in storage, but they will not last forever. Natalia had similar experiences as Imelda, where stored objects that held some kind of future potential were either left behind or were discarded after becoming useless. The strategy of storing things in these rather jumbled ways does not always work well. Such storage techniques as those in the household do not lead to a posterity but rather to possible loss, breakage, and abandonment. Such eventualities are seen as necessary casualties—things break, we need to move on, we need to leave things behind.

Natalia and the other members of the Queer Six are impossible subjects. They live in situations that are constituted in secrecy, fear, and shame. The conditions that brought Natalia into the crowded, packed household are different. The disarray of the apartment was due to circumstances that forced six unrelated people to live together and gather their possessions in one very limited space. Natalia was not strongly wedded or attached to the idea of a future utility and value of any one object. She firmly believed in the impermanence of things. But that is not to say that she did not have a desire for or an attachment to certain objects—it was a belief riddled with ambivalence, tempered by the reality of her undocumented status and scarred by previous struggles and losses.

What was clear from the discussion, and to which Natalia and Imelda would later confess, their aspirations and their practical stances were never clear-cut; they were murky and subject to swings or changes. Natalia argued that the bowl was a pivotal part of her daily life despite the fact that there was a big chance she would have to leave it behind due to her itinerancy. It would seem that the murkiness of feelings and attachments of the two women to their "stuff" was a way to take the edge off the cruel sting of loss, failure, and abandonment that has become almost a routine in their lives as undocumented immigrants. Unlike the "cruel optimism" that Lauren Berlant has attributed to the neoliberal malaise of people living in precarity whose almost fetishistic attachments to things, processes, ideas, and institutions are the very conditions that hinder them from thriving, I contend that the Queer Six rely on contrasting moments of detachments, letting go, moving away, the pleasure of discovery, and the reality that nothing is ever really permanent to enable themselves to move literally and figuratively through times and spaces, beyond days and rooms.[13]

Objects, bodies, and other materials may seem new, can bring pleasure, and can provide some kind of function while at the same time they all decay, rot, fall out of use, and get lost in the rubble. Objects, Natalia and Imelda agreed, have their allocated time and space. Once these objects go beyond their allocated temporal and spatial existence and usefulness, it is time to throw them out—albeit sometimes with a heavy heart. As Natalia astutely declared, she was always ready to move and "to get up and go." In itinerant lives such as those of the Queer Six, the burden of stuff and the weight of material paraphernalia are considered secondary to other concerns and other burdens—such as the fear of the federal government and its documents, possible arrests, prosecution, and deportation.

These fears and burdens point to the ephemeral and shifting sense of value. Value then is mercurial, subject to the vagaries of lives on the lam. At the same time, they also points to enduring structures of feelings, of moments of fear such as those with "official documents" and those moments of pleasure and wonderment such as finding "treasures" in the street. Despite the seemingly easy disposability of these objects, they do not in any way assuage the everyday struggles that both women recognized—the struggle to keep a job, pay the rent, send money to family back home, keep under the radar from the police and immigration authorities, and find some kind of pleasure somewhere. All these struggles are encased in the stuff but remain illegible if not invisible to a casual observer. What does one make of this apartment teeming with stuff and trappings of urban immigrant life? What is the "stuff" of an archival life? How does one begin to take these cluttered lives and spaces as an alternative archive?

Archiving Otherwise: Natalia's Archival Life and Queer Messiness

After going through the story of Natalia, a glaring question usually arises about how her experiences make up what I have been calling an archival life. After hearing my narration of Natalia's story as an illustrative case of an archival life, some people would inquire about how such a notion applies to other lives and other subjects. I would argue that Natalia's specific engagements with her immigrant and working-class status and her living conditions are indicative of her own openness to the muddled and fluid nature of precarity and uncertainty in modern times. In other words, an archival life like Natalia's involves witting and unwitting recalcitrance and a yielding approach to one's dwelling conditions. I am not proposing that Natalia's life is a unique exemplar of an archival life. Rather, I offer that her words and deeds are but a few of the various ways to reorient and displace normative perspectives in media and vernacular understandings of an archive as a controlled progressive accumulation of texts and objects—of stuff becoming a measurable metric of valuation and of worth.

An archival life therefore is an unadorned approach to possession and dispossession, to collecting and loss. It is not about a strict curation or an aestheticized connoisseurship. Natalia's seemingly nonchalant approach to stuff is not about an individualist privatized notion of ownership but is brought about by the challenges of gritty survival amidst attempts at flourishing and obtaining pleasures. Her ostensibly cavalier attitude about objects and their expendability is about the ephemerality of feelings, objects, and places. Such ephemerality results in a "turning away" from the controlled and ordered idea of an archive.

The ideal archive is about the management of the morass of memory. But what happens when disorder and chaos compose the elements that make up the archival space? What happens when instead of orderly catalogues, makeshift arrangements teetering on the brink of anarchy become the "dis-order" of things? What kinds of value get attached to lives, persons, and things that dwell in mess and disorder and how can they be dynamically reframed to think more broadly about political acts, aspirations, and stances? I now turn to the ways in which the ethnographic vignette about the dishes and the lives and spaces of the Queer Six may be a way to think differently about archives and the stuff in it.

Archives are vested with authority, as Derrida has astutely pointed out in *Archive Fever*, in terms of ordering time and space and storing. R. Vosloo, in a critical reading of Derrida's work, reemphasizes the need to recognize the archive not only as a site of power but also as a vantage for promoting social justice and ethical responsibility. Such responsibility involves an "openness to the future" and a recognition of the limitations and exclusionary impulses of state and other institutional archives that seek to "officialize" and tether historical knowledge or understandings of the past in terms that do not engage with views from below.[14]

Following Vosloo, this chapter is a way to center the lives and spaces of the Queer Six to promote a more sensitive and nuanced understanding of queerness and migration by upholding a particular notion of an archive enmeshed in clutter and disarray. The Queer Six household deviates from an idealized pristine archive that systematically stores, retrieves, and communicates information about past. The Queer Six's messy archive reflects the ways in which official state-mandated knowledge is embodied in the stuff of paperwork and how such a queer household/archive rejects the primacy of the document by refusing legibility and establishing an alternative (dis)order of things. The "undocumented" immigrant is not someone who does not have documents but rather is someone whose papers are in disarray or not in proper "official" state-sanctioned order. This mess or lack of documentary order is both the pivot of these queer immigrant lives and the burden they carry in the everyday.

The mess of the queer immigrant archive pivots on the "disorienting" effects of the various kinds of documents and objects as well as the swirling cauldron of feelings that inhabit the spaces, objects, and times of the queer undocumented immigrant.[15] The queer immigrant archive is an "archive of feelings" that echoes in more effective registers the ultimate truth of any and all archives—loss.[16] Loss can be seen in terms of the absence of access to the official discourses of the proper subject. For queer undocumented immigrants, the notion of origins, which is a fundamental fulcrum in the mobilization of citizenship, is not only unavailable but also impossible and perilous.

"Where are you from?" is a question that is posed to the foreigner, the non-citizen, and the queer. It is a question that comes from a power-laden state-centered vantage that demands a fixed reference, origin, or provenance from anyone seeking recognition. To accede to an "officializing" move and to answer such questions as to where one was born and if one was a citizen would make an undocumented person vulnerable and exposed to possible punitive actions from prosecution to deportation. The lack of fixed origins, which is often seen as a source of vexed perceptions and confusion, is at the same time a crucial component of queer as mess and a viable survival strategy for undocumented queer immigrants. For example, Natalia has often identified as Puerto Rican and Imelda has alluded to herself as Hawaiian to deflect any further inquiry as to their immigration status. They rely on messing up their identities in order to survive scrutiny and surveillance. Therefore, queer immigrant archives and the impossible lives of queer undocumented immigrants persist in a perpetual refusal of fixed origins and temporal and semantic legibility and are cast in in the whirling pool of often conflicting trajectories, desires, and aspirations.

The refusals of documentary "truths" of origins and legibility reside not only in the bodies of queer immigrants but also in their relationships with objects. In my accounts of the Queer Six household, I have tried to avoid normalizing notions about the relationship between persons and things. Scott Herring, inspired by Sara Ahmed's queer phenomenology, directs readers to the discrepant ways in which marginalized and impossible subjects like hoarders and queers have a wayward relationship to material objects.[17] Such "material deviance," as Herring astutely calls it, operates in ways that do not rely on the romanticized and normative expectations of how things "typically" work in people's lives or conversely how people's lives typically work on things. Allow me to go back to Natalia's dishes as a way to seriously engage with Herring's notion. Consider a situation when someone comes into contact with Natalia's plates and bowl encased with her other belongings—left behind in a moment of haste. What kind of interpretation can be made while holding the material objects on the one hand and the story of Natalia, Imelda, and the other Queer Six household members? Why should Natalia keep those dishes when she herself found the likelihood of using the implements in a "proper dining manner" to be either remote or nearly impossible, given her own living conditions? Is this just a case of unbridled hopefulness or is there something more?

To understand the archival usefulness of Natalia's dishes, it is important to repudiate a rational correspondence between the material value of the dishes, their functionality, and the various feelings and emotions that emerged from the moment when Natalia discovered the dishes and bowls on the street to the time she took them home, stared at them lovingly, and then stored them—never to be used at least in the couple of years I have known the Queer Six. It is more crucial to get a sense of the disjunctions between Natalia's words and her actions and not enclose them within a cause/effect framework, but rather to acknowledge the very muddled, illegible, and intractable lines between the material object, Natalia's own desires and aspirations, and the space of the apartment with the making of worlds and the creation of histories. I did not seek to "create order" out of the quagmire of Natalia's words and deeds, but to gesture to the workings of chaos, mess, and morass in ways that deflect simplistic questions of origins, functions, and value as part of a queering of the archive. This chapter does not clean up the mess but rather critically addresses the need to live with, against, and despite the mess.

Part of the problem that besets the queer immigrant archive, from the perspective of traditional historiography, is the validity of ephemera, material objects that are not indigenous to a particular group. Unlike an archeological dig of an ancient settlement, a contemporary observer coming into the Queer Six household will not have the delusional luxury of simplistically tying in objects with the people's habitus. The evidentiary problems of ephemera hearken to the issue of fixed origins discussed earlier. That is, any attempt to fix provenances and origins will ultimately fail if not be fruitless. The ephemera in the Queer Six household are precisely those that are impervious to clear itineraries of ownership and value. Things that are picked up in bargain stores, the Salvation Army, and trash bins in city streets have undergone multiple origins, transitions, and functions unlike those bought new at the mall or any other store. Indeed, objects bought in regular stores and at the mall may find their way to the trash and secondhand shops; hence ephemera do not allow themselves to be easily slotted into easy linear chronologies, singular narratives, or functional descriptions.

The significance of ephemeral evidence, such as Natalia's dishes, is not based on how it can be traced through a clear-cut genealogy and fixed strand of meaning; rather, its worth is based on how it embodies the fleeting, nomadic, messy, and elusive experiences and processes of self-making (and I may add history-making), particularly among what José Esteban Muñoz calls "minoritarian subjects" (which includes queers, people of color, immigrants, and many "others").[18] Muñoz astutely argues that ephemera go against preestablished disciplinary formations of evidence as they speak to illegibility and lack of clarity. Ephemera are to some extent about mess and clutter—of seemingly disposable and trivial stuff. Finally, ephemera, he elegantly offers, are about "traces, glimmers, residues, and specks of things."[19]

The glimmers and traces of Natalia's dishes can be gleaned through her attempts to appropriate these objects, bestow an alternative value to them (no longer somebody's trash), store them like treasure, and keep an eye on a future that may include a domestic scene of a dinner involving those implements or the possibility of loss and displacement. Following this line of thought about ephemera, the dishes together with the heaping mountains of possessions in the apartment combined with the stories of Natalia and the other members of the household hint at and subtly suggest the long, arduous process of resilient struggles, fleeting pleasures, hopeful aspirations, and manifold failures. The apartment, its objects, and its inhabitants, and the embodied relationships enclosed within the space, form a queer immigrant "living archive."[20] Such an archive initiates new ways of understanding history from below and fosters more expansive notions of queerness and migration. It also can help reorient activist and political discourses about time, space, and value—unfolding new vistas for what is significant and (im)possible for building new coalitions around immigration and queer issues. These objects, bodies, experiences, and practices do not foreclose or "fix" a future. There is *no* "No Future" among the Queer Six. This archive involves the gathering and interpretation of historical "matter" that includes the tragic, the repulsive, the uncomfortable, the banal, and the seemingly trashy, off-kilter objects and bodily practices that may hint at political potentials, gesture to alternative narratives, and enable an openness to multiple futures.

Notes

I would like to thank the editors for their patience and belief in the chapter. Gratitude and indebtedness to the following: Robert Diaz, Camilla Fojas, Billy Johnson-Gonzalez, Gayatri Gopinath, Allan Isaac, Anita Mannur, Ellen Moodie, Kevin

Mumford, Ricky Rodriguez, Karen Shimakawa, and Siobhan Somerville for their valuable support in the project. I also want to acknowledge the fruitful conversations with audiences at the University of Toronto, University of the Philippines, Indiana University, Duke University, McGill University, Ateneo de Manila University, University of Connecticut, Buffalo University and Brown University. Special thanks to Anne Allison, Denise Cruz, Roland Coloma, Scott Herring, Daniel Kim, Eng-Beng Lim, José Muñoz, Natalie Oswin, Cathy Schlund Vials, Roland Tolentino, Shane Vogel, and Cindy Wu for their wonderful comments and for inviting me to visit their respective campuses. During the final stages of writing this manuscript, the esteemed scholar José Esteban Muñoz passed away. This work is an archive of the feelings and ideas that he has made possible.

This chapter was previously published as "The 'Stuff' of Archives: Mess, Migration, and Queer Lives," *Radical History Review* 120 (Fall 2014): 94–107.

1 See the following works for a feminist and/or queer perspective on the archive: Arondekar, *For the Record*; Burton, *Dwelling in the Archives*; Cvetkovich, *Archive of Feelings*.

2 Home and Garden Television or HGTV is a cable channel devoted to home design, building, and interior decoration.

3 See Burton, *Dwelling in the Archives*, and Vosloo, "Archiving Otherwise."

4 See Manalansan, "Race, Violence, and Neoliberal Spatial Politics."

5 All informants have been given pseudonyms and some identifying markers have been changed.

6 Warner, *Fear of a Queer Planet*, xxvi.

7 My inspiration and thinking around impossibility, impossible subjects and desires have originated from the classics of Asian American studies, notably Ngai, *Impossible Subjects*, and Gopinath, *Impossible Desires*.

8 Ahmed, *Queer Phenomenology*.

9 I am grateful to Lisa Yoneyama for this felicitous phrase. For an excellent analysis of hoarders and queer material culture, see Herring, "Material Deviance," as well as his other essay, "Collyer Curiosa." See the vibrant critical literature on material culture especially Daniel Miller's work such as *Stuff* and *Home Possessions*.

10 Roe, *Making the Most*.

11 Law, *After Method*.

12 In the larger ethnographic project, I explore the ways in which fabulosity, a consumptive yet aspirational narrative about self-making, is made possible with and despite the marginalized conditions of these undocumented queer immigrants. Such moments as mundane as old gowns, cheap soap and furtive sexual escapades cut through the seemingly endless banal ordinariness of suffering and pathos.

13 Berlant, *Cruel Optimism*.

14 Vosloo, "Archiving Otherwise."

15 Ahmed, *Queer Phenomenology*, 25–64.

16 Cvetkovich, *Archive of Feelings*, 268; Burton, *Dwelling in the Archives*, 3–30.

17 Herring, "Material Deviance," 45.

18 Muñoz, "Ephemera as Evidence."

19 Muñoz, "Ephemera as Evidence," 10.
20 Roque Ramírez, "A Living Archive of Desire."

Works Cited

Ahmed, Sara. *Queer Phenomenology: Orientations, Objects, Others*. Durham, NC: Duke University Press, 2006.

Arondekar, Anjali. *For the Record: On Sexuality and the Colonial Archive in India*. Durham, NC: Duke University Press, 2003.

Berlant, Lauren. *Cruel Optimism*. Durham, NC: Duke University Press, 2011.

Burton, Antoinette. *Dwelling in the Archives: Women Writing House, Home and History in Colonial India*. New York: Oxford University Press, 2003.

Cvetkovich, Ann. *An Archive of Feelings: Trauma, Sexuality, and Lesbian Public Cultures*. Durham, NC: Duke University Press, 2003.

Gopinath, Gayatri. *Impossible Desires: Queer Diasporas and South Asian Public Cultures*. Durham, NC: Duke University Press, 2005.

Herring, Scott. "Material Deviance: Theorizing Queer Objecthood." *Postmodern Culture* 21, no. 2 (2011). http://www.pomoculture.org/2013/09/03/material-deviance-theorizing-queer-objecthood.

Herring, Scott. "Collyer Curiosa: A Brief History of Hoarding." *Criticisms* 53, no. 2 (2011): 158–88.

Law, John. *After Method: Mess in Social Science Research*. New York: Routledge, 2004.

Manalansan, Martin. "Race, Violence, and Neoliberal Spatial Politics in the Global City." *Social Text* 23, nos. 3–4 (84–85) (2005): 141–56.

Miller, Daniel. *Home Possessions: Material Culture Behind Closed Doors*. Oxford: Berg, 2001.

Miller, Daniel. *Stuff*. Cambridge: Polity Press, 2010.

Muñoz, José Esteban. "Ephemera As Evidence: Introductory Notes to Queer Acts." *Women and Performance: A Journal of Feminist Theory* 8, no. 2 (2006): 5–11.

Ngai, Mae. *Impossible Subjects: Illegal Aliens and the Making of Modern America*. Princeton, NJ: Princeton University Press, 2005.

Roe, Emery. *Making the Most of the Mess: Reliability and Policy in Today's Management Challenges*. Durham, NC: Duke University Press, 2013.

Roque Ramírez, Horacio. "A Living Archive of Desire: Teresita La Campesina and the Embodiment of Queer Latino Community Histories." In *Archive Stories: Fact, Fictions, and the Writings of History*, edited by Antoinette Burton, 111–35. Durham, NC: Duke University Press, 2005.

Vosloo, R. "Archiving Otherwise: Some Remarks on Memory and Historical Responsibility." *Studia Historiae Ecclessiastiae* 31, no. 2 (October 2005): 379–99.

Warner, Michael. *Fear of a Queer Planet: Queer Politics and Social Theory*. Minneapolis: University of Minnesota Press, 1993.

12. REASSESSING "THE ARCHIVE" IN QUEER THEORY

KATE EICHHORN

"The archive" has been deconstructed, decolonized, and queered by scholars in fields as wide-ranging as English, anthropology, cultural studies, and gender and ethnic studies. Yet almost none of the humanistic inquiry at "the archival turn" (even that which addresses "actually existing archives") has acknowledged the intellectual contribution of archival studies as a field of theory and praxis in its own right, nor is this humanities scholarship in conversation with ideas, debates, and lineages in archival studies.—MICHELLE CAS-WELL, "'The Archive' Is Not An Archives: Acknowledging the Intellectual Contributions of Archival Studies"

Since the mid-1990s, archives and archiving have gained significant import in queer theory. This preoccupation with queer archives, queer archiving, and what is sometimes simply referred to as "the queer archive" has resulted in the publication of dozens of books, edited collections, and special issues of journals. This volume, which was initiated in part due to the overwhelming response the editors received to an earlier call for papers for two special issues of the *Radical History Review*, is just one of the many examples of how archives and archiving continue to be taken up in the context of queer history and theory. To be clear, this chapter does not seek to question the importance of queer archiving or the concept of the queer archive, but it does seek to step back to ask some difficult and even contentious questions about why and how queer scholars have engaged in the archival turn. To begin, however, it seems appropriate to briefly account for this chapter's own long history.

This chapter was originally written for a panel on archiving feminist materials presented at the Protest on the Page Conference in 2012. The conference, hosted by the School of Library and Information Studies at the University of Wisconsin-Madison, brought together both social science and humanities scholars and librarians and archivists. After the first day of the conference, I decided to abandon the paper I had intended to deliver at the conference and to deliver instead an impassioned critique of how the concept of archives has been adopted by cultural theorists and specifically queer theorists over the past two decades. The decision reflected a desire to foster a more robust dialogue with my colleagues who are trained as archivists and librarians and as a result, engaged in the often tedious and difficult work of acquiring, describing, and preserving materials. Why do this? The answer is simple: because working in an archive or special collection entails a great deal of unglamorous work—work that is mostly invisible to scholars, even to those of us who frequently write about archives and archiving. Admittedly, even after writing an entire book on the topic, my understanding of what my colleagues who work as archivists and professional librarians do for a living remained partial at best.[1] What I do appreciate is that their labor is grossly undervalued both on an economic and epistemological level. After all, with few exceptions, archivists and librarians make much less money than academics with full-time tenure-track positions and with few exceptions, they are not afforded the same degree of epistemic status as academics (and this holds true in terms of how they are perceived and treated by academics as well as students). This chapter began, then, as a gesture intended to open up a productive conversation on the topic of archival labor and to critically reflect on how queer theorists' often utopian longing for the idea or ideal of "the archive" may be part of the problem.

Perhaps due to the context (a conference hosted by an information studies program), my original paper was well received. I soon discovered, however, that my critique of queer theory's preoccupation with archives was not to be as readily embraced by queer theorists as by archivists and librarians. Simply put, the paper, which had been well received in an information studies context, was considered too problematic for publication when brought into a queer history and theory context. Somewhat ironically, the very problem I wished to flag would be at least partially demonstrated in the essays that were eventually published in the *Radical History Review*'s double issue on queer archives. For all the phenomenal scholarship gathered together in these two issues, for every essay about an archival collection, there was at least one or more essays or photo essays focused more broadly on collections (private collections of ephemera, museum collections, and so on). While the editors, Daniel Marshall, Kevin Murphy, and Zeb Tortorici, very carefully grapple with what archives are or might be, reading across the two issues, one is left with the impression that in a queer context, "archive" is ultimately a highly flexible term and one with deep and resounding affective and political significance. Indeed, although the two issues do not entirely overlook the work of those professional archivists and librarians who work with special collections, in a majority of the essays, information professionals and their specific labor and contexts are not directly addressed.

In what follows, I present most of my original essay on the archival turn in queer theory, but with a few notable edits made in response to several rounds of review over an eight-year period. Here it is particularly important to note that since I first opened up this conversation in 2012, the conversation I hoped to initiate has evolved. The publication of Michelle Caswell's 2016 essay, "'The Archive' Is Not An Archives: Acknowledging the Intellectual Contributions of Archival Studies," which I now use as an epigraph to this chapter, has played a key role in expanding this conversation. Since 2012, a new generation of archival studies scholars has also brought archival studies scholarship more directly into dialogue with queer theory (e.g., this is evident in recent publications by scholars such as Marika Cifor and Jamie A. Lee).[2] Since 2012, several titles in Litwin Books' Series on Gender and Sexuality in Information Studies have also helped to draw attention to the important place of archival studies labor and scholarship in queer studies. I am thinking specifically about titles such as Lyz Bly and Kelly Wooten's *Make Your Own History* (2012), Patrick Keilty and Rebecca Dean's *Feminist and Queer Information Studies Reader* (2013), Alana Kumbier's *Ephemeral Material: Queering the Archive* (2014), and Rebecka Taves Sheffeld's *Documenting Rebellions* (2020). And to be clear, this is not an exhaustive list of scholars or titles bringing archival studies into dialogue with queer theory. Still, one thing remains clear: the dialogue between archival studies work and scholarship and queer theory still appears to be heavily driven by working archivists, librarians, and information studies and archival studies scholars bringing their insights into dialogue with queer theory rather than the other way around. In other words, while the dialogue has shifted over the past decade, work remains to be done on the part of queer theorists and, more broadly, scholars working in the social sciences and humanities.

Again, my intent here is not to dismiss any specific work on queer archives and archiving but rather to consider what material and even epistemological issues have at times been placed under erasure in queer theory's approach to archives. As much as archives are sites of resistance and imagination (and this is something I have consistently promoted in my own work), they are also sites defined by constraints (especially funding constraints), negotiations, and compromise. In this respect, this chapter doesn't necessarily reject José Muñoz's proclamation that "the archives is a fiction," nor his observation that "nobody knows that better than queers."[3] This chapter does call upon queer theorists and activists to recognize that archives are not merely a fiction. This chapter also calls upon queer theorists and activists to further acknowledge that the majority of our colleagues who work in archives and/or engage in archival studies scholarship aren't naïve about the history and workings of archives. Indeed, working archivists and archival studies scholars know better than anyone else the extent to which archives have at times produced and reproduced harmful fictions and excluded certain demographics.

Discovering "the Archive"

Over the past two decades, queer theorists have evoked archives as a powerful trope to grapple with subjects as diverse as collective trauma and queer subcultures. At the same time, a generation of queer artists born since the mid-1960s have turned to archives to explore the aesthetic and political efficacy of everything from everyday objects to the refuse of abandoned radical movements. On the ground, the preoccupation with archives and collections that have been labeled "archives" is also evident in a myriad of grassroots preservation efforts, which include both physical repositories and digitization projects. The apparent enthusiasm for archival endeavors of all kinds—theoretical, artistic, institutional, grassroots, and so on—among queer subjects is by no means surprising. Stubbornly persistent and often fetishistic, queers are at home in archives. We will survive but not without the right accessories, and in a sense, archives furnish us with no shortage of ephemera to appropriate and try on (hence, the "drag" in "temporal drag").[4] Archives, in a sense, enable us to try on the very things we have historically struggled to obtain, including a sense of belonging to an established history.

Without suggesting that there is necessarily a causal relationship between queer theory's archival turn and the preoccupation with archives and archiving among queer artists and activists, there is substantial evidence to suggest that theory and practice overlap in innumerable ways in the case of queer archives and archiving practices. As I suggest in this chapter, queer theory's call for us to reimagine archives as, in Jack Halberstam's words, a "floating signifier" has been deeply generative and in many respects, radicalizing.[5] The call gave at least some of us permission to look at our own personal collections as potentially valuable and legitimate material to donate to institutional archives while simultaneously encouraging queer researchers to enter archives with an increasingly open and generative appreciation for what archives might hold and, more importantly, do. Most significantly, the archival turn in queer theory and, more generally, cultural theory has dissolved long-standing understandings of archives and archival practice in ways that hold the potential to compromise future preservation efforts. Once understood as a repository for institutional knowledge, the concept of "the archive" has become shorthand for all kinds of things from films and art installations to bodies and communities of practice and dissent. Put into circulation in contemporary theory, art, and performance, what we think about as an archive has not only expanded but also started to come undone, drifting well beyond anything remotely recognizable in most professional circles. This chapter questions at what cost and more specifically, at what cost to whom? Reflecting in part on my own research on queer and feminist archives, I consider both what we have gained and placed under erasure by turning our attention to archives. Are queer theorists guilty of taking the labor of actual archivists and special collections librarians for granted? In our rush to assimilate archives into our theorizing, have we actually overlooked the fragility of documents and material artifacts? Will the legacy of the archival turn in queer theory be one that results in undermining rather than bolstering preservation efforts?

It is important to foreground the fact that I speak here both as a researcher who has written on the subject of feminist and queer archives, and as a writer who has adopted archives as a trope in various works. For all these reasons, I am complicit in the semantic drift I'm critiquing in this essay. Notably, like most researchers and writers, in the past I have frequently written about "the archive," a term few of my archivist colleagues would ever use. As a theorist and writer, I too have often approached archives as a conceptual framework and curatorial trope and, admittedly, as a deeply seductive imaginary—a nebulous framework in which to locate myself in histories I never experienced firsthand and to imagine possible worlds not yet realized.

Significantly, the archive's drift is by no means simply the work of queer theorists, though this is my primary focus here. In the 1980s to mid-1990s, largely thanks to the widespread circulation of Michel Foucault's earlier works, including *The Order of Things* and *The Archaeology of Knowledge*, archives were already being reconstructed as a site of enunciation—the law governing the sayable and knowable. The simultaneous French and English publications of Derrida's *Mal d'archive* and *Archive Fever* heightened interest in archives and not simply as a discursive structure but also as a concept that might enable us to think through the relationship between writing, technology, memory, forgetting, and trauma. By the early 2000s, in both literary studies and cultural studies there was a growing preoccupation with archives. During this period, it became increasingly common for academics to refer to their corpus (e.g., the texts referenced in a study) as their "archive." At the same time, a growing number of theorists began adopting archives (via Foucault and Derrida) to explore broader theoretical issues. If the archival turn in cultural theory was particularly attractive to queer scholars, however, it was likely because it gave queer theorists an opportunity to reembrace a materialism that had been abandoned under poststructuralism (archives are about documents, artifacts, and material life) without sidelining queer theory's preoccupations with desire, trauma, and longing.

In what follows, I explore a set of questions that queer theorists rarely consider but that our colleagues who work in archives and special collections have been asking all along. Has the semantic drift of the archive gone too far? What and perhaps whose narratives (including whose narratives of labor) are placed under erasure by this drift, and at what cost? Is this apparent democratization of archives necessarily in the interest of radical texts, subjects, and movements? And finally, what is at stake in this for the preservation of queer documents, artifacts, and lives? Asking these questions as a queer theorist who has both carried out research in archival collections and ethnographies of archives, including many contemporary feminist and queer collections, my objective is first and foremost to turn my attention in a more sustained way to the concerns expressed to me by the activist archivists and special collections librarians I have come to know and collaborate with in the context of my own research. As sociologist Dorothy Smith emphasizes, "the authority of the experiencer" can "inform the ethnographer's ignorance," and in many respects, without engaging in what Smith would describe as "institutional ethnography," this chapter responds to her call for researchers to take seriously the knowledge claims and perspectives that workers acquire by virtue of their location in specific institutions.[6]

Archives of Excess and Affect

To explore the questions I just posed, I first want to revisit two widely circulated citations about queer archives and archiving—passages that will likely already be familiar to most readers of this volume. Admittedly, these citations are also ones that I have cited in my own publications on several occasions, but again, this is precisely why I have chosen to use them as a "prop" here to consider some of the assumptions about archives and archiving that have become prevalent in queer theory. The first passage appears in the conclusion to *In a Queer Time and Place*. Jack Halberstam writes:

The nature of queer subcultural activity requires a nuanced theory of archives and archiving . . . Ideally, an archive of queer subcultures would merge ethnographic interviews with performers and fans with research in the multiple archives that already exist online and in other unofficial sites. Queer zines, posters, guerrilla art, and other temporary artifacts would make up some of the paper archives, and descriptions of shows along with the self-understandings of cultural producers would provide supplementary materials. But the notion of an archive has to extend beyond the image of a place to collect material or hold documents, and it has to become a floating signifier for the kinds of lives implied by the paper remnants of shows, clubs, events, and meetings. The archive is not simply a repository; it is also a theory of cultural relevance, a construction of collective memory, and a complex record of queer activity. In order for the archive to function it requires users, interpreters, and cultural historians to wade through the material and piece together the jigsaw puzzle of queer history in the making.[7]

The second passage I wish to consider appears in the introduction to Ann Cvetkovich's *An Archive of Feelings*:

This book's structure and materials are organized as "an archive of feelings," an exploration of cultural texts as repositories of feelings and emotions, which are encoded not only in the content of the texts themselves but in the practices that surround their production and reception. Its focus on trauma serves as a point of entry into a vast archive of feelings, the many forms of love, rage, intimacy, grief, shame, and more that are part of the vibrancy of queer cultures.[8]

Cvetkovich further emphasizes that "trauma's archive" necessarily incorporates "personal memories," including those found in oral and video testimonies, memoirs, letters, and journals.[9] The broad definition of archives embraced by Halberstam and Cvetkovich in the preceding passages is by no means insignificant. Indeed, I believe it is possible to trace an approach to feminist and queer archives and archiving that is rooted in the contributions of these queer theorists. Moreover, it is an approach that notably cuts across artistic, activist, and scholarly communities of practice. To begin, one might consider the ongoing and rich dialogue that has developed between queer theory and queer visual artists and performers.

Tammy Rae Carland adapted Cvetkovich's title, *An Archive of Feelings*, for a 2008 exhibit that featured, among other things, objects from Carland's own personal "archive."[10] Carland's *An Archive of Feeling* exhibit has subsequently been taken up in Cvetkovich's theorizing on archives published since Carland's exhibit. Archives and archiving also figure prominently in the work of other queer women artists born since the mid-1960s. Protest signs, photocopied political posters, and other refuse from abandoned political movements feature prominently in Sharon Hayes's work. In *Time Binds: Queer Temporalities, Queer Histories*, Elizabeth Freeman uses Hayes's redeployment of past political movements' slogans, fashions, and communication strategies (e.g., the leaflet and protest sign) to develop a theory of "temporal drag." As Freeman suggests, the collections of real and imagined political detritus accumulated and put back into circulation by Hayes effectively challenge assumptions about both history and the future by destabilizing "viewers from the present tense they think they know" and igniting "possible futures in light of powerful historical moments."[11] Hayes's sometimes collaborator artist Andrea Geyer has also played with the recirculation of the detritus associated with earlier political movements, as well as archival technologies and spaces, including contemporary news archives (Parallax, 2003) and collections of early twentieth-century photographs (Insistence, 2013).[12]

While Carland's, Hayes's, and Geyer's works most notably reference archival documents and objects, in the work of Canadian artist Allyson Mitchell, the space of a specific archival collection is brought into view. For a 2010 exhibit, *A Girl's Journey to the Well of Forbidden Knowledge*, Mitchell meticulously reproduced the spines of the books that appear on the bookshelves at the Lesbian Herstory Archives. At first, the line drawing reproductions may appear redundant but as anyone who has spent time at the Lesbian Herstory Archives knows, photography is strictly monitored in the space, including photography of archival materials. Mitchell's reproductions of the archive's bookshelves capture something about the archive and its policies. More importantly, by later reproducing the archive's shelves in public spaces (gallery and street settings), Mitchell also enacts a very queer displacement, resituating but not undermining the semi-public sphere of the LHA, which is open to the public but to this day occupies a Brooklyn row house and has rarely adopted regular visitation hours.[13]

The crossover between queer theory and queer artists' engagements with archives has as much to do with the institutional locations of the artists as it does with the overlaps between communities of practice. The artists mentioned earlier all hold full-time academic positions (Carland at the California College of Art, Hayes at the University of Pennsylvania, Geyer at the New School, and Mitchell at York University), and all of them are friends and collaborators with one or more of the theorists already mentioned in this chapter. While the dialogue between queer theory, art, and archiving is relatively transparent, the impact of queer theory on actual archival endeavors at the community level is both more difficult to track and more surprising. Community-based queer archives, like the Queer Zine Archive Project, have emerged as the result of all sorts of momenta, including a broader interest in activist archiving and the availability of new and accessible archiving technologies. However, queer theory's preoccupation with archives has also helped the founders of some community-based and DIY archives to more easily legitimize their projects and in some cases, even counter critiques from professional communities of practice.

In the meta-zine *Archiving the Underground*, Jenna Brager and Jami Sailor describe their mandate as one that seeks to offer "an intervention by underground cultural producers in the academic project of archiving and 'academicizing' the subcultural practices in which we participate."[14] Rather than rail against academics, however, Brager and Sailor go on to cite Halberstam's discussion on archives from *In a Queer Time and Place*, reiterating the claim that subcultures, especially queer subcultures, need to be archived from within, and reflect the structure of the friendship networks at the center of these communities. In an interview with Milo Miller from the Queer Zine Archive Project, a digital archive of queer zines, Brager and Sailor ask Miller about the supposed divide between "academics/archivists and underground artists and cultural producers." Again, Miller's response highlights the extent to which queer theory, art, and archiving are not easily disentangled: "I think this question sets up a false dichotomy. Many folks who are 'cultural producers' are also academics and archivists."[15] In *Ephemeral Material*, librarian-scholar Alana Kumbier is also generous in her engagement with queer theorists. She observes that despite the fact that these scholars may not always "engage conventional archives," we can nevertheless appreciate "how they draw our attention to the limits of existing archives."[16] Indeed, Kumbier suggests that the concept of "the queer archive" does not necessarily work against the mandates of actual material archives but rather simply reminds us that gay, lesbian, bisexual, and transgender records are often especially eclectic and may include all sorts of ephemera traditionally excluded from archives (e.g., buttons, T-shirts, and props used in political actions). She also acknowledges the important ways in which queer theory has helped working archivists become more attentive to some of the less obvious factors that shape archives, including feelings and collective experiences of trauma.[17]

Finally, it is important to foreground the material effects queer cultural theorizing on archives has had on the way queers look at their own bookshelves, boxes of papers, filing cabinets, and other detritus. While this is difficult to substantiate, as documented in my study on feminist archives, *The*

Archival Turn in Feminism: Outrage in Order, in the early years of the new millennium, coinciding with the archival turn in cultural theory, a growing number of feminists and queer activists and artists, many still in their twenties and thirties, started to donate their personal collections to university archives. Among many of the archivists and donors I encountered in my own study, there was a strong sense that their personal collections not only belonged in institutional archives but also that bringing their ephemeral materials to institutional archives constituted a powerful way to authorize such materials. Notably, as often as donors referenced community-based archives, such as the Lesbian Herstory Archives, as a sort of template for queer archival projects, they cited the work of queer theorists, such as Cvetkovich and Halberstam. Indeed, I discovered that definitions of archives and what might count as an archival collection appeared tangled up in complicated histories of queer archival initiatives and queer theorizing on archives and history.[18]

On this basis, I propose that the archival turn in cultural theory, and more specifically, queer theory in the late 1990s to early years of the new millennium functioned to radically unsettle how archives are understood and experienced. Books such as *An Archive of Feelings* and *In a Queer Time and Place* were taken up both as scholarly works and because they offered something else to their readers. Interweaving theory, history, references to lesbian feminist and queer films, music, art, and protest movements with the authors' own personal anecdotes, both Cvetkovich's and Halberstam's titles circulated in and outside the academy because they were not simply books that sought to theorize queer subcultures and histories. For queer feminist readers at least, both of these books functioned as types of archives—textual repositories of references to lesbian popular and underground cultures from the past few decades interwoven with collected testimonies. Unconventional in their movement across theory and popular culture, history and personal memoir, these titles also served as models of how one might write about history by paying homage to our messy archives rather than becoming fixated on the absence of queers from institutional archives. If the titles functioned to raise our awareness of archives, however, it is also because they led to so many other conversations about archives within queer and specifically, queer feminist communities—conversations that over time have arguably changed what counts as an archive and what counts as potential archival materials. At the risk of overdetermining the import of these two titles, I am suggesting that for many scholars, activists, and artists of my generation—queer women born in the late 1960s to early 1980s—these titles were important because they prompted us to take our own ephemera more seriously. However, when any discourse becomes too prevalent—too taken for granted—there is always a danger that other important narratives will start to be eclipsed, and it is what risks eclipse that I am concerned with here.

Returning to the two passages I cited earlier, I would like to suggest that the idea of archives produced in queer cultural theorizing over the past decade has been defined along two somewhat contradictory lines, both of which are as problematic as they are sometimes generative. On the one hand, the archive (usually in the singular) has been posited as a floating signifier. On the other hand, it has been adopted as a powerful trope to stand in for a much more narrowly defined set of phenomena. The archive, in queer theory, appears to be entirely open and at the same time, to have a specificity that exceeds the specificity of even archives proper. My concern, however, is less with the contradictions and more with the consequences this construction of archives may have on the preservation of queer documents, artifacts, and material lives in the future and on the extent to which the voices of archivists and other information professionals have at times been overlooked in this theorizing.

Materiality and Labor in the "Floating Signifier"

Halberstam's claim that the archive "has to become a floating signifier for the kinds of lives implied by the paper remnants of shows, clubs, events, and meetings" is deeply compelling. Returning to Claude Lévi-Strauss, the floating signifier appears as both the "limitation of all finite thought" and even more enticingly, to "all art, all poetry, all mythic and aesthetic invention."[19] It is more commonly understood, however, as a signifier with an unspecifiable or absent signified. A floating signifier, therefore, is unfixed, undefinable, and resistant to containment. It's plural, fluctuating, mobile, and of course, easily hijacked. To suggest that the archive has to become a floating signifier to accommodate queer lives may appear to make complete sense. If queer lives are uncontainable and synonymous with excess, shouldn't our archives be just as open? But if the archive points to nothing in particular but simply that which we desire it to be, what is it? More critically, what is lost when the archive, as we know it, is quite literally emptied out? Is this a democratizing move that enables archives to be filled up with materials that have traditionally been excluded from institutional collections? Or is it simply a way to express what queer archivists have been doing all along—to capture, for example, the curious collecting mandate of actual archives, like the Lesbian Herstory Archives, which collect materials related to lesbians, as well as any document or artifact that a lesbian finds meaningful?[20]

First, if archives can point to anything—any collection, any accumulation, any set of accumulated practices or objects or people—we risk forgetting what makes archives so compelling in the first place. Here it is critical to bear in mind that queer activists, artists, and theorists have been attracted to archives because they are sites of power. Calling something an archive or choosing to place a set of documents in an institutional archive is still a powerful act of legitimization and authorization. In my own study of contemporary feminist archiving practices, donors, including several of the women who donated their papers to the Riot Grrrl Collection at NYU's Fales Library and Special Collections, emphasized the fact that archives, especially those linked to established institutions, are more well equipped not only to preserve materials over time but to bring a certain degree of legitimacy to otherwise dispersed ephemeral items. When the Riot Grrrl Collection was announced, many fans were thrilled about the prospect of being able to visit the archives. Indeed, practically overnight, the collection, which at the time was still a set of boxes waiting to be processed, was being lauded as a sort of Graceland for riot grrrls—a place that fans might visit to pay homage to feminist punk idols like Kathleen Hanna and Johanna Fateman. But as Fales archivist Lisa Darms explains, greater accessibility for fans was not necessarily what was motivating her donors. Although Fales has a relatively open policy for access, as Darms emphasizes, researchers still need to make an appointment and whether or not they are academics, they need to be engaged in some sort of research project: "I have made sure that the donations have happened with an understanding that the materials will be accessed for scholarly projects. This has been the motivation for the donors so far—a recognition that the materials will support research. They haven't donated their materials to make them more accessible to fans."[21]

What the Riot Grrrl example illustrates is the extent to which part of the appeal of archives is their function as an authorizing apparatus. So what is lost when we open up archives to the extent that they come to operate as nothing more than a floating signifier? To begin, what is lost is a recognition of the fact that archives are deeply embedded in power structures, which is not to suggest they are necessarily oppressive but rather to suggest that they are engaged in the production of subjects, the conditions of language, and the possibility of alternative histories and countergenealogies. If archives are understood as one institution among many that play a critical role in "position-taking,"[22] the practice of defining and producing the value of a work, then the suggestion that they point to everything (or as the case may be, to nothing) risks divesting archives of the power that has historically made them a critical node in the field of cultural production. It follows that such a move may not, as assumed, be necessarily democratizing for subjects who have historically found themselves on the margins of the archival apparatus but rather disempowering to queers and other traditionally marginalized groups who continue to seek out a space for themselves in the archival apparatus.

The other obvious thing that is lost when archives are understood as nothing more than a floating signifier capable of absorbing anything and everything is that we stop paying attention to the function of archives as places dedicated to the preservation of specific types of materials, including printed documents but also reel-to-reel audio recordings, audio cassettes, beta video tapes, floppy disks, and an entire range of digital artifacts. Here, it is important to bear in mind that all the stuff that queers fetishize, including zines, posters, and what Halberstam calls "temporary artifacts," are highly vulnerable to the passing of time and to an entire myriad of temporally and spatially bound conditions, including moisture, excessive heat, dust, and of course, the obsolescence of media. Yet what does it mean to be drawn to such ephemera while simultaneously failing to be attentive to the very specificity of these material artifacts? However much we may celebrate grassroots efforts to collect beta videotapes of gay hardcore porn or reel-to-reel recordings of the Chicago Women's Liberation Rock Band, without remediation, there is no possibility of accessing these materials. As queer archivists, however, what we wish to preserve are not media artifacts (beta video tapes, reel-to-reels, LPs) but rather the content carried by these media, which requires an attentiveness to questions of preservation.

Celebrating ephemeral archives of all kinds may serve queers in the present by providing us with a powerful trope through which to make sense of otherwise eclectic materials and ideas, but is it necessarily in the interest of the documents and artifacts in the long term? Does it necessarily serve the interest of the communities in which these documents and artifacts originated? I would like to suggest that privileging the most open definition of archives rather than remaining attentive to preservationist concerns (the kinds shared by professional archivists and special collections librarians) may be symptomatic of a broader temporal orientation in queer theory, which variously depicts and celebrates queer culture as permanently in adolescence—a community that subverts the norms and constraints of heterosexual family time, for example—or one that apparently has "no future" because it is at once both deeply utopian and always already driven by a perversely hedonistic death drive. It follows that real material concerns, like the preservation of documents and artifacts, are not easily accommodated in this narrative, leaving their future also in question. As a result, despite the fact that queer temporality theorists, including Halberstam and Freeman, have produced some of the most compelling responses to the archival question, much of the theorizing on queer time also remains at odds with the materialist concerns at the center of archival projects, and this is a contradiction with which queer theorists have not yet fully grappled.

Perhaps the most troubling repercussion of the way in which archives have been taken up by queer theorists, however, is the extent to which queer theory has at times placed archivists and special collections librarians under erasure or near erasure. Again, as Halberstam suggests, "In order for the archive to function it requires users, interpreters, and cultural historians to wade through the material and piece together the jigsaw puzzle of queer history in the making."[23] Here, the emphasis is not on the collection and preservation of documents but rather exclusively on their use and interpretation. Yet there can be no use or interpretation without people collecting and preserving material culture in all its forms. One of the activist librarians I met in the context of my own research, Jenna Freedman, a special collections librarian at Barnard College, likes to remind academics (myself included) that those seemingly serendipitous encounters we have with materials in archives are rarely as serendipitous as they appear. As Freedman once declared on a panel at an academic conference on the subject of archiving, "We [archivists and librarians] spend a lot to time making sure that stuff floats to the surface!"[24] Writing as a researcher who has spent a tremendous amount of time in archives and special collections working with documents but also carrying out ethnographies in these spaces, I also appreciate the fact that much of what I do in archives is highly mediated by the interventions of archivists and special collections librarians. Workers in archives and libraries frequently encourage me to look at materials I would otherwise overlook, not always from the collections I have come to access in the first place. Workers in archives and libraries are also the source of the backstories and gossip surrounding collections—stories that sometimes prove just as prescient as the documents and artifacts themselves. The labor of these workers, of course, is rarely visible (usually taking place in processing facilities far away from the reading rooms frequented by researchers) and is mired in discourses and practices few researchers, even those who write about archives, know much about. At a moment when we continue to witness the deskilling of labor in the archival and librarian professions as the work of professionals is increasingly out-sourced, even off-shored, or simply redistributed to staff without formal training, it is important to consider what is at stake when cultural theorists insist on privileging uses and interpretation over an attentiveness to work entailed in collection and preservation.

Without necessarily downplaying the importance of uses and interpretation, I would like to make a strong plea for a new form of archival awareness that brings the everyday labor and contributions of working archivists and special collections librarians into view and takes seriously the consequences of assuming cultural theorists and historians, especially those engaged in queer and otherwise minoritarian research, can in the long term do their work without these other, mostly invisible, experts. Here, one only needs to bear in mind that some of the most compelling queer archives of subcultural excess—like Steven Fullwood's In the Life Archive (formerly known as the Black Gay and Lesbian Archives) housed at the Schomburg Center for Research in Black Culture[25]—are the products of both queer archival impulses (like so many queer collections, Fullwood's collection started in his own home) and archival expertise (Fullwood worked as an archivist at the Schomburg prior to becoming the Project Director of NYU's Center for Black Visual Culture). Similarly, it is important to point out that while the Lesbian Herstory Archives prides itself on being entirely volunteer run, many of its former volunteers are now archival professionals and many of its current and past volunteers and board members are archivists and librarians with day jobs working in established public and university collections. In short, even the most eclectic queer collections are often far more contingent on archival expertise than one might expect.

While the concept of archives has been, in many respects, emptied out as it has been taken up by queer theorists as a powerful trope that can stand in for almost anything, in other ways, it has also become overly invested with very specific kinds of meaning. After all, if archives point to nothing but that which we desire, it follows that archives are always already structured first and foremost by desire and more broadly by affects. But in this paradigm, what is brought into focus is not archives per se but rather feelings. Following along this line of thought, archives have also become a convenient trope through which to understand how feelings congeal around an entire range of objects and texts, events, and communities. While the preoccupation with archives of feeling and, more specifically, archives of trauma in queer theory is especially indebted to Cvetkovich's theorizing, interest in so-called affective archives is also a much broader preoccupation in cultural theory—one just as informed by Derrida as it is by the specific contributions of queer theorists, like Cvetkovich. *Archive Fever*, a book about a book about archives, and *An Archive of Feelings*, an archive that takes the form of a book about archives, may appear to share little in common, but both Derrida and Cvetkovich adopt archives as a trope to address something that resists naming—in this case, trauma.

To clarify, I have no interest in downplaying the importance of affective archives, which is a conceptual framework I have relied upon in my own critical and creative work to investigate an entire range of questions and problematics.

I do, however, think it is important to bear in mind the fact that there are many ways to read archives. Again, to return to Kumbier's work, there is no reason to dismiss the work of cultural theorists, including queer theorists, since their work has opened up new and innovative ways to understand and engage with archives. What is required is not a dismissal but rather a broader acknowledgment of the archival labor and practices that few scholars, activists, or artists ever witness.

Thus, despite the fact that I have written this chapter, I am not prepared to abandon queer theory's contributions to understanding archives. As I have emphasized here, I find these possibilities and concepts endlessly compelling and at times very useful. I am concerned, however, with the extent to which queer theory's understanding of archives and archiving has at times had a tendency to gloss over the realities faced by workers who toil away in actual archives and special collections. When we forget or fail to recognize that archives are also driven by a pressing need to preserve material culture, as well as a very practical need to bring order to materials that would otherwise remain unnavigable, we not only place the labor of archivists and special collections librarians under erasure, we place our own future research endeavors at risk.

Significantly, this chapter was originally written as a critical reflection on my own ethnographic work in contemporary feminist and queer archives. If I entered my research as a cultural theorist compelled by the potentiality of archives as a site of activism and locus of creation, I emerged from the research increasingly attentive to the conditions of labor and challenges facing archivists and librarians who bring an activist mandate to their professional practice, especially at a time when funding to archives, specifically those concerned with material objects rather than digital data, continues to diminish. This chapter, then, stands both as a critique of cultural theory's and queer theory's impact on archival practice and a call to other queer scholars to take more seriously the work of archivists, special collections librarians, and other information studies professionals whose mandate is not necessarily to reimagine "the archive" but rather to find ways to accommodate queer materials, practices, and legacies in institutional archives where "no future" is no option.

Notes

1   Since I first drafted this chapter in 2012, the relationship between humanities scholarship on archives and archiving and archival labor and archival studies scholarship has been addressed in a number of conference presentations and articles, including, most notably, Michelle Caswell's 2016 essay in *Reconstruction: Studies in Contemporary Culture*, "'The Archive' Is Not an Archives." Here, Caswell observes, and rightly so, that even humanities scholarship that recognizes archival labor (including my own writing

on this topic) largely ignores archival studies scholarship. Caswell further contends that it isn't by chance that archival labor and scholarship has been largely ignored by scholars in the humanities. As she writes, "the refusal of humanities scholars to engage with scholarship in archival studies is a gendered and classed failure in which humanities scholars—even those whose work focuses on gender and class—have been blind to the intellectual contributions and labor of a field that has been construed as predominantly female, professional (that is, not academic), and service-oriented, and as such, unworthy of engagement."

2 See, among other publications, Cifor, "Stains and Remains," and Lee, "A Queer/ed Archival Methodology."

3 Muñoz, *Cruising Utopia*, 18.

4 Freeman, *Time Binds*, 59–93.

5 Halberstam, *In a Queer Time and Place*, 169.

6 Smith, *Institutional Ethnography*, 138.

7 Halberstam, *In a Queer Time and Place*, 169–70.

8 Cvetkovich, *Archive of Feelings*, 7.

9 Cvetkovich, *Archive of Feelings*, 7.

10 Carland, *Archive of Feeling*.

11 Freeman, *Time Binds*, 61.

12 See Andrea Geyer, http://www.andreageyer.info (last accessed February 20, 2022).

13 Mitchell, *A Girl's Journey*.

14 Brager and Sailor, *Archiving the Underground*.

15 Brager and Sailor, "Archiving the Underground," 45.

16 Kumbier, *Ephemeral Material*, 21.

17 Kumbier, *Ephemeral Material*, 22–23.

18 Eichhorn, *Archival Turn in Feminism*.

19 Lévi-Strauss, *Introduction*, 63.

20 The Lesbian Herstory Archives, http://www.lesbianherstoryarchives.org (last accessed February 20, 2022).

21 Lisa Darms, personal correspondence.

22 Bourdieu, *Field of Cultural Production*, 30–31.

23 Halberstam, *In a Queer Time and Place*, 170.

24 Jenna Freedman, personal correspondence.

25 In the Life Archive (formerly known as the Black Gay and Lesbian Archives), Schomburg Center for Research in Black Culture, https://archives.nypl.org/scm/21212.

Works Cited

Bourdieu, Pierre. *The Field of Cultural Production*. Edited by Randal Johnson. New York: Columbia University Press, 1993.

Brager, Jenna, and Jami Sailor. *Archiving the Underground* (zine) (2011).

Brager, Jenna, and Jami Sailor. "Archiving the Underground." In *Make Your Own History: Documenting Feminist and Queer Activism in the 21st Century*, edited by Lyz Bly and Kelly Wooten, 45–55. Sacramento, CA: Litwin Books, 2012.

Carland, Tammy Rae. *An Archive of Feeling*. Jessica Silverman Gallery. https://
jessicasilvermangallery.com/exhibitions/an-archive-of-feeling/ (accessed April 7, 2022).

Caswell, Michelle. "'The Archive' Is Not an Archives: On Acknowledging the Intellectual
Contributions of Archival Studies." *Reconstruction: Studies in Contemporary Culture* 16,
no. 1 (2016). https://escholarship.org/uc/item/7bn4v1fk.

Cifor, Marika. "Stains and Remains: Liveliness, Materiality, and the Archival Lives of
Queer Bodies." *Australian Feminist Studies* 91–92 (2017): 5–21.

Cvetkovich, Ann. *An Archive of Feelings: Trauma, Sexuality, and Lesbian Public Cultures*.
Durham, NC: Duke University Press, 2003.

Eichhorn, Kate. *The Archival Turn in Feminism: Outrage in Order*. Philadelphia: Temple
University Press, 2013.

Freeman, Elizabeth. *Time Binds: Queer Temporalities, Queer Histories*. Durham, NC: Duke
University Press, 2010.

Halberstam, Jack. *In a Queer Time and Place: Transgender Bodies, Subcultural Lives*. New
York: NYU Press, 2005.

Kumbier, Alana. *Ephemeral Material: Queering the Archive*. Sacramento, CA: Litwin
Books, 2014.

Lee, Jamie A. "A Queer/ed Archival Methodology: Archival Bodies as Nomadic Subjects."
Journal of Critical Library and Information Studies 1, no. 2 (2017): 1–27.

Lévi-Strauss, Claude. *Introduction to the Work of Marcel Mauss*. London: Routledge &
Kegan Paul, 1987.

Mitchell, Allyson. *A Girl's Journey to the Well of Forbidden Knowledge*. Art Gallery of Ontario. October 2–November 28, 2010. https://ago.ca/exhibitions/allyson-mitchell-girls
-journey-well-forbidden-knowledge.

Muñoz, José Esteban. *Cruising Utopia*. New York: NYU Press, 2009.

Sheffield, Rebecka Taves. *Documenting Rebellions: A Study of Four Lesbian and Gay Archives in Queer Times*. Sacramento: Litwin Books, 2020.

Smith, Dorothy. *Institutional Ethnography: A Sociology for People*. New York: AltaMira
Press, 2005.

13. CROCKER LAND

A Mirage in the Archive

CAROLYN DINSHAW AND MARGET LONG

From the far northern tip of the Canadian Arctic Archipelago, famed Arctic explorer Robert E. Peary saw a snow-capped landmass shimmering in the distance. This was just the kind of big discovery he had hoped to make in the international territory-grabbing race to the North Pole. Peary had in fact failed to reach the Pole this time around, but he staked his claim to an exciting resource-laden new land by building a stone cairn on the spot where he stood as he gazed at the glimmering horizon. In the cairn he left a can stuffed with a scrap of an American flag and a note: "Peary. June 28, 1906."

Of all the accomplishments of that 1906 expedition, Peary ranked the sighting of this new land very high. It wasn't a continent, he conceded later, rather a mere island, yet nonetheless there it was, banana-shaped on the maps on which it was subsequently drawn.[1] Peary's expedition had been organized by the American Museum of Natural History (AMNH) and the American Geographical Society, funded in large part through donations from major industrialists such as railroad magnate George Crocker, who had contributed $50,000— over $1.6 million 2022 dollars—in return for which he got a new polar land as his namesake. Knowing full well that Crocker Land could be a mirage (because of the prevalence of atmospheric refraction in polar conditions, where steep temperature gradients refract light from a low-lying sun), Peary still made this claim of discovery.[2] He knew his claim would need to be confirmed, and he wanted to keep the American polar expedition industry flourishing: there was money to be made and national prestige to be gained. "My heart leaped the intervening miles of ice as I looked longingly at this land," he wrote about that moment of discovery, "and in fancy I trod its shores . . . even though I knew that that pleasure could only be for another."[3]

The follow-up expedition Peary imagined as he gazed out in the distance was organized several years later by the AMNH (with other institutional partners) and led by Donald B. MacMillan, who had assisted Peary on a previous expedition. The purpose of the Crocker Land Expedition was to confirm Peary's sighting and to explore all aspects of this new land, including the prospect of lucrative game and natural resources. Crucially, to document it all, they would take pictures with state-of-the-art cameras, both still photos and moving pictures.[4] They set out from the Brooklyn Navy Yards for the Arctic in the summer of 1913; in the fall of 1917, two years delayed, with vast sums spent and one Inughuit dead,[5] the last members of the expedition returned. The dispiriting news: Crocker Land was a mirage. Peary, they said, had been deceived by an optical phenomenon. They concluded this because they, too, had seen a mirage as they stood at Peary's cairn, the very point from which Peary had sighted Crocker Land. "We looked toward the distant horizon," MacMillan later recalled. "Glasses were not necessary. There was land everywhere! Had we not just come from far over the horizon we would have returned to our country and reported land just as Peary did."[6]

This story is well known to aficionados of Arctic exploration. It's in fact notorious, and the same questions always attend it: given the common nature of mirages in the Arctic—not to mention all the other difficulties in identifying anything on the Polar Sea, "that moving world of ice, with constantly rising mists"[7]—how could the very experienced Peary have been deceived into thinking he saw land? Did he see anything at all, or was it all just a ruse to get another expedition funded? Did he make this "discovery" under pressure to justify the failed 1906 expedition itself?[8] If he made it up, it wouldn't be the last time he falsified his achievements; there is strong evidence of his awareness that he did not actually reach the Pole when he claimed victory at last in 1909.[9]

What is not well known, though, is the sprawling photographic archive generated by the Crocker Land Expedition. There are 5,500 still photos as well as 12,000 feet of moving pictures. The explorers had not only the latest camera equipment but also a full darkroom in their headquarters in Etah, Greenland, in order to fulfill their photographic mandate. Everything about the Arctic— its human inhabitants, its flora and fauna, its geology, the whole stunning visual field—was new to all but team leader MacMillan; they observed, measured, and took photo after photo, each click of the camera meticulously logged. What can be found in that archive, and perhaps even more consequentially, what cannot?

We went to the archive to see what they saw and shot, and most pointedly, to look for a photograph of that legendary mirage—for mirages are physically real atmospheric events that can be photographed. And since a spectacular mirage is what Crocker Land turned out to be, we figured the explorers had photographed it. After all, photographs of mirages in Alaska had been published decades earlier; moreover, Arctic mirages were being photographed and published just as the Crocker Land Expedition was being planned.[10] We wanted to see that definitive shot confirming that Crocker Land was (in the unintentionally paradoxical language of the official report) "non-existent at 82° 30′ N, 108° 22′ W."[11]

This chapter narrates our archival pursuit of that mirage photograph. The mirage is the subject of our analysis, and it is also our heuristic, our way of seeing, our analytic. It refracts, duplicates, shifts, distorts, expands our vision. A mirage compelled the explorers, the AMNH officials, the benefactors toward what they didn't have and what they most wanted: a resource-rich land for the United States, Polar spoils for the museum and its benefactors, a place on the map with their own name emblazoned on it. The mirage motivated us as researchers, too, dazzled and drawn by this ephemeral visual phenomenon. It enticed us, and entices us still, into hours of looking. It pulls us. We get close and it vanishes. We can't control it. Partaking of the elusive nature of the North Pole itself—an imaginary point with no dimensions, unfixed to anything and undetectable in the visual field[12]—and partaking, too, of the irrationally wondrous nature of extreme northern latitudes, where north is south, where you can see five suns at once—the mirage reveals the queerness of archives themselves. It expresses the desire, the beckoning, the disappointment we felt in those most ambiguous places. And though that fleetingness and ungovernability have frustrated us, these qualities provoke us to think about archival practice in our current data-hungry, digital environment in which, as a rule, *everything* is collected and archived on a server somewhere. Because a mirage—a live imaging event— shimmers but cannot be corralled, contained, saved, or stored, it prompts us to reconceptualize archival practice as an ongoing, perpetual revelation.[13]

Part 1: "Our Old Friend the Mirage"

Among the papers that accompany the expedition photos, we found an Arctic expedition map at the American Museum of Natural History (see Figure 13.1).[14] MacMillan's proposed route to Crocker Land is superimposed onto a map of a Norwegian expedition that had claimed vast territories for Norway. Crocker Land is literally off the map, inked into the legend as a curved, blue line—the eastern edge of a shoreline of what could be either a limitless landmass, or almost nothing at all. The full contours, location, and existence of Crocker Land figure as sketchy, inexact, and provisional. Yet the very crudeness and intensity

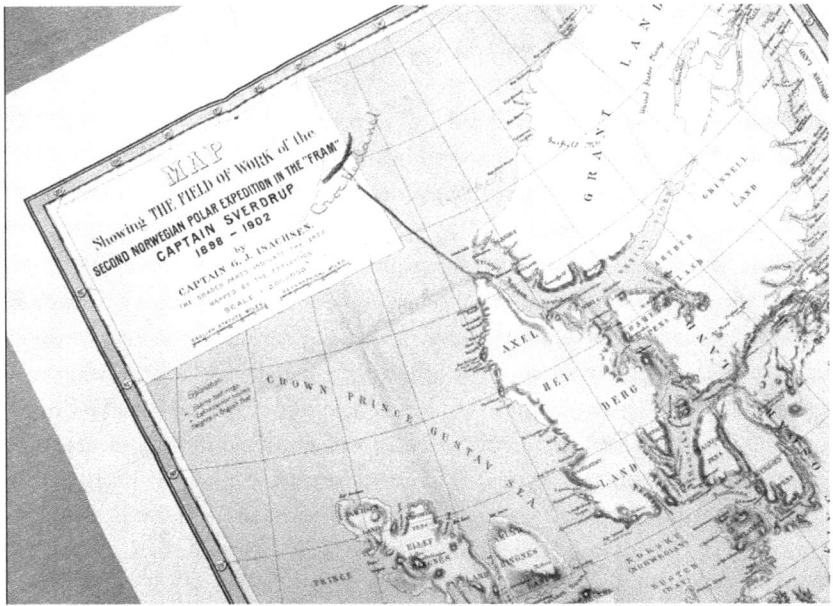

FIGURE 13.1. Expedition map with hand-drawn Crocker Land. Mss. C76, Box 17, folder 9. American Museum of Natural History Library.

of those hand-drawn lines express the imaginative pull of this unknown place, this hypothetical territory whose discovery and exploration could bring personal renown as well as geopolitical power, resources, and influence. As Eric Sundquist notes, Britain and Russia had dominated Arctic exploration in the early nineteenth century, but American "interest in the Arctic increased after Secretary of State William Seward, foreseeing geological wealth and a possible gateway to American control of Canada and parts of Asia, negotiated the purchase of Alaska from Russia in 1867."[15] Though "acquisition" exploration waned after global frontiers closed in the early twentieth century and professional geographers increasingly set research agendas, as Neil Smith reports, Peary and his followers doggedly persisted with their outmoded (and often meretricious) forms of "geographical conquest."[16]

In the spring of 1914, after months of hard travel from Brooklyn to Greenland and more months building their northern headquarters, Donald MacMillan and his team started the grueling journey across the polar ice toward the spot on the map where Peary had placed Crocker Land. Photos in the archive of the six-week-long "dash" across the Polar Sea to Crocker Land show the

FIGURE 13.2. Crossing the Polar Sea in search of Crocker Land. Image #233091-96, American Museum of Natural History Library.

final four-man crew (MacMillan, FitzHugh Green, and two very experienced Inughuit guides, Ee-took-a-shoo and Pee-ah-wah-to), dogs and sledges, igloo camps, and kills of musk ox and walrus; they give some sense (see Figure 13.2) of the daunting scale of the sea ice and massive pressure ridges, and the staggering challenges posed when crossing the Polar Sea at that time.

After forty-two days, MacMillan and crew finally approached the place on the map where Peary had pinned his new land. It was thrilling, as MacMillan later wrote in his memoir:

> April 21st was a beautiful day; all mist was gone and the clear blue of the sky extended down to the very horizon. . . . There could be no doubt about it. Great heavens! what a land! Hills, valleys, snowcapped peaks extending through at least one hundred and twenty degrees of the horizon.[17]

They walked and walked toward those snowcapped peaks but came no closer to them. The peaks came and went from sight, depending on the time of day and the angle of the sun.

Pee-ah-wah-to said that it was *poo-jok*, mist. He might also have added that it was an *ijiraq*, a shape-shifting creature in Inuit legends that appears with mirages. "Fabulous, transforming ijirait" were sometimes thought to be the cause of *taulittuq*, the experience of walking without getting any closer.[18] But MacMillan insisted they press on until he had to admit that they had passed the place on the map where Crocker Land was marked. Here's a deflated MacMillan later recounting his moment of reckoning:

> We had not only reached [Peary's] brown spot on the map, but we were thirty miles "inland"! You can imagine how earnestly we scanned every foot of that horizon—not a thing in sight.... We were convinced that we were in pursuit of a will-o'-the-wisp, ever receding, ever changing, ever beckoning.[19]

He wrote to Peary several months after their failure to find Crocker Land: "We were on the brown spot and not a thing in sight, not even our old friend the mirage."[20] Spectacularly deceptive mirages had accompanied them as they made their way across the Polar Sea; Green in his field notes recounts one mirage on April 27, for example, that had lasted for days, looking so much like land that he even descried mountains and valleys there.[21] With the rueful phrase "our old friend the mirage," MacMillan implicitly concedes that that's what both Peary and he had observed.

Once MacMillan reported to the museum that there was no continent, dozens of articles shot out over the wires: "Crocker Land Eludes Explorers," "Crocker Land a Mere Mirage."[22] For years afterward the AMNH tried to justify the huge expense of this four-year fiasco. The expedition had failed to find Crocker Land; this in itself could not have been a huge surprise in those days, because many nonexistent Arctic lands had been sighted and claimed over the years: Sannikov Land (Russia), Bradley Land (United States), even one called *Croker* Land (Great Britain).[23] But the expedition was an embarrassment to the museum: it had gone massively over budget, was marred by antipathies among expedition members and between the museum leadership and MacMillan, and faltered amid tensions between the Inughuit and the white men. The nadir of the enterprise was the senseless death of Pee-ah-wah-to at the hands of FitzHugh Green.[24] In order to defend their pursuit of Crocker Land, everyone involved with the expedition emphasized the geographical, botanical, zoological, geological, ethnographic, and other scientific findings. An ethereal landscape image had been used to sell the junket initially to prospective funders (see Figure 13.3). In publications after the expedition, a photographic image of a lone iceberg in the distance was used as a stand-in for the nonexistent Crocker Land.

FIGURE 13.3. Landscape suggesting Crocker Land. *Crocker Land Expedition to the North Polar Regions: Statement to Contributors*, 8.

In fulfillment of their scientific mission, the absence of Crocker Land notwithstanding, MacMillan and his team took pictures of just about everything under the Arctic sun. When the daylight receded for the winter and darkness came to stay, MacMillan said that they would keep busy during the perpetual night with their photography.[25] The Arctic visual field is stunning, with gleaming brightness and magnifyingly clear air, but also mists, fogs, clouds, and shimmering "water skies." The aurora borealis is the most legendary of visual effects, but phosphorescence, too, struck the expedition members with its incomparable beauty, and the drama of intense colors in the sky and reflected on the ice is remarked on by the explorers in their journals.[26] The midnight sun captivated the Crocker Land Expedition members, as did icebergs and glaciers and their reflections, of which there are many photographs. In an experimental mode, MacMillan shot striking multiple exposure photographs of the midnight sun (see Figure 13.4).

In addition to documentary photos of landscapes, plants, and animals, Mac-Millan and his team took photos of the expedition members themselves, indoors and out, and many photos—in the exploitive style of the ethnography of the day—of the Smith Sound Inughuit, on whose shores they built their headquarters and on whose labor they depended.[27] These photos range from "scientific" ethnographic head shots to documentation of hunting, sewing, and other everyday activities, to ostensibly affective photos of Inughuit children and puppies. They are exceptionally power-laden images, including, particularly, shots of an Inughuit woman suffering from "Arctic hysteria." We will discuss those shots in our next section.

What they didn't photograph, though, was the mirage. The archive, with its 5,500 still photos, is large for an expedition of that time. We looked at all of the still images, as well as the film clips, for an image of the mirage. It's not there.

233466

233467

233468

FIGURE 13.4. Expedition photos, including multiple exposure of midnight sun and polar loot. Image #233466-68, American Museum of Natural History Library.

Despite the accounts in field notes of how beautiful and real Crocker Land looked on the journey across the Polar Sea, no photo of it was taken. Instead of the photo we wanted to find, we found a picture MacMillan took at Peary's cairn, where MacMillan and his team, on their way back from the unsuccessful journey, reported seeing a dramatic, panoramic mirage. But curiously, rather than photograph that mirage, MacMillan shot this solid record, intended to be definitive: FitzHugh Green and the American flag (Figure 13.5). Intensifying the record, Green took one of MacMillan, in turn, and that flag.

There are many possible explanations for the lack of the mirage photo in the archive. We are convinced that MacMillan and crew knew they could photograph a mirage. Alfred Wegener, the brilliant German polar traveler and scientist, had made photographing mirages part of his scientific program on one Danish expedition in 1907–1908 (whose results were published in 1911) and another in 1912–1913 (see Figure 13.6).

But the American Anthony Fiala, too, an Arctic explorer well known to MacMillan, had published a photograph of atmospheric refraction in his 1906 book, *Fighting the Polar Ice*.[28] The numerous multiple exposure photographs of the midnight sun confirm the Crocker Land explorers' interest in atmospheric phenomena and their desire and ability to photograph them. But maybe they

FIGURE 13.5. FitzHugh Green at Peary's cairn. Image #233125, American Museum of Natural History Library.

FIGURE 13.6. Mirage, Gundahls Knold, February 1913. Danish Arctic Institute/Alfred Wegener.

didn't want an image of their failure to find a new land. Perhaps, committed to photography's veracity, they didn't use photography to document what they knew was *not* there. Or maybe there is a much more calculated reason: by not fixing the mirage on film, MacMillan and the museum may have tried to co-opt its illusory and shifty nature for their own benefit, deflecting or refracting away the shadiness of the entire enterprise: the dubious heroism, the loose relation to facts, the lack of accountability for Inughuit death, the profiteering via tax-free gift scheme that moved goods from the Inughuits into the museum and private collections, the territory-crazed attempt to prolong the age of "attainment" exploration even beyond Peary's claiming of the North Pole. If Peary was "nightmare American imperialism incarnate," MacMillan was his only begotten son.[29]

"Nationalism was and remains a central text of exploration," writes Neil Smith, and he goes on to quote a review of Mackinder and Lenin: "Even the few remaining 'empty spaces of the world are no longer non-political.'"[30] The mirage—distorting and displacing, always over there, in the distance, just out of reach—provides a perfect optic for the age of expansionism: for expansionist enterprises such as museum collections, nations, and empires (and in the case

330 · Carolyn Dinshaw and Marget Long

of the AMNH, institution and nation/empire are intimately intertwined), and for expansionist dreams. It beckons, but it can't ever be reached; approach too closely and it vanishes, remaining in the realm of desire. Always farther, finally ungraspable: Peary believed that Crocker Land "would become a gateway to other lands or seas"—and when he heard it was a mirage, he *still* held onto the belief that he had seen land.[31] The Crocker Land photographic archive is a refraction of the interests and desires that instigated the expedition: the drive of discovery, the urge toward knowledge, the imperative of territorial claim, the lust for resources—in short, imperialism and all its varied spoils. This archive is unwavering in its explicit promotion of American primacy—it is a "historical agent," to use Regina Kunzel's term, "organized around unwritten logics of inclusion and exclusion, with the power to exalt certain stories, experiences, and events, and to bury others" (such as the experiences of the Inughuit and the body of Pee-ah-wah-to above all)—and yet it was produced by a mirage, whose shimmering illusory unreal realness continues to call and confound us even now. "I wonder, too, if there isn't something queer about archives," Kunzel goes on to speculate, "the way they spark and frustrate our desires."[32] We looked for a photo of the mirage, as if the archive would reveal to us some truth about what really happened up there. Researchers with our own expansionist dreams of knowledge, we looked and looked. Turning over image after image, it was always going to be in the next drawer, the next folder. After pulling the last picture from the last filing cabinet, our prospects vanished. Ephemeral, partial, and distorted, the mirage isn't—and is—in the archive.

Part 2: It's the Ocean

How did we end up rifling through photographs in this strange back room? Our fascination with the infamous mirage that was Crocker Land didn't come out of nowhere. For the past several years I (Marget) have been chasing mirages in films, in texts, and with my camera over land and sea, often bringing Carolyn (with her own research interests) along for the ride.[33] Mirages are photographic—we'll explain that in a moment—and photographs pose problems of archiving with particular intensity. As an image-maker and image-consumer, I waver in my attitude toward photography: rivers, streams, oceans of pictures have diluted my sense of their presence and purpose in the world. I'm glued to the screen. I'm drained of all excitement. I resist the imperatives of social media. I can't stop posting to Instagram. Mostly, I have a lot of questions turning and turning in my mind. Why are we compelled to take all of these pictures? What do we want from them and what do they want from us?

FIGURE 13.7. *Carolyn Looking for the Mirage in the Museum.* Marget Long, 2014.

What can photographs—and more to the point here, the formal and informal archives they form—reveal about archival politics and priorities, past, present, and future? (See Figure 13.7.)

Seeing mirages is a way to get inside photography, to turn it inside out. A mirage is light interacting with matter in the world—a real, if intangible, imaging event that occurs when light is refracted in strange and unearthly ways. Refraction works like this: light rays, which normally move through space in a relatively straight line, are bent when steep thermal gradients are present in the atmosphere. The air acts like a giant lens and creates an inverted image (or sometimes multiple images, both inverted and upright) of a distant object. This mirage image is displaced from the object's geometric position in space and is sometimes quite distorted. In the case of a desert mirage, hot air just above ground is pressed up against cooler air above it; this intense thermal gradient bends the light emanating from the blue sky onto the ground. Because the image of the sky on the ground is blue(ish), we interpret it as water.[34] Arctic mirages occur when temperature differences over snow or ice refract an image of that snow/ice into the sky. In these instances, an observer might interpret the displaced snow or sea ice as a distant mountain or a land mass like the one Peary claimed to have seen.

Both physically and culturally, mirages are images tangled up with desire, imagination, illusion, deception, and disappointment. If we're in a burning desert, water is exactly the thing we most want to see. But the desire is not only ours: to chase a mirage is to chase image-making in a rudimentary but deeply sensory camera-less form, a queer mode where the earth makes distorted, displaced, and inverted new images of itself. As Kaja Silverman would say, this is the world showing us how it wants to be seen.[35]

Carolyn and I parked our rental car near the center of El Mirage Dry Lakebed, a flat expanse on the Mojave Desert in California. It was 112 degrees and the ground couldn't have been dustier or drier. Yet in every direction we saw what looked like beautiful rippling water. Shimmering blue oceans, hazy purplish lakes, and a row of Joshua trees in the distance formed an oasis. The scene was mesmerizing and hard to describe after the fact except to say that what was happening on the lakebed seemed to be both *supernatural* and *superphotographic*: supernatural because we were in the natural world and yet nothing, not even our own bodies, felt quite "natural" or "right" in the presence of the mirages, and superphotographic because when we looked out at the mirages both of us had the strange sensation of being inside of a giant camera and looking at a vast photograph.[36] With great anticipation and excitement we had flown across the country to photograph mirages. But once there I worried that a photograph might drain the liveness—the mirageness—of these alluring images. And yet I grabbed my camera, as we all do now. I clicked away.

Back in New York, though, reviewing these pictures filled me with ideas about what photography was, is, and can be. On one level, they offered a solid and unquestionable record of an atmospheric event on the lakebed: ordinary, old-school index. On another level, the subject of the photographs (the mirage) complicated and even mocked photography's own claims to fidelity. The "water" wasn't really water (see Figures 13.8 and 13.9), yet it could so easily be interpreted as such in the photograph. The tension in this photograph highlights the usefulness of the mirage as an analytic. While all camera-made photographs refer to something that undeniably took place in front of the lens, they simultaneously express unseen desires and imaginaries. For me, these mirage photographs illuminate one of the most interesting aspects of photography: its loose grip on reality. They point to a parallel image-world that might, as Charlotte Cotton has suggested, bend standard visual rules and social relations.[37] The mirage photographs are images of instability, conjecture, and disappointment—an image of photography itself.

To return to the photographic archive in the museum: the bronze busts, the magnificent wooden sledges atop beige filing cabinets, the carefully ordered record of a failed expedition—none of this would exist without Peary's false sighting of his false land mass. How, then, were we to understand what we were seeing? How were we to "read" these photographs? Certainly, a photographic archive instigated by a mirage does not have to be read according to conventional historical logics or standard visual rules. What if we were to turn a mirage's optics back onto it? What if we were to run the Crocker Land archive through a fata morgana machine? A fata morgana is a complex mirage; we appropriate "fata morgana machine" from Salomo Friedlaender's 1920 short story "Fatamorganamaschine," excerpted and disseminated by media theorist Friedrich Kittler.[38]

The sequence of six photos in the top image in Figure 13.10 appears on one sheet, and we've inverted and reversed that sheet on the bottom image. In the top image, you can see the label "PIBLOCTOQ ARCTIC HYSTERIA"; on the back "Inahloo pibloctoq" describes each of these six images. Now, *pibloctoq* (or *piblokto*) is a pseudo-Inuit term for what European and American explorers called "Arctic hysteria," a behavioral manifestation they noticed among Inuit women (pseudo-Inuit, because there is no such Inuit word; this is what Westerners transcribed). Robert Peary characterized it in *The North Pole* as a "nervous affection . . . whose immediate cause is hard to trace" but that might have to do with lost relatives or fear of the future.[39] Westerners multiplied theories about this phenomenon (psychoanalytic, environmental, nutritional, social,

FIGURE 13.8. *You Were Drifting*, video still. Marget Long, 2015.

FIGURE 13.9. *(Inferior) Mirage #11*. Inkjet print on Hahnemühle paper, 6 × 4 inches. Marget Long, 2013.

and cultural, as anthropologist Lyle Dick delineates).[40] And theories require pictures, evidence, documentation; thus this top image, imposing a Western European diagnostic gaze on this woman, named Inahloo, apparently unconscious, lying outside, away from any built structure. She is surrounded by a group of men and women (including Westerners) with dogs, and in the penultimate image, she is ministered to by three women along with two dogs.

There is in fact another picture being taken in one of the photos, suggesting that this was not a scene that the explorers just happened to come upon and shoot. Was this whole scene staged for those Western cameras? We know that on an earlier expedition Donald MacMillan—that's probably him, the tallest of the bunch—heard that a woman was in the throes of *pibloctoq* and grabbed his camera; her affect changed entirely at that point and she later insisted that she was faking and that she didn't want him to use her pictures because she was naked. Lyle Dick calls *pibloctoq* an "elusive entity," produced by Western imperialist agendas. Whose hysteria was it, anyway? The Crocker Land explorers were stuck up there for four miserable years; they argued, they pilfered surreptitiously, they killed.

Our deployment of mirage optics highlights the uncertainty about what was happening in front of the lens. When we put these images through our fata

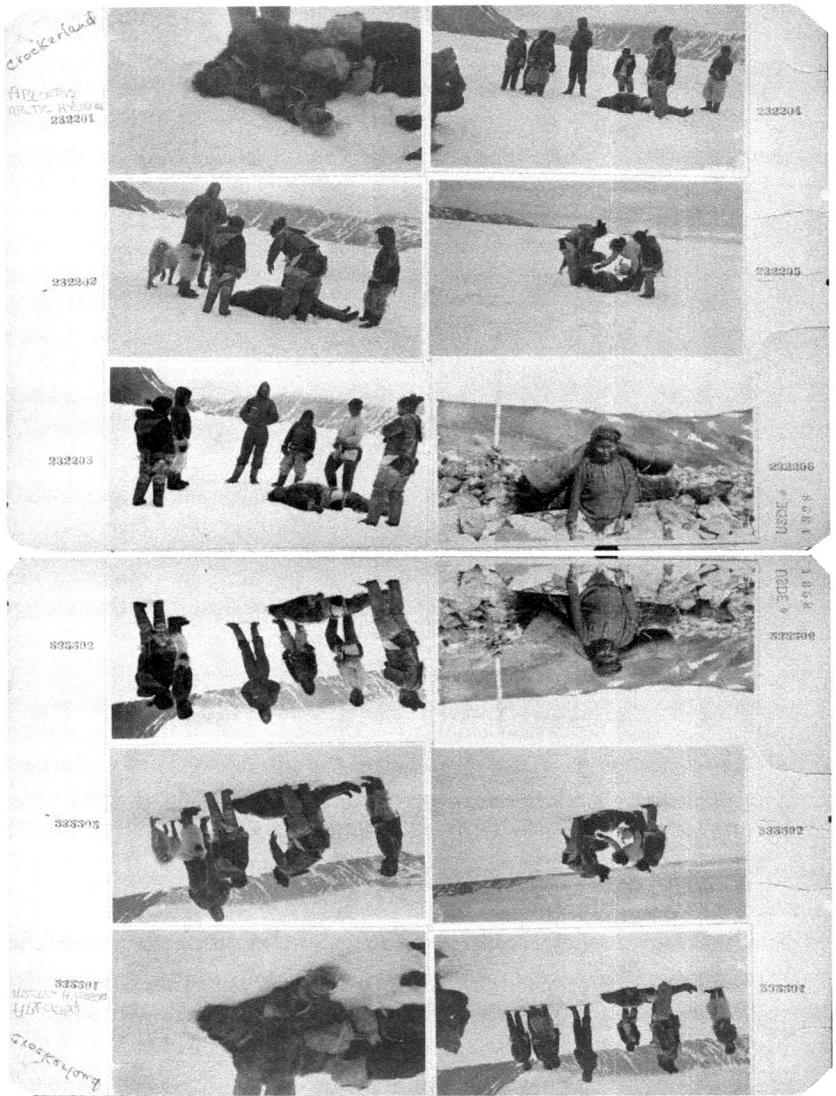

FIGURE 13.10. Pibloctoq Arctic Hysteria. Image #232201-06, American Museum of Natural History Library. Bottom image reversed and inverted.

morgana machine we see something distorted.[41] This distortion in the bottom image of Figure 13.10 allows us to imagine things beyond what a cultural critique will allow us to see. A woman looms above the onlookers. Her physical reality is completely changed; here she is outside the Western imagination. She is levitating, effortlessly dominant. One of the dogs levitates with her. The observers around her fall away, askew.

But that's not the "truth" of Inahloo, either. We may approach it, or her, but it vanishes. Beyond this loopy application of the mechanics of a mirage to this one photograph, the mirage insists that we understand all of the photographs in this archive as unstable, wavering mixtures of the real and the illusory. The expedition members had their own fata morgana machine: photography was not only a way of spending the long winter nights; it was also a lucrative meal ticket long after the expedition finally returned. Indeed, the lecture circuit was part of the funding machinery of the expedition industry, and MacMillan's lectures, copiously illustrated with lantern slides, were a major source of income for his life afterward. MacMillan took images up in the north and, fata morgana–style, displaced them into lecture halls, banquet rooms, and classrooms. Among his many different presentations, MacMillan gave a lecture titled "Removing Crocker Land from the Map." When we opened that folder for the typescript in the archive, it was empty.

Part 3: (Not) Saving Appearances

We had to go north ourselves as we chased our old friend the mirage. We drove up to Maine.[42] Bowdoin College's Peary-MacMillan Arctic Museum (PMAM) holds an archive of the Crocker Land Exhibition materials and had mounted a one-hundred-year commemoration of the expedition itself. As we ventured in, we glimpsed Crocker Land on the exhibition wall. Well, not Crocker Land, and not the mirage either, but a substitution—another stand-in. Just as the AMNH used a photograph of a landscape in place of Crocker Land, so Bowdoin's museum used a recent picture of a gigantic mirage over the water near Etah in place of the mirage MacMillan saw from Peary's cairn and didn't photograph (see Figure 13.11).

The caption tells of Peary's sighting the "faint white summits" in 1906 and states that he could not tell, as he stood there, whether he was looking at a mirage or not. But of course Peary never hinted at any uncertainty: whatever his actual experience and motives, he insisted that he had sighted a new land. The photo and caption in the exhibition try to settle the whole unsettled issue: here's a spectacular mirage, so real looking that such a vision fooled Peary. The exhibition

FIGURE 13.11. Exhibition photo of photo (by Dave Walsh, copyright 2009) of a fata morgana extending across the horizon. Carolyn Dinshaw, 2016.

gently saves appearances, so to speak: it uses a photo of a mirage retrospectively to install a question in Peary's mind and therefore to justify the Crocker Land Expedition.

This spectacular photo, when deployed thus, co-opts the mirage for institutional purposes, draining it of its liveness and ephemerality. Trying to present something of that liveness and ephemerality, though, the exhibition actually included a demonstration mirage located under a map of the Arctic: when you peer into a hole and press a button, a mirage appears. Presto! Yet the controlled, on-demand aspect of this mirage runs counter to the open-air, ungovernable aspect of mirages that we have been emphasizing; mounted at the height of a child, at least part of its function would seem to be to answer, jack-in-the-box–style, the demands of restless kids in a museum space.

The archival materials on which this exhibition was partly based are held by the museum; Special Collections in Bowdoin's library holds even more archival documents. We sifted through all these photos, journals, posters for lectures, lantern slides, and other material similar to—at times duplicating— the holdings in the AMNH. Day in and day out we looked, but again, there was no mirage photo to be found. By that time we were intentionally pursuing something that we already knew would fail us. We knew we were never going to reach solid evidence, grounded knowledge, the truth in the unstable, slippery realm that is an archive. *Not* finding something is, after all, a fundamental experience of working in archives. All archives are as much made of what is absent as what is present; we join many theorists and practitioners in this awareness.

But the mirage has moved our thinking further, beyond the realm of epistemological uncertainty and into a realm where we are ourselves superfluous. Mirages are images made without human activity; they are a "pencil of nature."[43] Their media are the earth, the air, and the sun. Images will continue to emanate from whatever is left after humans and all of our things are burned out and gone. If light and air still exist at the end of human time, the earth will continue to make its own upside-down pictures. Mirages don't need us. They can't and won't be saved and stored. So if mirages are crucial to our understanding of archives, what does all this mean?

In a short essay about imaging and modes of storage, Teju Cole ruminates on whether an image on Snapchat is a photograph at all, since the image disappears so quickly that it doesn't seem to fulfill photography's usual memorial function.[44] Snapchat, Cole goes on to say, meets his definition of photography because the image is saved, even if just for a moment. Even though these pictures vanish from our screens, he notes, they have an "optical afterlife" on a distant server, and the specter of these indelible photos haunts us. For Cole, a more revolutionary technology might be one without the capacity to save, thereby freeing us from "being subject to incessant visual notation," a form of surveillance. Mirages. They fade. They vanish. They can't be harnessed, saved, or capitalized in the usual ways. Maybe a mirage enacts Cole's radical ideal of image-making. A mirage is not reliant on anyone creating or consuming the image. It thus prompts us not only to consider the deeply contingent and partisan act of looking into any archive of photographs, but also to reevaluate the merits of saving images at all.

Acts of saving—amassing, sheltering, storing, retaining—are at the center of archival practice. These activities allow us to keep in touch with the ongoingness of the past; to learn about our present; to imagine possible futures. We would never suggest that the exploitive images of the Crocker Land archive should not be saved; we can learn from those photographs when they are properly contextualized. Nonetheless, many have argued the perils of saving (and displaying) such toxic materials. Veering away from that interminable debate, the mirage in the Crocker Land archive has enabled us to conceptualize future archival practices that value the *unsaveable*.[45]

We write in an era in which the manipulation of data and images by the United States government, particularly when Donald Trump was at its helm, has proven literally treacherous, economically catastrophic, and ultimately murderous. Trump grabbed and recirculated citizens' racist tweets; mined and exploited personal data on a whim; falsified maps; deleted entire realms of federal records; altered epidemiological data; and on and on. For the purposes of this chapter, we point to the administration's manipulation of 2017 protest records such that photographs of protest signs critical of the so-called president have been altered in the National Archives.[46] In this context, and as only one of many possible approaches to this threatened data landscape, we wonder what kinds of images might be created that *cannot* be subject to these odious ministrations, *cannot* be turned into commodities or otherwise exploitable forms of knowledge. Saving and stockpiling are fundamental to networked capitalism, data its most valuable commodity. Is there a yet-to-be-invented form of image-making and image-archiving that can elude this trap?[47] How can we use the liveness and ungovernability of the mirage to resist the co-optation of our images and ideas?

American Arctic explorer Frederick Cook, who claimed to have reached the North Pole before Robert Peary, wrote of his experiences in the far north: "Mirages turned things topsy turvy. Inverted lands and queer objects ever rose and fell, shrouded in mystery."[48] Huge mirages ever on the horizon, the Arctic was "a disappointing Sahara," where "strange contradictions" tantalized him and his companions. "What a world of paradoxes! All was queer. We were queer ourselves," Cook—or his ghost writer, who seems to have been gay—wrote.[49] A mirage, that geophysical phenomenon at once real and bound up with illusion, undoes conventional logics of here and there, now and then, nowhere and somewhere. With the mirage as our wavering, unreliable, but always provocative guide we have speculated about geographical exploration, about empire, about the promises and disappointments of archives—about places beyond anyone's grasp, animated by desire. After their experience in the Arctic, a place Frederick Cook called Eden, the Promised Land, and Paradise, their very bodies were different: "We were strange to ourselves and strange to others," he reflected. "Henceforth we were native to Nowhere."[50] Though we may still be caught up in our own expansionist dreams, a mirage points beyond. Its unreal realness is live and uncaptured image-making. It offers glimmers of an archive world of ongoing, evanescent revelation.

Notes

We thank the many research staff who generously and imaginatively helped us: Rebecca Morgan and Gregory Raml, the American Museum of Natural History; Susan Kaplan, Genny LeMoine, and Anne Witty, the Peary-MacMillan Arctic Museum,

Bowdoin College; and Jørgen Trondhjem and Stig Rasmussen, Danish Arctic Institute, Copenhagen.

1 Peary's letter to Crocker, April 14, 1907, quoted in Davies, *Robert E. Peary*, 165.

2 Danish polar explorers in 1907 had sighted an island that ended up with the name Fata Morgana Land; a fata morgana is a specific kind of spectacular mirage. Confirmation of the existence of that island was the goal of a subsequent Danish expedition. Higgins, *Exploration History*, 167.

3 Peary, *Nearest the Pole*, 207.

4 They brought an Ernemann motion picture camera plus a Graphlex still camera and hand cameras (Eastman Kodak 3A). See Kaplan, "Riding Shortwaves," 422.

5 Inughuit are native peoples of northwest Greenland.

6 MacMillan, "Geographical Report," 397.

7 Cook, *My Attainment of the Pole*, 3. Dr. Frederick A. Cook's claim to have reached the Pole before Peary set off controversy that was settled in Peary's favor by 1911, and Cook was regarded by the Crocker Land team as a charlatan. MacMillan notes the difficulty of judging distances in the far north in "The MacMillan Arctic Expedition."

8 Peary did not mention the sighting of a new land in his field notes, which subsequently disappeared, and noted that day that there was "no land in sight," according to Rawlins, "Contributions." The prospectus published by the museum, *Crocker Land Expedition to the North Polar Regions: Statement to Contributors*, justifies the projected expedition by referring to findings of a tidal expert, in addition to "Eskimo" traditions and prior reports of land in the area. MacMillan's *Four Years in the White North*, "Introduction," mentions evidence supporting Peary's belief. For the most skeptical critique of Crocker Land, see Rawlins, *Peary at the North Pole*, 67–77; see also Herbert, *Noose of Laurels*; Berton, *The Arctic Grail*, 564. The defense of Peary offered by Davies, *Robert E. Peary*, includes a section on Crocker Land (164–69).

9 See Rawlins, qtd. in Smith, *American Empire*, 98.

10 For discussion of Alaska mirage photographs of the late nineteenth century, see Pinney, *The Waterless Sea*. Pinney's book was published after we finished all major work on this chapter; it provides useful corroboration of many points we make here; it is particularly strong on mirages' association with racialization and orientalizing. For photography on Arctic expeditions in this period, including mirages, see Greene, *Arthur Wegener*, 127–54, 286–313.

11 MacMillan, "Geographical Report," 435.

12 Cook, *Return from the Pole*, 56; Bryce, *Cook and Peary*, xi.

13 The Crocker Land archive is an official, institutional archive of analogue materials owned and controlled by a large museum. But our critical analysis is not limited to this kind of archive. The mirage problematizes archival practices in both the analogue and digital spheres, as will become clear in Part 2.

14 AMNH, Crocker Land Expedition Papers, Mss. C76, Box 17, folder 9.

15 Sundquist remarks that US interests in Latin America and "sea routes to the Pacific" rendered the South Pole even more desirable than the North "in the era of manifest destiny." In Sundquist, "Exploration and Empire," ch. 1 of his *Literature of Expansion and Race*, 146–47.

16 Smith, *American Empire*, 85–86.

17 MacMillan, *Four Years in the White North*, 80.

18 Bennett and Rowley, *Uqalurait: An Oral History*, 152 and 155.

19 MacMillan, *Four Years in the White North*, 81. Punctuation altered for clarity.

20 Letter from MacMillan to Peary, August 21, 1914, qtd. in Davies, *Robert E. Peary*, 168.

21 Donald B. MacMillan Collection, Special Collections, Bowdoin College Library, M118.5 v. 25.

22 *New York Tribune*, November 25, 1914; "Mere Mirage," *Boston Daily Globe*, August 27, 1917.

23 "Sannikov Land" was a nineteenth-century "discovery" among the New Siberian Islands; "Bradley Land" was sighted by Cook in 1908 but revealed to be nonexistent; "Croker Land" was sighted on an 1818 expedition to find the Northwest Passage: Berton, *The Arctic Grail*, 591–92, 30–39.

24 Green was in a panic on the Polar Sea, fearing abandonment and expecting submission from the Inughuit. Compare Hunt, *North to the Horizon*, 55–57. Green may have "had designs on Pee-ah-wah-to's wife" (Kaplan and Searles, "Donald B. MacMillan," 127). On tensions between Inughuit and white men, see note in Kaplan, "Riding Short-waves." MacMillan's 1915 report in *Harper's* implies that Pee-ah-wah-to died in an avalanche or was otherwise buried alive; only later, in *Four Years in the White North*, did he acknowledge that Green, "inexperienced in the handling of Eskimos," had killed him (92). See Smith, *American Empire*, on the "racism" at "the core of Peary's organizational assumptions" (101); Peary was, of course, MacMillan's mentor and his organization of expeditions was the model for MacMillan's.

25 MacMillan, *Four Years in the White North*, 34–35.

26 See, for example, the journal of expedition member Walter Ekblaw, for August 2, 1913 (Bowdoin College, Peary-MacMillan Arctic Museum, Ekblaw journals, "Crockerland Expedition" [2011.16.264], 63–64).

27 The expedition enlisted Smith Sound Inughuit guides and hunters for help in exploration as well as hunting and trophy gathering, and depended on the sewing skills of the women.

28 J. P. Koch, the leader of the 1912–1913 expedition of which Wegener was a member, wrote in his diary for February 26, 1913, for example: "Wegener started photographing mirages, and he succeeded, despite the low temperature that puts so many obstacles on the Arctic photographer." Copenhagen, Danish Arctic Institute, A327.0.4, vol. 2, 191. Thanks to Jørgen Trondhjem for the English translation. For Anthony Fiala's photograph, see Fiala, *Fighting the Polar Ice*, 161.

29 It wouldn't be the first time an Arctic mirage had been used deliberately to deceive: Cook writes that he tries to keep his Inughuit companions going by telling them they're near land (but he knows it's just a mirage). Expedition member Hunt, disgusted by what he saw as the selfishness of the entire enterprise, wrote of the greed of MacMillan and of museum staffer Hovey, caring nothing of the Inughuit and only interested in money (Hunt, *North to the Horizon*). See Dick, *Muskox Land*, on MacMillan's efforts on behalf of a fur company (273). Peary had on an earlier expedition taken from the Inuit several enormous meteorites—their sole source of metal, now in the museum. On Peary as "nightmare," see Lloyd Rose, "Ice Follies," *Voice Literary Supplement*,

May 1989, 16, qtd. in Smith, *American Empire*, 107. Peary did beget sons of his own, including one with an Inughuit woman; our use of "only begotten son" for MacMillan is metaphorical.

30 Smith, *American Empire*, 108, 110.

31 Peary, qtd. in Kaplan and Searles, "Donald B. MacMillan," 122; Peary's comment reported in "Crocker Land Eludes Explorers," *New York Tribune* (second page of article).

32 Regina Kunzel, in Arondekar et al., "Queering Archives: A Roundtable Discussion," 214.

33 I've explored this elusive optical phenomenon through a series of interconnected artworks: mirages as the subject of photographs (http://www.margetlong.com/index .php/mirages/photographs-of-mirages-part-ii/), mirages experienced live in the landscape (http://www.margetlong.com/index.php/mirages/mirage-viewing-station/), mirages in film (http://www.margetlong.com/index.php/mirages/you-were-drifting/). Carolyn came to mirages a bit later, when she accompanied me to El Mirage Dry Lakebed on a shoot. Before embarking on this research on the Crocker Land archive, her research touched on impossible spaces such as the Earthly Paradise, located on medieval maps but inaccessible to ordinary humans.

34 A mirage is not only an optical phenomenon; it's a cultural refraction as well, as Pinney, *Waterless Sea*, demonstrates well. The word has been used to describe everything from shady financial doings to digital currency to the promises of an American president. The classic trope in film and animation presents a lost traveler on the desert, out of his mind with thirst, running wildly toward what he thinks is a body of water—only to have it vanish just before contact. In many twentieth-century desert narratives, the mirage magnifies racial and sexual stereotypes.

35 In *The Miracle of Analogy*, Kaja Silverman reminds us that image-making is not a strictly human activity. Leonardo da Vinci believed that there is an aesthetic capacity in all worldly things that allows them to generate images of themselves; Silverman compares these revelations to photographs.

36 Ann Reynolds describes such an experience in "At the Jetty."

37 Cotton, *Photography Is Magic*.

38 Kittler, *Gramophone*, 134–35.

39 Peary, *The North Pole*, 166–67. MacMillan's observations are reported in Brill, "Piblokto."

40 Dick, "Pibloktoq (Arctic Hysteria)."

41 A fata morgana is a complex mirage. We appropriate "fata morgana machine" from Salomo Friedlaender's 1920 short story, *Fatamorganamaschine*, excerpted in Kittler, *Gramophone*, 134–35. While Friedlaender imagines something like a virtual reality apparatus that visually dissolves the difference between optical effect and the "real" world, our mirage-creating instrument—crucially—distorts, refracts, displaces.

42 Bowdoin College bred Arctic explorers (Peary, class of 1877, and MacMillan, class of 1898) as well as their benefactors, such as businessman Thomas Hubbard, class of 1857.

43 *The Pencil of Nature* (1844–1846) is William Henry Fox Talbot's treatise illustrating his revolutionary process of printing on chemically sensitized paper. Talbot's vivid descriptions of "photogenic drawing" where "natural objects . . . delineate themselves" could also characterize the way a mirage works, the way it *writes itself* into the landscape.

44 Cole, "Memories of Things Unseen."

45 Our debt to the archival thinking of Ann Cvetkovich and of José Esteban Muñoz, that absent presence, is palpable here. Cvetkovich in *An Archive of Feelings* extends the idea of the archive to "cultural texts as repositories of feelings and emotions . . . encoded not only in the content of the texts themselves but in the practices that surround their production and reception" (7). Muñoz identifies the fleeting gestures of queerness that "are meant to be interacted with by those within its epistemological sphere—while evaporating at the touch of those who would eliminate queer possibility" in "Ephemera as Evidence" (6); he is writing in a "national and institutional moment of backlash" (7) that we find hauntingly relevant to our current moment of writing.

46 "National Archives Exhibit."

47 There are, of course, archives that have long existed resistantly outside this economy. The Lesbian Herstory Archives immediately comes to mind. This vibrant collection of the artifacts of lesbian lives and activities, for many years a strictly analogue enterprise, is now partly digitized. This will increase access to an already open, inclusive, and non-institutional collection. We recognize the value of access and at the same time wonder what moving materials from "the old table in Brooklyn" to the internet might mean for this archive's continued resistance to monetized uses and unwanted dissemination of its contents.

48 Cook, *My Attainment of the Pole*, 277. For discussion of the aesthetic that may have inflected Cook's descriptions, see Loomis, "The Arctic Sublime."

49 Cook, *Return from the Pole*, 71. For information about Cook's ghostwriter, see Dick, "Robert Peary," esp. 21–22.

50 Cook, *Return from the Pole*, 310.

Works Cited

Arondekar, Anjali, Ann Cvetkovich, Christina B. Hanhardt, Regina Kunzel, Tavia Nyong'o, Juana María Rodríguez, Susan Stryker, Daniel Marshall, Kevin P. Murphy, and Zeb Tortorici. "Queering Archives: A Roundtable Discussion." *Radical History Review* 122 (May 2015): 211–31.

Bennett, John, and Susan Diana Mary Rowley. *Uqalurait: An Oral History of Nunavut.* Montreal: McGill-Queen's University Press, 2004.

Berton, Pierre. *The Arctic Grail: The Quest for the North West Passage and the North Pole, 1818–1909.* New York: Viking Penguin, 1988.

Brill, A. A. "Piblokto or Hysteria among Peary's Eskimos." *Journal of Nervous and Mental Disease* 40, no. 8 (August 1913): 514–20.

Bryce, Robert M. *Cook and Peary: The Polar Controversy, Resolved.* Mechanicsburg, PA: Stackpole Books, 1997.

Cole, Teju. "Memories of Things Unseen." *New York Times Magazine*, October 14, 2015.

Cook, Frederick A. *My Attainment of the Pole.* New York: Polar Publishing, 1911.

Cook, Frederick A. *Return from the Pole.* New York: Pellegrini and Cudahy, 1951.

Cotton, Charlotte. *Photography Is Magic.* New York: Aperture, 2015.

Cvetkovich, Ann. *An Archive of Feelings: Trauma, Sexuality, and Lesbian Public Cultures.* Durham, NC: Duke University Press, 2003.

Davies, Thomas D. *Robert E. Peary at the North Pole.* Rockville, MD: Foundation for the Promotion of the Art of Navigation, 1989.

Dick, Lyle. *Muskox Land: Ellesmere Island in the Age of Contact*, Parks and Heritage 5. Calgary: University of Calgary Press, 2001.

Dick, Lyle. "Pibloktoq (Arctic Hysteria): A Construction of European-Inuit Relations?" *Arctic Anthropology* 32, no. 2 (1995): 1–42.

Dick, Lyle. "Robert Peary's North Polar Narratives and the Making of an American Icon." *American Studies* 45, no. 2 (Summer 2004): 5–34.

Fiala, Anthony. *Fighting the Polar Ice.* New York: Doubleday and Page, 1906.

Greene, Mott T. *Arthur Wegener: Science, Exploration, and the Theory of Continental Drift.* Baltimore: Johns Hopkins University Press, 2015.

Herbert, Wally. *The Noose of Laurels: Robert E. Peary and the Race for the North Pole.* New York: Atheneum, 1989.

Higgins, Anthony K. "Exploration History and Place Names of Northern East Greenland." *GEUS Bulletin* 21 (December 2010): 1–368. https://doi.org/10.34194/geusb.v21.4735.

Hunt, Harrison J. *North to the Horizon: Searching for Peary's Crocker Land.* Camden, ME: Down East, 1980.

Kaplan, Susan A. "Riding Shortwaves and Icy Seas: Practicing Science and Deploying Technology in the Arctic, 1913–24." In *North by Degree: New Perspectives on Arctic Exploration*, edited by Susan A. Kaplan and Robert McCracken Peck, 409–54. Philadelphia: American Philosophical Society, 2013.

Kaplan, Susan A., and Edmund Searles. "Donald B. MacMillan and the Polar Eskimos, 1913–1917." *Anthropological Papers of the University of Alaska* 25, nos. 1–2 (July 2000): 121–31.

Kittler, Friedrich. *Gramophone, Film, Typewriter.* Stanford, CA: Stanford University Press, 1999.

Loomis, Chauncey. "The Arctic Sublime." In *Nature and the Victorian Imagination*, edited by Ulrich C. Knoepflmacher and Georg Bernhard Tennyson, 95–112. Berkeley: University of California Press, 1977.

MacMillan, Donald B. *Four Years in the White North.* New York: Harper and Brothers, 1918.

MacMillan, Donald B. "Geographical Report of the Crocker Land Expedition, 1913–1917." *Bulletin of the American Museum of Natural History* 56 (1930 [for 1926–29]): 379–435.

"The MacMillan Arctic Expedition Returns." *National Geographic Magazine* 48, no. 5 (November 1925): 477–518.

Muñoz, José Esteban. "Ephemera as Evidence: Introductory Notes to Queer Acts." *Women and Performance* 8, no. 2 (1996): 5–16.

"National Archives Exhibit Blurs Images Critical of President Trump." *Washington Post*, January 17, 2020. https://www.washingtonpost.com/local/national-archives -exhibit-blurs-images-critical-of-president-trump/2020/01/17/71d8e80c-37e3-11ea -9541-9107303481a4_story.html.

Peary, Robert E. *Nearest the Pole: A Narrative of the Polar Expedition of the Peary Arctic Club in the S. S. Roosevelt, 1905–1906.* New York: Doubleday, 1907.

Peary, Robert E. *The North Pole: Its Discovery in 1909 under the Auspices of the Peary Arctic Club.* New York: Frederick A. Stokes, 1910.

Pinney, Christopher. *The Waterless Sea: A Curious History of Mirages.* London: Reaktion Books, 2018.

Rawlins, Dennis. "Contributions." http://www.dioi.org/cot.htm (accessed February 11, 2022).

Rawlins, Dennis. *Peary at the North Pole: Fact or Fiction?* Washington, DC: Robert B. Luce, 1973.

Reynolds, Ann. "At the Jetty." In *Robert Smithson: Spiral Jetty: True Fictions, False Realities,* edited by Lynne Cooke and Karen Kelley, 73–77. Berkeley: University of California Press, 2005.

Silverman, Kaja. *The Miracle of Analogy, or, The History of Photography, Part One.* Stanford, CA: Stanford University Press, 2015.

Smith, Neil. *American Empire: Roosevelt's Geographer and the Prelude to Globalization.* Berkeley: University of California Press, 2003.

Sundquist, Eric J. "Exploration and Empire." In *The Cambridge History of American Literature,* Cambridge Histories Online, edited by Sacvan Bercovich, 125–74. Cambridge: Cambridge University Press, 2008. http://dx.doi.org/10.1017/CHOL9780521301060.005.

Talbot, William Henry Fox. *The Pencil of Nature.* London: Longman, Brown, Green, and Longmans, 1844–46.

CODA: WHO WERE WE TO DO SUCH A THING?

Grassroots Necessities, Grassroots Dreaming: LHA in Its Early Years

JOAN NESTLE

In memory of Allan Bérubé, 1946–2007

In memory of Georgia Brooks, 1943–2013

The colonized draw less and less from their past. The colonizer never even recognized that they had one; everyone knows that the commoner whose origins are unknown has no history. Let us ask the colonized [herself]: who are [her] folk heroes, her great popular leaders, her sages? At most [she] may be able to give us a few names, in complete disarray and fewer and fewer as one goes down the generations. The colonized seems condemned to lose [her] memory. —ALBERT MEMMI, *The Colonizer and the Colonized*, 1967

We had rituals too, back in the old days, rituals born out of our lesbian time and place, the geography of the Fifties. The Sea Colony [a working-class lesbian bar in New York City] was a world of ritual display—deep dances of lesbian want, lesbian adventuring, lesbian bonding. We who lived there knew the steps. . . . But the most searing reminder of our colonized world was the bathroom line. Now I know it stands for all the pain and glory of my time, and I carry that line and the women who endured it deep within me. Because we were labelled deviants, our bathroom habits had to be watched. Only one woman at a time was allowed into the toilet because we could not be trusted. Thus, the toilet line was born, a twisting horizon of lesbian women waiting for permission to urinate, to shit.

The line flowed past the far wall, past the bar, the front room tables and reached into the back room. Guarding the entrance to the toilet was a short, square, handsome butch woman, the same every night, whose job it was to twist around her hand our allotted amount of toilet paper. She was us, an obscenity, doing the man's tricks so we could breathe. The line awaited us every night, and we developed a line act. We joked, we cruised, we commented on the length of time one of us took, we made special appeals to allow hot-and-heavy lovers in together, knowing full well that our lady would not permit it. I stood, a fem, loving the women on either side of me, loving my comrades for their stance, the hair hitting the collar, the thrown-out hip, the hand encircling the beer can. Our eyes played the line, subtle touches, gentle shyness weaved under the blaring jokes, the jukebox tunes, the surveillance. We lived on that line: restricted and judged, we took deep breaths and played.

But buried deep in our endurance was our fury. That line was practice and theory seared into one. We wove our freedoms, our culture, around their obstacles of hatred, but we also paid our price. Every time I took the fistful of toilet paper, I swore eventual liberation. It would be, however, liberation with a memory.—Joan Nestle, "The Bathroom Line" in *A Restricted Country*

I have been lucky enough in my own life to have participated in the beginning moments of a people's movement from private history to public discourse. I remember the early meetings in Boston, Manhattan, Maine, San Francisco, Buffalo and Toronto, where a handful of gay men and women gathered to share their discoveries and to agonize over how to find the money to continue their work, how best to share these discoveries with the communities they were documenting and how to balance the need for anonymity—a survival tactic of our people for so long—against the delight of revelation. I remember the flickering slide shows, capturing the lost faces and communal streets of other gay times, and the stunned recognition of audiences who were meeting for the first time with their own public story. In those days, we were not always sure that this fledgling idea of lesbian and gay history would find a home in the world.— Joan Nestle, introduction to *A Fragile Union*

Wars pound at my heart as I write this, images of lifeless Palestinian children being dug out of ruins, other bodies held hostage in farmer's fields, extreme nationalistic movements carving out who will survive and who will be driven into exile and the smug weapons-dealing power brokers reaping billions while pretending to be sad at the state of the world—always the push of unsettled histories, unresolved inequities. This uneasy terrain of invasion, diminution, and attempted erasure has been my background for all the conscious years of my life, let us say from 1950 until now, a time parallel with my queer fem coming out into the working-class butch-fem bars of New York City and in 1974, the cofounding of the Lesbian Herstory Archives (LHA), born at the juncture of gay liberation and the women's liberation movement.

> I know how to live in the shifting terrain of the margin, for there we knew more than the intruders, but I move very cautiously into the new territory that is being offered. Perhaps younger women will feel more at ease, more trusting of this new place, but they will not have the same memories, the same fears of betrayal, the same sense of comrades left at the border who could not cross over. How do I remain true to Maria, the bartender from Barcelona, who protected me from police entrapment in the early 1960s or to Rachel, the lesbian whore who lay in my arms dreaming of a kinder world, or the butch women I saw stripped by the police in front of their lovers? These actions happened in marginal

places, the reserves on which we were allowed to touch or dance or strut until someone decided enough of these freaks and took our fragile freedoms away. But this old country, as James Baldwin called his historical ghetto—the Jim Crow-ridden American South—is a complex and paradoxical place. I never want my lesbian daughters to find each other in bars where police brutality is rampant, to dance in a public place where a bouncer measures the distance between the partners to make sure no parts of the body are touching. I never want their nipples and clitorises measured by doctors convinced that lesbians were hormonal abnormalities, as was done in the 30s and 40s, and yet, while I know that living in the pre-liberation queer ghetto endangered my life, remembering it gives me life. (From "The Will to Remember: My Journey with the Lesbian Herstory Archives," 1998)

In the last ten years or so, it has been fashionable to show the faults of the liberatory impulse, to see it as a false narrative of beginnings and endings, but as I look over my lesbian queer archiving life, I can see how deeply the sense of what Didier Eribon called the daily insult to the gay self—I would add the working-class gay woman's self—propelled my involvement in the project called LHA. Throughout the late 1950s and 1960s we had taken to the streets to question the House Un-American Activities Committee and its punishing of deviant thinking, the brutalities of racial injustice, and the futility of war. This belief in committed group protest, in the collective power to refuse designated hatreds, this touch between endangered bodies—holding each other against the push of Reagan's mounted police, the feel of Mr. White's hand holding mine as we marched through Selma on the road to Montgomery, the shared water-soaked bandanas held to eyes seared with tear gas as we sat in front of the Pentagon, the push of women's bodies as we packed the streets of New York marching for abortion rights—these grassroots moments of protest and creation were the roots of my archival dreaming. We asked no permissions to announce our desires for change, we had no training except the lessons of life based on racial, gender, and class hierarchies, but living on the borders of the acceptable had shown me the richness of difference, the comradeship of the obscene. It was always the primacy of the endangered body and then the question, how do you imagine a grassroots site of appreciation for the shamed and the derided, for the defiant and the lustful?

Forty years later, the uniqueness of LHA still stands: its grassroots base, its refusal of governmental funds, its demystifying of the archives profession, its determination to keep lesbian as the all-inclusive noun, the collective ownership of its building which functions as a community cultural center, funded through small donations from many, its collective structure where consensus still rules—thus the building, the means of organization, its lesbian centeredness makes LHA its own kind of artifact. None of us in the founding collective were professionally trained archivists or librarians. Judith Schwarz, who joined us in the late 1970s, came the closest—she was a pioneer in the field of records management. None of us taught or attended queer/LGBT studies in traditional universities, but I did attend Jonathan Katz's class in gay history at the Alternative University in NYC. We were a band of independent "scholars" sharing our work often under the gaze of more professional gatherings like the Berkshire Women's History Conferences or the National Women's Studies gatherings. Sometimes we acted like the working-class kids we were. I remember one particular beautiful summer night on the campus of Smith or it could have been Bryn Mawr, Madeline Davis and I decided to strip and plunge into the lake that so beautifully framed the campus. We had waded far off shore, when our landed buddies started telling us to get out, but their shouts were drowned out by the roar of campus security vehicles screeching to a halt on the shore and in no time at all, Madeline and I, large women both, were bathed in a merciless spotlight and called to attention by the loudspeakers announcing that we had broken college rules—they kept the light on us for that very long walk back to shore and proper decorum. There were many moons that night.

*

The 1970s

The Sheer Joy of Collectivity

The apartment turned into a silk-screening factory for our first and only T-shirt with the word "lesbian" in over forty languages, with photographer-artist Morgan Gwenwald directing us, dozens of women working in every nook and cranny, washing lines draped through every room, festooned with T-shirts hanging out to dry. All of us learning a different aspect of the task, the great bustling of bodies in motion, of wonder at what we were creating. Turning inexpensive white cotton T-shirts into an international singing of the word "lesbian" in all its variety.

The Sheer Sexuality of It

Welcoming visitors to a private home that was a people's public space, the seduction of formality into comfort, my '50s fem self opening to the stranger, the researcher, the new volunteer, taking them in as I placed bowls of fruit before them, as I piled up the subject files they would need, as I took them on the tour of the archives-apartment, intimate living space transformed for that time into offered sites of desired resources, my bedroom, the audio-visual room of the collection, my bed heavy with bodies intent on studying the offered images, the erotics of it all, the fulfilment of want and longing for a touchable past.

The Sheer Grassroots Socialism of It All

Apartment 13A, the biggest living space I had ever had, giving home to my broken mother, my lover, and myself and still room for collective undertaking. Resources shared from purloined office materials; from the salaries of our daily jobs; from the boxes of materials left in front of the door; from the hands of travelers from across the seas who wanted to see this new thing, a Lesbian Archives. The "At-Homes" where lesbian cultural workers presented their creations to overflowing crowds, everything free, sometimes we had to have a second showing with women filling up the 1928 tiled hallway as they waited their turn. The kindness of neighbors in this rent-controlled building on 92nd Street, New York City in the grips of a depression, the well-off not wanting to live above 72nd Street, the city "dirty and filled with danger" as the 1970s have been described, "unwanted" people photographed in dark doorways—whores and drug dealers deplored in the right-wing papers—three sex workers lived on the same floor of LHA when we found the apartment, interracial couples abound in the building, a safe place for the different and no one questioned the steady stream of gender-questioning people through the doors of 215. A crack in the economics of a city allowed many grassroots collective undertakings to come to life. Womanbooks on the corner, a constant flow between this pioneering resource and LHA. How marginalities can speak to marginalities, again below the gaze of the Nationally Valued.

The Sheer Generosity of It All

Volunteers flooding the apartment on work nights, after long days of survival work, staying late, filing, talking, planning, welcoming, opening mail, preparing mailings, pasting up exhibits to be loaned, logging in journals, shelving books, Deb Edel always finding more room just when the apartment said no more and then after endless hours, out into the night for long subway rides back to Brooklyn, Queens. Keys left downstairs, materials left out on the archival table for researchers' use, the whole apartment theirs, nothing ever taken. I come home from teaching, never knowing who will be in the house, friends made for life. Artists bring their work, share their skills, always adding to the knowledges we need. The collection grows because of a community's appreciation at being seen, heard, housed. The interplay between generosities, moments of respite from struggling to survive in the city. From our newsletter, July 1980: "Georgia Brooks, a member of the collective, facilitated a weekly discussion group for Black Lesbians about Black Lesbian culture. Bibliographies and reading material were handed out on a wide range of topics including poetry, short stories, journal writings and individual authors such as Ann Allen Shockley, Audre Lorde and Lorraine Hansberry. This study group will be repeated this fall and more will be added!"

The Sheer Comradeship of It All

Around the country, gay history projects begin reaching out to each other. Sitting in a circle on the wooden floor in the early days of the San Francisco Lesbian and Gay History Project—listening to Allan Bérubé telling us of his work on passing women in California's gold rush years, seeing his groundbreaking work, "She Also Smoked Cigars," the delight Allan emanated touched us all, Eric Garber's face flushed with excitement as he outlined his thinking about the gay Harlem Renaissance, Maida Tilchin talking about her work with the 1960s paperback covers, again bodies shaped by a kind of mutual lust for the historical knowledges that seemed to be waiting for us just beyond the diurnal, John D'Emilio, Amber Hollibaugh, Gayle Rubin, Estelle Freedman, Martha Vicinus, Judith Schwarz sharing her work on the women of the Heterodoxy Club of New York City in the early twentieth century, a work engaged in after grueling hours of paid labor in the records libraries of legal firms, Pat Gozemba and the men and women of the Boston Lesbian and Gay History Project. The wonderful larrikin feeling that we had as we followed leads, shaped lines of inquiry, met in other countries, visiting Jonathan Katz in his old West Village apartment where his black-and-white seemingly-always-a-kitten cat strolled over the shoe boxes filled with thousands of index cards, the tracking of desire and punishment that would become *Gay American History*; attending our first workshop on how to do oral histories where Deb and I stood with Paula Grant, Liz Kennedy, and Madeline Davis, our backs leaning against the hard walls, Liz and Madeline already deep in their study of the working-class butch-fem community of Buffalo, New York. Bert Hansen calling us to say on his way home from work, he had found boxes of file folders with some papers still in them spilling out into the gutter in front of a Village apartment house and knowing we always needed folders, he wanted to bring them over. This was how we found the 1920 love letter written to the labor educator, Eleanor Coit, and Alice, the young woman who so loved her, "This is a 'very quiet' letter,

Eleanor dear, and you won't read it when you are dashing off somewhere in a hurry, will you—please." Helping each other without the possessive territoriality that so often marks academic endeavor. That was to come later, but now we laughed and worked and wondered at it all. LHA has a photograph of a group of us, queers all, the sun hitting our faces as we took a break from the Sex and the State Conference in Toronto. Before the world of academics and archival professions, there was Allan Bérubé, his moustache thick and smiling, an independent scholar who sang of class, history, and queer desire. It is his body I see now, in his just right fitting blue jeans, his flannel shirt, and his welcome, the twinkle in his devoted eye. These people, these projects, were the golden riches of my time.

The Sheer Womanness of It All, the Sheer Lesbianism of It All, All the Variations of Woman and Lesbian Welcomed

Again the photographs of this history so carefully posted now by Saskia Scheffer on LHA's website, so far from the boxy DOS-running computer we started with—a series of heads and upper bodies of women to be found in the work nights, visitors' weekends—twenty, thirty LHA visitors, many previously unknown to each other, all bodies pressed into a momentary intimacy to fit in the camera's frame. I look now from my new geography so far away from those 13A rooms, at one of these fading group images, looking back at the first decade of LHA and call out their names as best as I can remember—Pamela, Julia, Sahli, Georgia, Valerie, Lucinda, Linda McKinney, Polly, Alexis, Clare, Nancy, Beth Haskell, Irare, Amy Beth, Sam, Jan Boney, Ruth Pardo, Sabrina, Mabel Hampton, Deb Edel, Judith Schwarz, Morgan Gwenwald, Paula Grant, Arisa Reed, Leni, Marcyne, Rikki, Maxine, Joyce, Lisa, Teddy, multitudes more . . . and now new generations taking LHA into another kind of archival imagining. Maxine, Desiree, Flavia, Rachel, . . . and always Deborah Edel.

The Sheer Complexity of It All

LHA was born in my eyes as an anti-colonization project, what we called in the 1970s, lesbian separatism. A cultural, political undertaking to put us back into history, but always in our full complexity. Not in the service of lesbian purity but to provide one place where all who entered were for that time, lesbians. "Lesbian" becoming the noun that stood for all possibilities of queerness, for all possibilities of deviations. Lesbian sex workers, my comrades from the bars, were in my hands of inclusion. Not a role model lesbian history, not an archives of safe stories, always my own undertaking of keeping in the archives the tensions of lesbian difference, as we participated in the creation of lesbian feminist New York culture. This was the one place in my life where I stood for a lesbian specific world, and even though through the years, some of my queer archiving mates were uncomfortable with this specificity; Jonathan, Bert, Allan, Martin, Seymour, John, our early mates, helped in all the ways they could. In 1992 when LHA was holding a celebration in the Prospect Park pavilion to commemorate the opening of the new building, on a blistering hot day, amid two hundred women, I looked up to see John Preston coming toward me, two suitcases hanging by his sides, his face bathed in sweat, John in the last months of his struggle with AIDS, and with whom I was doing a book on relationships between gay men and lesbians, had detoured from his train trip back to Boston to be part of the celebration—"I know how much the archives means to you," he said as he bent down and I strained upward for our lips to meet. Here we were, at this moment, the two pornographers as we laughingly said, embracing amid hundreds of dancing lesbian feminists. I have never forgotten how much it cost John to make that pilgrimage that afternoon. The archives through its own kind of generosity brought into my life a multitude of inclusions.

The Sheer Politics of It All

Unfettered by institutional connections, we carried our LHA banner into the streets in support of a larger politic, first in anti-apartheid demonstrations, then in reproductive rights marches, in the Washington march against America's intrusions into Central America, wherever we felt seeing the words "Lesbian Herstory Archives: In Memory of the Voices We Have Lost" would refuse an absence, would remind others of the hidden history of lesbian activism. No one ever asked us to step out of the line of march. The sheer politics of refusing to have a board of directors or a letterhead with "famous" names, our search to find a social justice bank that would take a risk with us when after twenty-five years we had outgrown 13A and needed a permanent home and the politic of honoring our commitments. The forty-year-long commitment to never allowing lack of money deprive a woman from public LHA events. The politic of never wanting to be a national archives, that shifting thing of Nation, which in its generality, hides its specific exiles. Believing in regional lesbian archives which were also community centers, safe spaces for unsafe discussions, always creating cultures of place, believing in the internationality of the lesbian self: "send us something in the language you make love in." The books standing on the shelves in the alphabetical order of author's first names, to deny the power of patriarchy, we used to say. The archives as artifact.

To accommodate all the needs of full-time work, then the work of LHA—another full-time job, to rise in the morning and go to bed at night in full view of all that needs to be done. To raise the money to ensure best archival practices, then and still now.

October 5, 1981

The morning when I went to walk Perry before going off to work and found a death threat outside our door on a pile of sex magazines. "To the two female faggots . . . I hate fags of both sexes and my campaign of terror against you has just begun. You'll be hearing from me again and again and again. [Suggested sex acts for many lines.] Signed jack the ripper, the real one." We made the letter public in *Womanews*; many volunteered to be a protective brigade. We and the collection survived.

*

August 13, 2014

Trying to finish this written journey before we head off on one of our exhausting necessary trips, back to New York for LHA's fortieth anniversary celebration, for work on my history of LHA while it was in its first home, to see dear, dear friends separated from me now by continents, by twenty-three hours of flying, by aging body.

There is no end to my thoughts about queer archiving, though. No end to LHA, but new questions, new uncertainties about what we thought it all meant and what the future seems to be about. When Daniel visited the other day, I said to him, in the past we were worried about exclusion from history and now, I worry about inclusion—as more and more gay people turn to the right, as we are welcomed into the national fold, as we are no longer the unwanted deviant, but now courted for our votes, for our domesticities, for our support of national agendas of security—I am speaking in an American context, but in Europe too, the coalitions of the queer- and the migrant-hating have grown stronger. I have read the phrase, the activist archives, used to describe our projects of reclamation, the archives as a partner in the liberation of a people. But some of the most important collections in LHA to me are the documents of our failures, or our own exclusions, of the complex face of gender and sexual differences. Queer archives of the future perhaps will give evidence that it is harder to live with a history than without one. The trace-able arc of the public choices made, the markings of who we left at the border, the futility of thinking such words as "lesbian" or "man" or "woman" have fixed meanings.

The archiving that calls to me now, and perhaps always did, is the archiving of dissent. Times of war always call for unified fronts, and this is an endless time of war, an endless time of the policing of the borders. The queer archives must be a border crossing in all directions. I am saying good-bye now, this seventy-four-year-old Jewish working-class '50s fem lesbian-feminist who once helped bring a lesbian archives into being and who is now the archived. What did my over forty years of work with LHA teach me—to question or-thodoxies, the nation's and within our own communities; to refuse allotted places, to move into unknown waters with comrades on either side, to take on huge statements of No, to collectively say Yes to previously unthought-of equities, to take pleasure in new decipherings of old conversations, to compose homes in exile, to find the songs of the exiled who perhaps need another kind of body, to look always for the national absences, to keep alive the markings of the disappeared.

*

From My Haifa Journal, May 2007

Our friends in Haifa made us see with their eyes and so we saw through the landscapes to deeper histories. When we first traveled the roads between Tel Aviv and Haifa, our eyes fell off the scrub hills, but Hannah asked us to look again. "See those prickly pear cactuses," and she slowed the car down so we could focus our gaze, "every time you see a cluster of them, you are looking at the ruins of a Palestinian home. The farmers used the plants to form natural corrals for their grazing animals and also ate the fruit born at the tip of the rounded leaf." We started to look deeper, longer, and soon we could see the tracings of another people, a recently displaced people. Stone foundations started to ap-pear, buried in the living scrub. May you all have friends—and archives—that make you see again.

—JOAN NESTLE, Melbourne, August 2014

*

I am still here doing archival thinking at almost eighty inspired by the resis-tance movements all around me in America and here in Australia. Memory of the collective shouting no to state ugliness, the collective joy at the making of public kindness, this is the beating heart of our archival work.

—JOAN NESTLE, Melbourne, February 2020

Note

This chapter is a revision of "Who Were We to Do Such a Thing? Grassroots Necessities, Grassroots Dreaming: The LHA in Its Early Years." *Radical History Review* 122 (2015): 233–42.

Works Cited

Memmi, Albert, *The Colonizer and the Colonized*. Boston: Beacon Press, 1967.
Nestle, Joan. "The Bathroom Line." In *A Restricted Country*, 37–39. Ithaca, NY: Firebrand Books, 1987.
Nestle, Joan. *A Fragile Union: New and Selected Writings*. Jersey City, NJ: Cleis Press, 1998.
Nestle, Joan. "The Will to Remember: My Journey with the Lesbian Herstory Archives." In *A Fragile Union: New and Selected Writings*. Jersey City, NJ: Cleis Press, 1998.

.

Contributors

ANJALI ARONDEKAR is professor of feminist studies and codirector, Center for South Asian Studies, University of California, Santa Cruz. Her research engages the poetics and politics of sexuality, caste, and historiography, with a focus on Indian Ocean studies and South Asia. She is the author of *For the Record: On Sexuality and the Colonial Archive in India* (Duke University Press, 2009, Orient Blackswan, India, 2010), winner of the Alan Bray Memorial Book Award for best book in lesbian, gay, or queer studies in literature and cultural studies, Modern Language Association, 2010. She is coeditor (with Geeta Patel) of "Area Impossible: The Geopolitics of Queer Studies," *GLQ: A Journal of Lesbian and Gay Studies* (2016). Her book *Abundance: Sexuality, Historiography, Geopolitics* (forthcoming, Duke University Press) grows out of her interest in the archival figurations of sexuality, caste, and capital in colonial British and Portuguese India.

KATE CLARK is the lead artist and founder of Parkeology, a public art project that excavates shelved or buried social histories within museums, archives, and urban parks. Projects have included audio installations about LGBTQ+ cruising in parks, live face-casting events in anthropology museums, and permanent sculpture installations with salvaged artifacts from construction digs. Parkeology artworks have included projects with the National Museum of Natural History of the Smithsonian Institution, the Osage Nation Museum, Lambda Archives, the Oakland Museum of California, and NGBK Berlin. She is currently developing a public art master plan as artist in residence for Seattle City Light, and producing permanent public art commissions for 4Culture, the Washington State Convention Center, and the City of San Diego.

ANN CVETKOVICH is director of the Feminist Institute of Social Transformation at Carleton University in Ottawa, Canada. She was previously Ellen Clayton Garwood Centennial Professor of English, professor of women's and gender studies, and founding director of LGBTQ studies at the University of Texas at Austin. She is the author of *Mixed Feelings: Feminism, Mass Culture, and Victorian Sensationalism* (1992); *An Archive of Feelings: Trauma, Sexuality, and Lesbian Public Cultures* (Duke University Press, 2003); and *Depression: A Public Feeling* (Duke University Press, 2012).

CAROLYN DINSHAW is senior program officer in Higher Learning at the Andrew W. Mellon Foundation. Previously she was dean for the Humanities and Julius Silver Professor of Social and Cultural Analysis and English at New York University. She is the author of *Chaucer's Sexual Poetics* (1989), the first full-length feminist study of Chaucer, and two books that analyze desires for past times: *Getting Medieval: Sexualities and Communities,*

Pre- and Postmodern (Duke University Press, 1999) and *How Soon Is Now? Medieval Texts, Amateur Readers, and the Queerness of Time* (Duke University Press, 2012). With David Wallace, she edited *The Cambridge Companion to Medieval Women's Writing* (2003). And with David M. Halperin she founded and edited (1993–2005) the flagship journal of LGBT studies, *GLQ: A Journal of Lesbian and Gay Studies* (Duke University Press).

KATE EICHHORN is professor and chair of culture and media studies at the New School and the author of six books, including *The Archival Turn in Feminism: Outrage in Order* (2013); *Adjusted Margin: Xerography, Art, and Activism in the Late Twentieth Century* (2016); *The End of Forgetting* (2019); and most recently, *Content* (2022).

JAVIER FERNÁNDEZ-GALEANO is a historian of modern Latin America and Iberia. His interests include gender and sexuality, queer archives, diasporas and migrations, state violence, prison populations, and transnational activist politics. His first book project traces the erotic lives and legal battles of Argentine and Spanish gender-nonconforming people. He shifts the focus to nonelite actors—rural populations, recruits and prisoners, fans of flamenco music, and defendants' mothers—and to queer transnationalism in spirituality, folk music, fashion and performance, and visual and material culture. Fernández-Galeano has a PhD in history from Brown University, where he graduated as a Mellon/ACLS fellow; an MA in historical studies from the New School for Social Research, where he was a Fulbright scholar; and two BAs in history and anthropology (both cum laude) from the Universidad Complutense of Madrid. He has published in the *Journal of the History of Sexuality*, the *Latin American Research Review*, and *Encrucijadas*, among others.

EMMETT HARSIN DRAGER is a postdoctoral fellow of trans and queer studies in the Department of Women's and Gender Studies at the University of Missouri. Their writing can be found in *TSQ: Transgender Studies Quarterly*.

ELLIOT JAMES (they/them) is assistant professor of history at University of Minnesota Morris, formerly the West Central School for Agriculture (1910–1963), and the Morris Mission and Industrial School for Indians (1887–1909)—each occupying lands first inhabited by the Anishinaabe, Dakota, and Lakota peoples. Their scholarship engages everyone in theorizing and cocreating African and American indigenous, de-colonial, black feminist public histories for the purpose of remembering and honoring the past through the ancestors. They hold bachelor's and doctorate degrees in history from private and public universities at Mni Sota Makoce, in the heart of Turtle Island, on the banks of the Mississippi River. Their ongoing research explores histories of "people on the move" from the perspective of the Global South to engage questions about race and technology in the automobile era. They have published in *Kronos: Southern African Histories*.

MARGET LONG is a visual artist known for their exploration of the bodily impact and sensory politics of imaging technologies, past and present. They have screened and exhibited work at both national and international venues, including the Art Institute of Chicago, the Brooklyn Museum, British Film Institute, Exit Art, Anthology Film Archives, Kunsthaus Bregenz, and American Cinémathèque in Los Angeles. Long lectures frequently on photography and visual culture, most recently at University College London (with Carolyn Dinshaw), International Center for Photography, Yale University's Photographic Memory Workshop, and at the Center for Visual Cultures at University of Wisconsin-Madison. Their work has been published by *Afterimage*, *Social Text*, *Conveyor Magazine*, Art F City, and the Visual Studies Workshop. They are the author of *Flash + Cube (1965–1975)* (2012), and the self-published artist's book, *When I Was a Mirage* (forthcoming in 2022). Long received a BA from Harvard University and an MFA in photography from the Rhode Island School of Design, where they were the recipient of the T. C. Colley Award in photography. Long is an adjunct instructor at the Cooper Union in New York City, where they are also the director of the Paul Laux Digital Architecture Studio, an interdisciplinary maker's space for design, art, and architecture.

MARTIN F. MANALANSAN IV is the Beverly and Richard Fink Professor in Liberal Arts and professor of American studies at the University of Minnesota, Twin Cities. He has taught at the University of Illinois, Urbana-Champaign, University of the Philippines, New York University, New School University, and City University of New York. Manalansan is the author of *Global Divas: Filipino Gay Men in the Diaspora* (Duke University Press, 2003; Ateneo de Manila University Press, 2006). He is editor/coeditor of four anthologies: *Filipino Studies: Palimpsests of Nation and Diaspora* (2016), *Cultural Compass: Ethnographic Explorations of Asian America* (2000), *Queer Globalizations: Citizenship and the Afterlife of Colonialism* (2002), and *Eating Asian America: A Food Studies Reader* (2013). He has edited several journal special issues, including a special issue of the *International Migration Review* on gender and migration and more recently, a special issue of the *Journal of Asian American Studies* titled "Feeling Filipinos."

DANIEL MARSHALL is an associate professor in the writing, literature, and culture group in the School of Communication and Creative Arts at Deakin University, Australia. Daniel's publications include the edited/coedited collections *Queer Youth Histories* (2021), *Youth, Sexuality and Sexual Citizenship* (2018), *Secret Histories of Queer Melbourne* (2011; reprinted 2017), and two volumes on "Queering Archives" for *Radical History Review* (Duke University Press, 2014, 2015). Daniel has previously held positions as a Research Fellow at the Australian Research Centre in Sex, Health and Society at La Trobe University, as an invited Visiting Scholar at the Center for LGBTQ Studies (City University of New York) and at the Weeks Centre for Social and Policy Research (London South Bank University), and as a past president of the Australian Queer Archives.

MARÍA ELENA MARTÍNEZ was an associate professor of history and American studies and ethnicity at the University of Southern California. Her book *Genealogical Fictions: Limpieza de Sangre, Religion, and Gender in Colonial Mexico* (2008) received the American Historical Association's 2009 James A. Rawley Prize in Atlantic History and the Conference on Latin American History's prize for best book in Mexican history. Other work included the study of theories of race and sex, science, and the Enlightenment in the Spanish Atlantic world. Her fellowships for 2014–2015 included a Stanford Humanities Center Fellowship and an Advancing Scholarship in the Humanities and Social Sciences research and creative grant. Several articles of hers were published posthumously in the *Hispanic American Historical Review*, among other venues. The "María Elena Martínez Papers 1986–2015" are archived at the Hanna Holborn Gray Special Collections Research Center at the University of Chicago Library.

JOAN NESTLE, born in 1940 in the Bronx, came out into the working-class butch-fem bars of the 1950s in Greenwich Village; participated in the liberation struggles of the 1960s; taught writing in the Shirley Chishom–inspired SEEK Program at Queens College for twenty-nine years, where she learned of other histories of struggle and creation; helped form the Gay Academic Union in 1972; and cofounded the Lesbian Herstory Archives in 1974. She is the author of *A Restricted Country* (1987) and *A Fragile Union* (1998), and editor of *The Persistent Desire: A Fem-Butch Reader* (1992) and five other coedited collections on lesbian and queer culture. Her latest larger work was "Lesbians and Exile," edited with Yasmin Tambiah for *Sinister Wisdom* (2014). In 2002, Nestle followed her Australian lover, Di Otto, to new shores.

IVÁN A. RAMOS is an assistant professor in the Department of Theater Arts and Performance Studies at Brown University. His work brings together performance studies, queer and feminist theory, Latina/o/x American studies, and media and film studies. His first book, *Sonic Negations: Unbelonging Subjects, Inauthentic Objects, and Sound between Mexico and the United States* (forthcoming from NYU Press), examines how "dissonant sound" brought together artists and alternative subcultures on both sides of the border in the wake of NAFTA to articulate a politics of negation against larger cultural and economic changes. His work has been supported by fellowships from the University of California Humanities Research Institute, the National Humanities Center, and the Ford Foundation. In addition, his writing has appeared in the *Oxford Encyclopedia of Latina/o Literature*, *Third Text*, *Women & Performance*, *ASAP/Journal*, among others. He was also a contributor to the award-winning catalog for the exhibition *Axis Mundo: Queer Networks in Chicano L.A.*, sponsored by the Getty Foundation.

DAVID SERLIN is associate professor of communication and science studies at UC San Diego and affiliated faculty at the Center for the Study of Social Difference at Columbia University. His books include *Replaceable You: Engineering the Body in Postwar America* (2004), *Imagining Illness: Public Health and Visual Culture* (editor, 2010), *Keywords for Disability Studies* (coeditor, 2015), *The Routledge History of American Sexuality* (coeditor, 2020), and *Window Shopping with Helen Keller: Architecture and Disability in Modern Culture* (forthcoming). He was awarded the 2020–21 Rome Prize in Architecture from the American Academy in Rome.

ZEB TORTORICI is associate professor in the Department of Spanish and Portuguese Languages and Literatures at New York University. His monograph, *Sins against Nature: Sex and Archives in Colonial New Spain* (Duke University Press, 2018) received the John Boswell Prize from the Committee on LGBT History of the AHA and the Alan Bray Memorial Book Prize from the GL/Q Caucus of the MLA, among others. He has edited or coedited several books, including *Centering Animals in Latin American History* (2013); *Sexuality and the Unnatural in Colonial Latin America* (2016); *Ethnopornography: Sexuality, Colonialism, and Archival Knowledge* (Duke University Press, 2020); and *Baptism through Incision: The Postmortem Cesarean Operation in the Spanish Empire* (2020).

Index

gender identity: African feminism vs. trans feminism on, 195–96; cross-gender, 180n9; in government documents, 197; non-normative, clinical attempts at preventing, 166; origins of concept, 171; Stoller's theories on, 166, 171
Gender Identity Research Clinic (GIRC): establishment of, 166; female-to-male transsexuals at, 166–67; mission of, 166; nature of case files at, 169; sex reassignment surgery and, 170
genderqueer, meaning and use of term, 167
genitalia: of Aguilar, 33, 36–37, 44, 68, 71–72, 77; of hermaphrodites, 33; of Mrs. G, 166, 177–78; Spanish policing of photos of, 153
gentrification, 287
geographical conquest, 324
geographic transgenderization, 36
Germany, Esmarch bandage in, 272–79
Geyer, Andrea, 310
Ghaddar, J. J., 198
Giagni, Ann, 119, 131
Gil-Albert, Juan, 157
Gilliland, Anne J., 9, 67, 79, 88
Gilroy, Paul, 204
GIRC. See Gender Identity Research Clinic (GIRC)
Girgaum (India): "evil ladies" of, 18, 95–104; topography of, 101–2, 106nn29–30
Girgaum Memorial Memorandum, 101–2
Girl's Journey to the Well of Forbidden Knowledge, A (Mitchell), 310
Glavey, Brian, 145
glitter, 114
Global Pan-African Conference, 190
Global South, bootlegs in, 242
Goa (India), 98–100
Golove, Degania, 119
Gomantak Maratha Samaj, 97–100, 102–3
Gopinath, Gayatri, 199n18
Gordon, Angus, 218
Gordon, Avery, 179
Gozemba, Pat, 352
Grant, Paula, 352
grassroots archives, in partnerships with university collections, 112. See also Mazer Archives
Green, FitzHugh, 325–26, 329, 329, 342n24
Green, Richard, 166
Greene, Shane, 239, 240, 250

Greenson, Ralph, 166
Grier, Barbara, 113
Guatemala: Aguilar in, 34, 37, 85; national archive of (See Archivo General de Centro América)
Guatemala City, 68, 85
Guerra, José María, 68, 85–86
Guerra, Lizette, 131
guilt, space between desire and, 160
Guzmán, Daniel, 242–43; Boca, 244, 245–46. See also Remake
Gwenwald, Morgan, 350

Habell-Pallán, Michelle, 249
Haifa, 356
Halberstam, Jack, 217, 306, 308–9, 311–13, 315–16
Hall, Michael C., 225–26
Halperin, David, 277, 278
Hamilton, Carolyn, 188
Hanna, Kathleen, 314
Hansen, Bert, 352
happiness, of Aguilar, 69, 72, 86, 87
Harney, Stefano, 253
Harris, Verne, 171, 173
Harron, Mary, 243
Harsin Drager, Emmett: chapter by, 165–80; comments on, 20–21, 23, 146
Hartman, Saidiya, 181n32, 186, 191, 254
Hawaii, 196
Hayes, Sharon, 310
Haynes, Todd, 214–17, 220
Hefner, Hugh, 265
Hemispheric Institute of Performance and Politics, 74–76, 75, 86
heresy, sodomy as, 40
hermaphrodites: archival language regarding, 81, 82; study and display of, 41, 59n20. See also Aguilar, Juana
Hernández, Robb, 8
Herring, Scott, 297
hesitation, 179
Heterodoxy Club, 352
heterosexuality: archives' exposure of construction of, 42, 45; compulsory, 35; invisibility of, 278
Hilden, 273
Hilderbrand, Lucas, 241, 246–47
Hindutva, 93–94

photographs: of Arctic hysteria, 327, 334–37, *336*; from Crocker Land Expedition, 322–23, *325*, 327–30, *328*, *329*; instability of, 333–37; manipulation of, 340; in Mazer Archives, 122–30, *124*, *130*; of mirages, 322–23, 329, *330*, *334*, *335*, 342n28; problems with archiving, 331; reproductions of, 122; on Snapchat, 339; in Spanish policing of homosexuality, 152–53, 156–57; transcriptions of, 142, 153

physicians, objectivity of, 45, 47, 53

pibloctoq, 334–35, *336*

Pinney, Christopher, 341n10

piracy: of archives, 234; in Mexican economy, 233, 241. *See also* bootlegs

Pissing (Morioni), 244

pleasure: in archival work, 210–11; in queer archival turn, 16; in queer immigrant households, 294–96; in reading aloud of archives, 142–47, 160

PMAM. *See* Peary-MacMillan Arctic Museum (PMAM)

polar exploration. *See* Arctic exploration

Polar Sea, 322, 324–26, *325*, 329

policing, positivist approach to, 143. *See also* homosexuality, state policing of

pornography: ethno-, 70, 153; Spanish censorship of, 153

positivist school of criminology, 143

possessions, in queer immigrant households, 292–99

postarchival approach, 11, 16

postcustodial archives, 117

Potter, Clare, 118

Povinelli, Beth, 93

power: archives as institutions of, 188–89; classification as system of, 51–52; of clinical case files, 168; of naming, 187, 192–99; in production and preservation of documents, 34

Press (McCarthy), 233, 244, 245

Preston, John, 354

print cultures, in Mazer Archives, 113, 120–22, 128

problem-events, 94–95, 102–3

Probyn, Elspeth, 218

Prodigy, 120

profiteering, in Arctic exploration, 330, 342n29

Pro Infirmis campaign, 267–72, *268*, *270*, *271*, 278

pronouns: for Aguilar, 65–66; for Mrs. G, 180n6

property tax, in India, 101–2

prostitution, in India, 96–104

Protest on the Page Conference, 303–4

protest signs, 340

Protomedicato, 33

psychological tests, in state policing of homosexuality, 144, 147–52

Psychopathia Sexualis (Krafft-Ebing), 277

public sex, religious metaphors for, 145–46, 160–61

punk, 22–23, 249–53; bootlegs of, 240, 241, 242; emergence in Mexico City in 1980s, 233, 239–40; gaps in archives of, 235, 238, 249–50, 251; geographic origins of, 239; intersection of contemporary art and, 233–34, 241; meaning and use of term, 234, 239. *See also* Susy's Peleoneras Punk

Punk, 233

Punk and Revolution (Greene), 250

QPA. *See* Queer Pan-Africanism (QPA)

queer, meaning and use of term, 2–3, 40, 59n16, 260, 289

queer archival turn, 1–16, 303–18; archives as floating signifier in, 309, 313–15; being turned on in, 1, 16–17, 142; benefits and costs of, 307, 312–18; embodiment in, 4–5, 8; ephemerality of queerness in, 13; meaning-making in, 3–4; movement in, 11–12; pleasure in, 16; productivity of, 11–12; queer artists' role in, 306, 309–13; significance of act of turning in, 12–16; turning archival in, 6–7

queer archives: absences in, 174; assumptions in queer theory about, 308–13; as floating signifier, 309, 313–15; queer artists' use of, 306, 309–13; range of meanings of, 7, 205, 304–5, 307; as trope, 306, 307, 313, 315, 317; turn to (*see* queer archival turn); volume of scholarship on, 303

queer artists, archives used by, 306, 309–13

queer erasure, 174

queer history: designated sites of, 259–60; disappeared aesthetics in, 261; intersection of disability history and, 261–62, 265; possibilities and limitations of archives in study of, 38–43; role of imagination in, 74

queer immigrants. *See* immigrant households, queer

"Queer in Africa" conference, 189–92, 194

queering, meaning and use of term, 289

queer microhistory, 63

queerness: of act of turning, 6; "doing," 204, 208, 222; ephemera in transmission of, 204–12; ephemerality of, 13; mess as constitutive of, 289–92

queer of color critique, 3

Queer Pan-Africanism (QPA), 187, 191, 192, 198

queer reproduction, 217–27; through Bowie records, 208, 220–26; circulation of second-hand records as, 206–7, 212; genealogy and, 217–19; meaning of, 217–18; vs. queer production, 227

queer studies: in Africa, 188, 189, 195; African, 191–95; archival turn in (*see* queer archival turn); gender binary in, 167–68; materialism in, 3, 308, 316; possibilities and limitations of archives in, 38–43; postarchival approach in, 11; queer erasure in, 174; turning within, 3

queer subcultures, 205, 217

queer theory, 303–18; archival studies in dialogue with, 305–6; archival turn in (*see* queer archival turn); assumptions about archives in, 308–13; in emergence of trans studies, 167; queer artists' use of archives and, 309–13

queer transmission, ephemera in, 204–12

Queer Zine Archive Project, 311

"Race and Sex in the Eighteenth-Century Spanish Atlantic World" (USC symposium), 37–38, 44–45, 52–55, *54*, 74

racial differences, search for roots of, 41

racial discrimination: Du Bois on, 190–91; in South Africa, 185, 191

racial segregation: color line in, 190–91; de facto, 127

Radical History Review, 8, 16, 63, 78, 303, 304–5

Raghunathji, K., 99

Ramones, 251

Ramos, Iván A.: chapter by, 233–55; comments on, 22–23, 141, 150

Rao, Y. Sudershan, 94

Rawlins, Dennis, 341n8

Rawson, K. J., 165, 179

reading of archives: absences and gaps in, 254; aloud, 141–52, 160; critical, 42, 51; debates over, 93; against the grain, 39, 93, 169; along the grain, 93; shame and pleasure in, 142–47, 160

Real Audiencia (Royal Court), 33–34, 41, 55. *See also* Aguilar, Juana, trial of

realism, in clinical case files, 168

reality television, 290–92

realness, 192

Real Sala del Crimen, 85

Rechsteiner, Jasmin, 267, *270*

Reclaiming Afrikan (Matebeni), 189–90, 195, 197

records, vinyl. *See* secondhand vinyl records

recovery, in methodology of care, 178–79

Redefining Realness (Mock), 192–93, 196

Refiguring the Archives (Hamilton), 188

refraction, atmospheric, 321, 329, 332. *See also* mirages

Reid, Graeme, 192

religious metaphors, for public sex, 145–46, 160–61

Remake (Ortega and Guzmán), 243–49; access to canonical art and, 233–36, 254; artists referenced in, 233, 244–45; audience of, 246–48; as bootleg, 241, 248, 254; forms of distance in, 246–49; fragmentation in, 234, 242, 254; in *Punk* exhibition, 233; reasons for focus on, 235–38; sense of not having been there in, 234–35; sequence of action in, 244–46; sites used for filming, 247–48; sound in, 246, 248; still photos from, *245, 246, 249*; unreliability of recreations in, 238, 244, 254; version of history created in, 234–35, 238

remakes, in Mexican contemporary art, 233, 234

repertoire, archive and, 35, 45, 52–53

reproduction, queer. *See* queer reproduction

reproduction, sexual, in definition of men and women, 33, 40

reproductions: of archives through reading aloud, 141–52, 160; of photographs, 122

Resistencia Creativa, 35

Retter, Yolanda, 119

Rhodes, Cecil, 195

Rhodes University, 195

Ricco, John Paul, 260, 278

Rich, Adrienne, 35

Riot Grrrl Collection, 314

Rivera, Sylvia, 192–93

Robert J. Stoller Papers. *See* Stoller Papers

Roberts, George, 263

Robinson, Tom, 214, 220

www.ingramcontent.com/pod-product-compliance
Lightning Source LLC
Chambersburg PA
CBHW070841300326

41935CB00039B/1329